Developments in German Politics 2

Developments titles available from Macmillan

Patrick Dunleavy, Andrew Gamble, Ian Holliday and Gillian Peele (eds)
DEVELOPMENTS IN BRITISH POLITICS 4

Peter A. Hall, Jack Hayward and Howard Machin (eds)
DEVELOPMENTS IN FRENCH POLITICS (revised edition)

Gillian Peele, Christopher Bailey, Bruce Cain and B. Guy Peters (eds)
DEVELOPMENTS IN AMERICAN POLITICS 2

Martin Rhodes, Paul Heywood and Vincent Wright (eds)
DEVELOPMENTS IN WEST EUROPEAN POLITICS
(forthcoming)

Gordon Smith, William E. Paterson and Stephen Padgett (eds)
DEVELOPMENTS IN GERMAN POLITICS 2

Stephen White, Judy Batt and Paul Lewis (eds)
DEVELOPMENTS IN EAST EUROPEAN POLITICS

Stephen White, Alex Pravda and Zvi Gitelman (eds)
DEVELOPMENTS IN RUSSIAN AND POST-SOVIET POLITICS
(3rd edition)

If you have any comments or suggestions regarding this book or other *Developments* titles, please write to Steven Kennedy, Publishing Director, Macmillan Press Ltd, Houndmills, Basingstoke RG21 6XS, UK.

Developments in German Politics 2

Edited by

Gordon Smith
William E. Paterson
Stephen Padgett

First published 1996 by
MACMILLAN PRESS LTD
Houndmills, Basingstoke, Hampshire RG21 6XS
and London
Companies and representatives
throughout the world

ISBN 0–333–65902–3 hardcover
ISBN 0–333–65903–1 paperback

A catalogue record for this book is available from the British Library.

10 9 8 7 6 5 4 3 2
05 04 03 02 01 00 99 98 97

This book is printed on paper suitable for recycling and made from fully managed and sustained forest resources.

Copy-edited and typeset by Povey–Edmondson
Okehampton and Rochdale, England

Printed and bound in Great Britain by
Creative Print and Design (Wales), Ebbw Vale

This book is a direct replacement for *Developments in German Politics*, edited by Gordon Smith, William E. Paterson, Peter H. Merkl and Stephen Padgett, published 1992 by Macmillan Press Ltd.

Contents

List of Maps, Figures and Tables

Maps

Figures

Tables

Preface

Our purpose in *Developments in German Politics 2* is to provide a series of assessments of current trends in the Federal Republic in what can be described as the 'second phase' of unification. The first phase – the process of reunification and its immediate aftermath – was the subject of the 1992 edition of *Developments in German Politics*. The problems and perspectives are now somewhat different, and all the contributions to the present volume are entirely new.

Inevitably textbooks are frequently overtaken by events. In drawing largely on current material that is often available only in journal articles and German-language publications, the book seeks to give up-to-date accounts of leading issues. Nevertheless the discussion of individual topics is combined with sufficient background information to make the book accessible for readers who do not have a detailed knowledge of German politics.

As on previous occasions, we wish to thank our contributors – German, American and British – for their willing cooperation, despite all their other commitments.

June 1996

Gordon Smith
William E. Paterson
Stephen Padgett

Notes on the Contributors

Peter Cullen is Jean Monnet Lecturer in European Community Law at the Europa Institute, Faculty of Law, University of Edinburgh. With Klaus Goetz he has edited *Constitutional Policy in Unified Germany* (1995). He participated in a joint research project on European Police Cooperation at the University of Edinburgh; this has recently been published: in Anderson *et al.*, *Policing the European Union, Theory, Law and Practice* (1995).

Russell J. Dalton is Professor of Political Science at the University of California, Irvine, and Director of the Center for Study of Democracy at UCI. He is author of *The Green Rainbow: Environmental Groups in Western Europe* (1994), *Citizen Politics in Western Democracies*, 2nd edn (1996) and *Politics in Germany* (1992); and coauthor of *Germany Transformed* (1981); editor of *Germans Divided* (1996), *The New Germany Votes* (1993), *Challenging the Political Order: New Social and Political Movements in Western Democracies* (1984). He is now working on a comparative study of electoral choice in advanced industrial democracies.

Kenneth Dyson is Professor of European Studies at the University of Bradford, and Co-Director of its European Briefing Unit. He has written widely on European Politics and Political Economy. His recent publications include *Elusive Union: the Process of Economic and Monetary Union in Europe* (1995) and he is coauthor of *Culture First* (1996).

Christopher Flockton is Professor of European Economic Studies at the University of Surrey, where his main research and teaching interests cover the German and French economies and European economic integration. He has published widely in these fields.

Gert-Joachim Glaeßner is Professor of German Politics at Humboldt University in Berlin. He has written widely on problems of the communist and post-communist systems, German politics and German unification. Among his books are *The German Unification Process* (1992); *The German Revolution of 1989* (ed. with Ian Wallace) and *Demokratie nach dem Ende des Kommunismus* (1995).

Klaus H. Goetz is Lecturer in German Politics at the London School of Economics. He is the author of *Intergovernmental Relations and State Government Discretion* (1992), and co-editor of *Constitutional Policy in Unified Germany* (1995) and *A New German Public Sector?* (1996). He has recently edited a two-volume collection on German politics for the International Library of Politics and Comparative Government, and is currently writing a monograph on the German State.

Adrian Hyde-Price is Lecturer in Politics and International Relations at the University of Southampton, and was previously a Research Fellow at the Royal Institute of International Affairs. He has published widely on German and European security, and is the author of *European Security Beyond the Cold War: Four Scenarios for the Year 2010* (1991) and *The International Politics of East Central Europe* (1996). He is currently engaged in a research project on 'Security and Identity in Europe'.

Charlie Jeffery is Senior Research Fellow at the Institute for German Studies, University of Birmingham. He has edited a number of books on German federalism, including *Federalism, Unification and European Integration* (with Roland Sturm) (1993) and *The Challenges of Unification: German Federalism in the 1990s* (1996). He has written widely on the German Länder, German party politics and regional politics in the EU, including recent articles in *Political Studies, West European Politics* and *Parliamentary Affairs*. He is coeditor of *Regional and Federal Studies.*

Emil Kirchner is Professor of European Studies and Director of the Centre for European Studies, University of Essex. He is the author of *Decision making in the European Community: The Council Presidency and European Integration* (1992), coauthor of *The Recasting of the European Order: Security Architectures and Economic Cooperation* (1996) and coeditor of *The Future of European Security* (1994) and *The Federal Republic and NATO: 40 Years After* (1991).

Eva Kolinsky is Professor of Modern German Studies and Director of the Centre for the Study of German Culture and Society at Keele University. Recent books include *Women in Contemporary Germany* (1993), *Women in 20th century Germany* (1995), *Between Hope and Fear. Everyday Life in Post-Unification Germany* (1995), *Turkish Culture in German Society* (1996, with D. Horrocks). She is general editor of the *German Studies* series, coeditor with D. Horrocks of a new book series on *Culture and Society in Germany* and coeditor of the journal *German Politics*. Books in progress include *Social Transformation and the Family in Post-Communist Germany*, *Jewish Culture in German Society* and a social history of Germany from 1945 to the present.

Steen Mangen convenes the MSc in European Social Policy at the London School of Economics. Apart from research interests in German social security issues, his main research concerns inner city rejuvenation in Europe and the welfare state in post-Franco Spain. He is joint editor of *Cross National Research Methods in the Social Sciences* (with L. Hantrais, Pinter, 1986) and author of *Spain After Franco: Regime Transition and the Welfare State* (forthcoming).

Stephen Padgett is Professor of Politics in the School of Politics and Communication Studies at the University of Liverpool. He was previously Reader in the Department of Government, University of Essex. He has written widely on parties and party systems in Europe and Germany, and on public policy in the Federal Republic. His recent publications include *Parties and Party Systems in the New Germany* (1993) and *Adenauer to Kohl the Development of the German Chancellorship* (1994). He is an editor of *German Politics* and Chair of the Association for the Study of German Politics. He has recently completed a project on interest groups in post-communist Germany, supported by an ESRC Senior Research Fellowship.

William E. Paterson is Director of the Institute for German Studies at the University of Birmingham. From 1990–94 he was Director of the Europa Institute of the University of Edinburgh. Coeditor of *German Politics* and a member of the Steering Committee of the Königswinter Conference, he has published very widely on a wide range of German and European politics. His book with Simon Bulmer on *Germany in the European Union* will be published in 1996.

Peter Pulzer is Gladstone Professor Emeritus of Government and Public Administration at the University of Oxford. He has been Eric Voegelin Visiting Professor at the Geschwister-Scholl-Institut, Munich, and Visiting Professor at the University of Potsdam. His most recent books are *Jews and the German State. The Political History of a Minority, 1848–1933* and *German Politics 1945–1995*.

Gordon Smith is Emeritus Professor of Government at the London School of Economics. He has written extensively on European politics, comparative party systems and German politics. Besides coediting two journals, *West European Politics* and *German Politics*, he is associate editor of the International Library of Politics and Comparative Government.

Roland Sturm is Professor of Political Science at the University of Erlangen-Nürnberg. Most of his published work has been concerned with comparative politics, policy studies, political economy, and European, British and German politics. Amongst his most recent books are *Politische Wirtschaftslehre* (1995), *Europäische Forschungs- und Technologiepolitik und die Anforderungen des Subsidiaritätsprinzips* (ed., 1996) and *Großbritannien* (2nd edn, 1996).

Glossary of Party Abbreviations and Political Terms

Party Abbreviations

Bündis '90	Alliance '90
CDU	Christlich Demokratische Union (Christian Democratic Union)
CSU	Christlich-Soziale Union (Christian-Social Union)
FDP	Freie Demokratische Partei (Free Democratic Party)
PDS	Party for Democratic Socialism (former SED)
SED	Socialist Unity Party (GDR)
SPD	Sozialdemokratische Partei Deutschlands (Social Democratic Party of Germany)

Other Abbreviations

BDA	Bundesvereinigung der Deutschen Arbeitgeberverbände (Federation of German Employers' Associations)
BDI	Bundesverband der Deutschen Industrie
BKA	Bundeskriminalamt (Federal Criminal Police Office)
CSCE	Conference on Security and Cooperation in Europe
DGB	Deutscher Gewerkschaftsbund (Federation of German Trade Unions)
ECJ	European Court of Justice
EMU	Economic and monetary union
FRG	Federal Republic of Germany
GDP	Gross domestic product
GDR	German Democratic Republic
NATO	North Atlantic Treaty Organisation
OSCE	Organisation for Security and Cooperation in Europe
UN	United Nations
VDI	Verein Deutscher Ingenieure
WEU	Western European Union

Political Terms

Bundesbank	Federal Bank
Bundesrat	Upper house of federal parliament
Bundestag	Lower house of federal parliament
Bundeswehr	Federal armed forces
Land (pl. Länder)	Federal constitutent state
Mittelstand	Middle class
Ostpolitik	Policy towards the East
Rechtsstaat	State based on the rule of law
Sicherheitspolitik	Security policy
Sonderweg	Special path
Sozialstaat	'Socially responsible' state
Stasi	East German secret police
Stattpartei	Alternative Party
Technologierat	A round table for technology policies
Treuhand	Public Trustee Office
Volkskammer	People's Assembly (GDR)
Volkspartei	People's party
Volkspolizei	People's Police (GDR)

MAP 1 *Map of the Federal Republic and the Länder*

1

Introduction

The momentous events that took place in Germany in 1989 and 1990 and led to unification have now become a part of history. What seemed at the time to be a heady cocktail of idealism and rushed improvisation turned out to be remarkably successful. The social and economic disruption suffered in eastern Germany was inevitable, given the initial decision to make the transition as rapid as possible. Yet despite the upheaval and the heavy costs involved, the 'old' Federal Republic and its well-tried institutions have been successfully extended to eastern Germany. Nor, as many had feared, has the new Federal Republic immediately become an uncertain force in European affairs.

While its achievements have been considerable, it is apparent that Germany is not in a position simply to build on its past successes. Questions have to be faced about Germany's new role in Europe, both East and West. There is growing uncertainty about the performance and competitiveness of the economy, and the related difficulty of financing the welfare system. Whilst we are inclined to take Germany's political stability almost for granted, can the major parties continue to exercise their firm hold on the electorate? For the present these questions must remain unanswered, and it also remains to be seen how far the consensual style of policy making and the institutional structures can respond to these pressures.

The Federal Republic as a 'Normal' State

From the time of Germany's division in 1945 the question was how, and on what terms, could German unity be restored? Now it can be asked – as Pulzer does in the concluding chapter – is Germany at last a really 'normal state'? Some would reply that, considering the unhappy record of its predecessors, the Federal Republic can never be regarded, by itself or by its European neighbours, as a state like any other: its historical 'handicaps' will make Germany a special case for the indefinite future. International unease is compounded by the economic power of united Germany and its central geopolitical position within Europe. Thus whilst other countries can legitimately insist upon protecting their 'national interests', for Germany to do so would immediately cause concern, with accusations of 'arrogance' and renewed fears of German hegemony.

There is an alternative and sharply opposing evaluation: that contemporary Germany is a quite normal state in a rather 'abnormal' Europe. Countries in both Eastern and Western Europe are variously afflicted by deep economic problems, political fragility or national self-doubt. In fact from this viewpoint the Federal Republic – as a powerful and relatively normal state – has, if not a 'European mission', then at least a strong responsibility for providing leadership.

Components of the 'German Model'

The latter assessment has to be treated with caution, since it may be based on an overestimation of Germany's economic and political capabilities. Outside observers may be too optimistic, leading to uncritical acclaim of the successes of '*Modell Deutschland*' (German model) without properly appreciating its foundations or ramifications. The usual point of reference of the model is the economic sector: the set of framework conditions that have led to sustained economic growth, monetary stability and industrial harmony in Germany. Yet it is obvious that these conditions could not have been created in isolation from the wider society, that is, divorced from the whole institutional, political and cultural context in which they arose. Nor, for this reason, is the German economic model readily transferable to other countries.

The question of 'context' can be approached from various angles, but as both Glaeßner, in Chapter 2, and Goetz, in his examination of the Federal Constitutional Court (Chapter 6) demonstrate, the Basic Law (the constitution) is of utmost importance in controlling the institutional structure and the processes of decision making, and in setting the parameters for the conduct of politics. The Basic Law also has an 'expressive' function, as a focus of social aspiration and loyalty. That it has this overarching status is partly accounted for by legal norms being of overriding concern in German society. It may be an exaggeration to say that Germans prefer the certainty of law to the uncertainty of politics, but this leaning towards a 'legal culture' has certainly had a profound influence on German political development in the post-1945 era.

A further contribution of the Basic Law had been the construction of a system of 'institutional interdependence', which is far more sophisticated than older ideas of institutional control through constitutional 'checks and balances'. This interdependence, especially within the federal system, has had pronounced effects. One has been to make the processes of policy formulation and policy implementation subject to intensive and complex negotiations and adjustment. A readiness to compromise may initially have been absent, but the 'consensus-inducing' mechanisms of the institutional structure have left a strong imprint on the style of German politics. Thus the economic model should be regarded within the context of the framework provided by compromise rather than confrontation, and the relative depoliticisation of economic sector.

Another effect may prove less beneficial – rigid interdependence and the need to strike a careful balance among competing interests, any of which may be in a position to hinder progress, could lead to hesitant decision making and unsatisfactory outcomes – so the balance sheet of the German model must take account of this on its debit side. At present Germany is still tackling the economic and political consequences of reunification while simultaneously pushing for deeper and wider European integration, and therefore the demands made on the model will be intense.

The Contribution of Politics

Much of the success of the Federal Republic has been due to its political stability, whether as a cause or a consequence of its economic strength. Almost in contradiction to the emphasis on institutional interdependence, German chancellors – from Adenauer, through to Brandt and Schmidt and latterly Kohl – have been able to provide forceful political leadership and to act decisively in pursuing their goals. It could be argued that to an extent the Basic Law has given them sufficient scope to operate successfully. Alternatively it could be said that the Federal Republic has simply been fortunate in its choices. What is clear, however, is that the chancellors' position would have been far weaker had it not been for the strength and discipline of the two dominant parties, the Christian Democrats (CDU) and the Social Democrats (SPD), and the underlying consensus that they share. The parties' ability to hold the loyalty of the electorate has been largely responsible for the stability of the leadership.

Will that continue in the future? As Dalton concludes in Chapter 3, the electorate is becoming more diverse and fluid, less attached to individual parties, and that is especially true in eastern Germany. In addition both the CDU and SPD are finding it difficult to attract younger voters. As yet these electoral movements have not had a marked effect on the party system, but any substantial change could lead to weaker and less decisive governments than in the past with serious implications both internally and externally.

Sustaining Economic Success

Economic stability was the bedrock of certainty upon which the Federal Republic was built. In the early postwar years the economic miracle (*Wirtschaftswunder*) nurtured consolidation of the still-fragile political culture. Subsequently the Deutsche Mark became the symbol of 'economic patriotism'. Economic success was central to West Germany's national identity, offsetting as it did the truncated political stature of this 'semi-sovereign' state. The high-performance economy formed the foundation of the *Sozialstaat* (socially responsible state), promoting social solidarity and a sense of well-being in a cohesive society in which all had a stake. East Germany's desire for reunification was governed in large part by the economic and social success of the Federal Republic. Its allure was at least as powerful as the attractions of political democracy. Economic reconstruction will thus be the touchstone upon which the successs of reunification is judged. For all these reasons, the economic uncertainties now confronting Germany go to the core of the national psyche.

The uncertainties prevailing in the mid 1990s are threefold. The central question is the sustainability of the institutional and cultural foundations of the German model. As Kenneth Dyson shows in Chapter 11, the delicate balance between dynamism and conservatism at the heart of the German model has been undermined by changes in the international economy. Low growth rates, reduced export performance, a reluctance to invest and steep increases in unemployment are all indicative of an economy that has lost its competitive edge. In many aspects of economic life – corporate governance, banking and financial services, regulation, wage bargaining and the social state itself – German traditions are increasingly difficult to reconcile with the dynamics of economic globalisation.

A second set of doubts concerns economic take-off in the east. The new German Länder (provinces) represent a unique case of post-communist economic transformation. Other eastern European countries embarked upon 'shock therapy' strategies of transformation – economic liberalisation meant a strict regime of economic discipline, including currency devaluation, tight controls on state budgets and wage restraint. In eastern Germany, in contrast, the shock of adapting to a market economy was cushioned by the favourable terms of monetary union, a phased convergence with wage rates in the west and the Federal Republic's generous social benefits. The eastern German economy has grown by around 8 per cent per annum since 1992, but at the cost of financial transfers from the west totalling some DM600 billion. It is by no means clear how long it will take the economy in the east to generate self-sustaining growth.

A third set of questions relates to Germany's role in the European economic order and economic and monetary union. The European Monetary System (EMS) was based on Germany's economic strength, which enabled the Deutsche Mark to act as the anchor currency in the Exchange Rate Mechanism (ERM). The weakening of the German economy under the burden of reunification thus had far-reaching implications for the EMS. High Bundesbank (central bank) interest rates (an attempt to restore domestic economic discipline) set an impossibly high benchmark for Germany's neighbours, leading to the acrimonious disintegration of the ERM in 1992–93. Monetary union contains the potential for further conflict. The Bundesbank's insistence on a strictly disciplined approach to EMU is creating a straightjacket for aspirant members such as France that are struggling to meet the Maastricht convergence criteria. In the face of economic uncertainty the German public is clinging tightly to the Deutsche Mark as the symbol of monetary stability. Amongst German political elites the EMU consensus has begun to unravel. Germany's role in the EMU process is thus becoming problematical.

Economic Management

These three interrelated problem areas are uniquely difficult to manage. Meeting the EMU convergence criteria and reducing the burden on the 'real' economy means bringing budget deficits under control. Cutting budget deficits whilst at the same time protecting the fragile growth in the east and reversing the escalation of unemployment will not be an easy trick to bring off. To be sure, dexterous economic policy has rescued the Federal Republic from previous recessions, although each recovery stabilised at a lower level of economic performance than its predecessor. Successful policy management, moreover, was rooted in the underlying resilience of the economy. Present concerns are rooted in the growing conviction that the problems are inherent in the structure of the German model.

The core of the problem is located in the rigidity of the collective bargaining structures, regulated labour markets and a social infrastructure that bears heavily on the productive economy, all of which serve to discourage investment and blunt competitiveness. These problems are not in themselves new, having been on the neoliberal agenda since the early 1980s and receiving an extensive working over by the government-appointed *Deregulationskommission* (Deregulation Commission) between 1987 and 1991. Currents of liberalisation however, have been stifled by a pervasive tradition of *Ordnungspolitik* (economic order entrenched in a framework of rules), and by the fragmentation of authority across a highly pluralistic political system in which policy is based on bargained consensus. In this policy environment, structural change is inevitably gradual, since it is dependent on prerequisite shifts in the terms of the prevailing consensus.

Triggered by unemployment in excess of four million, there are indications that a modest shift may now be under way. Recent pay rounds have seen trade unions accept a virtual standstill in real wages. In some celebrated cases (such as that of Volkswagen) wage cuts and four-day working weeks have been agreed. Although the unions continue to defend the established wage-bargaining model, there is a greater readiness to accept a degree of flexibility. At the beginning of 1996 Chancellor Kohl's round table of employers, trade unions and politicians announced a joint initiative to tackle unemployment. This 'Alliance for Jobs' accords strongly with the German preference for bargained solutions to structural change. It is doubtful, however, whether this kind of bargained agreement can produce measures sufficiently radical to address the problems outlined above.

The Social Consequences of Structural Change

Germany may be a victim of its own economic success, with unprecedented affluence generating high expectations and stability breeding a deep fear of change. The reduced capacity of the German model will inevitably test social cohesion. Failure to confront the unmistakable signs of sclerosis can only result in a further decline in performance and an increasing gap between expectations and the capacity of the economy to deliver. Structural change, on the other hand, means sacrificing some of the welfare provisions flanking the market economy and underpinning the solidarity that characterises German society. Either way, distributional conflict is likely to increase, with unpredictable social consequences.

The effect this will have on the economic and social integration of the new Länder is particularly difficult to predict. Cushioned against the shock of economic transformation in the early stages of reunification, easterners were not conditioned to expect severe social hardship. The onset of deindustrialisation and mass unemployment in 1991–92 dispelled earlier illusions at the cost of sharp resentment and protest. Social attitudes have since stabilised, and sober economic expectations are now coupled with a cautiously optimistic perspective on the medium-term future, rooted in the growth of the regional economy since 1992. A loss of momentum in the recovery could lead to a resurgence of anti-western sentiment, and its attendant political fallout.

Post-reunification tension between east and west was rooted in the economic disparity between the two parts of Germany, coupled with a sense of cultural rejection amongst easterners. The east–west divide was entrenched in popular humour: 'We are one nation' says the easterner; 'so are we' replies his western compatriot. Easterners blamed reunification problems on selfishness and arrogance in the west. For their part the 'Wessis' derided the 'Ossis' for their lack of individual initiative and for clinging to a 'security culture' of state dependency. Since reunification easterners have had to adjust to the combination of rewards and uncertainties inherent in the market economy of the 1990s. Westerners may now have to undertake a similar reappraisal. The impact of economic globalisation may thus eclipse the more parochial issues of the post-reunification agenda.

The economic and cultural 'fault lines' in German society can be expected to shift, with increasing tension between those in the high-technology sectors of the economy with the skills and attitude to adapt, and the economically marginal upon whom structural change will bear most heavily. A more flexible economy is, in the short term at least, a less secure economy, and the reduced capacity of the state to cushion the effect of structural change will leave the weak vulnerable. Economic and social change can thus be expected to have some political fallout, with politics increasingly centred on the distribution of adjustment costs, and social groups mobilising to protect their interests. It is uncertain whether this heightened distributional conflict is compatible with the familiar consensus orientation of German politics.

The sense of crisis should not be exaggerated. Germany has retained its position as the strongest of the major European economies, symbolised by the resilience of the Deutsche Mark. It may be that the German model can be recreated along more flexible lines through the tried and tested political formulas of consensual adjustment. At present, though, the magnitude of the economic challenge is not being matched by a commensurate political determination.

Domestic uncertainties have repercussions in the wider arena. As France has shown, managing the EMU process against the backdrop of distributional conflict on the domestic front is far from easy. Social cohesion is a prerequisite of self-confidence in the international arena. Germany is unlikely to resolve the related questions of national identity and international role whilst beset by economic *Angst*. The earlier concern that Germany's economic might would spill over into political hegemony has been reversed. The German model has served as a role model for Europe and an anchor of European stability, but its sustainability raises questions that go far beyond the scope of this book.

Foreign Policy

> 'Germany, a former country in Central Europe' (Random House Dictionary of the English Language, 1986).

Since the creation of the Imperial German State in 1871, the *leitmotif* in German political development has been discontinuity and regime change. In the old Federal Republic there was nevertheless one element of continuity in foreign policy with previous regimes – its explicitly revisionist character in relation to its borders. All the German states, especially since the First World War, have striven to alter Germany's borders. There were, of course, huge difference in method and ambition between the Weimar Republic and the Third Reich in relation to foreign policy, but they shared the common goal of reversing the Versailles settlement. The Second World War, the ensuing territorial losses and the division of Germany in the postwar settlement ensured that territorial revision was an integral part of the foreign policy of the Federal Republic and no federal government could ever fully accept the permanence of the German Democratic Republic, though in practice the level of acceptance was very high between 1972, when the Basic Treaty between the two states was negotiated, and the breaching of the

Berlin Wall on 9 November 1989, which heralded the end of the German Democratic Republic.

What was new about the territorial claims was not the commitment to peaceful means in their pursuance (reunification in peace and freedom), since that had also been a feature of the foreign policy of the Weimar Republic, but the resolve of successive German governments to act in concert with other Western governments, especially the United States. The essential bargaining point at the centre of the Federal Republic's foreign policy was the underwriting by the Western powers of its aspiration to reunite the divided Germany. This was seen most clearly in the backing by the United States for the Hallstein doctrine, whereby states were forced to choose between having diplomatic relations with the German Democratic Republic or with the Federal Republic. The diplomatic weight of the United States ensured that between the inception of the Hallstein Doctrine in 1956 and 1969 when it was finally abandoned, very few states chose the German Democratic Republic, a choice that emphasised its continuing failure to gain legitimacy in the eyes of the West.

The dominant element of the foreign policy of the Federal Republic, however, was its marked multilateral and interdependent character. Foreign policy was made within the framework of NATO and the European Community and German interests were seen to coexist with these institutions and to be adequately articulated by them.

Post-reunification

German reunification can be seen as a triumphant vindication of the foreign policy claims and style of the Federal Republic, upon whose terms East and West won full restoration of sovereignty, including the right for the whole of Germany to be in NATO. Germany's commitment to multilateralism was rewarded by the whole-hearted support (after some hesitation by President Mitterrand and Mrs Thatcher) of the Western Allies for the reunification process. Perhaps even more strikingly, German reunification was endorsed by its neighbours in the East. This was a testimony to the positive experience of the Federal Republic these states had enjoyed through the *Ostpolitik* of successive federal governments, as well as the Federal Republic's territorial claims being limited to the German Democratic Republic. Germany's commitment to European integration was also of help, in two important ways. First, Germany's commitment to an integrationist, self-limiting policy served to reassure, where a neorealist, national-interest policy would have kept the shadows of the past alive. Second, and perhaps even more importantly in post-Yalta Europe, the states of Central Europe saw a unified Germany as the most powerful advocate of their goal to be included in the European Union and NATO.

German Foreign Policy and the Future

A major change in the foreign policy of the unified Federal Republic is that it unequivocally accepts the territorial status quo in Europe, and it thus can be regarded as the first non-revisionist German state since 1871. Some residual doubts about the finality of the borders with Poland surfaced during the reunification negotiations, but strong resistance from the four allied powers means that no ambiguity now remains in relation to the status of the present Polish–German border.

While there is no room for doubt on the border issue, the sustainability of Germany's multilateral institutional stance is more open to question. During the reunification process and its immediate aftermath the federal government restated its strong commitment to multilateral institutionalism. US and indeed British support for reunification was dependent on continuation of the NATO connection, and support on the European mainland was seen to depend on an even greater German commitment to integration, not that Chancellor Kohl and his government were in any way reluctant to embed Germany even more deeply in to the multilateral institutional framework. The EU's guiding principle remains that a policy based on the traditional state-centred system would threaten both Germany and other states in the system since Germany's size and power would render such a system inherently unstable.

There can be little doubt about the genuineness of the multilateral intentions of German policy makers, and questions about the sustainability of the multilateral model relate less to Germany's intentions than to its appropriateness in an altered international environment. Germany's stance was perfectly attuned to the bipolar Yalta Europe, but the passing of the Cold War has brought about fundamental changes in the geopolitical architecture of the European continent. Germany's commitment to NATO was a response to a perceived Soviet threat, but in the years following reunification the Soviet Union soon followed the Warsaw Pact into the pages of history. Ratification of the Maastricht Treaty, which firmly anchored Germany to a more integrated Europe, exposed a distance between government elites and mass opinion throughout Western Europe that imposed serious constraints on further progress.

The post-reunification years have been quite testing ones for German security Policy. The dilemma as Adrian Hyde-Price (Chapter 10), indicates is not whether Germany will pursue security policy through multilateral or national channels – the national channel will remain closed. One major dilemma – the question of which Western multilateral institutions will best be able to cope with new security problems in Central and Eastern Europe – is a very serious one, but it is shared with other Western states.

The central dilemma is more specifically German and is best illustrated by the federal government's inability to respond in a coherent manner to expansion of the geographical scope of Western multilateral military intervention. External expectations of an increased German contribution run counter to the view of the German public, which is attuned to Germany's role as a 'civilian power' and trading state. The federal governments at the centre of this field of forces have inched Germany towards greater international responsibility. So far the strategy has been relatively successful, but it would be seriously imperiled by any significant reduction of the readiness of the United States to continue to play its international role as the provider of security.

In the area of European integration the greatest immediate challenge as Emil Kirchner indicates (Chapter 9), is the question of economic and monetary union. Failure by France to sustain the policy would call into question the whole of Germany's European policy, which is predicated on the assumption that in return for Germany's agreeing to EMU and the single currency, France will agree to German policy on political union. Failure for whatever reason, including the hostility of German domestic opinion, carries the risk of a massive flood of foreign capital into the Deutsche Mark. It will, however, be far from easy to convince a sceptical German public of the benefits of giving up the Deutsche Mark, to which they remain very attached. There is also a problem with the eastward enlargement of the European Union, as the federal government's enthusiasm to extend the EU is shared neither by some of its EU partners nor by the majority of its population. The benefits to Germany of the European Union and the 'zone of stability' being moved further east are potentially huge, and lack of progress in this area would be much graver for Germany than any other EU member state.

Indeed Timothy Garton Ash divides Westernisation of the region into three historic phases. The first involved the Westernisation of the

Federal Republic. This has now been superseded by the process of Westernising former East Germany and the future task is to help Westernise the countries immediately to its east: 'It also needs to assist in the Westernization on which the new democracies to its east have themselves embarked, and to bring them into the structures of Western and European Integration to which the Federal Republic already belongs. If Germany really wants to be a normal country like Britain, France or American, then you need Western neighbours to the East' (Garton Ash, 1994, p. 81).

One very common fear amongst Germany's neighbours since the reunification is they will be faced with a much more assertive Germany. Much anxiety was caused by the very heavy pressure the German government exerted on the EU to recognise Croatia and Slovenia in December 1991. This proved to be an atypical act and German elites quite quickly drew the conclusion that it had been a mistake. It does, however, illustrate that in cases where the European institutions prove too weak, German power will become more evident.

The whole thrust of Germany's foreign policy reflects its economic weight. Its tendency not to choose between options (generally called *Genschering* after the former foreign minister Hans-Dietrich Genscher) and its preference for 'soft power' rather than 'hard power' solutions (as in Eastern Europe) reflect this mode in matters of security. This 'gentle giant' role is also exhibited by the European Union in its massive budgetary contributions and its use of side payments to elicit consensus and maintain the EU framework, which is of significant benefit to Germany in trade and other areas. Ultimately, then, Germany's foreign policy will depend on the German economy continuing to perform at a very high level. Despite these challenges the indications are that German unity and the end of a divided Europe, with Germany as the Eastern frontier of the West, and its replacement by one in which there is a greater correspondence between geographical and political Europe, with Germany at the centre of both, will not in the foreseeable future mean an end to the classic principles of multilateralism: 'tying Germany in' (*Einbindung* and *Westbindung*.)

PART ONE

The Institutional and Political System

2

Government and Political Order

GERT-JOACHIM GLAEßNER

The Federal Republic as a Semi-Sovereign State

In its early years the Federal Republic could be regarded as a classic example of a 'penetrated system' – a country regulated and controlled by external actors. Until the attainment of sovereignty in 1955, when the Federal Republic joined NATO, it was in the words of Peter Katzenstein (1987) only a 'semi-sovereign state', over which the Western Allies had a major influence on policy. The last remnants of these Allied rights, concerning Berlin and a solution to the German question, remained in force right up to reunification in 1990 and the arrangements made in the 'Two-Plus-Four Treaty', between the two German states and the four war-time allies.

Yet this limited sovereignty was not only the result of external compulsion. At its foundation in 1949 the Federal Republic's temporary constitution, the Basic Law, deliberately renounced some of the rights of a sovereign state. Thus Article 24 of the Basic Law states:

> (1) The Federation may by legislation transfer sovereign powers to inter-governmental institutions.
> (2) For the maintenance of peace, the Federation may enter a system of mutual collective security; in doing so it will consent to such limitations upon its rights of sovereignty as will bring about and secure a peaceful and lasting order in Europe and among the nations of the world.

The Basic Law came into force at a time when cooperation between the defeated Germany and its victorious western neighbours seemed scarcely conceivable. Nevertheless it showed the Federal Republic's constitutional readiness to learn from the experiences of national socialism and to develop a future political order for Germany, both as a whole and as part of the European order yet to be created.

The special quality about the development of the Federal Republic is that it has changed from being a 'penetrated system' into an 'integrated system'. Since the time when Germany joined the European Community (the European Coal and Steel Community in 1952, the European Economic Community and Euratom in 1957), national rights of sovereignty have gradually been handed over to supranational institutions. From being a restriction imposed from outside, semi-sovereignty became part of Germany's deliberate policy of restricting its own freedom of action – and not only in the field of foreign policy.

In contrast, until its demise in 1990 the German Democratic Republic, GDR (see Map 2) remained an 'occupation regime' (Huntington, 1968). Its existence was linked directly to the Soviet Union's political and military determination to support and defend it in a crisis. This the Soviets did with their tanks in 1953, but not in 1989. With that

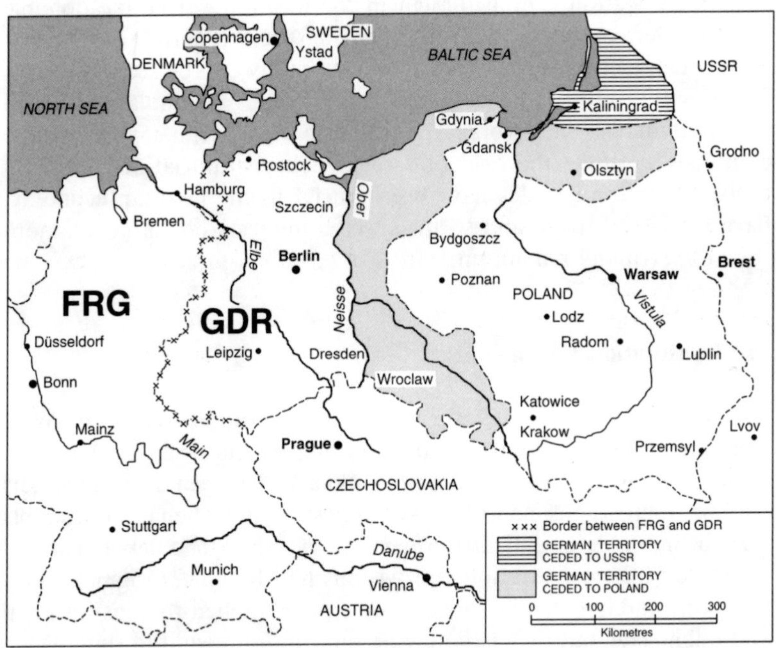

MAP 2 *Germany after 1949*

latter decision, what GDR propaganda had called 'the first workers' and peasants' state on German soil' was doomed.

The reunification of Germany in 1990, when the GDR became part of the Federal Republic under Article 23 of the Basic Law, removed the last formal limitations on sovereignty imposed by outsider powers on the two German states. However the limitation on sovereignty imposed by the Basic Law remained in place. For decades this self-limitation served as an excuse for a reluctance to take responsibility, for example as a member of the UN or NATO. Around 1989–90 many feared that reunification would lead Germany to make excessive use of its new opportunities, but this has not been the case. On the contrary, patterns of behaviour from the pre-1989 period still dominate foreign policy. In contrast, even prior to 1989 the Federal Republic took on a dominant role as the strongest economic power in Europe; and despite considerable economic constraints this has been no less true since reunification. In particular the criteria for European economic and monetary union, included at German insistence in the Treaty of Maastricht, as well as the influence of the Bundesbank on decisions of economic and monetary policy, show that this leading economic role has actually increased since reunification – even though in the meantime it is questionable whether Germany can itself fulfil the Maastricht criteria.

All these factors suggest that Germany today can be seen as a state that has not yet found a definitive role or clearly formulated its own national interests in Europe. The tradition of the semi-sovereign state continues to affect the field of foreign policy; transnational orientations, which for decades have been crucial to the German economy, have been reinforced, and so the specific interests of the new nation-state of Germany remain unclear.

The Constitutional Framework

In the years before 1989 there was a passionate debate in West Germany on the concept of 'constitutional patriotism', that is, what normatively justifiable relationship could exist between the state and its citizens when no German nation-state existed, and when clear attempts were being made to extend European integration. The debate showed how strong the constitutional provisions had become. Originally they had been purely formal and were principally applied to constitutional and public law, but they had now become not only vital to state order, but also to the understanding of politics and the state in West Germany.

In the Parliamentary Council of 1949 there was basic consensus on three guiding principles of the constitutional order: the new German state was to be a republic, based on federal structures; the principle of the rule of law was to be the general maxim of political and social activity; and the state should guarantee the social (or welfare) state. In this sense the Basic Law speaks of a 'democratic and social Federal state' (Article 20.1) and states that 'the constitutional order in the Länder must conform to the principles of republican, democratic and social government based on the rule of law, within the meaning of this Basic Law' (Article 8.1).

The Federal Republic of Germany

The constitution of the Weimar Republic of 1919 contained the short, sharp statement in Article 1: 'The German Reich is a republic. All state power emanates from the people'. The Basic Law employs no such wording. It refers to the republican principle indirectly (in Article 28.1), where there is mention of 'principles of republican, democratic and social government based on the rule of law', and in Article 20.1 it implicitly assumes that the federation should take the form of a republic and precludes other types of democratic state, such as a constitutional monarchy. This principle is also constitutionally anchored in the term chosen by the Parliamentary Council: 'The Federal Republic of Germany'.

The initial decision in favour of a republic still permited various options as to how the state would be organised – it could be constituted as a centralised state or as a federal structure. However Germany had no tradition of centralisation and there was no doubt that it would be a federal state, both in the light of German traditions and in the clear instructions of the Allies, who would not have permitted a centralised state. Another factor was the reconstitution of the Länder, which had already taken place. The fact that the Länder existed before the Federal Republic came into being is an historical element that continues to have effects today. The federal order and the autonomy of the Länder became the central structural principles of the Federal Republic.

The Rechtsstaat

The idea of the *Rechtsstaat* (a state based on the rule of law) has a long tradition in German political and popular thinking. National socialism had destroyed the validity of law, so it was therefore understandable that restoration of the rule of law became a vital condition for the political order of the Federal Republic. The essential elements of the principle of the *Rechtsstaat* are: 'the right to due process', confidence in legal norms, the preeminence of the constitution over all other legal norms, and the commitment of all state authorities to the law and the separation of powers.

The separation of powers, the commitment of the legislature to constitutional order (as set out in Article 20.3 of the Basic Law), and the commitment of the executive and judiciary to the law are taken for granted in established democracies. But in Germany after the Second World War this represented a new constitutional statement that had never before been formulated so unambiguously. This helps to explain the great importance attached to formal legalistic procedures in the German political culture. How well the separation of powers has been effected has to be assessed more cautiously. The classical idea of the separation of powers in the Basic Law has given way to a system of functional relationships. The political system of the Federal Republic is characterised by a *horizontal separation of powers* between the legislature, the executive and the judiciary and by a *vertical separation of powers* between the Federation, the Länder and the local authorities (*Gebietskörperschaften*). But at the same time the necessary cooperation between these different levels in a federal system leads to an intermeshing of the rights and competences of these powers (Figure 2.1). The basic idea of German constitutionalism, as laid down in the Basic Law, is of limited government, checks and balances, and a dispersion of decision-making authority through the principle of federalism.

The Basic Law treats the *Rechtsstaat* not only as a formal principle, as was the case with the conservative German doctrine of constitutional law, but also as one containing basic elements of a material kind. (The phrase 'a social *Rechtsstaat*' in Article 28.1 of the Basic Law is an illustration.) But opinions vary widely as to what specific elements are involved, and in particular what the 'social dimension' is and how far it should be taken. This poses a direct question about the social content of the *Rechtsstaat* and about the political actors who interpret it. It is a question of how widely the principle of the social or welfare state and that of democracy should be extended.

The 'Social State'

The principle of the welfare state (Article 20.1 of the Basic Law) is one of the entrenched constitutional clauses that are not subject to amendment (Article 79.3). The welfare state is of vital importance to the

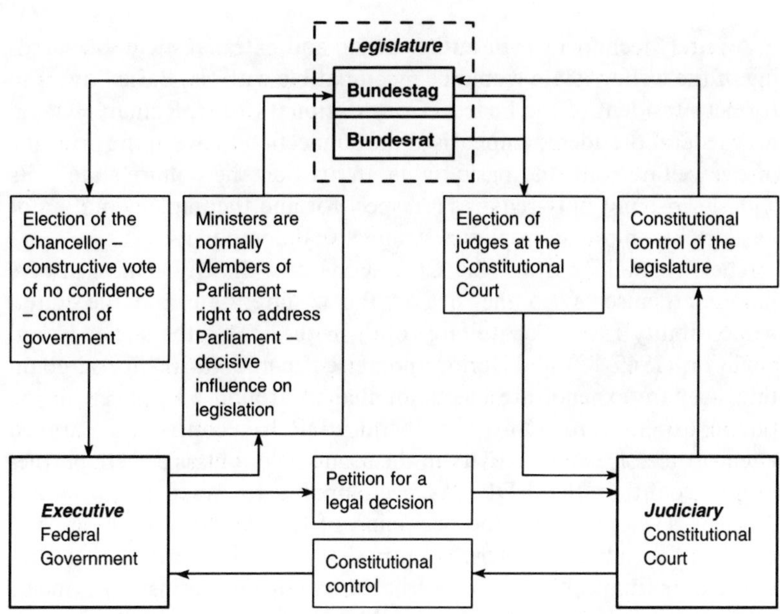

FIGURE 2.1 *Division and fusion of powers*

legitimacy of the political and social system, an importance that has increased since reunification because East Germans regard social welfare as a service provided by the state as a matter of course. For a long time its extent, significance and content were a matter of controversy. Whereas conservative theories of constitutional law interpreted the welfare state only as correcting the existing situation to make it 'more social', others saw the clause as a compromise formula, since those framing the constitution had been unable to agree on moral concepts.

Eventually, after extensive discussion and several legal judgements, particularly those of the Federal Constitutional Court, a degree of consensus emerged about the meaning of the 'welfare state' in the sense of the Basic Law: it was interpreted more as a broad set of targets than an agreement on its concrete shaping. There is still a general consensus that the principle of the welfare state places an obligation on the state to establish social justice, that is, a constitutional obligation to secure social justice in the sense of promoting equal opportunities and individual freedom. The inherent conflict between social rights and individual freedom has led to detailed discussions on German constitutional theory.

A purely technocratic or authoritarian and paternalistic understanding of the welfare state would be incompatible with the Basic Law. The former president of the Federal Constitutional Court, Roman Herzog, now federal president, emphasised the connection between the principle of the welfare state and basic rights. In his view the welfare state in its widest sense not only requires a respect for and the implementation of basic rights, but also implies a strong social component.

The two main parties, the CDU–CSU and the SPD, have always pledged themselves to the idea of the welfare state and the state's responsibility for social welfare. Both in the era of the social–liberal coalition (1969–82) and during the present conservative–liberal coalition, welfare expenditure has amounted to around 50 per cent of all public expenditure. Only the liberal FDP has consistently argued against excessive state activity in the social field, but as a mere partner in the coalition the FDP has been unable to make major policy changes. However since the beginning of the 1990s, as is the case in other industrialised Western countries, the social security system has reached its financial limits, exacerbated by immense transfer payments to eastern Germany – more than DM600 billion since 1990. The new debate on 'reconstructing' the welfare state is in reality a discussion about 'cutting it back'. This will have far-reaching consequences for the political self-perception of the Federal Republic, since it owes its political stability very largely to the way in which it has been able to maintain a high level of social welfare.

Democracy and the Basic Law

At first sight, what the Basic Law means by 'democratic' seems straightforward enough. Thus the Basic Law asserts that 'All state authority emanates from the people' (Article 20.2). The phrase 'emanates from the people' does not mean *conducted* by the people. The process takes place 'by means of elections and voting and by specific legislative, executive and judicial organs' (Article 20.2). The Basic Law provides for state authority to be exercised directly by the people only in the case of Article 29 on redrawing the territorial boundaries of the Länder as happened in 1952, in the case of Baden-Württemberg, and then in Berlin and Brandenburg in 1996. The constitutions of the various Länder contain different and generally more extensive arrangements for citizens to participate directly.

The constitutional order of the Federal Republic is based on the principle of representation. After the experience of national socialism, which was initially supported by the majority of the population, the founding fathers of the constitution were sceptical about direct participation in politics by the citizenry. Until now that decision has made it difficult to develop forms of political decision making based on popular participation and consultation. After the positive experiences of the citizens' rights movement in the GDR in 1989–90, many had expected that constitutional reform would lead to the introduction of elements of direct democracy, especially in relation to public petitions, citizens' action groups and referenda. This has not happened, mainly because the CDU–CSU raised objections and thus the two-thirds majority necessary to amend the constitution was not forthcoming.

Until 1989 reunification was a distant goal, to be attained only within the framework of a future European peace order. The Basic Law had worked out a complicated procedure: 'This Basic Law shall cease to be in force on the day on which a constitution adopted by a free decision of the German people comes into force' (Article 146). A constitutional assembly, elected by the citizens of both German states, was supposed to devise a constitution, which was then to be ratified by a referendum. As a result of the pressure of events in 1990 it was not this 'clean' procedure that was chosen – however well it would have fitted in with democratic theory – but a different method of reunification. As with the Saarland in 1956, the GDR acceded to the Federal Republic under the terms of Article 23 of the Basic Law which provided for the voluntary accession of former German territories to the Federal Republic.

The democratically elected, final government of the GDR insisted in the Unification Treaty that amendments to the Basic Law resulting from accession should be implemented. In Article 5, concerning future amendments to the constitution, the Unification Treaty 'recommends' to the legislative bodies of the united Germany (that is, Bundestag and Bundesrat) 'that within two years they should deal with the questions regarding amendments or additions to the Basic Law as raised in connection with German unification in particular'. The main subjects listed in the treaty were the relationship between the Federation and the Länder, the possibility of restructuring the Berlin/Brandenburg area, the introduction of 'state objectives' into the Basic Law, and procedural questions as to whether a referendum should be held on amending the constitution.

The last two points were especially important for the democratically elected government of the GDR. In early 1990 a constitutional draft had been approved by the 'Round Table', providing for extensive state objectives (*Staatsziele*) and far-reaching rights of participation. These proposals matched ideas for reform that had arisen in West Germany in the 1980s. The arrangements made in the Unification Treaty, however, turned out to be only a formal concession.

The 'Joint Constitutional Commission of the Bundestag and Bundesrat' was only able to agree on a few changes to the constitution. The idea of the GDR, and in particular of the civil rights campaigners, to expand the catalogue of basic rights in the Basic Law with an extensive list of state objectives fell on stony ground; they succeeded only in having environmental protection listed as a state objective in the new Article 20a, and for equal rights for men and women to be extended through the introduction of a clause obliging the state to help remove existing inequalities (Article 3.3).

All the other constitutional changes concerned the organisational part of the Basic Law and mainly strengthened the authority of the Länder. Since they involved constitutional law, the Unification Treaty and the other constitutional changes following from reunification required a two-thirds majority in both the Bundestag and the Bundesrat. Thus the Länder were able to use their position in the latter body as a bargaining chip.

Features of German Federalism

The federal order of the Federal Republic is characterised by three leading elements: legislative competences are allocated to both the federal governments and the Länder, administrative tasks are divided between the federal government and the Länder and financial resources are shared between the two branches of government. In principle the Basic Law proceeds from the assumption of responsibility of the Länder: 'The Länder shall have the right to legislate insofar as this Basic Law does not confer legislative power on the Federal government' (Article 70.1). In practice, however, an ever greater shift of legislative activity has taken place from the Länder to the federal government, which was achieved by the latter exploiting the authority of the general provisions of the federation and extending the provision for 'joint tasks'.

The federal system not only allocates concrete and clearly differentiated legislative competences to the federal government and the Länder. It also allows administrative tasks to be distributed, on the basis of subsidiarity, to the individual corporate bodies – the federation government, the Länder and the local communities and their associations. The essential characteristic of the German administrative system is that while the federal government has an administration of its own in just a few – though important – areas, the majority of administrative tasks are conducted at the Land or local authority level in the towns, districts and regions (Table 2.1).

Exclusively federal administration exists in only a few areas, such as the Foreign Office, financial administration, the army, the federal border guard and other security bodies. These institutions, when necessary, have offices of their own at the Land and local authority level (for example the army has administrative offices in the Länder and with local authorities). Apart from these few exceptions, the Länder are solely responsible for applying federal law. This provides the main autonomous function of the Länder, along with the exclusive legislative authority accorded to them, although this is limited to a few spheres.

TABLE 2.1 *Administrative structure of the Federal Republic*

Federal Administration with its own administrative substructure (Article 87 of the Basic Law)	Foreign Office Federal Financial Administration Federal Railways and Post Office (before privatisation) Federal Waterways Federal Security Authorities 'Indirect' Federal Administration (social insurance organisations)
Länder Administration on behalf of the Federation (Article 85 of the Basic Law)	Executing federal laws on behalf of the Federation Supervising the Federation (for legality and effectiveness) Responding to the federation's right to issue directives The federation pays the cost of this administration
The carrying out of federal legislation as the Länder's own responsibility	The federation has no right to issue directives, except in special cases with the agreement of the Bundesrat Federal supervision (for legality only) Administration costs are borne by the Länder
Joint Tasks (Article 91a of the Basic Law)	Participation of the Federation in Land responsibilities through 'joint framework planning' (e.g. new university buildings, regional economic structure) Costs are shared by federation and Länder Participation in Land administration to carry out Federal laws
Local authority administration	Tied to instructions of the Land supervisory organisations

The federal system provides not only for a sharing of tasks and responsibilities between the federal government, Länder and the local authorities, but also for a corresponding division of financial resources. The Basic Law precisely regulates the division of tax revenues between federation and Länder (right down to the 'Beer Tax') and the allocation of financial resources to the local authorities. The idea developed in the Basic Law of a 'democratic and social federal state' and 'joint tasks', 'which are important for society as a whole' and 'where federal participation is necessary for the improvement of living conditions' (Article 91a.1), require the sharing of revenues between the corporate bodies. The financial relations between the federal government, the Länder and the local authorities involve the following principles:

- Vertical equalisation, that is, federal payments to poorer Länder.
- The sharing of common tax revenues by the federal government and the Länder.
- Federal payments to the Länder to cover the cost of administering federal law.
- Horizontal equalisation between the Länder, where federal legislation 'shall ensure a reasonable equalisation between financially strong and financially weak Länder, with due account being taken of the financial capacity and financial requirements of local authorities and local authority associations (Article 107.2).
- Intergovernmental grants for joint tasks, for example, improvement of regional economic or agricultural structures.

This system, combined with special infrastructure programmes for structurally weak regions, has led to a considerable reduction in regional disparities in West Germany.

When the GDR joined the Federal Republic there was a shift in the balance of influence among the Länder, shown above all in their relative financial status. The accession of the five new Länder meant that the system for allocating financial resources, which had been carefully balanced over a period of decades, was thrown into confusion. For a long time to come Brandenburg, Mecklenburg-West Pomerania, Saxony-Anhalt, Saxony, Thuringia and Berlin will require considerable financial support. This has turned Länder, such as the Saarland, which previously received funds through the financial equalisation mechanism, into states that now have to pay considerable sums in financial equalisation to Länder in the east. For this reason the introduction of the West German financial arrangements, according to

Article 7 of the Unification Treaty, was delayed until 31 December 1995. A final date had to be set, since prolonged, special treatment of the eastern Länder would not only have endangered social peace in the unified Germany, but would also have been impossible to reconcile with the basic rules of the federal political system. The eastern Länder were reestablished in 1990 more out of feelings of nostalgia than with an eye to economic and political rationality, and they will be dependent on financial help from the federal government and the western Länder for much longer than originally anticipated. Since, as with the eastern Bundestag representatives, they are in a minority position, they need to find allies among the western Länder, but they too are experiencing increasing financial constraints and are coming under political pressure.

The transfer of sovereign rights to the European Union has had a considerable effect on the German federal system. The criterion of 'subsidiarity' developed in the Maastricht Treaty means that, according to the Basic Law, the principles of federalism have to be respected and the agreement of the Bundesrat, (the upper house of the federal parliament), has to be obtained, or in other words the agreement of the Länder. This required an amendment to the constitution (Article 24), which *inter alia* provides for the Bundesrat to be expressly included in the 'formation of political will' in the affairs of the European Union. Furthermore, within the EU framework the responsibility for decision-making in matters that affect the exclusive legislative authority of the Länder (for example, questions of education) are to be transferred from the federal level to a Länder Committee appointed by the Bundesrat. The increasing regulatory activity of the EU is restricting the rights and authority of national parliaments, but these rights are *not* being transferred to the European Parliament. This democratic deficit is becoming all the more serious in federal systems, where the authority of constituent states is being undermined.

The Federal Constitutional Court, in its ruling on the Maastricht Treaty, produced a series of clarifications in its judgement of 12 October 1993. It declared: 'The democratic principle does not hinder the Federal Republic from membership in supranational international communities, provided that legitimation and influence emanating from the people, the validity of basic rights and the principles of the "democratic and social federal state" of Article 20.1 of the Basic Law are not affected'. When all these internal and external factors are taken together, it is clear that Germany's federal system is facing a severe test.

Government at the Centre: Parliamentary Institutions

Two fundamental structural decisions shaped the two-chamber governmental system of the Federal Republic. Firstly, unlike the semipresidential system of the Weimar Republic, a parliamentary system was established that stressed representation on rather than direct democracy, and provided a strong position for the government and the chancellor. Secondly, the representation of Länder interests was not entrusted to a second chamber whose membership would be decided by popular vote, but to the Bundesrat, which is composed of representatives of governments and seats are allocated according to the population size of the Länder (see Table 4.4, p. 69). In contrast, the Bundestag is directly elected by universal suffrage for a maximum four-year term.

This basic structure has not been fundamentally affected by reunification. However the changed balance of voting in the Bundesrat after reunification has caused problems for the western Länder. Before 1990 each of the large Länder – Bavaria, Baden-Württemberg, North-Rhine Westphalia and Lower Saxony – had five seats in the Bundesrat, and together the four held a blocking majority. This strategic advantage would have been lost through the accession of the new Länder, even though in total the latter only have the same number of inhabitants as North-Rhine Westphalia, the largest of the Länder. To preserve their strategic position, in 1990 the large Länder agreed to sign the Unification Treaty only if the voting ratio in the Bundesrat was changed in their favour. Finally, the accession of the new Länder, and above all the different development of the party system and voter behaviour in East and West Germany, has led to new differences between the Länder and new problems in the relationship between Bundestag and Bundesrat (see Chapters 4 and 5).

The German version of the parliamentary system is based on an historically understandable but problematic analysis of the Weimar constitution, which despite its institutional weaknesses (emergency decrees, the strong position of the president and so on) was a modern constitution for a parliamentary republic. Some peculiarities of the postwar German parliamentary system can be explained by the fact that the 'modern' constitution of the Weimar Republic which, despite the provision of various safeguards in the constitution, did not prevent the overthrow of the democratic system by the National Socialists (Nazis).

In institutional terms the Bundestag is the leading legislative organ. In practical, everyday politics 'classic' legislation – that is, laws dealing with basic questions of the political, social and judicial order – comes second to bills that adapt existing regulations to changing conditions. By and large the civil service initiates this type of legislation. Thus the Bundestag, as well as the Land parliaments, *de facto*, have been reduced to a control function, rather than having an initiating role. The Basic Law sets out the areas of exclusive and concurrent legislation of the federation, in which the Bundesrat participates (Figure 2.2). The various areas are specified in a detailed catalogue (Articles 70–74). In addition the federal government can make general provisions in particular fields, such as public sector pay and nature conservation.

The Bundestag is responsible for electing the chancellor and the governing majority has a decisive influence over appointments to ministerial posts. However, as bodies such as the national executive, Land associations and special working groups enjoy growing influence, conflicts increasingly arise over the respective roles of the national party and the parliamentary party and the power of the head of government to set the general parameters of politics has been undermined. At the same time the emphasis on the importance of 'chancellor candidates', 'leadership candidates' and 'government teams' means that the ability of parliamentarians to elect leaders of their own choosing is effectively weakened. The opportunity to remove a serving chancellor (and the government) is severely restricted and can only be achieved through a 'constructive' vote of no confidence whereby the majority vote for an alternative leader.

A vital element of liberal democratic systems of government is the responsibility of government to parliament and the control of government by parliament. The brief provisions of the Basic Law allocate

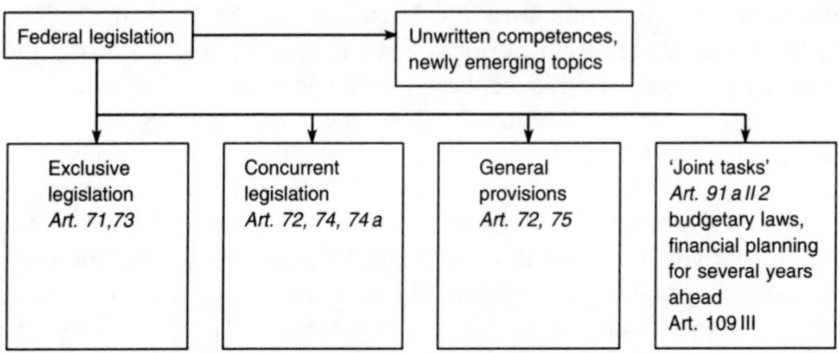

Note: In certain areas the Länder have the power to legislate as long as the Federation does not exercise the powers for itself.

FIGURE 2.2 *Legislative competences of the federation*

only secondary importance to parliamentary control of the legislative process. The Bundestag's most important control instrument is the right to advise on and to control the budget. The Bundestag and each of its committees can demand the presence of a member of the government (Article 43.1), set up committees of inquiry (mostly with only moderate results), and as a last resort can vote the chancellor out of office. In controlling the general political direction taken by the cabinet, the executive government and the majority parties of the coalition in the Bundestag are dependent on one another; they can only succeed by sticking together. This has led to government deputies exercising their control function only internally, within the governing parties, if indeed at all. Thus it is left to the opposition to try to embarrass the government and gain as much publicity as possible in the process. The opposition can also look for support from Land governments of the same party in the Bundesrat, an important aspect of opposition in the context of German federalism. Controls of public administration allows deputies from the government *and* the opposition parties to act together, and because of the federal structure of the administration they play a greater role in the Land parliaments than in the Bundestag. In practice, government and parliament, federation and Länder very often work closely together so that the relevant literature refers to 'cooperative federalism' and the 'governmental functions of parliament' rather than a strict dichtomy of government and opposition.

The legitimacy of parliamentary opposition is recognised, and is mentioned in some new Land constitutions, but is not separately identified in the Basic Law itself. It is questionable whether the idea of an 'alternative government' power, borrowed from the British model, really conforms with the intentions of the Basic Law. The fundamental decision to adopt a federal system, together with the nature of the relationship between government and parliament, have structural elements that have led to the contemporary system of 'political intertwining' (*Politikverflechtung* – the complex process of negotiation involved in policymaking). It has also led to cooperative methods of conflict-solving as an opposition strategy. However, bringing all parliamentary parties, including the opposition, into the political decision-making process has had a considerable effect on the ideal model of the 'dual system', in which political outcome is fashioned through a contest between the government majority and the opposition. Since – via the Bundesrat – the opposition actually participates in the process of government, the system may be described as one of 'shared leadership of the state'.

The Bundesrat is in an extremely strong position with regard to legislation planned by the central government. Since its members are mandated delegates of the Land governments, acting on instructions from them, the direct participation of the Land governments in federal legislation is secure. Thus in addition to their functions in public administration, the Länder also play an important legislative role at the federal level.

The Constitutional Court (*Bundesverfassungsgericht*) was created by the Basic Law as a strong controlling authority *vis-à-vis* both government and parliament (see Chapter 6). The Constitutional Court has the authority to rule on the conformity of legislation with the constitution, to ensure that basic rights are guaranteed and maintained, to interpret the Basic Law and to decide whether federal law is compatible with international law. It rules on constitutional complaints made by individual citizens, on the so-called compatibility of statutory law with the Basic Law (*Normenkontrollverfahren*), and on disputes between other constitutional organs, such as the Länder. Its decisions are binding, which means that the Constitutional Court also possesses a *de facto* right to amend legislation. But above all the Constitutional Court is the guarantor of the constitution, particularly of the basic rights laid down in Articles 1–20. In this respect it has proved an effective brake on attempts to restrict or alter basic rights for purely political reasons.

However this sweeping degree of responsibility has also produced additional problems. Frequently the Constitutional Court is brought in to mediate in cases of dispute between government and opposition, between federal and Land authorities, and even within the government coalition itself. Those who have been defeated in the decision-making process hope that the Court will make amendments in their favour. Thus in spite of its inclination to exercise judicial self-restraint, the Court is provided with an authority that forces it into the role of a referee. This role was not intended by the constitution: 'It shall be [the] final arbiter in ruling between competing interests but not replace parliamentary decisions and competences'.

The Role of the Chancellor

In most parliamentary democracies the head of government has a prominent position, and in the German political system the chancellor's position is particularly strong. This is one reason why in more than forty years the Federal Republic has had only six chancellors, of whom two, Konrad Adenauer and Helmut Kohl, governed for over ten years. The powerful position of the chancellor is established by a series of Articles in the Basic Law.

First, the right of the chancellor to determine policy guidelines (*Richtlinienkompetenz*): 'The Federal Chancellor shall determine and be responsible for the general policy guidelines. Within the limits set by these guidelines, each Federal Minister shall conduct the affairs of his department autonomously and on his own responsibility' (Article 65). Because most of the chancellors have remained in power for several years, and have had great authority in the cabinet, the relationship between the right to determine policy guidelines and the personal responsibility of ministers has changed. Strong chancellors tend to define the right to determine policy in broad terms and to interfere with the work of individual ministries. Helmut Kohl, in particular, has in recent years declared an increasing number of ministerial decisions to be 'a matter for the boss', so that a *de facto* shift of competence from the ministers and the cabinet to the chancellor has occurred. Just as during the Thatcher era in Britain, tendencies that undermine parliamentary practices and replace them with quasipresidential decisions have become marked.

Second, above all, the chancellor's strong position, provided he has a parliamentary majority, resides in the 'constructive vote of no-confidence' (Article 67), as a reaction to the 'negative majorities' of the Weimar Republic. This instrument has been used only twice in the history of the Federal Republic – in the unsuccessful attempt to bring down Willy Brandt in 1972 and in the successful overthrow of Helmut Schmidt in 1982; in this way Helmut Kohl became chancellor. It is almost impossible to remove a chancellor from one's own party merely because he is regarded as too weak and 'past his sell-by date', as, for instance, Helmut Kohl was perceived in the early summer of 1989. An internal leadership battle would inevitably split the governing party and make it difficult for any challenger to forge a parliamentary majority.

Nevertheless the chancellor is also subject to major constraints:

- With one exception (1957–61) no party has had an absolute majority in the Bundestag. Every chancellor needs coalition partners, but if the parliamentary arithmetic permits the partners can threaten to leave the coalition and side with the opposition.
- The chancellor and government majority have to contend with the Bundesrat, which may well have a different political complexion,

since different coalitions exist in the Länder. But even if the governing parties have a majority in the Bundesrat too, the decisions of Land governments are often dictated more by the interests of the Länder themselves than by party loyalties.

- The complicated legislative procedure and the structure of public administration make necessary a permanent search for cooperation and harmony between government and Länder, and reduce considerably the ability of the former to shape political decision making.
- All government decisions are subject to control by parliament, but above all by the Constitutional Court, as shown in the case when the Court ruled positively on whether German soldiers could serve in the Balkans.
- The Federal Republic has a powerful central bank (the Bundesbank), which by law pursues an independent monetary policy and thereby exerts a crucial influence on the economic and financial policy of the government.
- The scope for activity of all governments in the European Union is becoming ever narrower, as European laws and decisions by the Commission and the Council of Ministers are gaining increased importance.

As mentioned above, governments and chancellors in the Federal Republic tend to stay in power for a comparatively long time (Table 2.2). The first chancellor, Konrad Adenauer, remained in office for 13 years, Helmut Schmidt governed for eight years, and in 1996 Helmut Kohl had been in office for 14 years. The unhappy chancellorship of the previously successful economics minister and 'Father of the Economic Miracle', Ludwig Erhard, lasted only three years, as did the chancellor of the Grand Coalition (1966–69), Kurt-Georg Kiesinger. In his five short years as chancellor, Willy Brandt achieved historical success with his policy towards the East *(Ostpolitik)*.

The lengthy chancellorship of Helmut Kohl and the equally extended spell in opposition of the SPD show there is a close relationship between parties and government and that the act of governing has important consequences for government and opposition parties alike. The CDU, which under the leadership of Helmut Kohl in the late 1970s became a modern party with an effective programme and party apparatus, today appears nothing more then a support organisation for the government and the chancellor. As a result of the offices of chancellor and party leader being combined, the CDU, as in the days of Adenauer, has degenerated into an 'organisation to re-elect the chancellor', with comparatively little life of its own.

TABLE 2.2 *Coalitions and federal chancellors, 1949–96*

Term of government	*Chancellor*	*Coalition*	*Changes during term of office*
1st Legislature, 1949–53	Adenauer	CDU/CSU–FDP–DP	None
2nd Legislature, 1953–58	Adenauer	CDU/CSU–FDP–DP–GB/BHE	GB/BHE quits coalition 1955; FDP splits, ministers form FVP and stay in government; the party leaves coalition 1956
3rd Legislature, 1957–61	Adenauer	CDU/CSU–DP	Most of the MPs of DP join the CDU in 1960
4th Legislature, 1961–63	Adenauer	CDU/CSU–FDP	Adenauer resigns in Oct. 1963
4th Legislature, 1963–65	Erhard	CDU/CSU–FDP	None
5th Legislature, 1965–66	Erhard	CDU/CSU–FDP	FDP leaves government in Oct. 1966; minority government until Dec. 1966
6th Legislature, 1966–69	Kiesinger	CDU/CSU–SPD	'Grand coalition'
6th Legislature, 1969–72	Brandt	SPD–FDP	After defections from coalition and a failed 'constructive vote of no confidence' early elections in 1972
7th Legislature, 1972–74	Brandt	SPD–FDP	Brandt resigns in May 1974
7th Legislature, 1974–76	Schmidt	SPD–FDP	None
8th Legislature, 1976–80	Schmidt	SPD–FDP	None
9th Legislature, 1980–82	Schmidt	SPD–FDP	After FDP defects Schmidt coalition is deposed by a vote of no confidence
9th Legislature, 1982–83	Kohl	CDU/CSU–FDP	Voted into office by new coalition
10th Legislature, 1983–87	Kohl	CDU/CSU–FDP	Early federal elections
11th Legislature, 1987–90	Kohl	CDU/CSU–FDP	None
12th Legislature, 1990–94	Kohl	CDU/CSU–FDP	First all-German elections
13th Legislature, 1994–	Kohl	CDU/CSU–FDP	None

Coalition Government

The political system of the Federal Republic is characterised not only by continuity of political leaders, and in particular of chancellors, but also by the remarkable stability of government coalitions. From 1949 to 1966 a right-of-centre coalition was in power, usually involving the Free Democrats (FDP). From 1969 until the break-up of the coalition at the end of 1982, the Social Democrats formed an alliance with the FDP, but then the latter changed its coalition partner and brought the present government to power. The effect of the political structure is that just one change of government has come about through an election – the socialist-liberal coalition in 1969. The others took place through the break-up of a coalition by action taken by the FDP, or in the case of Helmut Kohl in 1982 by a constructive vote of no-confidence in which a partner in the earlier coalition participated – the FDP again. This situation, which is somewhat problematical when measured against criteria of democratic theory, results from the constitutional features of the government, the strong institutional position of the chancellor and the *de facto* as well as *de jure* strength of the parties.

The Bundestag has never been a place for the exercise of party sovereignty. It is the party organisations rather than parliamentary parties, that have a decisive influence on the political constellations that lead to particular government coalitions. Party committees rather than parliamentary groups decide on coalitions. Once governments have been voted in, members of parliament are generally held to owe them their loyalty. Changes of coalition have been a far from routine event, instead they are turned into 'decisions about a new political direction'.

Yet despite the domination by Chancellor Kohl over his own party and the governing coalition, changes in the party system and voting behaviour are evident, with uncertain effects on coalition formation, not least because of the decline of the Free Democrats, (see Chapter 4). The altering situation is especially evident in the different development of the party system in West and East Germany: the post-communist PDS will remain a force to be reckoned with. In particular there are the changes in voting behaviour, weakening and shifting party loyalties, together with protest voting, as for example, the case of the right-wing Republicans (see Chapter 3).

All these developments will make both government and government formation more difficult than in the early 1990s, and that is to be expected in view of the economic and social problems: they will demand answers of entirely new dimensions from parties and governments. Institutionally the Federal Republic is stable enough to cope with the challenges, and the popular commitment to democracy justifies optimism. Nevertheless, it remains to be seen whether these assets will be sufficient to solve new problems at the turn of the century.

3

A Divided Electorate?

RUSSELL J. DALTON

German reunification brought together two publics from vastly different political worlds. The people of West Germany had matured and prospered under a democratic political system and a social market economy (*Sozialmarktwirtschaft*). This had transformed the values of West Germany, creating a democratic, pluralist and liberal electorate (Baker *et al.*, 1981; Conradt, 1980). Under the system of the German Democratic Republic (GDR) the people had been socialised into a 'socialist personality' that stressed socialist economics, communist political principles and solidarity with the Soviet Union. While the GDR ostensibly had a multiparty system and national elections, true democracy had been just an illusion – political power had been firmly held by the communists. Then, within only a few months in 1989–90, political life was transformed in the East. East Germans celebrated the new freedoms of democracy but also began to learn the responsibilities that accompanied these new rights, and the benefits and costs of West Germany's market economy. The last five years have shown that this adjustment has been difficult at times.

German reunification raises questions about how well these two different publics have been integrated into the political system of the Federal Republic. Public opinion surveys indicate that easterners accept the political and economic institutions of the Federal Republic, but they often hold different expectations about how these institutions should function. Moreover easterners view contemporary political issues, such as welfare reform or the conflict in Bosnia, in the context of political experiences and histories that are different from those of westerners.

This chapter focuses on the electoral behaviour of the German public and examines the political differences between westerners and easterners. Elections are a useful setting to study political attitudes and behaviour, because they require citizens to think about political issues and make political choices. During elections, citizens express their judgements about the past accomplishments of the political parties and make choices about the future course of the nation. Elections also mobilise and display the political cleavages existing within a society. A study of the voting behaviour of westerners and easterners can tell us a great deal about the political legacy of Germany's divided history. To what extent has 40 years of life under different economic and political systems created a divided electorate that is manifested in voting behaviour?

In addition, electoral research can highlight one example of how reunification may have altered the democratic politics of the Federal Republic. There is a long history of electoral research on western Germany. To what extent has the addition of several million new voters from the east altered the calculus of electoral politics, changing the patterns noted in earlier studies?

We begin our analysis by examining the factors that are normally described as stable and long-term influences on electoral politics: social group ties and partisan identification. These factors provide the enduring basis of party competition, and voters often use them to simplify their choices. Then we study the role of issues in guiding voting behaviour, and in defining policy contrasts between easterners and westerners. In the conclusion we discuss the implications of these findings for the German party system and German democracy.

Social Cleavages and Voting Behaviour

Electoral research often begins by examining the linkage between social characteristics and partisan choice. As Seymour Lipset and Stein Rokkan noted in their seminal work, party systems normally arise from the social divisions existing within a nation, and the strategic choices social groups make in courting party allies (Lipset and Rokkan, 1967). Because of this, many people use their social position or their judgments about the social leanings of the parties as a guide to their voting choices. A Ruhr steelworker who votes for the Social Democrats, or a Bavarian Catholic who supports the CSU, is reflecting his or her own values as well as the political choices available at elections. Thus social characteristics are often a good surrogate for studying differences in political values within a nation, as well as the importance of alternative social networks as influences on political behaviour.

Two social divisions have historically structured the electoral politics of the Federal Republic: class and religion. These cleavages have displayed extraordinary stability through the various institutional changes of the past century. They emerged in the constitutional monarchy of the German *Kaiserreich*, stabilised in the presidential democracy of the Weimar Republic, survived the Nazi dictatorship and were revitalised immediately after the Second World War in the first elections of the Federal Republic (Schmitt, 1993, 1994). The German Democratic Republic, however, attempted to restructure these social cleavages. The class system of a capitalist society was replaced by a socialist order and an officially classless society; the GDR consciously attempted to remove religious influences from East German society. Thus a comparison of social divisions in voting behaviour across regions provides a first assessment of whether unification has created two distinct electorates.

Social Status: East–West Contrasts

The Federal Republic's party system is partially built upon the traditional class conflict between the bourgeoisie and the proletariat, and more broadly the problems of providing economic well-being and security to all members of society. These economic conflicts were important in defining the initial structure of the party system. Moreover the CDU and the SPD are embedded in their own network of support groups (business associations and labour unions) and offer voters distinct political programmes catering to these group interests.

Despite the historical importance of the class cleavage, four decades of electoral results point to an unmistakable decline in class voting differences within the FRG's party system (Dalton, 1996a, ch. 8). At the height of class-based voting in 1957 the SPD received a majority of working-class votes (61 per cent) but only a small share (24 per cent) of middle-class votes. In overall terms this represented a 37 per cent gap in the class bases of party support, rivalling the level of class voting found in Britain and other class-polarized party systems. Over the next two decades the level of class voting steadily decreased. By the 1980s class voting differences averaged around 10 per cent. Voting differences based on other class characteristics, such as income or education, displayed a similar downward trend in their influence.

The top panel of Table 3.1 presents class voting differences for the western electorate in 1994. Class voting patterns were relatively unchanged in the west after German reunification. The working-class gives the bulk of its support (55.9 per cent) to the Social Democrats. Indeed, one of the SPD's successes in 1994 was to recapture its

TABLE 3.1 *Class voting patterns, 1994 (per cent)*

Party	*Worker*	*Self-employed*	*Salaried employees*	*Combined middle class*
Western Germany:				
CDU–CSU	37.2	59.7	38.6	42.9
FDP	1.1	17.1	8.0	9.9
SPD	55.9	14.6	39.4	34.5
Alliance 90/Greens	3.6	5.9	12.7	11.5
Other (REP/PDS)	2.2	2.6	1.4	1.1
Total	100.0	100.0	100.0	100.0
(N)	(264)	(98)	(391)	(489)
Per cent	35.1	13.0	51.9	
Eastern Germany:				
CDU	51.5	39.1	33.5	34.3
FDP	2.5	9.4	3.9	4.6
SPD	34.1	26.6	32.5	31.6
Alliance 90/Greens	1.8	7.8	8.0	8.0
PDS	9.8	17.2	21.6	21.0
Other (REP)	0.3	0.0	0.5	0.4
Total	100.0	100.0	100.0	100.0
(N)	(396)	(64)	(388)	(452)
Per cent	46.7	7.5	45.8	

Source: September 1994 Politbarometer Study, conducted by Forschungsgruppe Wahlen for the Zweite Deutsche Fernsehen (ZDF). The salaried employee category in the West includes civil servants.

traditional electoral strongpoints in western industrial districts. In contrast western middle-class voters give the largest share of their vote to the Christian Democrats (42.9 per cent). If we simply calculate the difference in the percentage of leftists (SPD and Greens) between the working class and the combined middle class, the 14 per cent gap in party support in 1994 is very close to prior elections in the west.

Past research has stressed the differences in social position and political behaviour between the traditional middle class (the self-employed and professionals) and the modern middle class (salaried employees and government workers) (Baker *et al.*, 1981). In more recent elections the modern middle class vote has been split between left-wing and right-wing parties. This pattern was repeated in 1994, with a less than 1 per cent difference in the CDU–CSU and SPD vote share within this stratum.

It is less clear, of course, how the class cleavage should affect electoral politics in the east. During the first democratic elections of 1990 the easterners understandably had a difficult time using the class cues that guide electoral choices in the west. It was hard to apply western notions of social class to the occupational structure inherited from the communist GDR. The economy had overwhelmingly comprised state-owned enterprises; the GDR had proclaimed itself as a classless society. Similarly, in place of the modern middle class of service workers and white-collar employees in the west, the east had party functionaries, governmental appointees and managers of state enterprises. Thus the traditional contrast between the bourgeoisie and proletariat in a free market economy had been largely irrelevant in East Germany.

To the extent that capitalist class distinctions could be applied to the eastern electorate in 1990, researchers found striking evidence of a *reversal* of class voting patterns among easterners (Dalton, 1992). The eastern CDU won most of the working-class vote and fared less well among the middle class. Conversely the leftist-oriented parties – the SPD and the PDS – garnered more votes among the middle class than among their 'normal' working-class constituency. The Alliance 90/Greens also gained greater support from the middle class. The few self-employed professionals in the east supported the CDU, but white-collar salaried employees in the east disproportionately endorsed leftist parties. Eastern voters thus began their experience with the FRG's party system with the opposite of the class voting pattern found in western Bundesrepublik and almost all Western democratic party systems.

This reversal of the class cleavage in the new Länder may have been a temporary phenomenon. Reactions to German reunification overshadowed ongoing public interest in the structure of social welfare programmes, social benefits, issues of environmental quality and many other topics (Kuechler, 1993). In addition the intermediary institutions that could link the parties to class groups, such as the unions and business associations, were themselves still developing in late 1990. Consequently the easterners displayed considerable uncertainty about the partisan leanings of business and labour groups in the 1990 elections.

The 1994 *Bundestagswahl* (federal election) was the first test of whether the class voting anomaly of easterners in 1990 had converged with voting alignments in the west, or maintained its own course. The lower panel in Table 3.1 shows that the reversal of class voting patterns in the east carried over to 1994. The eastern CDU drew a disproportionate share of its voters from workers (and the lesser-educated) – exactly the opposite relationship found in the west. The bulk of the eastern middle-class vote went to parties of the left. The SPD gained a near equal number of middle-class and working-class votes among easterners, and the core of PDS support was located in the eastern middle class – more than a fifth of the middle class in the east voted PDS. The worker–middle-class gap in class voting in 1994 was a negative 15 percentage points, even greater than in 1990. Moreover time-series analyses by Dalton and Bürklin (1996) show that these class patterns remained stable between the 1990 and 1994 elections.

How did this class reversal develop? In part it reflects the different historical experience of the people in the east. Despite the rhetoric of the GDR being a state for farmers and workers, its system disproportionately benefited the party elite and intelligentsia. Especially in the last decade, the GDR showed characteristics of a politically stratified, elitist society. The political system did not allow these conflicts to surface, but they began to manifest themselves in the democratic system of the Federal Republic. The ideological heirs of the GDR – the parties of the left – represent some of the same principles espoused by the Socialist Unity Party, (SED), albeit in moderate and democratic forms. Because of this their core support comes from groups that had supported the old regime. This can be seen in the concentration of PDS support in east Berlin districts that were formerly identified with government employment and SED membership.

Historical experience also gives a different meaning to a working-class identity in the east. Faced with the failure of the GDR, the workers in the new Länder gave their support to the party group that promised a change and improvement in their situation. In early 1990 the leading figures in the SPD were hesitant to offer a dramatically new vision of the future, thinking more of a partial stabilisation of the socialist model via a confederal solution (*Staatenbund*). Thus eastern workers were suspicious, fearing that a vote for the SPD would not bring about real change. In contrast the CDU leadership promised a radical and immediate change in the economic and political conditions in the east. The CDU (that is, the Alliance for Germany) thus gained the support of many easterners in the elections of 1990, and the CDU still benefits from this image.

Because of the centrality of class to German politics and the political identity of the parties, these contrasting East–West class voting patterns are a striking finding. Moreover these patterns have endured across two national elections and many more state elections. The continuity from 1990 to 1994 suggests that this is not a transient phenomenon. A new class cleavage has developed in the east, and it is grounded in citizen identification with the parties. Voters participating the next election will carry predispositions based on these class patterns.

On the one hand this contrasting pattern of class cleavage is weakening the overall importance of class-based voting in the unified electorate, and when the class voting patterns of both regions are merged this reinforces the long-term decline of class voting in the Federal Republic.

On the other hand real class voting differences do exist within each region – but they are contradictory. The contrasting nature of this cleavage has implications for intraparty relations between eastern and western factions of the political parties. Taking the CDU as an illustration, the CDU's electorate in the west largely comprises middle-class voters, especially members of the new middle class. This provides a political base for the Christian Democrats' conservative economic policy, a preference for limited social spending and other conservative policies.

In the east, however, the bulk of the CDU's support in 1994 came from working-class voters. If CDU deputies reflect this political base, an eastern wing of the CDU that is oriented towards the ideal of Christian socialism would strengthen the labour-oriented wing of the party (*Sozialausschüsse*) and could create new policy strains within the union. If CDU deputies do not represent these eastern views, it will create problems of democratic representation for the east.

The SPD faces a similar problem establishing its identity among easterners. A middle-class-oriented SPD in the east might fit in with the modernising image of the current party leadership. However this eastern constituency could handicap the SPD's efforts to renew its working-class constituency in the east and west. Similarly there are growing signs of tension between the eastern and western wings of the Alliance 90/Greens, partly because of the divergent constituencies in the two regions.

To sum up, differences in the class bases of electoral support in the east and west are creating internal tensions within the political parties. Moreover, with the passage of time social cleavages will tend to institutionalise themselves in patterns of partisan alliance and support. Hence, these class divisions may be an ongoing feature of contemporary German politics.

Religious Imbalance

Historically, religion has provided another basis for partisan division within the Federal Republic. This conflict goes back to the *Kultur-*

kampf of the 1870s and continues in the current political debates on the separation of church and state. This historical division is still exerting a strong influence on voting patterns in the west. The gap in SPD voting support between Catholics and Protestants has remained within the 20–25 point range for most of the past three decades. Furthermore, public perceptions of the Catholic Church's leanings towards the CDU–CSU suggest that religious cues remain distinct.

The impact of religion on eastern voters is uncertain because of the GDR's history. Although the GDR followed a policy of separating church and state, the government also replaced formal religious rites such as *Taufe* (baptism) and *Konfirmation* with secular rites such as, *Jugendweihe*, an initiation rite that marked the passage of 14-year-olds to adulthood. The churches' right to exist was not questioned, but they were under strict government control. It was unclear whether religious cleavages could persist in such an environment. Reunification changed the religious balance of politics in the Federal Republic. Catholics and Protestants were roughly equal in number in the west, but the east was heavily Protestant. Thus reunification significantly altered the overall religious composition of the new Germany.

Table 3.2 shows the distribution of votes by religion in the west and east in 1994. Among westerners, a 16 per cent gap separated Protestants and Catholics in their support for leftist parties (the SPD and the Greens). The voting gap between religious and non-religious westerners displayed a similar divide. Both patterns were similar to the results for 1990 and other recent Bundestag elections.

In the east, Catholics and Protestants disproportionately support the CDU. The voting gap between denominations is 18 per cent in leftist voting preferences – almost exactly the same as for the western electorate. The more relevant dimension for easterners involves the secular–religious divide or religious attachments such as church attendance. Secular voters favour leftist parties by a large margin; the size of this gap is similar to that in the west.

Thus the religious vote apparently follows a similar pattern in west and east, yet this commonality overlooks a basic difference in the composition of the two electorates. The GDR government successfully created a secular society during its forty-year rule. For instance the 1990 World Values Survey finds that 63 per cent of westerners believe in the existence of God, compared with 33 per cent in the east; 54 per cent of westerners consider themselves religious, but only 33 per cent of easterners do likewise (Dalton, 1996a, ch. 6). Only a tenth of the western public say they are non-religious, compared with two thirds of easterners! In summary, the GDR was a much more secular society

TABLE 3.2 *Religious voting patterns, 1994 (per cent)*

Party	*Catholic*	*Protestant*	*No religion*
Western Germany:			
CDU/CSU	49.5	37.4	30.7
FDP	7.8	4.2	5.7
SPD	31.9	49.2	42.0
Alliance 90/Greens	9.0	7.9	17.0
Other	1.7	1.4	4.5
Total	100.0	100.0	100.0
(N)	(372)	(356)	(88)
Per cent	45.6	43.6	10.8
Eastern Germany:			
CDU	72.7	56.5	32.1
FDP	4.5	2.5	3.9
SPD	18.2	29.1	34.5
Alliance 90/Greens	2.3	6.1	5.1
PDS	2.3	5.7	20.7
Other	0.0	0.0	3.6
Total	100.0	100.0	100.0
(N)	(44)	(244)	(588)
Per cent	5.0	27.9	67.1

Source: September 1994 Politbarometer Study; conducted by Forschungsgruppe Wahlen.

than western Germany, even though the west experienced its own secularisation trend.

The sharply different religious preferences of easterners and westerners is clear evidence that two separate electorates now exist. The western electorate is still relatively religious; the eastern electorate is predominately secular. The different religious composition of the two electorates is creating two distinct constituencies within the major political parties. In the west the majority of CDU–CSU voters are Catholics; in the east the majority of CDU voters describe themselves as having no religious attachment. Among Western democracies, this is probably the only party explicitly espousing religious values that has such a secular base.

In summary, the social cleavages that have traditionally structured voting patterns in the Federal Republic are decreasing in electoral importance, and the inclusion of new voters from the east has further attenuated these cleavages. The declining impact of class and religious cleavages has arisen from compositional changes that have reduced the number of voters integrated into traditional social groups, and presumably from declining reliance on group cues as criteria for electoral decisions. These social group networks are even weaker in the east.

Social and partisan networks may strengthen in the new Länder as the democratic political system takes root, but reunification has generally weakened the impact of the social cleavages that traditionally framed electoral politics in the Federal Republic.

Our findings also highlight the social and political contrasts between the western and eastern electorates. Class voting differences, for example, may be modest in both regions, but they work in opposite directions. Even the same political party – whether the CDU–CSU or the SPD – draws upon different constituencies in the west and east. Such contrasts are invariably creating tension within the political parties, tension between regions, and the potential for further political change.

Partisan Attachments

Social cleavages may provide the foundations of modern party systems and electoral choice, but they are only one factor in electoral decision making. Electoral research has found that people develop more direct personal attachments to their preferred political party, which guides their voting and other aspects of political behaviour (Dalton, 1996a, ch. 9). Researchers call this a sense of 'party identification'. Party identifications is generally instilled early in life, often as part of a family political inheritance, and then reinforced by adult electoral experiences.

These party ties are important because they can structure a voter's view of the political world, provide cues for judging political phenomena, influence patterns of political participation and promote stability in individual voting behaviour. This concept of party identification has proved to be one of the most helpful ideas in understanding the political behaviour of contemporary electorates.

Prior research has tracked two distinct phases in the postwar development of party attachments in the Federal Republic. The stabilisation and consolidation of the party system during the 1950s and 1960s strengthened popular attachments to the political parties (Baker *et al.*, 1981; Norpoth, 1983). During the 1980s, however, this trend towards partisanship slowed, or even reversed. A decreasing proportion of westerners expressed strong feelings of partisan identity, and a growing number did not feel attached to any political party. There were other signs that party loyalties were weakening: vote switching between elections increased,. and there was an increase in the number of voters switching parties between their first (*Erststimme*) and second votes (*Zweitstimme*).

Several factors seemed to account for this decline in partisanship. After decades of growth and policy accomplishments, recently the political parties have had to struggle with economic recession and the rise of new political issues (Zelle, 1995). Other political bodies – such as citizen action groups and public interest lobbies – arose to represent new political interests and challenge the political parties. In addition a series of political scandals at the national and state levels tarnished party images (for example a series of party finance scandals and an election dirty tricks scandal in Schleswig-Holstein). The political parties appeared to be self-interested and self-centred, which led to feelings of antipathy among the public. In short these developments created doubts about the ability of political parties to represent public interests effectively.

In addition the growing sophistication of the western electorate has weakened individual party ties, mainly among the politically sophisticated and better educated (Dalton and Rohrschneider, 1990). With growing interest in and knowledge of politics, people are better able to make their own political decisions without depending on party attachments. Furthermore, as voters begin to focus on particular issues as a basis of electoral choice, they are more likely to diverge from their normal party predispositions, which will then erode these predispositions and make further defections even more likely. This general pattern is described as a 'dealignment' of long-term party attachments in the Federal Republic.

German reunification is likely to have accelerated this process of dealignment. Kohl's narrow victory in 1990 represented a less than enthusiastic endorsement by the voters. Moreover, no sooner had the votes been counted than the longer-term costs of his election became apparent to the Christian Democrats and the German public. Kohl had promised the eastern voters that no one would be made worse off by reunification but the reality has been different. Kohl had promised western voters that reunification could be accomplished through a second *Wirtschaftswunder* (economic miracle) and without new taxes; but in January 1991 Kohl's government introduced a surcharge on income taxes and increased other government fees. The Social Democrats criticised the government's actions, but offered no viable alternatives. Many Germans on both sides of the former border have been disturbed by the political and economic problems resulting from German reunification, and they see the political parties as unable or unwilling to address these problems in an effective and convincing way.

In addition to the problems of German union, continuing scandals have further undermined the parties' stature and contributed to these negative images. For example the leader of the Social Democrats, Bjorn Engholm, resigned his position in 1993 because of his complicity in the cover-up of a Schleswig-Holstein dirty-tricks scandal. Erwin and Ute Scheuch (1992) published a damning study of local party structures in Cologne, illustrating the self-centredness of the parties and their collusion to ensure their mutual access to government. Reacting to these events, President Richard von Weizsäcker took the unusual step of criticising the political parties for being obsessed with power (von Weizsäcker, 1992). He reprimanded the parties for pursuing their own self-interest instead of pursuing the nation's interests.

For many westerners this pattern of poor performance and party scandals confirmed their doubts about the vitality of the German party system, and even their own partisan loyalties. For many easterners, these events raised fundamental questions about how democracy really functions.

In fact we should expect the partisan orientations of easterners to be different from those of westerners (Kaase and Klingemann, 1994). Easterners are just beginning their democratic experience with the Federal Republic's parties, so few easterners should (or could) display the deep partisan loyalty that constitutes a sense of 'party identification'. Although some research suggests that many easterners have latent affinities for specific parties in the Federal Republic, these are not the long-term attachments born of early life experiences that we normally equate with party identification.

Table 3.3 enables us to monitor this dealignment trend by tracking party identification among western voters (1972–94) and eastern partisanship (1991–94). The western data indicate a slight erosion in the strength of party attachments during the 1980s, which accelerated in the 1990s. In the 1972 election, for instance, 55 per cent of the electorate felt 'strong' or 'very strong' party ties. By 1990 this group had declined to 40 per cent of the public, and by 1994 to 36 per cent. This is reflected in the fact that while only 20 per cent of westerners were non-partisan in 1972, this rose to 27 per cent in 1990 and 31 per cent in 1994. Not only did the overall percentage of those expressing partisan attachments decrease over time, but the strength of partisanship within each partisan camp also decreased (Dalton and Rohrschneider, 1990).

Regular measurement of partisan attachment did not begin in eastern surveys until early 1991. By then most voters already had significant electoral experience with the federal parties, having participated in two national elections – the March 1990 Volkskammer (GDR People's Assembly) and the December Bundestag elections – as

TABLE 3.3 *The strength of partisanship, 1972–94 (per cent)*

	West							*East*	
	1972	*1976*	*1980*	*1983*	*1987*	*1990*	*1994*	*1991*	*1994*
Very strong	17	12	13	10	10	11	12	4	6
Strong	38	35	33	29	31	29	24	22	19
Weak	20	35	29	35	31	31	31	35	34
No party, don't know	20	16	19	22	25	27	31	37	40
Refused, no answer	5	3	6	4	3	2	2	3	1
Total	100	100	100	100	100	100	100	100	100

Source: Data from German election studies conducted by the Forschungsgruppe Wahlen for the Second German Television (ZDF).

well as regional and local contests. Still, eastern voters were significantly more hesitant to express a sense of party attachment. In 1994 eastern partisanship remained weak: only 25 per cent of easterners claimed to have 'very strong' or 'strong' party ties, and two fifths of the public (40 per cent) were explicitly non-partisan.

In summary, both publics display evidence of weak psychological ties binding them to the political parties, but these findings can be interpreted differently for west and east. The continuing decrease in partisanship among westerners is similar to the situation in several other advanced industrial democracies (Dalton, 1996a, ch. 9). This suggests that we are observing a general pattern of partisan dealignment, and the special problems of reunification may have simply added to this process.

In contrast we might describe easterners as a prealignment electorate. Democratic politics is still a relative new experience for eastern voters. Party attachments normally strengthen through repeated electoral experiences, especially in newly formed party systems (Converse, 1969). Thus the current situation in the east might be closer to that of the Federal Republic in the immediate postwar period. We should therefore expect the partisan attachments of easterners to strengthen over time, but the dealigning forces of the contemporary party system may slow this process. The rapidity with which easterners develop party attachments will be an important measure of their developing stable political orientations and their integration into the Federal Republic's party system.

Comparing Political Beliefs

We have seen that the long-term determinants of electoral behaviour, such as group cues and party attachments, have decreased in impact among the western electorate and remain underdeveloped among easterners. As these long-term factors diminish in electoral decisions the individual views of voters will become more important as a basis of political decision making.

Until 1989 both the FRG and the GDR tried to create distinct political values among their respective publics. To the extent that these efforts were successful, German reunification represented the merger of two different electorates, with different political norms and different expectations for society and the political system. Thus the most direct test of the similarities between east and west is a comparison of the political values of both publics.

We can of course compare easterners and westerners on a virtually unlimited set of political attitudes (see the evidence collected in Niedermayer and Beyme, 1994). The two publics display sharp differences in their perceptions of the process and prospects of German reunification. Religious values and perceptions of the economic situation vary sharply across the two regions. Other research, however, finds remarkably similar profiles in social values, certain political norms and even images of the superpowers. Any comparison of east–west political beliefs will inevitably present some evidence of similarity and dissimilarity.

Therefore we will focus our attention on two sets of political attitudes that we think tap essential (and interrelated) political values and illustrate the mix of abstract agreement and specific disagreement displayed for many other political attitudes.

We will begin by comparing the broad orientations towards the contrasting socioeconomic systems and past socialisation patterns of the Federal Republic and the German Democratic Republic. Figure 3.1 presents the opinions of both easterners and westerners on a set of fundamental political and economic principles. The figure presents the results of a 1995 survey that replicated questions asked in 1990 (Dalton, 1992, p. 74). The dominant pattern in these data is the broad similarity in political values across regions. East–west differences on most questions are modest, suggesting that forty years of separation did not create two separate electorates.

Comparisons with 1990 show that east–west opinions have generally converged on these questions. This convergence partly reflects the erosion of easterners' initial enthusiasm for capitalism. In 1990 easterners actually expressed greater support than westerners for a society that relies on a free market economy, rejects income equality in favour of performance criteria and ties living standards to an individual's economic contributions. By 1995 easterners were displaying greater

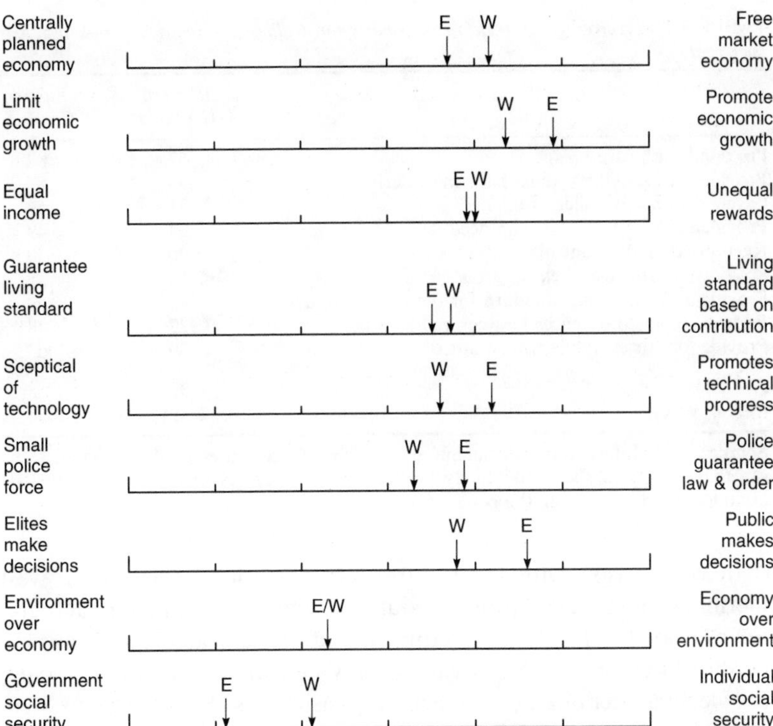

Source: IPOS Survey 1995. Data provided by Dieter Roth, Forschungsgruppe Wahlen.

FIGURE 3.1 *Social values of the German electorate, 1995*

reservations about these capitalist principles, although a small east–west gap remained. Ironically, easterners are more likely to endorse a society where people participate in political decisions even if this leads to delays; westerners lean towards a society that leaves important political decisions up to those who are responsible for them and who can decide quickly.

This convergence on the broad economic and political principles does not mean that both regions agree on the norms and performance of these systems. To illustrate this, Table 3.4 compares perceptions of the role of government between east and west. The perceived responsibilities of government are a central topic in the historical left–right political divide, and thus serve as an important measure of citizens' political identity and political goals. The table displays the percentage who think the government is 'definitely responsible' for dealing with specific social problems.

TABLE 3.4 *Perceived government responsibility for dealing with political problems (per cent)*

	Western Germany	*Eastern Germany*
Provide health care	57	82
Provide decent living standard for the elderly	54	85
Give aid to needy college students	31	59
Provide housing for those who need it	24	49
Keep prices under control	20	50
Provide industry with help to grow	12	35
Provide a decent living standard for the unemployed	19	52
Reduce income differences between rich and poor	22	48
Provide job for everyone who wants one	30	63
Average	32	58
(No. of cases)	(2812)	(1028)

Source: 1990 International Social Survey Program. Table entries are the percentage who say that each area should definitely be the government's responsibility. Missing data excluded when calculating the percentages.

In comparison with most Europeans (Dalton, 1996a, ch.6), west Germans have reservations about extensive governmental activity. Even in areas where the government is a primary actor, such as care of the elderly and unemployment, only half of westerners view these problems as definite government responsibilities. East Germans were conditioned by the GDR to expect a large government involvement, and despite their rejection of socialism and a planned economy (Figure 3.1), easterners still have very high expectations of government. Half believe the government is definitely responsible for providing for health care, a decent standard of living for the elderly, keeping inflation in check, helping needy students, reducing unemployment and helping industry to grow. In short, while both easterners and westerners accept the basic principles of Germany's social market economy, the former emphasise the *social* dimension and the latter emphasise the *market*.

This pattern of agreement on abstract principles and disagreement on the specifics of policy also applies to other political areas. The two publics share a common belief in the principles of democratic government, but interpret these principles in different terms (Dalton, 1994). Both publics approve of German unification, but differ widely in their interpretation of the reunification process. Rather than treating one side of these contrasting beliefs as erroneous, we think that such contrasts may be accurately describing the present nature of the eastern public. Easterners endorse the principles underlying the Federal Republic and its political and economic systems. Yet easterners are learning what these principles mean in concrete terms. They favour democracy, but they are learning how the democratic ideal translates into the sometimes less than ideal processes of federal politics; they favour the social market economy, but only through experience are they learning how this system functions. In addition there is considerable disagreement even among westerners about how the nation's social and political ideals should be translated into specific policies. Easterners' attitudes towards the responsibilities of government retain an image of 'big government' that has carried over from the German Democratic Republic. This does not mean these attitudes are undemocratic or incompatible with a capitalist economic system – the same survey found that British attitudes towards government closely matched those of the east Germans (Dalton, 1996a, ch. 6).

The German Electorates

This chapter has highlighted two broad characteristics of electoral politics in the contemporary Federal Republic. First, our findings underscore the considerable potential for electoral change that now exists. For the past two decades, long-term influences on electoral choice have diminished in influence. Social class, religion, area of residence and other social characteristics are having a diminishing impact on voters behaviour. Similarly, a dealignment trend is signalling a decrease in the influence of enduring partisan loyalties on electoral decisions. Fewer west German voters now approach elections with fixed party predispositions based either on social characteristics or partisan ties acquired early in life. It is not that voters lack partisan predispositions, but the nature of these predispositions is shifting from strong ties (group and party attachments) to weak ties (particular issues, candidate images and perceptions of party performance). Much like the findings of US and British electorate research, this erosion in the traditional bases of partisan support has occurred without producing new, enduring bases of support that might revitalise the party system (for example, Wattenberg, 1996; Rose and McAllister, 1989). Indeed it is the lack of a new, stable alignment that appears to be the most distinctive feature of contemporary party systems (Franklin *et al.*, 1992).

The citizens in the five new Länder, of course, have a much different electoral history. Rather than an erosion of previous social and partisan ties, the eastern electorate is still learning about democratic politics and the rough-and-tumble of partisan campaigns. Easterners understandably began this experience with weaker party ties and less certainty about the general structure of political competition. One factor to watch is how quickly they adapt to the political structures of the west, or whether they remain only weakly tied to the party system. In the years since these patterns were first observed (Dalton, 1992), little has changed.

The modest impact of long-term determinants of party choice is likely to strengthen the role that policy preferences play within the German electoral process. Although most voters will still habitually support a preferred party, the slackness of these bonds will increase the potential that a particular issue or election campaign may sway their electoral choice, at least temporarily. More and more, the parties' stand on particular issues and their political images will influence voter choice, as a substantial group of floating voters will react to the political stimuli of individual election campaigns. There is even some evidence that candidates' images are playing a growing role in voters' decisions, especially among easterners (Norpoth and Roth, 1996; Anderson and Zelle, 1995). This shift towards issue-based voting behaviour is likely to make policy considerations a more important aspect of elections while injecting considerable fluidity into electoral politics – at least until (if ever) a new, stable group-basis of party support forms.

A second implication of our findings concerns the contrasts between western and eastern Germans. As discussed throughout this chapter, there are two distinct electorates within the one German nation. The western electorate is fairly religious, as well as conservative on economic and social issues; the eastern electorate is secular and liberal on social issues. In addition, the reversal of the normal class alignment among eastern voters is creating different constituencies within the same parties in the west and the east.

These partisan and political contrasts between west and east may also reinforce a regional identity in the new Länder. Regardless of their party attachment, eastern CDU and SPD voters may feel that their views are not being well represented in the present party system, and such experiences could strengthen feelings of regional solidarity. This failure of representation undoubtedly contributed to the PDS's success in 1994 as spokesperson for the disenfranchised east.

When we first observed this sharp regional contrast in the 1990 elections, we speculated that it might be a passing phenomenon linked to the unusual circumstances of reunification and the undeveloped nature of democratic politics in the east (Dalton, 1992). Now we are more inclined to think that these patterns will remain a feature of the two electorates unless there is major political intervention. Repetitive voting experience will strengthen party ties and lead to a partisanship that will endure between elections. Moreover, even with the anomalous partisan alignments of the east, once partisan networks and support groups start to develop they will create a framework for perpetuating these alignments. State and local politicians and party activists realise who their voters are, and are building ties with them that strengthen with each new election.

These regional differences can create sharp intraparty tensions. For instance, because CDU voters in the new Länder are significantly less religious and less Catholic than their western counterparts, their attitudes towards abortion and other social issues conflict with the policy programme of the western CDU. If CDU politicians from the east represent these views, it places them in conflict with the party's official policies. If eastern CDU deputies do not reflect these views, then this produces a representation deficit for easterners. The SPD and the other parties face similar problems in representing contrasting constituencies in west and east. Thus, the complex relationship between horizontal integration with the national party elite, and vertical integration between party elites and their social constituencies has been unbalanced by German unification.

Taken together, the patterns of partisan fluidity and contrasting political alignments across regions do not lend themselves to a simple prediction of the future of the party system. The already complex situation in the 1980s has become even more complex in the 1990s. It appears that electoral politics will be characterised by continued diversity in voting patterns. A system of frozen social cleavages and stable party alignments is less likely to develop in a society where voters are sophisticated, political interests are diverse and individual choice is given greater latitude. Even the new political conflicts that are competing for public attention seem destined to create additional sources of partisan change rather than recreate the stable electoral structure of the past. This diversity and fluidity may in fact be the major new characteristic of German electoral politics and the contemporary electoral politics of other advanced industrial societies.

Note

This research was partially supported by a grant from the Center for German and European Studies, University of California, Berkeley. The survey data utilised in this chapter were made available by the Inter-University Consortium for Political and Social Research (ICPSR) in

Ann Arbor, the Zentralarchiv für empirische Sozialforschung in Cologne, and the Forschungsgruppe Wahlen in Mannheim. Neither the archives nor the original collectors of the data bear responsibility for the analyses presented here. I would like to thank Wilhelm Bürklin for his collaboration on a study of German voting behaviour, which influenced many of the ideas presented here.

4

The Party System at the Crossroads

GORDON SMITH

Any country that has had the same government for 14 years through four elections must find the possibility of radical change remote. In the case of the Federal Republic this continuity amounts to an awesome stability. Moreover the CDU–CSU/FDP coalition, first formed in 1982 and led since then by Chancellor Kohl, has never looked like falling apart in the intervening years. This record is all the more striking considering the likelihood of upheaval following reunification in 1990. Quite apart from the problem of merging two societies with their contrasting socioeconomic systems, the addition of 12.5 million voters in eastern Germany to the electorate of 45 million in the west presented a formidable challenge to the established pattern in the old Federal Republic. Yet from a later perspective, after the reunification election of 1990 and the first normal one in 1994, it could perhaps be concluded that the German political 'model' has the look of indestructibility.

The Inherited Structure

At the level of the party system the components of this model can be summarised as follows:

- Throughout the life of the Federal Republic two principal parties, the CDU–CSU and the SPD, have been dominant. They – the so-called *Volksparteien* (people's parties) – have a moderate, pragmatic outlook and tend to minimise their differences. Their broad electoral appeal and integrative character make it difficult for parties with a strong ideological or sectional basis to compete successfully.

TABLE 4.1 *Elections to the Bundestag, 1949–94*

	1949	*1953*	*1957*	*1961*	*1965*
Electorate (millions)	31.2	33.1	35.4	37.4	38.5
Turnout (%)	78.5	86.0	87.8	87.7	86.8
			% Zweitstimmen/list vote		
CDU/CSU	31.0	45.2	50.2	45.3	47.6
SPD	29.2	28.8	31.8	36.2	39.3
FDP	11.9	9.5	7.7	12.8	9.5
Greens	–	–	–	–	–
Others	27.8	16.5	10.3	5.7	3.5

Note: For 1990 the vote for the West German Greens and the East German Greens and Eastern and Western Germany, 1990 and 1994. 'Others' in 1990 and 1994 includes the

- Although they contest vigorously for political power, their political strategies and the style of electoral competition imply a centripetal party system rather than a polarised one.
- The dominant position of the CDU and the SPD has led to their periodic alternation in government. In German circumstances, however, as neither party has been able to win an absolute majority since 1957, the alternation is imperfect because both parties have had to rely on the small FDP to form a coalition majority.

Although the *Volkspartei*-dominated system took root early on, the two-and-half party system – alternatively a 'frustrated' two-party system – dates from the beginning of the 1960s. In 1983 the Greens won their first federal representation, but it did not alter the essentials of the model or the basis of coalition formation. The same applied in 1990, when the former communist party, the PDS, had electoral success. In the 1994 election the Greens and the PDS together mustered around 12 per cent of the total vote. Thus, although now nominally a five-party system, the model has continued to be operated by the three established parties of government (Table 4.1), but with less room for manoeuvre than in the past.

While it is important to stress the persistence of the broad features of the party system inherited from the earlier years of the Federal Republic, it is also an oversimplification since it obscures the growing complexity of party relationships and electoral behaviour (see Chapter 3). The cumulative effects of these changes are now becoming apparent and have the potential to affect the model quite fundamentally. The changes, however, need not lead to a fragmenting multi-partyism or to polarisation through the rise of extremist forces. Indeed the complete

1969	*1972*	*1976*	*1980*	*1983*	*1987*	*1990*	*1994*
38.7	41.4	42.0	43.2	44.0	44.9	60.4	60.5
86.7	91.1	90.7	88.7	89.1	84.4	77.8	79.0
46.1	44.9	48.6	44.5	48.8	44.3	43.8	41.4
42.7	45.8	42.6	42.9	38.2	37.0	33.5	36.4
5.8	8.4	7.9	10.6	6.9	9.1	11.0	6.9
–	–	–	1.5	5.6	8.3	5.1	7.3
5.5	0.9	0.9	0.5	0.5	1.2	6.6	8.0

Bündnis '90 has been combined. See Table 4.2 p. 59, for the distribution of votes in PDS, with 2.4% in 1990 and 4.4% in 1994.

failure of the extreme right-wing parties in the 1990 and 1994 federal elections points rather to a consolidation of the existing five-party system.

The 1994 Federal Election: Crumbling of the Model?

Not unreasonably, the results of the 1990 election were widely regarded as a personal triumph for Chancellor Kohl, thanks to his role in securing German reunification (Smith, 1992). It is worth noting, however, that the CDU–CSU share of the vote, at 43.8 per cent, was its lowest since 1949. The FDP, its coalition partner, with 11 per cent, benefited both from the Kohl effect and – especially in eastern Germany – through the popularity of the foreign minister, Hans-Dietrich Genscher. Neither the CDU nor the FDP could count on the reunification bonus lasting another four years; for this reason the 1994 election appeared to be far more open.

It could have been expected that the SPD, so long in opposition, would be able to mount a strong challenge. In 1990 the SPD's then chancellor candidate, Oskar Lafontaine, had warned against the high costs of reunification (his forecasts proved accurate: large-scale unemployment in the new Länder and additional tax burdens in the west), but to no avail: the SPD vote in 1990 fell to 33.5 per cent, also its lowest since 1949. Chancellor Kohl's optimistic beliefs proved sufficient to lull the electorate at the time. For the 1994 election the SPD concentrated on its programme and policies, but it was a lacklustre performance. How anyway, it was pointedly asked, could the SPD hope to recover sufficient ground to be in a position to forge a coalition majority – and with whom?

The SPD's poor showing in 1990 meant that it would have to make massive gains in 1994 to overhaul the CDU–CSU, and there were no signs that the FDP was willing to desert the CDU. A left-facing alternative, towards the Greens, was equally problematic, both in policy terms and electoral arithmetic: the Greens in western Germany had fallen below the 5 per cent barrier in 1990, and even if they were to make a spectacular recovery in 1994, a large increase would be mainly at the expense of the SPD.

The survival of Kohl as chancellor in 1994 can in part be ascribed to the weakness of the SPD, for Helmut Kohl's fortunes and popularity reached a low ebb early in 1994, and it was chiefly the signs of economic recovery that boosted the government's chances. But to say that the CDU was successful in 1994 largely 'by default', because of the lack of credibility of the SPD challenge, ignores the skilful way the CDU's campaign managers capitalised on Helmut Kohl's image, not just as the architect of German reunification, but as the country's experienced leader and one who had acquired the stature of a European statesman (Boll, 1995). This high-profile campaign was sufficient to compensate for the long-term weakening of the CDU–CSU's 'structural majority' within the electorate of western Germany, typically the links of Christian democracy in sections of the electorate with a firm religious affiliation. Even so, the CDU–CSU share of the vote fell once more to a new low since 1949 of 41.7 per cent (39.9 per cent of the eastern vote, against 46.1 per cent in the west). Its coalition partner, the FDP, suffered severe losses in both eastern and western Germany. As the election campaign progressed it even became doubtful whether the party would achieve the necessary 5 per cent of the vote, and this doubt was reinforced by the fact that in preceding Land and European elections the FDP had lost heavily and failed to retain its seats in the new Länder and the European Parliament. There was even a sense of surprise when the FDP managed to score 6.9 per cent at the federal election.

Differences in party performance in eastern and western Germany, evident in 1990, persisted in 1994 (see Table 4.2). They were less evident for the CDU than other parties, and the greatest differences, relatively speaking, were for the FDP and the Greens. The persistence of the differences can largely be accounted for by the advance of the PDS to almost double its share in 1994 (from 9.9 per cent to 17.6 per cent). But viewed overall, the deficits of the other parties in eastern Germany are not so significant because the electorate is much smaller: 13.5 million in the east compared with around 47 million in the west. Another factor that helped boost the PDS was the lower turnout in the new Länder:

TABLE 4.2 *Election results, 1990 and 1994, East and West Germany (per cent)*

	1990			*1994*		
	West	*East*	*FRG*	*West*	*East*	*FRG*
CDU–CSU	44.2	42.6	43.8	42.2	38.5	41.4
SPD	35.9	25.0	33.5	37.6	31.8	36.4
FDP	10.6	12.5	11.0	7.7	4.0	6.9
Greens	4.7	6.2	5.1	7.8	5.3	7.3
PDS	0.3	9.9	2.4	0.9	17.6	4.4
Republicans	2.3	1.5	2.1	2.0	1.4	1.9
Others	2.0	2.0	2.1	1.9	1.3	1.7
Turnout	78.4	75.5	77.8	80.6	73.4	79.0
Electorate (mills)	46.6	13.9	60.4	46.9	13.5	60.5

73.4 per cent compared with 80.6 per cent in the west. The PDS can count on a large number of committed supporters, whereas the population at large is less interested in party politics: the lower the turnout, the more impressive the PDS's performance looks.

None of the results of the three 'natural' parties of government did anything to strengthen the trusted model, and their relative weakness was the obverse of the modest success of the Greens and the PDS. In 1990, a 'green' presence was maintained in the Bundestag by the eastern Greens/*Bündis* '90. The western Greens failed largely because 'new politics' concerns were seen as less relevant in the year of reunification. However, that was a temporary eclipse; the party's basic strength lies in the Länder (unlike the FDP), and that has not faltered. By 1994 issues relating to the environment, civil and minority rights and the wider problems of German society had again moved up the political agenda. The Greens, with 7.9 per cent in 1994, have become the third largest party in the Bundestag.

The return of the Greens was widely expected, but the PDS was in a different category. In 1990 the PDS needed only to win 5 per cent of the vote in the new Länder to qualify. But in 1994 the 5 per cent requirement was extended to cover the entire Federal Republic, and since support for the PDS was not extensive in western Germany its exclusion seemed probable – except for one possibility: the electoral law stipulates that a party winning at least three constituency seats by direct mandate is entitled to its proportional share of Bundestag seats. This provision was a gift to the PDS: the strong concentration of the party's followers in east Berlin made its task far less difficult than an attempt to find sufficient favour throughout the whole of Germany. Thus in 1994 the overall vote for the PDS was 4.4 per cent, with 20.5 per cent in eastern Germany, but a mere 0.4 per cent in the west. Yet as

Peter Pulzer has pointed out, 'the PDS's votes in the west should not be ignored. One per cent of the eastern vote equals 86 000 votes; one per cent of the western vote equals 385 000. Two out of every 11 PDS votes came from the west, as did five of its 30 seats. Support for the PDS in the western Länder may be insignificant in terms of western votes, but not in terms of total PDS votes' (Pulzer, 1995a, p. 149).

The CDU, SPD and FDP were the real losers in 1994. For the CDU that was not so readily apparent, for despite the continued decline of its share of the vote it remained by a margin the largest party. For the FDP there was little comfort at all. The party's decline in the east was particularly severe, from 12.9 per cent in 1990 to 3.5 per cent in 1994. In contrast the SPD made a modest recovery in both parts of Germany. However it is still 'underperforming' in the new Länder (in 1994, 31.8 per cent in the east compared with 39.7 per cent in the west) partly because of competition from the PDS, but also because, unlike the CDU and other 'bloc' parties in the former German Democratic Republic, it had no organisational or membership base upon which to build: in 1946 it had been forcibly merged with the communists (KPD) to form the 'Socialist Unity Party'.

If attention is focused on all three 'core' parties, then their relative decline over the years becomes apparent, as Table 4.3 shows in aggregate for the two major parties and all three together. The high point of concentration in the party system was reached in the mid 1970s, and there has been a gradual decline since then, both for the two *Volksparteien* and for all three established parties.

The extent of their decline needs qualifying: meanwhile the electorate has grown substantially, from 42 million in 1976 to 61 million in 1994. On this rendering they have been successful in attracting a large number of new voters, a fact that is missed by concentrating solely on their percentage of the vote (Mair, 1993; Smith, 1993). Nevertheless, from the perspective of the party system it is their relative performance in comparison with other parties that counts.

TABLE 4.3 *Aggregate vote of leading parties, 1976–94 (per cent)*

	Two-party (CDU–CSU+SPD)	*Three-party (CDU–CSU+SPD+FDP)*
1976	91.2	99.1
1980	87.4	98.0
1983	87.0	94.0
1987	81.3	90.4
1990	77.3	88.3
1994	77.8	84.7

Contrasts of Party Leadership

A comparison of the recent experience of leadership in the CDU–CSU, FDP and SPD reveals some of the factors affecting their performance. An ineffective leader will weaken a party, even though its policy positions are acceptable. The difficulties encountered by the FDP and the SPD since reunification can in part be explained by Helmut Kohl's towering presence in government and as party leader. But their weaknesses have also been of their own making.

Kohl's control over party and government became stronger as a result of the reunification process. From the time he boldly issued his 'Ten-Point Plan' aiming at German reunification in late 1989, and reinforced by election victories in 1990 and 1994, Kohl has made full use of his constitutional powers to determine the guidelines of policy on *Ostpolitik* and the European Union, as well as domestic policy. The fact that he is probably prepared to stay on until after the next election (due in 1998) means that the question of succession has been shelved. It remains to be seen whether his likely nominee, Wolfgang Schäuble, leader of the parliamentary party, will prove acceptable to the party at large. However, the CDU has faced a succession problem once before: after Konrad Adeneur finally stepped down in 1963 (he had been chancellor since 1949) it took several years to resolve the leadership issue, and the obvious 'crown prince', Ludwig Erhard, did not survive long in office.

To account for Kohl's supremacy in the party it is necessary to appreciate his skills in party management, isolating critics and using tactics of 'divide and rule', while at the same time being able to placate competing interests in the party (Clemens, 1994). Christian democracy represents a coalition of interests, and the leader has to maintain a delicate balance. Kohl has been able to tame the party leaders in the Länder, usually the source of unrest, and for the present the CDU's 'polycentrism' (Schmidt, 1990) has been suppressed. He has also been fortunate that, since the death of Franz Josef Strauss in 1988, the Bavarian CSU has been a relatively docile partner. Theo Waigel, CSU party leader and finance minister since 1989, has proved to be 'federally minded' rather than intent on pushing Bavarian interests. The prominence he has achieved as finance minister and working amicably with Kohl is in sharp contrast to the time when Strauss threatened to make the CSU a federal-wide party (Jesse, 1996).

How vital the quality of leadership can be is shown by the catastrophic decline of the FDP. The older generation that gave the party federal strength in the 1970s and 1980s left no obvious successors. After the retirement of Otto Graf Lambsdorff, the party leader, and Hans-Dietrich Genscher, foreign minister from 1969–92, the mantle passed to Klaus Kinkel, who combined both posts – foreign minister and party leader – even though he had joined the party only in 1991! Above all, the FDP needs a strong federal profile to compensate for its weakness in the Länder, yet neither Kinkel nor the other FDP ministers were able to capitalise on the party's role in government. Kinkel, as foreign minister, lacked the political astuteness of Genscher, but the international situation too had changed, and *Ostpolitik* had lost its place in the headlines.

Part of the FDP's difficulty was it had served too long in comfortable harness with the CDU at the expense of its own identity, and seemed to be in danger of becoming a 'client party' of the CDU. Yet when it sought to block CDU policies the party received little public credit. For a long time the FDP (with the SPD) opposed a CDU constitutional amendment aimed at restricting the unqualified right of political asylum. Only when the number of asylum seekers reached a dangerous level, alienating public opinion, did the FDP and SPD agree to the constitutional change, finally made in 1992. Indeed on most disputed issues with the CDU the FDP ultimately gave way (Søe, 1995). Following the severe losses at the various elections in 1994, Kinkel finally relinquished the party leadership in 1995, but that move alone is unlikely to improve the FDP's standing with the electorate.

A similar problem of 'generational succession' has afflicted the SPD, though in its case reference is usually made to 'Brandt's grandchildren'. Ever since Helmut Schmidt was ousted from office in 1982, the SPD has searched for a formula to restore its fortunes. Thus far it has failed both to produce an attractive chancellor candidate and a convincing set of policies. The crushing defeat with Lafontaine in 1990 led to the replacement of Hans-Jochen Vogel as party chairman by the much younger and promising Bjorn Engholm, minister-president of Schleswig-Holstein. He set about making internal party reforms, and would probably also have become chancellor candidate in 1994. However Engholm was forced to resign in 1993 as chairman and minister-president following revelations of a scandal in his own state.

The SPD then experimented with grass-roots democracy – a consultative vote of party members to elect a new chairman. The successful candidate, Rudolf Scharping, formerly minister-president of Rhineland-Palatinate, also became chancellor candidate for the 1994 election. It turned out to be an unfortunate choice: he was a colourless campaigner, a weak tactician, and no match for Kohl. Scharping survived the 1994 defeat, but dissatisfaction within the party persisted and came to a head during the Mannheim party conference of October 1995. After Scharping made an unconvincing speech, the delegates were treated to a rousing performance by Lafontaine. It became clear that more was at stake than the leadership, that in fact the whole style of the SPD had to change. Peter Lösche (1996) has argued that such a change would require a shift from the party's 'programmatic fixation' towards concentration on a single, overarching theme – such as economic competence – and a deliberate emphasis on the personal qualities of leadership. These both imply a weakening of the traditional features of a mass party. Shortly after the Mannheim conference, the results of the Berlin election drove home the need for decisive change: the SPD's vote slumped to a miserable 23.6 per cent – and that in a city that had once been an SPD stronghold. The resignation of Scharping and his replacement by Lafontaine (the defeat in the 1990 federal election forgiven) was the first sign of the SPD's commitment to a new course.

By their nature and origin, the Greens, with their emphasis on decentralisation and aversion to elite power, differ from the other parties in the low priority they accord to party leadership; even so, in Joschka Fischer ('speaker' of the parliamentary party), they have a figure who is rated highly in the opinion polls. The strength of the Greens lies not only in their concern for ecology, civil rights and protection of the *Sozialstaat* (socially responsible state), but more generally in presenting to the younger generation a 'cultural modernity' that the traditional parties are unable to offer. But this success in western Germany is not matched in the new Länder, where these priorities are not so pronounced and where the PDS, rather ironically in view of the latter's past history, is a strong competitor. Although the fusion of eastern *Bündis* '90 with the Greens in 1993 has proved harmonious (Schoonmaker, 1995) the weakness of the merged party may lie precisely in the disinclination of the Greens to promote a strong national leadership so as to avoid 'the cult of personality'.

The PDS has apparently succeeded in transforming itself into a democratic party. That can in part be ascribed to the new, acceptable face of postcommunist leaders who promote a democratic image: Lothar Bisky, the party chairman, and Gregor Gysi, leader of the parliamentary party. However the role they play should not be divorced from other factors that have contributed to the party's resurgence in eastern Germany. The new leadership has in reality been grafted on to a party with enduring features. The PDS inherited the strong organisational structure of the old SED as well as its considerable financial wealth, and these underpin its electoral success in the new

Länder: reliance on a core 'loyalist' vote, combined with a wider appeal to a specifically 'eastern' identity that is attractive both to those who have 'lost out' through reunification and to younger voters wanting a radical alternative (Betz and Welsh, 1995). The PDS, freeing itself from its Stalinist past, is still a radical party in aiming at the 'transformation' of the capitalist system. In principle this radical alternative could be attractive in western Germany, but it is clear that, without the organisational infrastructure the PDS has in the east, the leadership by itself is unlikely to secure a substantial federal-wide following.

The Parties in a Two-Bloc System

If the inherited structure of the party system is being eroded, what is likely to take its place, and how will the individual parties react to the challenges of a new-style system? One possibility is a move towards two distinctive blocs of parties. The emergence of a two-bloc system has been mooted in the past (Padgett, 1989), but forecasts of this kind proved premature, partly because of the effects of German reunification. The development would entail a line-up of parties on a clear left–right basis and with consequent effects on government formation. This division has not been evident in the Federal Republic, largely because the *Volksparteien* do not have a strong ideological basis. The moderation has been reinforced by the 'coalition triangle' (Pappi, 1984) and by the constraining influence of the FDP, while effectively imposes a 'centripetal bind' on the two major parties.

The changes in the relative strength of the parties, the presence of the Greens and the PDS, and in particular the possible demise of the FDP, all give new impetus to the idea of a two-bloc model. The performance and composition of left and right-orientated groupings over the last three federal elections is shown in Figure 4.1.

There are several comments to be made about these strictly notional alignments. Most obvious is that the gap between them was at its widest at the time of reunification in 1990 and narrowest, almost reaching parity, in 1994, and in fact narrower than it had been since the CDU–CSU/FDP coalition was first formed in 1982. These groupings are useful in showing the changing balance of the party system, but there are limits to what they can say about the basis of likely governing and opposition formations in the future. It is worth examining them chiefly to see how the parties may react to the possibilities – and dangers – of working in alliance with other parties.

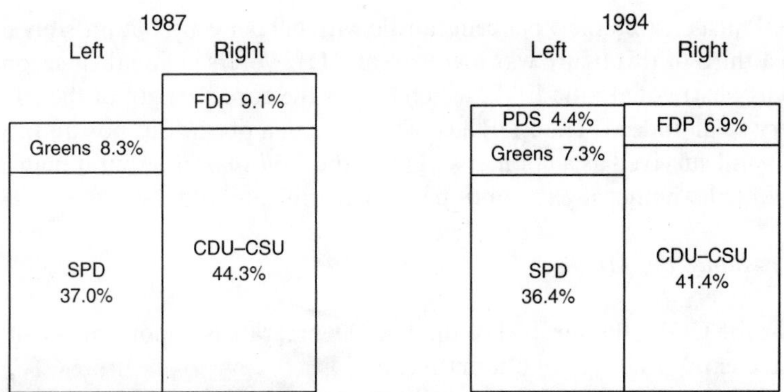

FIGURE 4.1 *Performance of left and right blocs, 1987 and 1994*
Note: In 1994 the Republicans, with 1.9 per cent, could also be added to the 'right' bloc.

Alignments on the Right

Although the existing coalition between the CDU–CSU and the FDP is best classified as being on the 'right', neither the CDU nor the FDP would accept that they are right-wing parties. The CDU, as a *Volkspartei*, seeks to occupy the centre ground, and the FDP – as is typical of most European liberal parties – is resistant to being pushed into either left or right categories, combining elements of both. The CDU is perhaps best seen as belonging to the moderate centre-right, but there are a number of different elements in the party that have to be accommodated. On the left of the CDU there is the 'social wing', and the absence of an established party to the right, conservative-nationalist rather than extremist, means that the CDU, and more particularly the CSU, span this orientation as well (Smith, 1995).

At present most attention is focused on the FDP and its future, with three possibilities usually being mentioned. The first is that the FDP will continue in secular decline; the second is that the party, although surviving, will have no future outside a coalition with the CDU; the third is that the FDP – acutely aware of both these dangers – will seize an opportunity to break with the CDU and join a left alignment, preferably in a governing coalition solely with the SPD. Unless the FDP is able to recover its electoral support and its standing *vis-à-vis* the CDU, a switch in alignment may appear the best course. The danger here is that the party would lose those voters who favoured the coalition with the CDU (as happened in reverse after the party deserted the SPD in 1982), without necessarily winning new voters. In 1994 the

FDP just cleared the 5 per cent hurdle with 6.9 per cent, but possibly up to a third of this figure was made up of CDU voters giving their second (party list) vote to the FDP, which makes the core strength of the FDP very small indeed. The FDP has often been in a precarious position, yet has still survived as a counterweight to the *Volksparteien*, but it may be doubted whether it can continue to perform this role.

Straddling the Middle

For the CDU, the survival of the Free Democrats is important because there is no other ready alternative, and the falling share of the CDU–CSU vote makes the party even more dependent on finding a reliable partner. Neither the CDU nor the SPD would be interested in forming a grand coalition, except for a limited period and in special circumstances – for instance if there was no other way of securing a governing majority. Their reservations do not stem from a basic incompatibility of their policies; on the contrary, over a range of policies there is not much to distinguish them or to make compromise difficult. It is rather their fear of the probable consequences of their joint rule: the rise of extremist and protest parties, with the warning parallel of the only previous occasion of a grand coalition from 1966–69 when extremes of right and left temporarily won support.

The SPD, despite its weak performance in recent years, is in an altogether more favourable position. It would, in fact, benefit from a short period in coalition with the CDU, because that would be one way of making a return to federal office. Again there is a parallel: the SPD was continuously in opposition from 1949–66, and after the grand coalition broke up in 1969 the SPD wrested power from the CDU.

Alignments on the Left

It may appear that, if a choice could be made by the SPD, the Greens would be a preferred coalition partner, but the SPD has only had the experience of centre-leaning coalitions, and to take a decisive step to the left would be a new departure and one that might still be resisted by many of the 'old left' in the party. For several years, too, the Greens were regarded as a maverick force (*unberechenbar*), and not suitable to assume the responsibilities of government (*nicht regierungsfähig*). Yet there are at least three factors that have altered attitudes towards the Greens. One is the experience the two parties have had of coalitions at the Land level; a second is the absorption of some elements of the Green agenda into mainstream thinking; the third is the changing character of the Greens themselves, and this last aspect is perhaps the most important. The earlier emphasis on direct action, spontaneity, wide involvement in decision making throughout the party, suspicion of parliamentary elitism – all these attributes were antithetical to the conventional politics favoured by the SPD. Within the Greens the fundamentalist wing, the so-called *fundis* had an important influence, and it was not until the realist wing, or *realos*, gained the upper hand that the party came to adopt a conciliatory and parliamentary strategy.

Nevertheless a link with the Greens would still pose problems for the SPD. On the local and Land levels cooperation is often successful because it does not involve the 'big' issues of politics, and it is these that would be most disruptive for federal government. Economic policy, for instance, would lead to tensions between the traditional SPD demand for economic growth and the basically hostile attitude of the Greens, partly but not only rooted in the priority they give to environmental concerns. Conflicts would also occur in the fields of security and foreign policy and in relation to the European Union. The Greens, too, could be uncomfortable entering into a federal coalition with the SPD: hard compromises made by the leadership and accepted by the Bundestag *Fraktion* (parliamentary group) would run the risk of being denounced by those outside, fearful of seeing their movement succumb to the 'parliamentary embrace'.

The picture becomes all the more complex if the PDS is brought into the calculation. The three-party alignment of the left bloc might work in opposition, but if they were to make a preelection commitment to form a coalition, it could be difficult to convince voters that stable government would result. Moreover any hint that the PDS could be an acceptable partner for the SPD would be ammunition for the CDU. In the 1994 campaign the CDU made effective use of this tactic, drawing a parallel with the situation after the Land election in Saxony-Anhalt, where a minority SPD–Green coalition took office but was dependent on PDS support for a majority. Rudolf Scharping had to declare that he would not accept election to the chancellorship if it came about through the votes of PDS deputies. It is anyway still difficult for the SPD to contemplate an alliance with the PDS. The SPD and the forerunner of the PDS, the KPD, are historical enemies, a hostility that reaches back to the German Revolution of 1918, persisted throughout the Weimar Republic and was renewed in 1945. The SPD in the new Länder has fewer reservations about cooperating with the PDS and is more prepared to regard it as a legitimate expression of popular interests in eastern Germany. The PDS itself has everything to gain from becoming 'rehabilitated'.

One conclusion that can be drawn in outlining the implications of a two-bloc model is that neither the CDU nor the SPD would be entirely happy with the outcome. The SPD might well look back with nostalgia to the security and predictability of coalition with the Free Democrats. For its part the CDU would be content to have the FDP as a permanent partner, but fearful of being relegated to a minority position if the FDP should collapse. Other alignments can be envisaged, such as the CDU with the Greens (Betz, 1995), which has some plausibility given that in the future the Greens could play the pivotal 'third party' role, as it has been practised by the FDP.

Trends in the Länder

There is now little correspondence between the party systems and composition governing coalitions in the individual Länder and even less with the federal coalition. This growing complexity is in part a result of reunification and the increase in the number of Länder, but it has become all the more marked following the elections held in 1994 and subsequently. Table 4.4 gives details of the parties serving in Land governments in April 1996. The most notable features are as follows:

- There are no fewer than eight kinds of governing formation, ranging from those where one party has an overall majority to the quite exceptional case of Saxony-Anhalt, which has a minority coalition of SPD and Greens supported by the PDS.
- In contrast to an earlier phase, there are no cases of three-party coalitions. At first sight this development might imply a simplification of Länder politics, but that is a deceptive impression.
- The SPD has an outright majority in three Länder and the CDU–CSU only in two. The relative weakness of the CDU in the Länder, which has been evident for some years, admits of no one explanation, except that, with the CDU so long in power federally and heavily dependent on the personage of Helmut Kohl, there is a slippage in favour of the opposition in the years between federal elections.
- The SPD is in government in 13 of the 16 Länder, four of them with the Greens.
- There are only two coalitions involving the FDP, and only one that reflects the federal coalition.
- A large group, four Länder in all, consists of grand coalitions between the CDU and the SPD; in the past this was an exceptional occurrence.

TABLE 4.4 *Composition of Land governments and Bundesrat seats, 1996*

Land	*Election year*	*Governing parties*	*Bundesrat seats*
Baden-Württemberg	1996	CDU–FDP	6
Bavaria	1994	CSU	6
Berlin	1995	CDU–SPD	4
Brandenburg	1994	SPD	4
Bremen	1995	SPD–CDU	3
Hamburg	1993	SPD–STATT	3
Hesse	1995	SPD–Greens	5
Lower Saxony	1994	SPD	6
Mecklenburg–West Pomerania	1994	CDU–SPD	3
North Rhine–Westphalia	1995	SPD–Greens	6
Rhineland–Palatinate	1996	SPD–FDP	4
Saarland	1994	SPD	3
Saxony	1994	CDU	4
Saxony–Anhalt	1994	SPD–Greens (PDS)	4
Schleswig–Holstein	1996	SPD–Greens	4
Thuringia	1994	CDU–SPD	4

Note: There is a minority coalition in Saxony-Anhalt, with the support of the PDS. Total number of seats in the Bundesrat = 69.

There are two ways of interpreting this unusual diversity. One is that it marks a stage of transition in German politics: the situation is at present confused, but this will soon give way to new, firm patterns of alignment. Yet the alternative interpretation is equally valid: diversity may become a permanent feature, resulting from changes in electoral behaviour to accord more with local circumstances and concerns rather than purely federal ones, and that would most obviously be the case for the new Länder. Partly, too, it is a consequence of the disparity between voter turnout at federal and Land elections: the lower turnout in a Land election gives those parties that represent minority or local issues far greater significance than at a federal election. A good example is the *Stattpartei* in Hamburg, which in 1993 gained 5.6 per cent of the votes, and is now in coalition with the SPD. It was formed as a protest (*statt* means 'alternative') against the government of the city-state and discontent with the running of the CDU, but with votes coming also from SPD supporters.

Individual politicians also have a strong effect, positively or negatively. Thus two with a pronounced favourable rating are the minister-presidents of two neighbouring Länder, Brandenburg and Saxony, Manfred Stolpe and Kurt Biedenkopf respectively. The two Länder are not greatly dissimilar, and yet in Brandenburg the SPD commands an absolute majority, as does the CDU in Saxony. Stolpe is attractive as a representative of an east German identity, whereas Biedenkopf's favourable reputation owes much to the fact that he is a *Wessi* (West

German) who has nevertheless succeeded in identifying himself with the interests of his 'adopted' Land. This personality effect is a feature more in eastern Germany because there the electorate feels little attachment to the political parties, and the reputation of political leaders is of greater importance.

These factors can have lasting effects and indicate a growing and possible lasting disjunction between politics at the federal and Land levels. Yet whilst it is true that the party systems in the Länder all display individual characteristics, Länder politics are also closely related to what happens at the federal level – and in the other direction, developments in the Länder affect the course of federal politics:

Firstly, Land elections are also contests between the federal parties, and they test the relative standing of the parties in federal government and those in opposition, giving a guide as to how the parties will fare at a subsequent federal election, sending warning signals that should be heeded. Thus earlier in 1994, prior to the October federal election, the FDP lost its representation in six Länder; in Saxony-Anhalt it plummeted from 13.5 per cent to 3.6 per cent. It was probably impossible for the FDP to take drastic remedial action at that stage, but the fact that the party was able to survive at the federal election was probably the shock its supporters received after the party's serious setbacks in the preceding Land elections, and the prospect of the FDP's demise encouraged some of the CDU to split their votes.

Secondly, the outcome of Land elections can have specific political consequences. The Berlin election of October 1995 provides a good illustration. The SPD suffered a serious defeat: its vote fell from 32.1 per cent to a miserable 23.6 per cent in 1995. This failure led to the ousting of Rudolf Scharping.

Thirdly, changes in the composition of Länder coalitions may foreshadow changes in federal alignments. This was so in the past when the FDP switched in Land coalitions from the CDU to the SPD, and vice-versa. At the present time there are three Land coalitions involving the SPD and the Greens: in Saxony-Anhalt, Hesse, and – most importantly – in the largest of all the Länder, North-Rhine Westphalia. These formations could be the precursors of a new federal coalition.

Finally, the most direct impact on federal politics is the effect of changes in Länder governments that lead to an alteration in the composition of the Bundesrat and thus affect the balance between government and opposition at the federal level (see also Chapter 5). Since 1991 the balance has swung decisively in favour of the SPD. It is either in sole control or with the Greens in seven Länder, whereas the CDU–CSU control only three states – as Table 4.4 above shows, the difference in voting strength depends on the relative size of the individual Länder and the number of votes each Land is allocated. In the remaining six there are mixed or cross-cutting coalitions, and this large group modifies the sharp imbalance, since how the votes of these Länder will be used depends on the issue to be decided and the extent to which the interests of an individual Land are likely to be affected.

In this situation it is less the case of the SPD majority defeating the legislation of the federal government, but rather using its position to extract favourable concessions and compromises. By the same token, however, the SPD-controlled Länder also have to accept responsibility for the decisions finally agreed. Moreover the federal government is not altogether helpless: it can use its resources as a bargaining counter to trade for votes – especially to win over poorer eastern Länder. Although this kind of fluidity has always been present to a degree, formerly a much clearer division existed between those Länder supporting the federal government and those in opposition.

A 'Cartel' Democracy?

Richard Katz and Peter Mair have advanced the argument that, 'the recent period has witnessed the emergence of a new model of party, the cartel party, in which colluding parties become agents of the state (the party state) to ensure their own collective survival' (Katz and Mair, 1995). In this process the parties loosen their links with civil society and the electorate at large as a means of support; instead they anchor themselves to the state, drawing on the state's resources to provide their financing and opportunities for party patronage, and use legislative means to secure their position. As the parties become more dependent on the state, they act less as the representatives of civil society and have weaker links with the electorate. This process also affects the parties themselves – their organisation and the part played by their members. The 'new model' cartel party would mark a further stage in the development of party systems following on from the two earlier eras – those of the 'mass party' and its successor, the catch-all or *Volkspartei* party.

Whether or not the cartel party proves to be a new type, its leading features are certainly relevant to the Federal Republic, and might even be taken as a forerunner of developments elsewhere. One reason is that German parties already have closer connections with the state than in many countries because they operate within a tight, controlling legal framework that on the one hand regulates their activities, but on the other gives them a privileged role in society. This framework was in fact integral to the formation of the original West German state, and it is enshrined in – or implied by – the provisions of the Basic Law, and subject to the jurisdiction of the Federal Constitutional Court.

The 'officialisation' of party politics through the Basic Law belongs to what Thomas Poguntke describes as a 'legalistic political culture' (Poguntke, 1984), but it was also a direct reaction to the failure of democratic parties in the Weimar Republic. Of cardinal importance is Article 21 of the Basic Law, which sets out the criteria for deciding whether a party is 'democratic' and therefore eligible to compete; the detailed internal ordering of the parties was regulated by the Party Law of 1967.

The parties are also 'elevated' in the sense that they are charged with an educative function in society (*Politische Willensbildung*), which has had the important consequence of justifying the state-financing of parties, directly in order to assist them to contest elections, and indirectly via the various party-related 'foundations' that engage in a range of activities not specifically aimed at boosting the parties' electoral fortunes.

Over the years the parties have increasingly supplemented their income from membership fees, corporate and individual donations and by recourse to public funds. On numerous occasions the Federal Constitutional Court has intervened to limit the extent to which the parties have sought to 'help themselves' from the state. Although membership fees are still an important source of finance, the state-dependency of the parties has shown inexorable growth.

A new Party Law (1994) changed the basis of direct state financing to a 'general funding' of party activities, instead of, as previously, for campaign expenditure alone (Gunlicks, 1995). Now less weight is given to a party's electoral performance by also taking into account the success of parties in generating their own income. Thus the new system is a combination of (1) a subsidy of DM1.30 for each vote for the first five million votes a party receives (federal, Land and European elections) and DM1 for each additional vote); and (2) a subsidy related to the income a party derives from membership subscriptions and individual donors (the latter to a limit of DM6000).

The sums involved are large. At present the limit is set at DM230 million, to be divided among the parties. The major parties naturally take the largest share. In 1995 the amounts (in millions of Deutsche Marks) were SPD 90, CDU 74, CSU 16, Greens 15 and FDP 14. The many minor parties that failed to win federal representation (although some were successful in Länder elections) were also compensated; the Republicans for instance, were entitled to DM5 million.

On one level this system of rewarding parties is perfectly equitable. On another, however, the effect is quite different: the largesse flowing to the leading parties helps them further to consolidate their position, so that the strong imbalance in their favour is maintained. If the amounts were small and only a minor proportion of a party's income, the distortion would not be great, but in the German case the sheer scale of subsidisation is a persuasive explanation for the continuing dominance of the *Volksparteien*.

In a detailed assessment of party financing Poguntke (1984, pp. 196–7) concludes:

> The one very unambiguous message that emerges is that German parties are to a very substantial degree dependent on the continuous flow of public money. . .. If we add the income of party foundations and the subsidies to the parliamentary parties in the Bundestag, the self-generated income on the *national* level become negligible, falling from around 20 per cent to less than 10 per cent since 1970 in most cases.

The extent of state financing is the most significant aspect of cartellisation, but it also applies to the wide scope for patronage that is available to the parties, especially evident in a federal system. Party-related appointments are common in a range of public bodies and semi-official organisations both at federal and Land levels: the top ranks of the civil service, broadcasting authorities, Länder banks, to mention just a few, and often a form of *Proporz* operates, whereby the major parties share out appointments between them. That is the case with appointments made by the Bundestag and Bundesrat to the Federal Constitutional Court. It well illustrates the blurred division in Germany between the parties and the state.

If there is an interpenetration of parties and the state, does it amount to a collusion to ensure their collective survival? It can be argued that the present position belongs to a continental tradition that is quite different from countries where the lines separating state and society are more clearly marked. According to that view the idea of emerging cartel parties may be misplaced. However the 'state inheritance' could facilitate such a development and simply mean that Germany is in the vanguard of the new type.

German parties, like those elsewhere in Europe, are less able to rely on stable electoral support. Declining levels of party identification, electoral volatility, issue voting and falling electoral turnout have affected the established parties. In Germany there is also the phenomenon of *Politikverdrossenheit* – a general disillusionment with party politics. The parties are becoming detached from civil society and the electorate, and with the erosion of social cleavages, voters are more heterogeneous. Electoral campaigns are consequently increasingly professional and the party leadership is less dependent on party activists and a large membership.

Yet party membership is comparatively high (see Table 4.5). To this extent German parties are still firmly anchored to civil society, despite the fact that the CDU and the SPD have both lost a significant number of members in recent years. The two weakest parties – that is, those with a low proportion of members to voters – are the Greens and the FDP; the PDS is by far the strongest.

The most striking contrast is between the new and old Länder. In the east, only the PDS qualifies as a mass membership party. Thus the CDU has around 77 000 members, the FDP about 29 000 (probably on the optimistic side) and all three have experienced a steep decline compared with their former existence as 'bloc' parties in the GDR. The SPD has a mere 27 000 members and can scarcely hope ever to become a 'mass' party in the new Länder. For their part the Greens, with some 4000 members, have never made formal membership a high priority. The federal structure of the German state compensates for the weakening of the mass party, since party organisations in the Länder have a degree of independence from the national leadership, an insulation that gives party members a greater role.

Katz and Mair (1995) leave open the possibility that the cartel party may itself be challenged by parties not willing to become part of the cartel: a relative outsider could attract voters away from the main parties if it attacks the style of politics that has given rise to electoral discontent. That role is unlikely ever to be taken by the PDS: as a former 'state party' *par excellence* it would have no problems with the

TABLE 4.5 *Party membership and ratio to voters, 1994*

Party	*Votes (mills)*	*Members (thous.)*	*Votes/members ratio*	*Organisational density (%)*
Greens	3.42	44	78.1	1.28
SPD	17.14	850	20.1	4.96
CDU	16.08	671	24.1	4.17
CSU	3.42	176	19.1	5.14
FDP	3.26	90	36.1	2.76
PDS	2.07	124	17.1	5.99

cartel club, once accepted by the other parties. The most obvious pretenders are the Greens, in view of their history and their 'anti-party' origins. Yet their record over the past few years – in coalition at Land level, hopeful of joining a federal coalition, and (with a low membership) dependent on their share of state funding – is an indication that cartellisation may be an insidious process.

5

The Territorial Dimension

CHARLIE JEFFERY

The quest to divine the post-reunification future of the German federal system was a growth industry among academic commentators in the early 1990s. Unusually, the prognosis was remarkably consistent: reunification posed an 'acid test' (Benz, 1991; Gunlicks and Voigt, 1991; Hesse and Renzsch, 1990; Klatt, 1993) that the federal system was unlikely to pass unscathed. The task of integrating the new Länder of eastern Germany would strain and, in all likelihood, rupture the consensualism that had shaped relations between the Länder in West Germany prior to reunification and guaranteed their role as a counterweight to the Federal Republic's central political institutions, in particular the federal government. Moreover the prognosis was made bleaker by the concurrent problems posed by deepening European integration, which in the run-up to Maastricht threatened to erode Länder competences without offering them adequate compensatory input into the European-level policy process. The federal government, secure in its seat in the Council of Ministers, again stood to gain at Länder expense.

With the luxury of hindsight, such judgements might now seem a little overhasty. There has not been an overt lurch towards some more centralised form of government since 1990. The integration of the new Länder into the structures and procedures of German federalism has proceeded without dramatic disruption. And the Länder proved able to mobilise effectively in and around Maastricht to turn the tide of disadvantage with which European integration has typically burdened them since the 1950s. This chapter suggests, however, that the effect of unification has yet to become fully apparent. It argues that a number of trends can be identified that broadly confirm the thrust of the prognoses made in the immediate aftermath of unification. Taken collectively, these trends highlight a growing disjunction between a federal decision-making process that has traditionally been predicated on consensus, and a widening differentiation and divergence of Länder interests. The nature of this disjunction, and its likely long-term impact, are examined below under five headings: the structures of German federalism; patterns of interest divergence and policy differentiation in the Länder; questions of resource distribution; party-political factors, and the role of the Länder in the European integration process.

The Structures of German Federalism

The constitutional foundations of the German federal system have changed remarkably little as a result of re unification. The Treaty of Unification expanded the number of Länder to sixteen by providing for the accession of the five new Länder of eastern Germany (Brandenburg, Mecklenburg-West Pomerania, Saxony, Saxony-Anhalt and Thuringia) to the Federal Republic on 3 October 1990 and the establishment of East and West Berlin as a unified Land. It also rejigged the voting weights of the Länder in the Bundesrat (which are loosely related to population size) as a result of pressure by the larger western Länder to retain their relative decision-making weight after unification (see Table 5.2 below). Otherwise the Treaty of Unification required no further constitutional changes in relation to the federal system. It did, however, recommend that consideration be given 'within two years' to additional constitutional changes that would merge the Länder of Berlin and Brandenburg and more broadly reconsider 'the relationship between federation and Länder' in the light of post-reunification circumstances. In neither case was the timetable adhered to. Following protracted negotiations, Berlin and Brandenburg held referenda on merger in May 1996 only for it to be rejected. And reconsideration of 'the relationship between federation and Länder' was subsumed in wider discussions on constitutional reform that were finally completed in October 1994. These ultimately amounted to a 'non-reform' (Jeffery, 1995a) of the federal system, at least with regard to the federal–Länder relationship in domestic politics (though, as discussed in the final section of this chapter, significant changes were made in the field of European integration policy). Among the limited changes made in the domestic arena were the following: a minor reallocation of competences in favour of the Länder; tougher rules for the justification of federal-level legislation in the field of 'concurrent' powers (fields of policy in which both federation and

Länder may both legislate, but where the federal authorities have typically been able to claim a dominant position); and a number of technical amendments to legislative procedure at the federal level designed to strengthen the capacity of the Länder, acting through the Bundesrat, in the federal legislative process.

The net impact of reunification on the constitutional structures of German federalism has been, then, relatively modest. The expanded, post-reunification community of Länder in other words operates within a constitutional framework that in most respects is unchanged from the pre-reunification situation in West Germany. The impression of continuity is reinforced by the pattern of administrative structures and procedures established in the new Länder. These, constructed with considerable fraternal input from the western Länder, drew substantially on existing West German models (Goetz, 1993). Combined with an extensive west–east transfer of personnel – particularly of civil servants, but also, in some cases, of politicians seeking to revive careers and reputations that had been treading water in the west – the process of administrative transfer has produced a group of new Länder seemingly well-placed to ensure continuity in the practices of federal politics established prior to reunification.

These practices were encapsulated in a dense process of intergovernmental coordination between the Länder governments and their counterpart at the federal level. Variously described as 'cooperative federalism' or, more pejoratively, *Politikverflechtung*, an 'entanglement' of the two levels of government (Scharpf *et al.*, 1976), this coordination process typically imposed high consensus requirements in intergovernmental relations. These had a number of sources. The first three were based in the constitutional division of labour between the federal level and the Länder.

Firstly, postwar German federalism has not been based primarily on the parcelling out to each level of government of exclusive competences in separate policy fields. Although the federal level and the Länder have each had exclusive fields of competence, these – especially in the case of the Länder – have not been extensive. Far more prevalent has been the shared exercise of competence in the same policy fields, with the federal level responsible for the bulk of law making and the Länder governments largely responsible for the implementation of those laws. This division of labour between legislation and implementation tended to produce a high degree of interdependence between the two levels of government.

Secondly, the degree of interdependence was made more intense by the role of the Bundesrat in the federal legislative process. The

Bundesrat is a forum of the Länder governments that acts as the second legislative chamber at the federal level. It possesses the right of absolute veto over around 60 per cent of federal laws (and a suspensive veto over the remainder). The scope of its absolute veto power typically required the federal government, as the main initiator of legislation, to secure the agreement of the Länder governments prior to the introduction of legislation. The two levels of government were thus bound together – or 'entangled' – in a perpetual process of coordination designed to secure the consensus necessary for federal legislation to be accepted in the Bundesrat and then to proceed to the implementation stage in the Länder.

Thirdly, in some fields of policy – the 'joint tasks' of federation and Länder and other joint policy-making mechanisms – federal–Länder interdependence was further institutionalised with the creation of detailed joint legislative, planning and financing procedures following constitutional reforms in 1969–70. The special procedures of the joint tasks, and more broadly the role of the Länder governments in legislative implementation and, through the Bundesrat, the formulation of federal legislation, together imposed a *prima facie* requirement on the federal government to secure agreement on policy with its counterparts in the Länder. However, and fourthly, this *prima facie* requirement could only be made active if the Länder governments achieved a unity of purpose among themselves. Their power of veto and their role in legislative implementation and the joint tasks could only be translated into genuine and sustained influence on the federal government if they maintained a united voice. Consensus between the Länder was therefore a necessary precondition for any extensive Länder role in the federal policy process. Inter-Länder consensus was thus the cornerstone of the wider practice of cooperative federalism. It was secured in a complex mass of policy coordinating committees, centred on the Bundesrat, which in part overlapped with and fed in to a further mass of federal–Länder policy coordinating committees designed to secure federal–Länder consensus (c.f. Leonardy, 1991).

Patterns of Interest Divergence and Policy Differentiation

As noted above, the constitutional framework from which the consensus orientation of the pre-reunification federal system derived has remained in essence unaltered since reunification (as indeed has the committee structure of inter-Länder and federal–Länder coordination).

In other words the structural foundations of cooperative federalism persist. A significant question mark hangs, however, over the capacity of the Länder to maintain sufficient levels of consensus among themselves to guarantee the forms and scope of influence over the federal government they had exercised before 1990. The central problem concerns the inevitable divergences of interest between old and new Länder, which may prove too wide to secure high levels of inter-Länder consensus in the post-unity federal system and thus help to promote a pattern of policy differentiation inimical to the practice of cooperative federalism. A foretaste of this kind of problem was given with the emergence of tensions in the practice of cooperative federalism in the West German Federal Republic of the 1980s. These are briefly worth recapping in order to place the new all-German situation into perspective.

These West German tensions had two main and in part connected sources. The first was a growing divergence in economic performance in the Länder. Long-term structural weaknesses in former core industries – coal, steel and shipbuilding – finally hit hard in a group of mainly northern Länder during the 1980s at the same time as a mainly southern group was developing a new and successful emphasis on high-technology and high-growth sectors employing advanced electronics. The nascent north–south divide between smokestack and silicon chip, clearly observable in contrasting growth and unemployment rates (Benz, 1989, p. 205), was then overlaid by a second factor: the neoliberal drive for cutting (central) state expenditure and thus 'rolling back the state'. While neoliberal forms of policy making were never implemented in the Federal Republic with an intensity comparable to Thatcher's Britain or Reagan's United States, they nevertheless had two important implications for the federal system. They led on the one hand to the disengagement of the federal government from parts of the joint federal–Länder policy apparatus established in the late 1960s. On the other they redirected some of the burden of state expenditure away from the federal level and on to the Länder, in particular in the field of social security.

The combined effect of economic change and 'rolling back the state' was a growing strain on the inter-Länder solidarity upon which cooperative federalism rested. Those Länder with more buoyant economies placed increasing emphasis on autonomous policy making. Facilitated by the withdrawal of the federal government from aspects of joint policy making and sustained by the tax proceeds of economic growth, they sought in part to disengage from the structures of cooperative federalism and commit their superior resources to increased policy discretion, in particular in industrial policy, regional planning and research and technology policy (Benz, 1989; Götz, 1992). In contrast Länder facing structural economic decline were confronted with declining tax revenues at the same time as having to pick up a growing tab of social welfare expenditure imposed on them by federal government cutbacks. The inevitable result was increased indebtedness, which in turn inspired the partially successful quest to secure the selective reengagement (contrary to the neoliberal vogue) of federal government funding to cover the shortfall, most notably in the Structural Aid Law of 1988. More broadly, the divergences of interest and priority arising from contrasting economic backgrounds led to intense inter-Länder conflict, in part carried out in constitutional litigation, over resource distribution within the federal system (as discussed in the following section).

The wider significance of these West German tensions should not be overstated. The structures and procedures of cooperative federalism, though increasingly under strain, remained by and large intact. However the underlying trends – economic strength and growing emphasis on policy discretion versus economic weakness and growing financial dependence on the federal level – do act as a reference point for the post-reunification situation. The post-reunification economic divide between east and west is far starker than the old West German north–south divide. The new Länder have a far lower per capita GNP than the western Länder, and on average a far higher unemployment rate. And although growth rates in the east are much higher, they are calculated from a far lower base following the collapse of manufacturing industry in the east in 1990. The catching-up process for the east will not be a short one. The potential for a rupturing of cooperative federalism is clear. The new Länder are, and have to be, far more concerned with the problems of economic regeneration than with seeking consensus with their western counterparts. Unsurprisingly this has led them to formulate common positions on policy fields where the post-communist transformation process has placed particular burdens on them, and on which their interests do not easily coincide with the western Länder. Also unsurprisingly they have sought – and in part secured – joint policy initiatives with the federal government in policy fields that emphasise the disjunction between east and west in policy-making practice. Since reunification a range of joint policy inititiatives has been selectively focused on the east, for example in health-care provision (Hildebrandt, 1994) and higher education (Neuweiler, 1994). Others have offered special dispensations for the new Länder within all-German joint policy-making frameworks, the latter funded in part by reduced access of the western Länder to the fruits of joint policy, for example in the joint task on Regional Economic Development (Toepel, 1995).

In addition, the method and pace of reunification produced separate policy structures in certain fields that grant the federal government policy roles in the new Länder it does not possess in the west. The prime example concerns the *Treuhandanstalt*, the federal agency set up in 1990 to execute the restructuring, privatisation or liquidation of former GDR state industries. Despite a policy remit embedded in the heart of what would normally be seen as Länder competence in regional economic policy, the new Länder made relatively little real impact on the work of the *Treuhand* (or of its successor institutions, now that its main task of industrial privatisation has been completed). The reasons for the limited input of the new Länder into the work of the *Treuhand* are symptomatic (c.f. Seibel, 1994). Firstly, the Länder were excluded from a full role because the *Treuhand* was set up before they were in 1990; the sheer speed of the reunification process established a *fait accompli.* Secondly, they failed to challenge the *fait accompli* with any degree of vehemence partly because of the vast sums the federal government was pouring into industrial subsidies, which they could not conceivably have taken over, and partly because they wished to distance themselves from coresponsibility for unpopular decisions made by the *Treuhand* on restructuring and, in particular, liquidation. The end result has been, and remains, a degree of federal involvement in the management of the economies of the new Länder that is incomparably greater than the situation in the west.

The degree of federal financial and policy commitment to the new Länder has inevitably had an impact on the western Länder, most obviously, as indicated above, in the scaling back of joint task and other cofinancing programmes to compensate for new eastern commitments. In contrast to the cutbacks of the 1980s, however, little prospect of selective compensation for the economically weaker western Länder exists beyond limited adjustments through federal grants awarded in the financial equalisation procedure (see below). As a result, even the economically weaker western Länder have been forced to develop a greater degree of policy autonomy and discretion, drawing on the models established by their stronger counterparts in the 1980s. The transformation has been such that even the perennially straitened Lower Saxony, the leading *demandeur* for additional federal government support in the 1980s, has developed a highly innovative, autonomous policy profile in the fields of regional economic development and employment.

Assessments of the divergence of Länder interests and policy roles since reunification have varied. The close relationship and financial dependence of the new Länder on the federal government and the growing, in part enforced, emphasis of the western Länder on self-reliance and policy discretion has certainly broken down some of the density and rigidity of the cooperative federal relationships characteristic of the pre-reunification Federal Republic. Given the scale of post-reunification disparities, the Länder are now less able and arguably much less concerned to secure consensus among themselves on key policy issues. This has led some to identify the emergence of a 'two-class' federal system in which inter-Länder divisions between 'rich' west and 'poor' east can only benefit the federal level and create a 'disguised unitary state' whose federal structure is nominal rather then real (Abromeit, 1992). Others have been more sanguine, seeing a more or less natural development towards a 'territorially differentiated policy regime' which may well provide a useful and positive mechanism for reducing east–west disparities over the coming years (Goetz, 1995b, pp. 158–9). A final assessment would undoubtedly endorse aspects of both judgements, but first questions of resource distribution, the role of party politics and European integration need to be addressed.

Resource Distribution in the Federal System

The question of resource distribution is central to any federal system. The distribution of competences between two levels of government requires an appropriate distribution of resources sufficient for those competences to be exercised. Prior to reunification this question was regulated by a complex system of financial equalisation, under whose formulae tax revenues were distributed between the federal level and the Länder and between the Länder themselves. The system of financial equalisation was particularly significant for the practice of cooperative federalism. It was designed to even out resource differentials between the Länder so that each, in theory, was able to fulfil its competences on a more or less equal financial basis. The Länder could then embark on the process of policy coordination with the federal government without being divided against each other over differences in financial capacity.

The question of financial equalisation was, self-evidently, a key issue following reunification. A means had to be found to equip the resource-weak new Länder with sufficient resources to fulfil their competences without at the same time undermining the ability of the old Länder to do the same, and without introducing enduring conflicts of financial interest that might undermine the capacity of the Länder to secure consensus among themselves. The initial solution to this problem was to defer it with the creation of a German Unity Fund, cofinanced by the federal government and the western Länder, which was designed as a stop-gap until a renewed system of all-German financial equalisation could be devised. Negotiations between the federal and Länder governments, conducted within the framework of the 'Solidarity Pact for the Reconstruction of the New Länder', finally produced such a renewed system in March 1993 that came into effect on 1 January 1995.

The renewed system of financial equalisation was remarkable in that it left intact the objectives of the pre-reunification equalisation system. As before unification, the various mechanisms of equalisation were designed to ensure that each Land ultimately has a more or less equal financial capacity, measured in terms of tax income per head of population, in order to fulfil its obligations. There are two key equalisation stages. The first is designed to bring the financial capacity of each Land up to a level of at least 95 per cent of the average financial capacity of the Länder as a whole. Prior to reunification this stage was effected primarily through inter-Länder transfers from those with higher financial capacities to those with lower financial capacities. However this was not a feasible option given the economic weakness – and therefore the severely limited tax receipts – of the new Länder: even in 1995 the new Länder could generate only around 50 per cent of the average financial capacity of the Länder as a whole. The solution was to plunder the federal coffers through a massive redistribution of VAT revenues from the federal budget to the Länder. VAT receipts had hitherto been shared between the federal level and the Länder in the ratio 63:37; the new ratio from 1995 was to be 56:44. This increased the volume of funds available for inter-Länder transfers sufficiently to boost the financial capacity of the new Länder to 92 per cent of the Länder average before the western Länder had to dig into their own resource base. It thus provided a realistic basis for the achievement of the 95 per cent objective through the established process of transfer from the revenue-richer (that is, western) to revenue-poorer Länder. In the second stage of equalisation, federal complementary grants (*Bundesergänzungszuweisungen*) are awarded from the federal-level budget as an additional 'safety net' to ensure that the financial capacity of each of the Länder reaches at least 99.5 per cent of the Länder average.

The net effect of the equalisation process for 1995 is shown in Table 5.1 (including a range of other measures also adopted as part of the Solidarity Pact). The remarkable feature of the financial transfer flows

TABLE 5.1 *Financial equalisation flows for 1995 (in DM million)*

Measures	*Federal level*	*Western Länder*	*Eastern Länder*
VAT redistribution	–17500	–900	18400
Inter-Länder transfers		–12800	12800
Federal Complementary Grants	–26740	7770	18970
German Unity Fund Annuities	2100	–2100	
Other	–7775		7775
Total	–49915	–8030	57945

Source: Calculated from figures presented in Peffekoven, 1994, p. 304.

is the relative contribution of the federal budget to the task of resourcing the new Länder – some 85 per cent of the almost DM 59 billion headed east – compared with the 15 per cent contribution made by the western Länder. The figures are all the more remarkable given that the initial federal government proposal for the Solidarity Pact negotiations foresaw a mere 60 per cent contribution from the federal budget to net equalisation transfers to the eastern Länder (Bundesrat, 1993, p. 9).

Unsurprisingly, this outcome was greeted as a great triumph in the Länder. The new Länder had received as much as they could have expected, while the western Länder had successfully limited the impact of reunification on their equalisation obligations. The federal government, on the other hand, was judged to have lost 'hands down' (Webber and Sally, 1994, p. 26). This is true to the extent that the Länder won a short-term victory over the federal government in the context of the Solidarity Pact. However a longer-term perspective on the implications of the renewed equalisation system demands a little more circumspection. Aside from the redistribution of VAT revenues from federation to Länder and a number of other relatively minor adjustments (Peffekoven, 1994), the equalisation system operating since 1995 is the same as that in operation before reunification. And prior to reunification the equalisation system was seen by different groups of Länder as deeply unsatisfactory, sufficiently so for a number of cases to be brought before the adjudication of the Federal Constitutional Court. The reasons for this are worth recapping.

Firstly, equalisation is income-oriented. It ensures that each Land has a minimum of 99.5 per cent of the average per capita income of all Länder taken together. It takes no systematic account of the differing per capita expenditure commitments of the Länder. This was a problem acutely felt in the 1980s by a number of western Länder faced by problems of structural economic decline. The per capita shortfall in revenue-raising capacity caused by economic decline was addressed by equalisation, but the additional per capita expenditure burdens caused by economic decline – above all on social security – were not. Economically weak Länder felt as a result that their particular needs were not being met by equalisation and were prone, as a result, to seek redress at the Constitutional Court and/or separate and selective support from the federal government (for example in the 1988 Structural Aid Law).

Secondly, equalisation transfers are not targeted at specific forms of expenditure. They accrue to the general budgets of the Länder concerned. They are therefore not necessarily used to address the problems that led to financial weakness in the first place. They could, in theory, merely sustain a financially incompetent or profligate Land administration. This was certainly a perception held in the 1980s by those economically buoyant Länder that supplied the bulk of inter-Länder transfers. Their feeling was that they were being penalised for their economic success, while their recipient counterparts faced no real disincentives to mismanagement or any other contributions they may have made to their own economic and financial weakness. The response of the economically stronger Länder was to seek to limit their fraternal obligations to their economically weaker counterparts, again in part by recourse to the Constitutional Court.

Despite the promptings of a vigorous academic debate (c.f. Jeffery, 1995a, p. 264), no real attempt was made in the negotiations leading up to the Solidarity Pact to address the expenditure blindness of the equalisation process or the absence of penalties for incompetence in economic and financial management. The equalisation system therefore remains unsatisfactory for the economically weaker payee Länder with high expenditure commitments, which, in post-reunification terms are those in the east, plus Bremen and Saarland in the west. It remains unsatisfactory too for the economically stronger payer Länder, that is the remainder of the western Länder. These, despite the successful damage limitation exercise at the Solidarity Pact negotiations, are paying far more now than before reunification into a system whose transfer flows are not ring-fenced against the effects of maladministration. As Rolf Peffekoven (1994, p. 295) notes with some exasperation: 'One does not have to be a prophet to foresee further dispute about these [equalisation] rules'.

An additional factor that is likely further to stoke up the potential for dispute is the attitude of the federal government. As Table 5.1 shows, the federal government was a massive loser in the Solidarity Pact negotiations. It will want to claw funds back and has already taken steps to do so in the following ways (Peffekoven, 1994, p. 306): by raising taxes whose proceeds are not shared with the Länder; by cutting its commitments to joint federal–Länder programmes (though not primarily to those it undertakes selectively with the new Länder); and by relocating expenditure commitments from the federal level to the Länder (in particular, as in the 1980s, in the field of social welfare). Ring-fencing new revenues out of the reach of the Länder and imposing new expenditure burdens on them can only exacerbate the inherent tensions of the financial equalisation system. It will create conditions ripe for a return to the 'litigious' federalism of the 1980s (Jeffery and Yates, 1993, p. 65) which saw inter-Länder conflicts carried out in law before the Constitutional Court rather than through negotiation within the structures of cooperative federalism. More broadly, it will confirm and widen the divergence of Länder interests and practices noted in the previous section of this chapter. In order to meet their expenditure needs, the weaker Länder, especially in the east, are predisposed by the nature of the equalisation system to seek enhanced support from, and ultimately dependence on, the federal government. And the stronger Länder are equally predisposed to serve notice on past practices of inter-Länder solidarity in order to protect their resource base from further depredation by their equalisation obligations.

Party Politics and the Federal System

This conclusion points further towards a situation in which the trends towards inter-Länder divergences of interest following reunification are likely in some measure to outweigh the incentives for inter-Länder cooperation and consensus inherent in the constitutional structure of German federalism. The likelihood of such a development is enhanced by post-reunification developments in the party-political dimension of German federalism.

Much has been written over the years about the potential conflict between the federal logic of nationally organised political parties and the territorial logic of Länder politics. In particular, concern has been voiced about the 'invasion' of Bundesrat decision-making processes by federal party imperatives at the expense of territorial Länder imperatives. It was certainly the view of Gerhard Lehmbruch (1976) that the CDU–CSU illegitimately used its Bundesrat majority as an instrument of federal opposition during the period of SPD–FDP government after

1969. Similar concerns were raised that the CDU–CSU-dominated Bundesrat acted, as it were, as Helmut Kohl's 'poodle' during the renewed era of Christian Democratic federal government after 1982 (Klatt, 1991).

In retrospect these concerns seem somewhat overstated. The 1970s and 1980s certainly saw a stronger element of party-based coordination (by both the CDU–CSU and the SPD) in the Bundesrat. Rather than being primarily an instrument of federal party politics, for which the evidence is rather inconclusive (Sturm, 1996), such coordination acted much more as an additional means of coalition building and consensus formation in cooperative federalism. The groupings of so-called SPD-led 'A-Länder' and CDU or CSU-led 'B-Länder' acted as 'pillars' that provided points of contact between other divides around which shared Länder interests might form: for example between revenue-richer and revenue-poorer Länder, or larger and smaller Länder. In this pattern of – to use the terminology of electoral studies – 'cross-cutting cleavages', the party 'pillars' provided permanent points of contact between Länder located in different interest constellations. Party politics thus facilitated the overall process of consensus formation in the Bundesrat, whose results could then be brought to bear in interactions with the federal level.

The party-political dimension of coalition building in the Bundesrat presupposed, though, a pattern of governmental composition in the Länder that could be organised along the lines of the government–opposition divide at the federal level. For the most part, this was the case during the 1980s, when there was typically a straightforward situation of a group of Länder led by the Christian Democrats alone, or in coalition with their federal coalition partners, the FDP, and another group of single-party SPD governments. It has not been the case since reunification. The post-reunification period has seen significant changes in the landscape of Länder party politics that have produced the following features: the two big *Volksparteien*, the CDU and the SPD, have experienced untypically high fluctuations in the level of their vote; the subnational electoral base of the FDP has become extremely fragile, leading to a series of failures to secure Land parliament representation; the Greens, on the other hand, have consolidated a strong presence, in the western Länder at least; protest voting has become widespread, periodically elevating parties of the far right and other, looser, non-extremist groupings into Land parliaments in the west; and in the east the post-communist PDS has, contrary to some expectations, maintained itself as a strong third force behind – in some cases only just behind – the CDU and the SPD.

The volatility of the party-political situation has substantially complicated the process of government formation in the Länder, producing a range of coalition alignments in part incongruent with the government–opposition divide at the federal level. The situation in April 1996 is shown in Table 5.2. Alongside a group of single-party SPD, CDU and CSU governments, the dictates of electoral arithmetic and the unpalatability of alternative coalition partners has led to the formation of grand coalitions of the CDU and the SPD in Bremen, Berlin, Mecklenburg-West Pomerania and Thuringia. The SPD has demonstrated a high degree of coalition versatility elsewhere by joining forces with the Greens in Hessen, North Rhine-Westphalia and (controversially 'tolerated' as a minority government by the PDS) in Saxony-Anhalt, with the FDP in Rhineland-Palatinate, and with the bourgeois protest grouping, the *Stattpartei* (Instead-of-a-Party!), in Hamburg.

The ability to collect a 'weird and wonderful' range of governmental partners has given the SPD, which remains anchored in opposition in the Bundestag, a nominal majority in the Bundesrat since early 1991.

TABLE 5.2 *The Parties in the Bundesrat (April 1996)*

Land Government composition	*Land*	*Bundesrat votes*
SPD-led Länder		
Single party SPD	Brandenburg	4
	Lower Saxony	6
	Saarland	3
SPD–Green	Hesse	5
	North Rhine-Westphalia	6
	Saxony-Anhalt	4
	Schleswig-Holstein	4
SPD–Stattpartei	Hamburg	3
SPD–FDP	Rhineland-Palatinate	4
SPD–CDU	Bremen	3
Total SPD-led Länder		42
CDU/CSU-led Länder		
Single party CDU	Saxony	4
CDU–FDP	Baden-Württemberg	6
Single party CSU	Bavaria	6
CDU–SPD	Berlin	4
	Mecklenburg-West Pomerania	3
	Thuringia	4
Total CDU/CSU-led Länder		27
Total		69

Source: Adapted from Klatt (1995).

The SPD's majority has raised a concern, like that expressed by Lehmbruch in the 1970s, that the Bundesrat will be exploited as an instrument of federal opposition. This concern is again overstated (c.f. Klatt, 1995). It has to be qualified by the fact that the SPD's majority is not easily mobilisable. Until the end of 1995, when Hessen unexpectedly won another Bundesrat vote by virtue of increase in population since the previous census, the SPD-led Länder could only summon a majority if it secured the support of either the FDP in Rhineland-Palatinate or the CDU (or, prior to the establishment of the grand coalition, the FDP) in Bremen. Given that Land coalitions that cut across the government–opposition divide at the federal level have abstention clauses in case of disagreement, the achievement of an SPD majority in the Bundesrat counter to a CDU–CSU/FDP majority in the Bundestag could not easily be secured. Equally the current SPD majority, won by the reproductive powers of the people of Hesse, is not secure given, (1) the need still to secure Green and *Stattpartei* consent, and (2) the combination of declining SPD opinion poll fortunes in 1995–96 with the approach of a further raft of Land elections in the spring of 1996.

A rather more important feature of the fluid party-political situation in the Länder are the obstacles it places before the party-political dimension of coalition building in the Bundesrat. As Table 5.2 clearly shows, there is no longer a neat divide between 'A-' and 'B-Länder'. The confused pattern of coalition alignments in the Länder has undermined the basis for party-based coordination. It has thus increased the potential for policy differentiation irrespective of party and lent added impetus to the divergences in Länder policy interests and priorities, which have become especially marked since reunification. In other words, the post-reunification pattern of party politics in the Bundesrat has supported the emergence of a rather more fluid and competitive policy environment within which shifting coalitions of Länder form – and dissolve – from one issue to another. As Roland Sturm (1996) concludes: 'More than ever before in German post-war history economic interest and political diversity, not party-political manoeuvres, have become the driving force behind the political moves of the Länder in the nineties'.

The Länder and the European Union

The above discussion has highlighted a pattern of continuity of federal system structures alongside one of change and differentiation in the formation and articulation of Länder interests. The field of European integration policy provides a partial contrast in that the structures for Länder input into the European policy process have been quite radically reformed since 1990. In both the domestic and European-level negotiations surrounding the Maastricht Treaty on European Union, the Länder were able to secure important new rights of input into European policy making. These collectively plugged what the Länder termed the 'open flank' of the federal system, the 'blindness' of the European policy process to the domestic constitutional status and competences of the Länder. From the foundation of the European Coal and Steel Community in 1952 onwards, this 'blindness' led to the transfer of Länder competences to European institutions without offering the Länder adequate compensatory mechanisms for the exercise of those competences in the European policy process. The federal government, on the other hand, was able to coexercise such competences alongside the other member states on the basis of its seat in the Council of Ministers. In other words, the result was, an indirect transfer of competence from the Länder to the federal level and an erosion of the status of the Länder as 'efficient' units of government.

The Länder, however, were able to 'strike back' (Jeffery, 1994) in and around Maastricht. The scope of the emergent Maastricht Treaty was so extensive that it would fall under a Bundesrat right of veto in the domestic ratification process in Germany. The potential of the Bundesrat veto was sufficient for the Länder both to claim a place on the Federal Republic's delegation in European-level negotiations and to secure a number of domestic constitutional changes in European policy in the constitutional review process that followed reunification. At the European level the Länder, in part with the support of other regional governments in the EU, won the following: a partial remedy to the 'Länder blindness' of the European policy process with the recognition of the principle of subsidiarity in the Maastricht Treaty; the establishment of the Committee of the Regions as a consultative organ, offering for the first time a direct route of input for subnational tiers of government into European policy making; and the possibility of the Länder formally representing the Federal Republic in the Council of Ministers.

These achievements were then complemented by domestic constitutional reform, in particular the new Article 23 of the Basic Law. Article 23 offered protection to the 'open flank' of the federal system by assuring a Bundesrat veto over sovereignty transfers to European institutions and by making the wider European policy process in essence subject to the forms of procedure that would apply if policy were being made domestically. In particular it gave the Länder, acting through the Bundesrat, the right to bind the federal government in European policy matters that would otherwise fall under their domestic legislative or administrative competence, and the right to sit for the Federal Republic in the Council of Ministers in the (relatively few) policy fields in which the Länder have exclusive domestic legislative competence. The latter provision thus fleshed out the possibility of Council representation won at Maastricht.

A further point to note is the consolidation by the Länder of the network of information offices they have all established since the mid 1980s in Brussels. These have evolved into effective 'antennae' of the Länder within the EU institutions, particularly the Commission. They equip the Länder with early, first-hand information on the emergence and progress of European policy initiatives that can then be employed to enhance the quality of input they are able to make under Article 23.

The above are impressive achievements that have certainly done much to ameliorate Länder concerns about the European integration process (Goetz, 1995a). However a number of caveats need to be entered. Firstly, the Länder's experience of the Committee of the Regions has been a disappointing one. The Committee was initially seen in the Länder as a 'decisive breakthrough' (Hoppe and Schulz, 1992, p. 33) for the Länder. It was a first step in establishing a fully institutionalised 'third' or regional-level voice in EU affairs, which had the potential to evolve powerful legislative rights alongside Council and Parliament. This enthusiasm did not last long. The Committee consists of representatives of both regional and local government in the EU. It has proved difficult from the Länder's perspective to bridge the differences of interest and mentality that exist between the regional and local levels and to build effective coalitions of interest in the Committee in support of their aims. The frustration that has resulted has led to a clear downgrading of the Committee, and of the direct route to 'Brussels' it was supposed to provide, in Länder European policy priorities. Their concern has turned much more – in particular in the run-up to the 1996 EU Intergovernmental Conference on the review of the Maastricht Treaty – to the creation of optimal conditions in the European treaties for the exercise of their domestically grounded European policy role under Article 23 (Jeffery, 1995b).

This leads to a second caveat: Article 23 has essentially extended the procedures of cooperative federalism to European policy making. This route into the European policy process passes through the Bundesrat and, prior to debate in the Bundesrat, through a Conference of European Minsters of the Länder created in October 1992 to prepare and coordinate the European policy business of the Bundesrat. For the full force of Article 23 procedures to become operative, a high degree of inter-Länder consensus is required, just as in the traditional realm of cooperative federalism. Although the pattern of post-Maastricht European policy practice has not yet become entirely clear, it seems likely that the kinds of divergence of policy and financial interest that have challenged the operation of cooperative federalism domestically will also feed through into the European policy arena. Substantial differences of European interest clearly exist between the Länder. At one end of the spectrum – there are highly Euroactive Länder in western Germany – in particular Baden-Württemberg, Bavaria and North Rhine-Westphalia – that are always keen to point out that they have bigger populations and economies than a number of fully-fledged EU member states, and that are keen to play a decision-making role commensurate with their size and weight (an aspiration linked, in the case of Bavaria, to periodic expressions of a robust Euroscepticism aimed at the restriction of further transfers of competences to the EU). This Euroactivism has been reflected in the redesignation of the Brussels Information Offices of these Länder as 'Representations', a term calculated to imply a superior diplomatic status. This – as was no doubt intended – has deeply irritated the federal government, which, outside Article 23, emphatically reserves for itself the right to 'represent' the Federal Republic externally. Another example is the concern of these Länder to defend the remaining exclusive competences of the Länder from erosion by the EU, as illustrated in the vigorous mobilisation of Länder opposition by Bavaria to European-level regulation of media policy (Blair and Cullen, 1996).

At the other end of the spectrum are the new Länder. Their priorities are not to enhance the profile of their presence in Brussels or even to protect exclusive competences – which in any case they can barely fund themselves – from absorption by the EU. Their overriding European policy concern is the far narrower one of securing Structural Fund flows from Brussels to feed into the economic reconstruction process. This they have achieved so far, initially with an *ad hoc* support programme and subsequently, for the period 1994–99 by being awarded the generously funded 'Objective One' status (structural adjustment for regions whose development is lagging behind). Importantly, decisions on 'Objective One' status are politically sensitive enough to be reserved to the Council of Ministers, effectively making the Structural Fund fortunes of the new Länder dependent on the goodwill and representation of the federal government on the Council. This contrasts strongly with the 'Objective Two' status (economic conversion of industrial areas in decline) enjoyed by parts of some of the western Länder: Objective Two allocations are the preserve of the Commission, and are much more open to independent Länder lobbying outside the control of the federal government (c.f. Conzelmann, 1995, pp. 146–51).

A 'Two-Class Federalism' or a 'Differentiated Policy Regime'?

The width of the spectrum of Länder interests in European policy, in other words, has led to the replication, at least in outline, of the pattern of policy differentiation that is increasingly evident in the domestic politics of German federalism. The inevitable conclusion is that the forms of cooperative federalism that have so clearly distinguished the German federal system in the past will be increasingly difficult to maintain. The structures and practices of inter-Länder cooperation and consensus formation were honed in a much more homogenous Federal Republic. They were not designed to accommodate the clear differences of interest that arise from high levels of divergence in the economic background and performance of the Länder. This was becoming evident in the increasingly heterogenous West German Länder community of the 1980s. It is especially true now, given the starkness of the east–west divide in united Germany.

This does not mean that the Länder will inevitably be thrust into conflict with one another and that the practice of cooperative federalism will be abandoned wholesale (though conflicts over financial equalisation will be difficult to avoid). It will mean, though, a growing differentiation in the character of political interaction in the federal system. On some issues Länder unity *vis-à-vis* the federal government will be maintained, and on others a 'Sinatra doctrine' will prevail, with the Länder separately 'doing it their way', some, particularly in the east, seeking a close association with the federal government, and others, particularly in the west, pursuing autonomous policy priorities. Goetz' (1995b) 'differentiated policy regime' is certainly emerging in an essentially pragmatic adaptation of inter-Länder and federal–Länder interactions to the different needs of east and west. In a sense this implies the realisation of the 'two-class' federalism identified by Abromeit (1992). The western Länder have in part sought and in part been forced into more autonomy and discretion in policy making, less 'entangled' with the federation and with one another than before reunification. The eastern Länder have rather less policy discretion, at least in high-expenditure policy fields, by virtue of their financial dependence on the federal government.

Whether this amounts to an irrevocable transformation of federalism into Abromeit's 'disguised unitary state' is less certain. The federal government has certainly seen some of the constraints hitherto imposed on it by cooperative federalism become less stringent wherever the Länder have proved unable to bridge and reconcile their divergent interests. To that extent the centralising effect of reunification implied by Abromeit's 'disguised unitarism' and which lay at the heart of the prognoses of the early 1990s has happened. But it has not happened without cost. The degree of centralisation is more or less directly dependent on the size of federal government financial assistance to the new Länder. In an era of budgetary restraint – and in particular of feverish pursuit of the budgetary convergence criteria of European economic and monetary union – this is not obviously a welcome development for the federal government. A centralisation process is an expensive commodity. One suspects that it will be reversed as and when the situation in the new Länder makes it politically feasible.

6

The Federal Constitutional Court

KLAUS H. GOETZ

There is a long and well-established tradition of placing the Federal Constitutional Court at the centre of political life in Germany. As the authoritative interpreter of the Basic Law (*Grundgesetz*), that is, the federal constitution – and the final arbiter of constitutional disputes, the Court exercises substantial political power. The scope and volume of constitutional regulation in Germany mean that political, economic and social conditions are strongly affected, and often determined, by constitutional law. As a consequence of this reliance on the directive capacity of the Basic Law, constitutional interpretation and arbitration have assumed vital political importance.

Political scientists and lawyers are therefore agreed that it is impossible to explain the Federal Republic's political system 'without taking proper account of the part played by the Court' (Johnson, 1982, p. 237). By international standards the Court seems unusually influential: a well-known American commentator considers it the 'most active and powerful constitutional court in Europe', arguing that 'the Court has managed to colonize spheres of law and politics that only the most ardent supporter of judicial review would have thought possible' when the Court was established in 1951 (Kommers, 1994, pp. 470–1). Some even speak of an 'extensive constitutional jurisprudence unparalleled throughout the world' (Stern, 1993, p. 22). Undoubtedly the Court is politically influential. In fact it is sometimes held that the Court's position is supreme, as it has the authority to control the executive, the legislature and the ordinary judiciary. Accordingly the Court is seen as a superlegislature, ultimately more powerful than the federal parliament, the Bundesrat, the federal government and the federal president combined. According to this view the Court is not just the guardian

(*Hüter*) of the constitution, but has evolved into its master (*Herr*), against the intention of the framers of the Basic Law and with problematic consequences for the health and vitality of German democracy.

The Potential of Constitutional Review

The strictly limited scope of constitutional review during the Empire and the Weimar Republic provided little positive inspiration for the definition of the extensive powers, responsibilities and prerogatives that the Court has exercised since 1951. The Court therefore represented a genuine institutional innovation. The legal bases for its position are found in the Basic Law itself, notably in Chapter IX (The Administration of Justice), and in the Act on the Federal Constitutional Court of 12 March 1951, which has since been amended on a number of occasions and contains detailed provisions concerning the Court's powers, organisation and procedures. Of the 15 principal types of case listed in Article 13 of the Court Act, the following five have been of particular importance:

- *Disputes between institutions of the federation*: these are constitutional conflicts regarding the rights and duties of the highest federal bodies (federal president, federal government, Bundesrat and Bundestag). This provision also includes other institutions who have been vested with independent rights by the Basic Law or by the rules of procedure of a high federal body. The latter includes, for example, the parliamentary parties represented in the Bundestag, which may bring a case against, say, the federal government if they allege that the federal executive has acted unconstitutionally.
- *Federation–Länder disputes*: these relate to rights and duties in the relations between the federation and the Länder, particularly with regard to the implementation of federal laws by the Länder and their supervision by the Federation (see Blair, 1981, 1991).
- *Judicial referral* (sometimes referred to as concrete norm review): this occurs when an ordinary court, when considering a case that has been brought before it, alleges that the law upon which that case has to be decided contravenes the constitution. In such cases the proceedings are stayed, and a decision must be sought from the Federal Constitutional Court.
- *Abstract norm review*: under this provision the federal government, a Länder government or a group of at least one third of the members

of the Bundestag can challenge the constitutionality of any federal or Länder law. The review is 'abstract' since it does not involve a particular case arising from the implementation of the law in question.

- *Constitutional complaints*: any person who claims that one of their fundamental rights guaranteed by the Basic Law has been violated by a public authority can bring a complaint of unconstitutionality before the Court. Such violations can comprise all forms of public action, including all acts, decisions and decrees by executive authorities, judicial decisions and even parliamentary statutes.

In addition, the Court has repeatedly had to decide on a range of other types of case, notably those concerning the scrutiny of elections to the Bundestag and the prohibition of political parties that 'by reason of their aims or the behaviour of their adherents, seek to impair or abolish the free democratic basic order or to endanger the existence of the Federal Republic of Germany' (Basic Law, Article 21.1. The wide range of formal powers with which the Court is entrusted, combined with the broad access to constitutional review that the Basic Law affords, make it difficult 'to conceive of any constitutional argument that could not be brought before it for an authoritative decision' (Simon, 1994, p. 1647). Moreover the Court's decisions are immediately binding on all public authorities, and in many instances they have the force of law.

Extensive formal powers, responsibilities and prerogatives, easy access and the formal authority of judicial decisions are important preconditions for a politically influential Court, but they cannot in themselves fully account for the Court's formative influence on the political system (Schlaich, 1994). To understand the Court's political impact, at least two further conditions must be mentioned. The first relates to the openness or indeterminacy of legal norms. Many constitutional provisions, in particular those regarding basic rights, are both vague and highly abstract. Consider, for example, Article 2.1 of the Basic Law, which guarantees that 'Everyone has the right to the free development of his personality insofar as he does not violate the rights of others or offend against the constitutional order or against morality'. The material substance of this basic right, and especially its relevance and implications for a particular decision, will rarely be self-evident. In other words, to be effective basic rights need not just to be applied, but also interpreted. It is this prerogative for the authoritative and final interpretation of constitutional norms that allows the Court substantial scope for developing the content of the written constitution.

Constitutional interpretation often implies the creation of legal norms. The Court's innovative definition of many basic rights provides a good example (Böckenförde, 1991, pp. 175–203; Currie, 1994). Classical constitutional theory has tended to view basic rights as essentially defensive, that is, designed to protect the individual against unjustified state interference. According to this understanding, basic rights equal, first and foremost, personal freedoms *vis-à-vis* the state. While fully upholding this conception of basic rights, the Court has also progressively imbued them with a positive character. This means that the Court has imposed 'a variety of affirmative duties on the state to protect one citizen against the other and even on occasion to overcome organizational, technical, or financial obstacles to exercise a fundamental right' (Currie, 1994, p. 13). In line with this 'welfare-state theory' of basic rights, the state becomes responsible for creating 'the necessary social conditions for the realisation of the liberty enshrined in the basic rights' (Böckenförde, 1991, p. 196). At the same time the individual citizen is thought to be entitled to such public services as are necessary for realising the basic right. For example freedom of education may require the state to subsidise private schools; freedom of religion may necessitate public support for religious communities; and the special protection the Basic Law guarantees to 'marriage and family' may oblige the state to provide tax privileges to these forms of social organisation.

The second fundamental prerequisite for the Court's prominent role in the political system lies in the quality of the law it is asked to interpret. Contrary to what its designation as a 'Basic Law' may seem to suggest, the federal constitution is much more than a skeleton framework content with stipulating the principles governing the relations between state and society and the organisation of state power. Rather the Basic Law is seen as constituting a fundamental societal order, expressing the ultimate aspirations of the body politic and at the same time guiding and shaping political, social and economic reality. It embodies and seeks to secure the realisation of a distinct value order that unites state and society and centres on the principles of the 'democratic and social federal state', committed to the rule of law and the protection and furtherance of basic political, economic, social and even cultural rights. This value order is comprehensive in that it encompasses the entirety of social relations, including those between private individuals; and it is authoritative in that constitutional law is directly applicable and takes precedence over all other legal norms. Therefore, political and social disputes are necessarily also arguments about constitutional values. Consequently the realm of constitutional review extends well beyond the confines of conflict resolution between state institutions and the protection of the individual against undue state interference.

The Court as a Judicial and Political Institution

The most visible expression of the favourable conditions for constitutional review in Germany is the extraordinary case load the Court has faced (see Table 6.1). By the end of 1994, 101 268 cases had been brought before the Court, of which approximately 80 per cent were resolved through a Court decision. The bulk of cases resulted from constitutional complaints and judicial referrals. In 1994 alone a total of 5324 cases were added. To deal with this huge stream of cases, efficient organisation of the Court's work is imperative. Above all, this will require an effective division of labour. The Court consists of two senates, each with eight judges. Each senate deals autonomously with the cases brought before it, that is, it decides for the Court as a whole. The distribution of cases between the two senates is regulated in the Court Act, but the Court as a collegiate body may decide to deviate from these provisions if the resulting case load is unbalanced. In the past it has repeatedly made use of this possibility in an attempt to balance the weight of incoming cases. Thus the customary designation of the first senate as the *Grundrechtssenat* (basic rights senate) and the second senate as *Staatsrechtssenat* (public law senate dealing with interinstitutional conflicts) suggests a relatively clear-cut division of substantive responsibilities, but which in reality has become progressively blurred by considerations of expediency.

A second major organisational–procedural device to rationalise the Court's work are the so-called chambers. Both senates have established several chambers, each of which consists of three judges. Their main function is to act as a filter or screen for constitutional complaints and judicial referrals, limiting the number of cases that the senate as a whole needs to decide. The first such bodies designed to screen cases before they reach either senate were established in 1956, and their powers have since been progressively extended (Faller, 1995). In respect of constitutional complaints, the chambers are entitled to reject a complaint without explanation if either of two conditions are not met: the complaint must raise a matter of fundamental constitutional importance (*grundsätzliche verfassungsrechtliche Bedeutung*) or the alleged violations of the complainant's rights must have particular weight. The chambers can also uphold a complaint without a senate

TABLE 6.1 *Proceedings before the Federal Constitutional Court, 1951–94*[1]

Type of case	*Legal basis*	*Cases brought*		*Decided through Court*	
Forfeiture of basic rights	Art. 18	4	(–)	2	(–)
Unconstitutionality of political parties	Art. 21 (2)	5	(–)	2	(–)
Election cases	Art. 41 (2)	89	(–)	73	(–)
Presidential impeachment	Art. 61	–	(–)	–	(–)
Federal Interinstitutional cases	Art. 93 (1 No. 1)	107	(8)	51	(3)
Abstrct norm review	Art. 93 (1 No. 2)	124	(2)	68	(–)
Federation–Länder cases	Art. 93 (1 No. 3); 84 (4)	26	(–)	14	(1)
Other public law cases	Art. 93 (1, No. 4)	69	(1)	31	(3)
Impeachment of judges	Art. 98 (2, 5)	–	(–)	–	(–)
Constitutional disputes within a Land	Art. 99	14	(1)	10	(–)
Judicial referral	Art. 100 (1)	2901	(55)	959	(28)
International law cases	Art. 100 (2)	12	(–)	6	(–)
Referrals from Land Constitutional Courts	Art. 100 (3)	7	(–)	4	(–)
Cases regarding the continued validity of federal laws	Art. 126	151	(–)	19	(–)
Provisional orders and other matters	Art. 93 (2); Court Act Art. 32	751	(63)	509	(46)
Constitutional complaints	Art. 93 (1 Nos. 4a, 4b)	97007	(5194)	80 767[2]	(4790)[3]
Plenary matters	Court Act Art. 16 (1)	1	(–)	1	(–)
Total		101268	(5324)	82 516	(4871)

1. Figures in brackets refer to 1994 only.
2. Of these cases, 3750 were decided by the senates, the remainder by the chambers or their precursors.
3. Of these cases, 22 were decided by the senates, the remainder by the chambers.

Source: Secretariat of the Federal Constitutional Court.

decision, if it is obviously justified and the relevant subject matter has previously been decided by the Court. Since 1993 the chambers have also been able to dismiss most judicial referrals. The practical importance of this screening procedure is borne out by the fact that in 1994 only 22 constitutional complaint cases were decided by the two senates, whereas a total of 4768 were settled by the chambers.

The ever-increasing number of cases reaching the Court is a first, and not very reliable, indicator of the importance of constitutional review. What matters much more are the substance of decisions, their impact on political decision makers, notably government and parliament, and their consequences for the development of the polity. A review of more than four decades of judicature by the Court provides ample evidence of its centrality in the political system. In fact much of the political history of the Federal Republic, both in domestic and international affairs, and many important chapters of its social and economic history can be written through the Court judgements. The Court began to make its mark soon after its foundation. In terms of domestic politics, early judgements regarding the principle of federalism, the separation of powers, the principle of representation and democracy, and the role of political parties were of decisive importance in fleshing out the provisions contained in the Basic Law (most of these landmark cases are reproduced in English in excerpts and with very useful comments in Kommers, 1989). As regards international affairs, for much of its existence the Court has tended to grant the federal executive and parliament very substantial discretion, an approach established early on in the Court's existence (for an collection of case excerpts see Federal Constitutional Court, 1992).

A look at some of the key decisions taken by the Court since reunification may help to illustrate its central contribution (Cullen, 1996; Johnson, 1994). In substantive terms, these cases have concerned reunification-related matters; foreign policy and international relations; and domestic political controversies.

Reunification-related Matters

Several judgements by the Court have been of critical importance in providing constitutional backing for the federal government's reunification policy, as laid down in the Unification Treaty. They have included:

- The decision of 18 September 1990, which declared that the changes to the Basic Law contained in the Unification Treaty could be adopted as part of the treaty ratification process and did not need to pass through a separate legislative procedure.

- The decision of 29 September 1990, which confirmed the special regulations governing the first post-reunification general elections. These provisions enhanced the chance of new East German parties to enter the Bundestag as they allowed the creation of joint party lists (*Listenvereinigung*) and applied the 5 per cent threshold for parliamentary representation separately to western Germany and the territory of the former GDR.
- The decision of 23 April 1991 in which the Court upheld Article 41 of the Unification Treaty, which declares irreversible the expropriation without compensation of property under Soviet authority between 1945 and 1949.
- The decision of 24 April 1991, which in principle approved the provisions of the Unification Treaty regarding the suspension and termination of the employment of persons formerly working in the GDR administration, but nullified them insofar as they conflicted with the rights of pregnant women and young mothers. Moreover the Court stressed that the special circumstances of handicapped and older employees, single parents and similar groups needed to be taken into account. These principles were also stressed in a decision of 10 March 1992 on the employment of former members of the Academy of Sciences.

Foreign Policy and International Relations

Since reunification the Court has made two landmark judgements clarifying central aspects of German foreign policy:

- The decision of 12 October 1993 on the constitutionality of the Maastricht Treaty. The Court dismissed the constitutional complaints against the Treaty on European Union, but at the same time reemphasized that European integration must not undermine the central principles of the Basic Law, notably the democratic principle (Foster, 1994; Herdegen, 1994).
- The decision of 12 July 1994 on the external use of German armed forces. Here the Court argued that there was nothing in the Basic Law to prohibit the use of German forces outside the NATO area as part of a collective security system, including all types of armed UN operations. With this judgement the Court laid to rest the political consensus view that been prevalent up to the late 1980s, according to which 'The Constitution should be so construed as to rule out any

external use of German armed forces except in cases of individual self-defence or collective self-defence' (Kress, 1995).

Domestic Political Controversies

The majority of cases dealt with by the Court have concerned domestic political and social disputes. Those with broader political implications have included the following rulings:

- The decision of 16 July 1991 on a case brought by the PDS, which specified the rights of groups of Bundestag members other than parliamentary parties, notably with reference to their rights to be represented on Bundestag committees.
- The decision of 9 April 1992 on party political finance, which partly revised the Court's previous judicature in this area by recognising that public funds could be made available to political parties for part of their general expenses rather than election expenses only.
- The decision of 27 May 1992 regarding intergovernmental fiscal relations, which clarified the responsibility of all members of the federation to come to the financial aid of individual Länder experiencing an 'extreme budgetary emergency'.
- The decision of 28 May 1993 on the Abortion Reform Act (see below).
- The decision of 16 May 1995, which declared unconstitutional the mandatory placing of crucifixes in non-denominational state schools.

There is no doubting the political implications of these judgements, and they testify to the Court's decisive contribution to the post-reunification political agenda. The judgements also underline the fact that the Court is more than a judicial institution and must be considered amongst the key political decision makers. This is not just because its judgements have political consequences. Constitutional law itself is political law, and therefore its interpretation necessarily has a political element to it. Moreover many of the cases referred to the Court, notably interinstitutional and federal–Länder disputes, but also many constitutional complaints, are essentially about political conflicts that constitutional review is expected to settle in an authoritative fashion. Thus 'a major political role is imposed on the Court simply by virtue of some of the procedures under which issues can be referred to it' (Johnson, 1982, p. 240).

The pacifying effect of many decisions in politically controversial matters confirms the Court's important role in political compromise making, arbitration and the maintenance of societal peace. The ability to perform this important function reflects the judges' sensitivity to the political and societal context in which they operate and the very detailed consideration of the arguments put forward by all parties to a case. As a result there are often no straightforward winners and losers in cases before the Court. Frequently, allegations of unconstitutionality are only partly upheld or rejected, so that both sides can draw comfort from the judgement. Even when a claim of unconstitutionality is rejected *in toto*, the Court's reasoning will clarify the grounds upon which the decision has been reached and acknowledge the concerns of the complainant. Moreover, since 1971 the Court has published signed dissenting opinions, which, though by no means the rule, also help to underline the fact that constitutional interpretation is not a straightforward business with foregone conclusions.

The Court, then, finds itself in a very delicate position. It cannot avoid becoming involved in political conflicts, but it must scrupulously avoid any impression of partiality. It needs to take account of political and societal realities and sensitivities, and yet must not be seen simply to do what a majority of politicians and citizens, however large and vocal, may expect. It has to ensure the acceptability and ultimately the legitimacy of its role, yet as a judicial body it cannot draw on the democratic legitimation enjoyed by parliament and the government. It is reactive rather than proactive in that it can only decide on issues brought before it; at the same time, in its interpretative function, it is responsible for developing constitutional law in such a way as to maintain its vitality and relevance to the body politic.

The Court under Scrutiny

Considering the difficult tasks the Court is called upon to perform and the inevitable tensions arising from its dual nature as a judicial and political body, it can occasion no surprise that from its beginnings the Court has been the object of critical attention, and at times harsh condemnation. Already in 1952, the then federal minister of justice, Dehler, in connection with a case regarding the European Defence Community, accused the judges of 'having departed from the paths of the law in a shocking manner', and throughout the Adenauer era, relations between the Court and the government were often tense (Häußler, 1994). Equally, during the Social Democrat–Liberal coalition of 1969 to 1982 the Court was repeatedly charged by political supporters of the government, but also some academic commentators, with undermining the central planks of the government's reform programme, thereby doing the opposition's bidding (Däubler and Küsel, 1979; Lamprecht and Malanowski, 1979). Even with the passage of time, critics of the Court blamed it for a 'blockage of societal development', obstruction of policy innovation, and 'disintegrative' decisions during the Brandt and Schmidt chancellorships (Biehler, 1990, p. 197f.)

More recently the Court's decisions on abortion, the permissibility of the statement 'soldiers are murderers', and the legality of so-called sitting blockades, by which demonstrators seek to impede the free movement of others, have led to harsh *Urteilsschelte* (criticism of judgements) from some quarters. The most scathing and perhaps most damaging comment in recent years has been reserved for the Court's decision of May 1995, which forbids the state from placing crucifixes in classrooms of non-denominational schools. It ignited what, according to *Die Zeit* (22 December 1995), was the most passionate public debate in 1995. Chancellor Kohl called the judgement 'incomprehensible', the Catholic Church branded it as a 'kowtow to the *Zeitgeist*', and leading CSU politicians suggested that the decision ought to be circumvented and the powers of the Court curtailed.

Judicial Review and the Democratic Principle

If one tries to systematise the criticism aimed at the Court over the years, two themes emerge. First, the Court shows too little restraint in exercising its powers and responsibilities, and thus encroaches on the rights of parliament and government. Second, politicisation and, in particular, party-politicisation cast doubt on the Court's status an as an independent and neutral judicial institution. While legislative action to restrict the Court's formal powers has sometimes been proposed, most criticism is directed not at the range of the Court's powers, but at the manner in which it chooses to exercise them. This applies, first, to the Court's tendency to go beyond the concrete case to be decided by putting forward general policy principles that, because they are part of the judgement, constrain future parliamentary and governmental decision making. A recent example is the decision on the Maastricht Treaty, which discussed in detail possible future scenarios for the development of the European Union and sought to define the constitutional parameters within which future integration policy has to proceed if it is not to conflict with the Basic Law. There is indeed a danger that individual cases may merely serve as a welcome opportunity for laying down general policy precepts. This temptation is especially pronounced in the case of constitutional complaints. Almost every conceivable issue of public policy is at some stage the subject of a constitutional complaint and as noted above the Court enjoys wide discretion in accepting or rejecting cases for detailed consideration. It is therefore only a slight exaggeration to argue that a suitable case can be found if the Court wishes to pronounce on a particular matter.

The temptation to cross the dividing line between judicial control and judicial policy making is partly inherent in the Court's powers. It is able not only to declare any public act totally or partially unconstitutional and void, it can also stipulate the conditions under which, and the limits within which, such an act can still be considered compatible with the Basic Law. Even more importantly, if the judges nullify a legal provision or, more typically, parts of it, they may stipulate interim regulations that are immediately and directly applicable until parliament passes a revised act. In this instance, norm-making replaces judicial interpretation. If a legal provision is declared unconstitutional it does not immediately cease to be law, but the Court can set parliament a deadline by which new legislation has to be enacted.

Evidently these competences need to be exercised with caution if the proper separation of powers between parliament and government on the one hand, and the judiciary on the other, is not to be jeopardised. In other words the democratic principle must not be undermined by the cumulative effect of the Court's monopoly of authoritative constitutional interpretation and norm making. One oft-cited example of a highly sensitive public policy question where the Court is held to have repeatedly failed to show the required degree of self-restraint is the abortion issue (Landfried, 1992, pp. 54–4; Prützel-Thomas, 1993). In its 1975 judgement on the Abortion Reform Act adopted by the Social Democrat–Liberal coalition in the previous year, the Court argued that it was not within the power of parliament to dispense with punishment for abortions, even if they were performed within the first three months of pregnancy (English excerpts in Kommers, 1989, pp. 348–62). Although there were conditions under which an abortion could be deemed legal, for example if the pregnancy endangered the mother's life or was the consequence of rape, an abortion would in principle remain illegal and punishable.

This judgement was heavily criticised not just for the inclusion of a binding list of conditions (*Indikationen*) under which the Court would be prepared consider abortion legal, but also, and in particular, for postulating a duty of the legislature to enact legislation for punishment for abortion. In a dissenting minority opinion, two judges of the Court stressed that by imposing such a duty on parliament the Court had misinterpreted the constitution and was clearly infringing the rights of the legislature. Thus judges Rupp-von Brünneck and Simon pointed out that

> Under no circumstances can [one] deduce from the Constitution a state obligation to subject the termination of pregnancy to punishment at every stage . . . . Any contrary interpretation is incompatible with the freedom-oriented character of the constitutional norms and, in a measure fraught with consequences, transfers decisional authority to the Federal Constitutional Court . . . . The authority of the Federal Constitutional Court to annul decisions of the parliamentary legislator demands restraint in its use in order to avoid a dislocation of power among the constitutional organs. The command of judicial self-restraint, which has been termed the 'life-giving elixir' of the judicial function of the Federal Constitutional Court, applies when a case does not involve warding off encroachment by governmental authority but rather involves the court issuing directives for the positive development of the social order to the popularly elected legislature by way of constitutional review. In this instance the Federal Constitutional Court may not succumb to the temptation to assume the functions of the organ to be controlled if, in the long run, the status of constitutional jurisdiction is not to be endangered (quoted from Kommers, 1989, pp. 356–7).

The Court as a whole showed little inclination to heed this advice, as is borne out by its second abortion judgement of May 1993 on the 1992 Abortion Reform Act. This Act, which replaced the Act of 1976 that had been modelled on the Court's judgement of the previous year, was made necessary by reunification. In the GDR abortion on demand was legal, and during discussions on the Unification Treaty, GDR negotiators, supported by the western Social Democrats, held out against the simple extension of West German law to the East. As a result the Unification Treaty envisaged that the GDR law should remain in place until a common law for the whole of Germany could be enacted. The legislation finally adopted by the Bundestag declared that abortion during the first three months of pregnancy was 'not illegal' in principle, and stipulated a counselling procedure all women would have to undergo before a termination could be performed.

In a classic instance of an attempt to use the Court to overturn a considered decision by a parliamentary majority in both the Bundestag and the Bundesrat, 248 CDU–CSU Bundestag members and the Bavarian government challenged the 1992 Abortion Reform Act by means of abstract norm review. In its decision the Court declared key parts of the new law unconstitutional and void; reemphasised that abortion must in principle continue to be regarded as wrong, and therefore illegal, though it was permissible that during the first 12 weeks such an illegal act would not be punished; and laid down immediately applicable and very detailed guidelines for the counselling women had to obtain, under specific conditions, before they could be granted a legal abortion.

The politically highly charged abortion issue demonstrates the way in which interested parties can use the Court to obtain policy outcomes they have been denied by the parliamentary process. In both 1975 and 1993 parliamentary minorities challenged acts that majorities in both houses, after lengthy and careful deliberation, had approved. In this way the Court is drawn into a political controversy that it cannot avoid, since it must not refuse to hear abstract review cases. At the same time the abortion judgement shows that the Court cannot always resist the opportunities for activist public policy making and the usurpation of the prerogatives of other political institutions that the judicialisation of the German political process affords.

The Politicisation of the Court

For many critics the politicisation of the Court is the inevitable, if undesirable, obverse of the judicialisation of politics. In discussing the politicisation of the constitutional judiciary, three related but analytically distinct issues must be addressed: the Court's role as a political institution; party-political influence on the appointment of judges; and the partisan orientation of the Court itself. As argued above, the Court's task of interpreting political law inevitably invests it with a dual institutional character, partly judicial, partly political. In this sense politicisation is indeed a necessary and desirable corollary of constitutional review.

It is much more contentious, however, whether the political functions of the Court also imply that the appointment of judges should be as heavily dominated by political parties as it is at present. Members of the Court are elected for a non-renewable period of twelve years, and must have an advanced legal qualification. Half of the members are elected by the Bundesrat, the other half by the Bundestag, which has delegated this task to a small selection committee. In both houses a two-thirds majority is needed for a candidate to be approved. This rule means, firstly, that the selection and appointment procedure is entirely in the hands of political parties, and secondly that cross-party consensus is needed for any appointment to be made. In response a practice has evolved whereby the CDU–CSU and the SPD each claim the right to propose four judges per senate; the Liberals nominate one candidate from the contingent of their coalition partner at the federal level. It is also common practice for candidates on a party ticket to be a member of that party, although by convention one candidate per ticket is exempt from this rule.

As regards their background, judges are drawn almost exclusively from other federal courts (at least three per senate), academe and politics. The recruitment of formerly active politicians, in particular, is often viewed as problematic. The current president of the Court, Jutta Limbach, for example, was formerly the SPD minister of justice in the Berlin Land government, and her predecessor, Roman Herzog, had been minister of the interior in Baden-Württemberg. It needs to be kept in mind, however, that both were former professors of law, and that, as Landfried has pointed out, the number of politicians in the Court has tended to decrease over the years (Landfried, 1988, p. 149).

Perhaps surprisingly, both the attention paid to the party affiliation of prospective judges and the parties' monopoly in the choice of appointees have, for much of the Court's history, done little to undermine its authority and public standing. This is partly because the bargaining surrounding judicial appointments takes place behind firmly closed doors, and partly because most judges have in the past carefully sought to avoid the impression that their own political preferences might determine their decisions. In recent years, however, these conditions appear to have been to some extent eroded. Thus in 1993 the appointment of a successor to the Court's vice-president, Mahrenholz, who had reached the end of his tenure, was delayed for nine months, as the CDU–CSU and the SPD quarrelled in public about who was to succeed him. The CDU acknowledged that it was the SPD's turn to put forward a candidate, but took exception to their eventual choice of nominee, Herta Däubler-Gmelin, the deputy chairwoman of the SPD. The CDU, led by the leader of the parliamentary party, Wolfgang Schäuble, vetoed the SPD's choice, arguing that Däubler-Gmelin was too much of an ingrained party politician to make a neutral judge, while the SPD asserted its 'customary right' to have its nominee elected. After months of mutual recrimination Däubler-Gmelin finally withdrew as candidate, but not before a public debate had set in on the horse trading that characterises judicial appointments.

This controversy and the furore caused by some recent judgements have also led to a public climate in which the Court's impartiality, and thus its most important quality as an accepted arbiter of constitutional disputes, is increasingly called into question. Knowledge about judges' party-political leanings, it is alleged, allows fairly accurate predictions about the outcome of pending cases; in other words judicial decision making is party-politically biased. Thus one prominent commentator on the constitution has argued that in most cases that have a political effect it is possible to predict more or less accurately 'how the individual judges decide: liberal, conservative, liberal-conservative, liberal-progressive, left or right' (Karl Doehring in the *Frankfurter Allgemeine Zeitung*, 25 August 1995). Another well-known academic lawyer has suggested that in important cases there is increasingly a 'collective confrontation between the four SPD-nominated judges and the opposite side proposed by the CDU–CSU' (Thomas Oppermann in *Frankfurter Allgemeine Zeitung*, 6 September 1995).

Such charges are, in principle, nothing new, although of late they have assumed greater prominence than during the 1980s. Nor are they undisputed: members of the Court are themselves at pains to stress their neutrality and impartiality, and the majority of observers would probably still agree that 'party membership and social background do not influence the judicial decision-making process to any great extent' (Landfried, 1988, p. 149). It should also be kept in mind that times of intensive scrutiny and criticism of the Court, amongst which the mid 1990s undoubtedly count, have in the past been regularly followed by periods of calm and near-universal approval. The growing unease in recent years with the Court's performance may, however, be indicative of something more than periodic unhappiness provoked by specific judgements. Beyond the recurrent questioning of the Court's powers, their proper use and politicisation, there are indications that its traditional functions might be subject to more fundamental challenges that call for a partial reassessment of its role in the German political system.

Decline of the Basic Law?

The forces most likely to reshape, and perhaps reduce the Court's position in the coming years are not, in the first instance, directed at the institution of constitutional review itself. Rather they affect the status of national constitutional law as the ultimate reference point for the regulation of political, economic and social life. To the extent that the

Basic Law ceases to be capable of such authoritative steering and control, the Court's own position as supreme and final arbiter is called into question. Externally, the rise of international legal frameworks, notably European Union law, is gradually undermining the primacy of national constitutional law. At the same time, internal changes affecting state, society and their interrelationship are confronting constitutional law with regulatory challenges that it is not necessarily well-suited to meet (Goetz and Cullen, 1994). The eventual result may be, in the words of one of the Court's judges, an external and internal weakening of the Constitution (Grimm, 1995, p. 144), which threatens gradually to reduce its centrality to the political process. According to another former judge and prominent commentator on the Basic Law, the Court faces a reduction 'in its tasks, its position within the system of public powers and its opportunities for influence' (Hesse, 1995, p. 169).

The Effect of European Integration

Partly by design, partly by implication, the process of European integration, first and foremost within the framework of the European Union, is restricting the sovereignty of national public institutions, which are ceasing to be the supreme authorities for political decision making. The member states' constitutional law is not exempt from this process. In fact it is amongst the national institutions that are most immediately affected by the integration process, since the latter relies heavily on the use of law to achieve 'an ever closer union'. It is widely held that the EU laws automatically take precedence over national laws, including the constitution, although the Federal Constitutional Court does not fully subscribe to this view. While the Court has repeatedly acknowledged the supremacy of EU law in principle, its 1993 Maastricht judgment emphasises that EU acts, including legislation, only apply to the Federal Republic if they do not exceed the limitations established by the Treaty. Undoubtedly, however, the regulatory objectives and capacities of national constitutional law and its interpretation are, by now, inextricably intertwined with the European legal framework. To date their interrelation could probably be more accurately described in terms of coregulation, rather than European legal supremacy and national subordination. However, as Grimm has pointed out, the more the EU moves towards becoming a federal entity, the more 'national constitutions will become of peripheral importance' (Grimm, 1995, p. 141).

Integration implies a reduction in the scope of matters regulated independently by national political institutions, whereas the policy-making capacities of European institutions increase. Accordingly the range of public acts to be controlled by the German Court is gradually narrowing, while the European Court of Justice (ECJ), which controls the application of European law, is assuming greater importance. This Europeanisation effect is further accentuated by Germany's status as a signatory of the European Convention for the Protection of Human Rights and Fundamental Freedoms, which is placed outside the EU framework and enforced by the Strasbourg-based European Court of Human Rights. Although the Federal Constitutional Court does not consider the convention to be of the same rank as the German constitution, the convention is an important guideline for national constitutional review. Where, as in a recent case concerning the equality of men and women (Bleckmann, 1995), the Strasbourg Court's views conflict with earlier judgements of the German Court, the latter appears willing to reconsider and revise its former position.

Change in State and Society

The second, perhaps less visible but in the longer term no less significant challenge to constitutional law arises from its threatened capacity to establish, distribute and control state power and provide a binding framework for state–society relations. This problem can only be hinted at in the present context (for details see Grimm, 1990; Goetz and Cullen, 1994, pp. 26–30). Briefly, constitutional law has traditionally been chiefly directed at the state with a view to ensuring the citizens' fundamental human and political rights. The core of constitutional regulations - the definition of the powers of the major state institutions and the stipulation of basic rights protecting individuals and society against state interference - serves this purpose. Accordingly, effective constitutions assume a reasonably clear distinction between a sphere of state institutions on the one hand, and a private and societal sphere on the other. Changes in state and society, however, make this assumption questionable. Privatisation and the growing reliance on paragovernmental institutions, 'hybrid organisations' and indirect administrations mean that public powers are increasingly exercised through non-public institutions, which operate at least partly outside the traditional realm of constitutional–public law. Moreover state regulation has by now permeated all spheres of societal and private life, including intimate family and sexual relations. At the same time society is reaching deep into the state, notably through the channels of political parties and interest groups, which in practice partly assume public powers. In short, the etatisation of society is accompanied by the socialisation of the state.

Constitutional law is not well-suited to be an authoritative means of guiding and controlling the resultant complexity. It is preoccupied with establishing clear institutional boundaries, regulating interinstitutional relations and the protection of individual and society spheres from state interference. As a consequence the gap between the normative substance of the written constitution and the actual political, social and economic constitution is likely to widen. This is not to argue that constitutional law and constitutional practice increasingly conflict; rather the normativeness of constitutional law is restricted to only part of constitutional reality.

Acquiescence, Reassertion or Cooperation? The Future of the Court

The contextualisation of the Basic Law within a wider European and international legal setting and the changes in state and society call for adaptation on the part of the Federal Constitutional Court. There are two closely linked issues at stake. First, how should constitutional interpretation best respond to the changing status of national constitutional law? Second, how should the Court define its relations to other judicial bodies, notably the ECJ, national state institutions and the public? At least three strategies are conceivable: acquiescence, reassertion, and cooperation. Acquiescence accepts that national constitutional law is gradually becoming more marginal to the body politic and implies an increasingly limited role for the Federal Constitutional Court. In contrast, reassertion rejects the assumption of a slow decline and, by making extensive use of the powers and interpretative discretion of the Court, seeks to preserve its centrality.

While the Court is plainly unwilling to accede to managed decline, evidence of reassertion is not difficult to find. This is particularly the case in relation to European integration. Here the Court's Maastricht judgement of 1992, mentioned above, not only spelled out the substantive procedural conditions the European integration process has to meet in order to be compatible with German constitutional law, thus seeking to establish binding parameters for future integration policy. The Court also directly challenged the prerogative of the ECJ to decide on the legality of EU actions (Ress, 1994). The Court declared that:

> if European institutions or organs were to utilize or develop the Treaty of European Union in a manner not covered by this Treaty and the German implementing legislation based upon it, the resulting obligations could not be binding within Germany's sovereign sphere. Accordingly, the German Federal Constitutional Court will examine whether legal acts of the European institutions and organs are within the limits of the competences granted to them or whether they exceed those limits.

It is, then, not surprising that the Court's judgement is seen by many to have resulted in 'rather dramatic restraints upon the future development of the European Union by its members, its political organs and the European Court of Justice' (Herdegen, 1994, p. 231). So far the Court has not made use of the self-assigned power to control EU acts, and in the discussions on the revision of the Maastricht Treaty the Court's decision does not feature prominently (Goetz, 1996). The Court's strictures should therefore not be overdramatised (Cullen, 1995). Nonetheless the intention of assertion is unmistakable, as is the potential of serious conflict with EU institutions, Germany's European partners and German decision makers who favour the creation of a European federal state.

Whether such a strategy can, in the long run, be successful without overstretching the inherent limits of constitutional regulation and interpretation is debatable. The Court enjoys very wide discretion in the use of its powers, and if it so chooses it can impose severe restrictions on the choice of policy options by government and parliament. It is, however, itself subject to constraints that it cannot ignore without jeopardising the bases upon which its past contributions to the development of the German polity have depended. It is called upon to control public activity rather than initiate public policy; it has to interpret the Basic Law rather than act as a constitutional legislator; and it needs to respect the limitations arising from its status as a non-elected institution in the democratic division of powers. If it fails to accept the restrictions this implies, the acceptability and the effectiveness of its judicature are in danger.

In order to continue to contribute positively to the stability and vitality of the German political system, the Court will therefore have to take full account of the need for cooperation. This does not equal conflict avoidance; rather it requires an appreciation of the functional limitations of constitutional legislation and review in a Europeanised democratic nation state and of the political and societal underpinnings of constitutional interpretation. First, in relation to the European integration process and the ECJ, cooperation necessitates a clear and unequivocal recognition of the competences of the European Court; attempts by national courts to call the ECJ's prerogatives into question must inevitably lead to legal and political uncertainty. Equally importantly, while it is reasonable to demand that European integration must not undermine Germany's character as a 'democratic and social federal state', the Basic Law, as the constitution of a nation state, may act as an inspiration, but must not be construed as an imperative precept for the constitutional evolution of the European Union as a unique political entity.

Second, cooperation involves careful observation of the prerogatives of national governmental and parliamentary institutions. The Court is charged with controlling their actions and not to act in their stead, however unsatisfactory their performance may appear. The decision on the Abortion Reform Act may be cited as an example of the Court encroaching on these prerogatives and calling into doubt its respect for the constitutional separation of powers.

Finally, and most importantly, the Court is ultimately reliant on the public acceptability of its judgments, its awareness of and sensitivity to public opinion. Since it possesses no electoral legitimation and its procedures are generally unfamiliar to the public at large, the Court's positive evaluation depends critically on its ability to reconcile the demands of constitutional law with public perceptions of right and wrong. This does not imply trade-offs between constitutionality and public opinion; also, not every decision will please, or even be acceptable to, the majority of citizens. On the other hand, effective arbitration and pacification require the Court to use judiciously the wide interpretative discretion which it enjoys. If the Court is to remain a focus for the resolution rather than the generation of conflict in the German political system, and if it is to retain broad public trust, the careful nurturing of its somewhat strained relations with European and domestic institutions and the German public will be its foremost task in the coming years.

7

Continuity and Change in the Policy-Making Process

ROLAND STURM

The German policy-making process exhibits a surprising degree of institutional continuity and a 'dominant' policy style of consensus (Richardson *et al.*, 1982). It allows pressure groups to play an important role in decision making, especially with regard to the legislative detail of policy. In order to explain policy making it is necessary to ask the following questions. Who are the decision makers? What is the role of consensus and compromise in policy making? And what is the usual pattern of the so-called policy cycle? Procedural stability, however, is only one side of the coin. In the history of the Federal Republic policy making has had to respond to a number of challenges provoking changes both of policy priorities and policy instruments.

Reunification has created a new and special situation for policy making. The first reaction of German policy makers was simply to treat eastern Germany in the way economically backward regions have traditionally been treated in the west. It soon became apparent, however, that policies aiming at equalising living conditions with those in the west (*Angleichung der Lebensverhältnisse*) had to operate differently. Success depended upon two factors: the transformation of the east Germany economy from state socialism to a market economy, and the adaptation of political and administrative structures to the western model. Moreover an important but often neglected factor was that the impact of financial transfers from the west was not always exclusively linked to their size, but also to their timing. If the latter was inadequate large sums of money were wasted or misdirected away from essential investment. For example local government in particular is confronted with the problem and costs of oversized investments in industrial sites. Reunification not only created the need for policies tailored to the special situation in the east, it also produced a hitherto unsolved strategic problem for policy makers. There is a legal principle that policy should be non-discriminatory. This principle is easy to defend in homogenous societies such as the 'old' Federal Republic. Acute inequalities between the two parts of Germany after reunification, however, meant that from an east German perspective at least, formal equality merely reinforced the disparity between east and west.

The Decision Makers

Policy making in Germany has always been a very complex process and German citizens are confronted with a confusing variety of policy actors. Among the more independent rule makers are the political parties. They do not usually govern alone, but in coalitions based on agreements that summarise the political priorities of the government and often contain quite a lot of policy details. Coalition treaties tend to be unstable political compromises. Shifts in the relative power of the coalition partners can lead to quite significant changes in the policy agenda. Moreover multiparty government is compounded by multilevel government. European, national, Land and local government do not act independently of each other, but are interconnected. Like coalition politics, multilevel government involves compromise to bring about decisions, and it also lacks transparency.

There are two principles for the cooperation of different levels of government. One is a clear separation of powers, as is the case in cultural policies for example. Culture, the media, education, the police and public administration are the policy arenas in which the Länder are the major policy makers. In these matters they are not only independent from the federal government, in 1992 they even secured for themselves a voice at the European level. Article 23.6 of the Basic Law stipulates that in these matters a representative of the Länder – selected and instructed by the second chamber of parliament, the Bundesrat – will speak for the Federal Republic in Brussels.

A second principle is the institutionalisation of joint responsibilities between different levels of government. Policy making in Germany is highly interconnected. In addition to the coordination of decision making between the Länder, a wide range of tasks are jointly financed by the Länder and the federal government, sometimes with the involvement of European and local actors. The joint tasks (*Gemein-*

schaftsaufgaben) of the federal government and the Länder are listed in Article 91 of the Basic Law. Whereas Article 91 focuses on infrastructure policies, Article 104a gives the federal government a free hand to offer both the Länder and local government financial support for investment policies it would like to see.

Multilevel government is intensified by the legislative role of the Bundesrat, in which the Länder are represented, and which is able to exercise an absolute veto over 50–60 per cent of legislation (Schindler, 1994, p. 848). A very efficient tool to win over the Länder or local government for joint policies is the principle of additionality. The Land government may offer a municipality money for investment, for example, but only if a certain amount comes from the local government's own budget.

The multiplicity of actors in the policy process is intensified by public institutions such as the Bundesbank or the Federal Cartel Office (*Bundeskartellamt*), whose independent role is entrenched in law. Though parliament cannot control these institutions, politics nevertheless plays a role. Key appointments are political, and the institutions can be susceptible to the political climate. The Bundesbank exercises exclusive control over monetary policies. The Cartel Office is the major national actor in competition policies, although it is important to note that whereas the decisions of the the Bundesbank are final, Cartel Office decisions can be challenged by the Courts. In 1992 Article 88 of the German constitution was changed. It now includes a clause that allows parliament to transfer the responsibilities of the Bundesbank to the planned European Central Bank of the European Union.

Also participating in the policy process are the so-called parapublic institutions, such as the Chambers of Commerce (*Industrie- und Handelskammern*), the associations of artisans (*Handwerkskammern*), or the professional organisations of physicians (*Ärztekammern*). These institutions not only lobby for the interests of their members and provide expert advice to law makers, they are also self-regulatory in character. They set the norms and standards of their professions. Chambers of commerce and artisans' associations are responsible for most vocational training in Germany, including the quality and procedure of exams.

The Federal Constitutional Court is a key policy actor. Although it can only act if cases are referred to it, its decisions weigh heavily because they represent definitive judgements on the constitutionality of a policy, or the dividing line between the competences of competing institutions. Very often the Court also lays down the guidelines for future decisions of policy makers. The Constitutional Court was never meant to be a policy maker, but its role in policy making has grown, because politicians often shy away from the political costs of decision making and ask the Court for guidance. It is impossible to predict the political inclination of the Court. Whereas in the case of abortion rules (see Chapter 6) the Court has come under attack by pro-choice activists and liberal and left-leaning parties, it has recently been sharply criticised by Conservatives for defending the antimilitary slogan 'soldiers are murderers' as an expression of the right to free speech, and for ruling against the compulsory presence of crucifixes in Bavarian classrooms.

Consensus and Compromise

The degree of involvement of these decision makers in the policy making proces depends on the characteristics of the policy field, the amount of public controversy, and the economic and social costs involved. All actors select their preferences in accordance with routines, conventions and traditions of decision making, in other words in accordance with an established policy style (Sturm, 1985). Though there may be different styles in different policy fields, research has shown that policy makers in Germany have developed certain preferences that shape their decisions. The most important features of the German policy style are the consensus orientation and the search for compromise. German policy makers prefer non-decisions, incrementalism (Sturm, 1989, p. 291ff.) and the middle ground (Schmidt, 1990) to radical change and zero-sum games, and they believe in long-term solutions. Strategic thinking of this kind is based on the tacit assumption of lasting social and political stability. In other words, if Germany got it right in principle at the beginning, policy making afterwards only means adjusting to the changing social and political environment. Policy making does not a *priori* include the possibility of a fresh start.

If political compromises cannnot be found, conflicts are expected to be resolved by the use of supposedly 'neutral' legal instruments. Much has been written about the legal culture of German politics. Germans have been described as a very law- and courtminded people (Greiffenhagen and Greiffenhagen, 1993, p. 88). The neutrality of the law is a topos that not only plays a pivotal role in cases of conflicts of interest, it is already present in the early stages of the legislative process. What is 'possible' in policy making depends very much on what the staff of ministries, almost exclusively lawyers, believe to be possible and what they believe can survive a test in the Constitutional Court.

The German inclination to prefer cooperation to competition in policy making was based on unprecedented postwar economic success and a broad consensus on the welfare state. What we witness today is increasing controversy over what policy makers should achieve. The task of finding compromises has become much more difficult.

One reason for this new development is German reunification, which broadened the spectrum of expectations with regard to policy making and its results. In 1994, Article 72.2 of the German constitution was changed. The old article had stipulated that in those policy fields where both the federal government and the Länder have potential responsibilities, it was the task of the federal government to initiate laws whenever the uniformity (*Einheitlichkeit*) of living conditions seemed to be jeopardised. Written in view of the problems such a demand would cause after reunification, the new article requires only *comparable* (*gleichwertige*) living conditions. But apart from such legal changes, burden sharing in united Germany is an unresolved problem, not least psychologically. As long as the categories of east and west remain central to every official statistic, as they still do, and as long as laws exist that define different levels of benefits for west and east Germans, policy making will provoke comparisons and tend to define winners and losers (Sturm, 1995). Some of the remaining policy differences between east and west are that there is no business tax (*Gewerbesteuer*) at the local government level in the east, that the costs of public transport and rented housing in the east are kept below west German levels, that old-age pensions are calculated so as to avoid new poverty in the east, at least up to 1996, and that it will take at least until 1996 for wages in the east to rise to western levels. East German parliamentarians regularly form pressure groups inside the parties to negotiate policy privileges and exemptions in favour of the new *Länder*. Cooperation amongst eastern *Länder* minister-presidents has similar aims.

A second reason for the erosion of consensus politics concerns the definition of winners and losers. The German economy is no longer growing at the high rate of the 1960s and 1970s. At that time it was possible to rely on a policy-making style that combined weak regulatory interventions with generous distributive policies. Politicians only had to decide which social group was to benefit most (this in order to help the governing coalition to get reelected). In the 1980s and 1990s policy making has been about redistribution. It has also accepted to some extent the world-wide scepticism of the welfare state, the prejudice against social policies and the belief that the general welfare of society is closely connected to the needs of industry.

A third reason for the difficulty German policy makers are presently having in finding compromises is the steady erosion of what used to be a very strong idea of the common good. On the one hand German society has become much more individualistic during the last two decades. As a result more and more groups with a temporary interest in a very limited number of issues dominate the public debate. None of these groups are concerned about whether their demands conflict with what the majority may want, nor with the consequences of their demands for the future of the polity as a whole. On the other hand policy makers have become more corrupt (Claussen, 1995). Almost all the major institutions in Germany, including the unions and the parties, have been involved in financial scandals. The reputation of Bundestag members is at a record low. In such a climate it is easy for critics to argue that policy makers are only interested in their careers and individual rent-seeking. In this view policies are no longer based on a greater political project or vison.

A fourth reason is the gradual disappearance of the party political and social consensus on the boundaries of state intervention in society and the role of the public sector (*die öffentlichen Aufgaben*). In the 1980s privatisation in Germany made some progress. Between 1984 and 1989 the number of firms in which the federal government held shares was reduced from 808 to 132. Privatisation income amounted to DM 9.7 billion (OECD, 1990, p. 43). Article 87 of the constitution was changed to allow the privatisation of the Post Office and the federal railway system. In addition there is a debate on the financial limits for sustaining the state-regulated health sector, the universities and subsidised housing. Reformers also want to reduce the number of tasks reserved exclusively for civil servants. With the privatisation of the Post Office and the railway system the status of their staff has changed from civil servant to employee. It is argued, that the same should apply to the staff of schools and universities, in order to introduce flexibility, a changed incentive structure and greater productivity. Financial difficulties at all levels of government have increased the attractiveness of contracting out public services to private firms. In this context some of those involved in the debate have even come out in favour of private infrastructure investment, for example in roads, which would then to be bought back over time by the state.

The Policy Cycle

Nowhere in the world does policy making follow predetermined patterns. Still, for analytical purposes policy research uses categories that characterise certain stages of the decision-making process. A distinction can be made between the initiation, implementation, and evaluation of policy (Table 7.1). Evaluation might be expected to lead to the amendment of the original policy or its termination and replacement with a new policy initiative. Policy learning is supposed to connect the end to the beginning of the cycle. This of course, does not exclude feedback at earlier stages of the policy-making process.

In Germany ideas for new policies formally originate from government ministries, parliament or the chancellor's office. One should not, however, underestimate the influence that pressure groups, new social movements and even public opinion at home and abroad have on policy initiation. A very important new source of influence, which has stimulated many policy changes, has been the European Union, especially after the member states agreed on the aim of the post-1992 Single Market with the Single European Act of 1986.

Pressure groups have a strong informal role in policy making and more than 1500 pressure groups are registered as lobbying organisations in Bonn. Ministries have a rule that only allows them to deal with national representatives of special interests. This was meant to reduce the number of possible interventions, but has only served to increase the number of pressure groups with national representation. It is impossible to say how many of the details of certain pieces of legislation are directly influenced by pressure groups. Occasionally pressure groups are the virtual authors of bills especially when the policy

TABLE 7.1 *Examples of German policy making as a three-step decision-making process*

Policy	*Initiation*	*Implementation*	*Evaluation*
Deregulation of the electricity supply industry (Sturm and Wilks, 1996)	EU (Single Market), Cartel Office, Economics Ministry	Prevented by interest groups	No Evaluation
Health reform (Döhler 1995)	Health Ministry	Health sector groups (doctors, hospitals, pharmaceutical industry health insurance)	*Konzertierte Aktion im Gesundheitswesen* (Corporatist self-regulation of the health sector)
Policies to increase investments in the housing sector (Wollmann, 1985)	Pressure groups of landlords and private investors, Liberal Party (FDP), CSU and parts of the CDU	Market forces	Pressure group of tenants (*Mieterbund*), Unions and Social Democrats

decision has a low public profile or pertains to a bill regulating a matter that requires specialist knowledge of a kind that is at first sight incomprehensible to bureaucrats trained only in the law. Though it is difficult to draw a line between information and influence with regard to the input of pressure groups in the decision-making process, it can safely be said that before a bill reaches parliament all relevant pressure groups will have had a chance to present their views and propose alternative policies.

Policy implementation is primarily the task of Länder bureaucracies. The most important institutions still under the exclusive control of the federal government are the military (*Bundeswehr*), the federal police force (*Bundesgrenzschutz*) and the secret services, the federal railway and the Post Office having been privatised. In some policy fields, such as health and some social services, there is greater reliance on outside experts, self-help and social groups (above all the churches). In some sectors, such as housing and culture, the state has reduced its public policy role, relying instead on the market.

Increasingly, government regulations are becoming less intrusive, laws and regulations being seen as the traditional instruments of a pervasive state. Since the late 1980s Helmut Kohl's government has advocated deregulation at both the national and the European level.

Laws have always be seen as potentially dangerous instruments when it comes to steering the economy. Economic policy making in Germany has tended to reply on financial incentives, and occasionally on moral pressure. Government attempts to encourage western companies to invest in eastern Germany for example, have adopted the latter strategy, though with limited success. In technology policy, governments at all political levels only define a very general aim, namely sectoral modernisation. They do, however, try to identify those sectors that should be given special incentives to expand rapidly. Environmental policies are a typical case where mixed instruments are used. On the one hand there are sets of standards for pollution control, and on the other there are a wide range of disincentives – ranging from extra taxes on petrol to user fees – aimed at changing social behaviour in order to reduce pollution levels.

In the German federal system not only policies but also the implementation of policies may be different from one Land to another. Examples of policy variation are the differences in the legal framework of universities and legislation aimed at increasing women's employment opportunities. With regard to policy implementation, for example, at least on some occasions there are observable differences between the way in which the police in Bavaria and Lower Saxony control violent crowds, and between the degree of attention Hesse and Rhineland-Palatinate pay to pollution caused by the chemicals industry.

Policy evaluation is very rarely exercised by German policy makers. The greatest degree of interest in policy output is shown by interest groups. Policy makers often lack the necessary criteria for evaluation. For them the best policies are those that do not cause conflict, that further their careers and are accepted by the client groups. In some policy fields, especially agriculture, close relationships have developed between politicians, bureaucrats and clients (often termed 'iron triangles' at the cost of the (in this case European) taxpayer. In situations where the clients are more numerous but less powerful, bureaucrats often use another yardstick for measuring success. They are content when a programme arouses the interest of client groups, for example a programme to finance research in biotechnology. The faster public money can be spent on applications from industry, the more important a programme seems to be.

Policy results and strategies that increase the probability of success of political programmes are rarely debated. The German National Audit Office (*Bundesrechnungshof*) should in theory only identify cases of fraud or ones, in which public money has been wasted by bureaucrats, its focus being on the way policies are implemented and financed. Still, since the 1970s advising parliament and the federal government (*Vorprüfung*) has become a very important part of its work. The auditors usually look into the costs and benefits of several policy alternatives. Though in theory they only concentrate on the question of how public money can be most wisely spent, in practice separating the financial aspects of a policy from its political component is difficult to do (Diederich *et al.*, 1990, p. 74). With its early evaluation of the possible consequences of different policy choices the *Bundesrechnungshof* contributes more to the readiness of bureaucrats to learn from past experiences than it does with its annual reports. The latter criticise policy mistakes but although these are debated in a sub-committee of the Bundestag budget committee, this activity is merely symbolic because it has consequences neither for the person nor the institution concerned.

Since the 1980s, and especially since reunification, a greater diversity of policy preferences between the Länder has emerged. This was seen as necessary both because the federal government no longer had the financial means to dominate the political agenda and because of the regional flexibility needed to cope with the problems of reunification. There is also inter-Länder competition; for example through industrial policies they seek to attract investment capital into their regions. In the

1980s, when the federal government still relied exclusively on the market as the driving force behind economic modernisation, the Länder tried to bring together regional and local technology coalitions of universities, administrators, local banks and firms, and small and medium-sized companies. In Länder governed by the Social Democrats the unions also played a role.

In the late 1970s the federal government cut back its financial support for industrial modernisation (Sturm, 1991). The first Land to react with its own initiatives to improve its infrastructure in research and technology was Baden-Württemberg in 1977, followed by North Rhine-Westphalia in 1978, Hamburg and the Saarland in 1979, Bavaria, Lower Saxony and Berlin in 1980, Schleswig-Holstein and Bremen in 1982, and Hesse and Rhineland-Palatinate in 1985, the last of these having sent a commission of experts to Stuttgart to study the Baden-Württemberg model (Sturm, 1991, pp. 66, 96). Now policy learning in this field has extended to the federal level: in 1994 Chancellor Kohl set up a *Technologierat* (a round table for technology policies), which brings together the same groups that organise economic modernisation policies at the Land level.

Policy Making

Though Germany's past economic success has often been attributed to forms of corporatist interest intermediation (Bulmer and Humphreys, 1989), for economic policy making this arrangement restricted to the lifetime of the so-called *Konzertierte Aktion*, (1967–76), after which the forum comprising representatives of employers, labour and the government degenerated into little more than a public relations event with no capacity for serious decision making. However in the 1990s, post-reunification economic difficulties led to the resurrection of the idea of *Konzertierte Aktion* (concerted action) in relation to economic modernisation in the east (Pilz and Ortwein, 1992, p. 150). To this end the Kohl government came to an informal agreement with industry and the banks to mobilise support for eastern reconstruction. The banks promised (within 'reasonable' limits) to provide access to risk capital for investments, and industry promised to train young east Germans applying for apprenticeships. However these promises were more symbolic than real, and what was achieved was a far cry from the success of the tripartism of the late 1960s.

In two other policy areas the Kohl government was, however, the driving force behind a revival of round-table politics. As mentioned above, in 1994 Kohl copied the idea, successful in the *Länder*, of a *Technologierat* at the federal level. The 17-member *Technologierat* comprises scientists, representatives of industry (Degussa, Orpegen Pharma, Harting Elektronik, SMH, Trumpf, Siemens, BMW) and the unions (IG Chemie, IG Metall) and politicians (Chancellor Helmut Kohl, of the CDU, the economics minister, Günter Rexrodt of the FDP, the technology minister, Jürgen Rüttgers of the CDU and the Bavarian minister of culture, Hans Zehetmair of the CSU). So far the *Technologierat* has met only a few times. It is too early therefore to evaluate its impact on policy making.

More important has been the *Konzertierte Aktion im Gesundheitswesen* (KAiG), which is an instrument for decision making in the health sector. Intended primarily as a mechanism to bring about voluntary costs control, the KAiG has not influenced policy making in a positive way. Corporatism in German policy making today has more to do with coordinating than decision making. It may create (negative or positive) incentives, but its effects are not convincing enough to serve as a role model for policy making in more than a few policy arenas. In addition today's corporatism is heavily biased in favour of the strongest groups in society. Neither the unions nor the patients, the latter being both consumers and financers of health service provisions, have a voice in corporatist interest intermediation.

With regard to higher education, cost control has become the yardstick of recent reform initiatives. In the 1980s and 1990s the so-called 'education summits', where the *Länder* ministers responsible for education have meetings with the federal government have not produced a single decision on the future role of universities in society.

Housing as a policy responsibility was taken off the agenda in the 1980s, when the federal government publicly declared that the German housing problem was solved. Chancellor Kohl's Liberal coalition partner and influential interest groups, above all the well-organised National Association of Real-Estate and Home Owners (*Zentralverband der deutschen Haus-, Wohnungs- und Grundeigentümer*), argued that any new housing shortages that might arise could be resolved if there was enough flexibility in the housing market. The state should therefore cease to finance costly housing programmes and concentrate on the deregulation of housing markets. Central to deregulation should be the abolition of rent controls and a weakening of the legal rights of tenants.

Housing policy was more or less handed over to the market in a situation where demand was growing rapidly because the baby-boom generation of the 1960s needed cheap housing for young families, the number of so-called 'guest workers' with large families was increasing, and in general young people were leaving home earlier. Since the mid-1980s the situation in the housing market has deteriorated rapidly. New pressures on the market were caused by an increase in mobility (for economic reasons), the break-down of the traditional family, and the inflow of hundreds of thousands of asylum seekers and ethnic Germans with their families. Reunification added new problems, for example the poor housing stock in the east, and the westward migration of large numbers of easterners with housing needs. The removal of government responsibility for housing policy has created a new policy problem: homelessness. In 1991 an estimated 130000 people were without a home, of whom 40000 were sleeping in the streets (Hanesch, 1994, p. 88).

In some policy fields where the government plays only a very weak role, policy making by private-sector policy makers can have far-reaching consequences for society. Two examples of successful private policy making within a broad legal framework set by the state are the industrial policies of the banks and the electricity supply policies of German energy producers. In each case, public policy functions are carried out by private economy actors.

Though formally under the regulatory control of the *Bundesaufsichtsamt für das Kreditwesen* (Federal Credit Office) in Berlin, German private banks have a long tradition of autonomous policy making. German banking is controlled by the big three: Commerzbank, Deutsche Bank and Dresdner Bank. Empirical studies have shown that representatives of these banks or their board members control up to two thirds of the votes of the first hundred German joint-stock companies (*Aktiengesellschaften*) (Pfeiffer, 1993, p. 73). The most active and important bank is the Deutsche Bank, but all the large private banks have played a role in the merger and acquisition of companies. No research has so far disentangled their combined role as financers and initiators of changes of property rights in industry. Arguably, in industrial restructuring the large private banks play a role that is comparable to that of the state in France. It was certainly remarkable that in the course of a few months in the mid 1980s, the Deutsche Bank was involved in the biggest merger in German postwar history (that of Daimler-Benz, AEG, Dornier and MTU), in the conversion of the last of the great family-owned private firms into a joint-stock company (Flick), and in the financial restructuring of Germany's then politically most influential media company (Springer). Because of the lack of transparency in this process, one can only guess at the mixture of competition and collusion that existed.

Another policy field with a relatively high level of autonomy from the state and a quasi-state regulatory structure is energy, especially electricity supply. In contrast to Britain, the German electricity supply industry has always been privately owned, but although there is a multitude of electricity suppliers they do not compete (Sturm and Wilks, 1995). Rather they have carved up individual territories, over which they have exclusive jurisdiction. At first sight this seems to imply that the common interests of the electricity supply companies dominate when it comes to policy making in the field, especially if one takes into account the existing degree of interlocking ownership. However in the last few years the sectoral cohesion between the electricity companies has been reduced because the European Commission and the federal government have started initiatives that threaten to break up the existing monopolies. The big producers in particular have diversified their activities, and are major competitors in other sectors, such as telecommunications or the recycling industry. As a consequence some of the electricity companies have come to accept a greater degree of competition in the policy field. As in banking, interest in self-regulation and oligopoly is coming into collision with 'new' competitive pressures. Stephen Padgett (1990, p. 189) therefore identifies a 'dual policy style' in the electricity supply sector:

> An associational style of policy-making is intrinsic to relations between the state and the sector in which the state abstains from direct intervention, delegating functions to broadly encompassing sectoral interest organisations. The structure of interest representation is also conducive to an associational policy style. Sectoral interest organisations are geared to self-concertation, the balancing of interests and the negotiation of mutually acceptable outcomes. Sectoral solidarity, a precondition of the associational order, is fostered by a network of interlocking ownership in the sector. However, the ownership/market structure also contains the potential for sectoral hegemony on the part of sectoral leaders.

The findings of Wolfgang Rüdig (1988) support the hypotheses that a surprising degree of private sector decisions is the central feature of energy policy making. Rüdig has studied policy styles in nuclear technology and concludes that it is characteristic for policy making in Germany that government and quasi-governmental organisations confine their role to nuclear research and are not extensively involved in technology development and dissemination, that the nuclear construction industry is closely involved with the initial research work and takes the dominant role at the development stage, and that the main decisions at the dissemination stage are left to the electricity companies (Rüdig, 1988, p. 421f.)

Recent Developments in Policy Making

Helmut Kohl's election victory in 1983 was seen by many of his supporters as the beginning of an initiative to reduce the role of the state in society. Supply-side economics, however, has been slow to influence economic policy making. Anti-union legislation was restricted to a change of Paragraph 116 of the *Arbeitsförderungsgesetz* (Employment Protection Law). Workers laid off as a result of strike action in a related firm or industry are no longer allowed to claim unemployment benefit. In 1984 and 1985 working hours and employment rules were to some extent deregulated. In 1994 the Employment Office lost its monopoly over finding jobs for the unemployed. Though not through government intervention, workplace flexibility has increased dramatically because of agreements between employers and employees at the level of the firm.

Before reunification, policies to reduce the burden of taxation appeared to be making some progress. Corporate taxes in particular were reduced. There was also a three-step reform of income tax in the years 1986, 1988 and 1990, from which most Germans benefited. Privatisation got off the ground in the mid-1980s, although it did not initially attract much public attention.

In the 1980s the booming world economy saved the Kohl government from financial problems that would have forced dramatic cuts in social policy. Nonetheless health benefits, for example, were reduced and pensioners were obliged to contribute to their health insurance. Pensions remained indexed, but instead of being linked to the *gross* average income of an employee, they were linked to *net* average income. In years with small increases of income this meant that pensions rose slower than the inflation rate, or even decreased. In spite of benefit cuts a last-ditch effort was made to broaden the reach of social security legislation by the introduction of a special insurance, which since 1994 has subsidised care for the elderly and disabled (*Pflegeversicherung*).

Political observers have often criticised the Kohl government for its wait-and-see attitude. Kohl's policy style in the 1980s was certainly mainly reactive, characterised by muddling through and the struggle for political survival. Little energy was invested in new perspectives and agenda setting. The government was more or less forced to innovate in the field of environmental policies. The German debate on nuclear accidents, summer smog and the ozone layer has triggered environmental legislation and has given the Environmental Office (*Umweltbundesamt*) in Berlin an important role, at least in technical matters. The tension between ecology and the economy is a dominant factor in the general framework in which policy choices are made today. A typical example is the 1995 decision of the federal government to ignore the plans of its own minister for the environment, Angela Merkel, who wanted an ecologically oriented reform of the tax system. The cabinet plans instead to introduce new criteria for the taxation of cars, based on emission levels and not on engine capacity, a proposal identical with the car industry's own preferences.

Another topic that society has imposed on the government is gender discrimination. Though the Kohl government believes that the state should not be in the forefront of this issue, at Land level Kohl's party has actively supported the cause of women.

For a number of years in the late 1980s and early 1990s the influx of asylum seekers to Germany made the headlines. Germany had a very generous legal provision in Article 16 of its constitution: 'Everyone who is in danger because of her or his political views has the right to asylum'. After much debate this was amended and the right to asylum is now no longer granted to asylum seekers who come to Germany via a state in which human rights are guaranteed. This, however, has not solved the social problems that gave rise to the asylum debate. What has been suggested is a law to stop illegal immigration and define some rules for new arrivals.

Post-reunification Germany has inherited the economic problems of the east. Policy now concentrates on transforming the East German economy and improving its competitiveness. The federal government has invested large sums in infrastructure projects and the Länder have helped to rebuild public administration. The tension between ecological and economic needs is even greater in the east than in the west. Financial transfers to the new Länder, combined with economic crisis resulting from the loss of international markets and in unemployment growth has radicalised the Conservative social and economic agenda.

Cutbacks in social policies have been more openly debated and more often implemented in the 1990s. The losers of modernisation policies – the older unemployed, young people without any training, the children of immigrants or low-paid employees – are ignored by policy makers. Today's policies are redistributing wealth not only from west to east, but also from poor to rich.

The new Germany has to live with a strange policy mix in order to cope with the double challenge of the post-modern policy problems of multiculturalism and equal opportunities on the one hand, and the problems of low industrial growth on the other. Priority setting for policy makers has become incredibly complex, especially if they hope to mobilise broad societal support. Policies that are popular in western Germany seem to be of marginal importance to many easterners. Westerners argue that policy makers in the east seem to be inclined to repeat western mistakes, for example with regard to the dominance of the motor car, rather than coming up with new ideas. Suboptimal solutions, however, have often resulted from the pressure of western interests, as in the reorganisation of the health sector in the new Länder, where the more cost-effective GDR system of health care was abandoned and the western problem of exploding costs was imported (Manow-Borgwardt, 1995). For ideological reasons the government sees an easy solution in reducing its own policy role by reducing the responsibilities of the state in society. Political realities make it hard, however, for the government to distance itself from acute social problems. Helmut Kohl has even personally guaranteed the survival of certain chemical firms in the east to avoid the devastating effects of deindustrialisation on the regional economy. This kind of interventionism is, however, neither goal-oriented nor systematic and therefore difficult to predict as a variable for policy making.

PART TWO
Germany and the World

8

Beyond Bipolarity; German Foreign Policy in a Post-Cold-War World

WILLIAM E. PATERSON

> Poor Germany, too big for Europe, too small for the world (Henry Kissinger).

The collapse of the Yalta system and the recreation of a united Germany was accompanied by a heady mixture of high expectations and barely suppressed concern inside and outside Germany. How different would the new Germany be and what would the implications of any changes be for Germany's neighbours and allies? The internal changes have been less than expected and a near complete process of 'institutional transfer' has taken place between the old Federal Republic and the five new Länder. Internally the future shape and character of the new Germany is no longer an open question; it is simply the old Federal Republic writ large (Webber, 1995).

Externally, the picture is much less clear. The foreign policy of the Federal Republic had been framed by the constraints of a bipolar system and indeed it could be argued that this was a central reason for its success. Free from the illusions that historical memory had bequeathed to a number of other states, it felt totally at home in the alliance and European community context and harboured no wider aspirations. The breaching of the Brandenburg Gate on 9 November 1989 and the steady achievement of full sovereignty just under a year later on 3 October 1990 opened a series of questions that were thought to have been foreclosed.

Over the past century the 'German question' has had two dimensions. The first, which was concerned with whether it was possible to establish a stable liberal democratic political order, was answered in the affirmative in the course of the first four decades of the history of the Federal Republic, though it found some very faint echoes in the heated debates within Germany surrounding the question as to whether Bonn or Berlin should be the future capital following unity. Some of those opposing the move to Berlin argued that a return to Berlin would transform the shadows of the past into the shadows of the future and would reawaken external fears about Germany's permanent commitment to the West. This was a misperception since external confidence was sufficiently robust not to be dependent on the site of the future capital.

The other dimension of the German question – the compatibility of a unified German state with its external environment – became much more of an open question with the ending of the bipolar international order. NATO had been founded, as Lord Ismay famously and not entirely inaccurately remarked, 'to keep the Russians out, the Americans in and the Germans down'. While the problem of keeping the Russians out appeared to have been solved by the implosion of the Soviet state, the end of the Cold War certainly raised question marks about the other two goals of NATO policy.

In the reunification process and in its immediate aftermath the German government attempted to reinforce Germany's commitment to multilateral institutions, especially the European Union, where the metaphor constantly employed was that of an anchor. The accent, as in domestic policy, was on continuity rather than change. However, unlike domestic policy, many doubt that this will be possible in the long term and Germany is now confronted with a series of dilemmas in relation to both the goals and the style of foreign policy.

The first dilemma relates to the issue of national interest: should Germany persist in forswearing explicit pursuit of national interests and continue to follow a policy of framing its interests within multilateral contexts? Further dilemmas are raised by the continued role of historical memory and whether Germany can continue to define itself as a 'civilian power' rather than expanding its external options through acceptance of a much wider range of security responsibilities. The 'bonfire of certainties' in 1989 necessarily involved recasting Germany's relations with the United States and Russia, but crucial questions remain as to the pace and direction of the adjustment process. Finally, Germany's increasing power raises the question of whether it is acquiring a global role.

The National Interest Debate

> Germans have too much consideration for foreigners and too little national prejudice (Madame de Stael, *De l'Allemagne*, 1810).

For most analysts and practitioners in the Anglo Saxon world, the influence of realist and neorealist conceptions is sufficiently strong for them to find it difficult to imagine that Germany will not in the course of time seek to deploy its enhanced power resources more openly. This would constitute an overdue return to normality. No state, in their view, would opt permanently to punch below its weight. A structuralist or integrationist on the other hand is much more impressed by the diminished role of states in general and the imperatives of interdependence. Foreign policy in this view is about managing the institutions of interdependence and it is the postnational, postmodern, multilateral foreign policy stance of the old Federal Republic that defines normality rather than what they would see as the atavistic and self-defeating policies of a more realist state such as Britain.

The German foreign policy community has been deeply marked by the thinking of the second school, and most of the arguments conducted within it point to a persistence of this mind set and policy preference.

With the exception of the issue of German unity, foreign policy in the old Federal Republic was notable for the almost complete absence of explicit recourse to national interest as an organising principle of foreign policy formulation. Initially this could very largely be explained by the Federal Republic's contingent dependent sovereignty – a foreign policy in search of a state rather than a state in search of a foreign policy.

In a postwar Europe characterised by increasing economic interdependence and very marked security dependence on the United States, all states were semisovereign, but the Federal Republic was more semisovereign than the others. Semisovereignty was the defining mark of the Federal Republic. The factors adding up to semisovereignty included the vulnerability of West Berlin *vis-à-vis* the Soviet East and the dependence that this induced on Western allies, the total nature of the Federal Republic's incorporation into the North Atlantic Treaty Organisation, the absence of any independent strategic planning capacity, the stationing of the bulk of allied forces in Germany and its participation in the European Community. Of course, participation in the European Community was a feature shared with the Federal Republic's fellow members, but the situation of the Republic as a new state in a divided and defeated Germany and the forging of its identity around a European vocation led German political elites to reject a 'realist' stance in relation to European institutions. In contrast to the United Kingdom, where the imperatives of collective memory reinforced a discourse of national interest, multilateralism was the dominant theme in the German case, and as Anderson and Goodman stated in their article 'Mars or Minerva', 'in the eyes of German political elites, institutional memberships were not merely instruments of policy, but also normative frameworks for policy-making' (Anderson and Goodman, 1993, pp. 23–4).

The Pull of Memory

> The story of the evolution of a foreign policy is that of experiences becoming maxims (Waldemar Besson).

The analogy with Gulliver often employed by analysts of the Federal Republic's international role suggests its semisovereignty and resultant commitment to multilateralism were exclusively externally imposed conditions that would alter as soon as the bonds were cut. In fact, unlike Gulliver, the Federal Republic actively sought internal and external restraint, and far from being a crippling condition it brought significant benefits to Germany. Paradoxically, by pursuing a policy of espousing semisovereignty the contingent, dependent sovereignty of the infant Federal Republic had by 1990 been formally transformed into the fully sovereign, unified Germany. The first compelling reason for expecting a continuation of the present policy style is therefore its track record.

A second powerful ground lies in the impact of history. Historical memory is a key organising principle in the making of foreign policy and nowhere more so than in Germany. The defining historical memory focuses on the lessons to be drawn from 1945:

> The total defeat of the Third Reich was a traumatic experience common to all the policy-makers of the Federal Republic after 1949, though the present generation of policy makers now remember it, if at all, as teenagers rather than as adult participants. The key lesson that they drew was the necessity for Germany not to exploit its full power potential, which would only unite other powers against it, but to associate the exercise of the power of the nascent state with the

> emerging alliance and institutional structures. In this sense, the Federal Republic's lack of 'giant' status represented a deliberate choice (Paterson, 1992, p. 139).

This historical memory was associated with a very negative view of balance-of-power policy (*Schaukelpolitik*) and what its practice had meant for Germany and its neighbours between 1871 and 1945. Germany could only be secure by identifying itself unequivocally with the West and adopting policies within Western institutions at the opposite end of the spectrum from De Gaulle's classic realist maxim that 'War is against one's enemies while peace is against one's friends'.

As direct personal memories begin to fade and generational change takes place, historical memory becomes more plastic and more open to the reinterpretations of academic historians and journalists. In the final years of the former Federal Republic a bitter dispute took place on the historical status of the Third Reich, in which conservative historians such as Ernst Nolte questioned the uniqueness of the Third Reich while their adversaries, for example Jürgen Habermas, argued strongly that the only historical memory that should positively shape policy in the Federal Republic was postwar experience, and that political loyalties should be based on postnational, constitutional patriotism.

None of the central contributions to the *Historikerstreit* (historians' dispute) explicitly addressed in any depth the implications of a particular view of history for foreign policy, though Habermas' position implicitly backed the prevailing foreign policy orientation. Half a decade after reunification, the climate has altered. One indication of this change is given in the contrasting views of Karl-Dietrich Bracher and Hans-Peter Schwarz, his successor in the chair of Political Science at the University of Bonn.

Bracher and Schwarz are among Germany's most distinguished contemporary historians. Bracher, who made his reputation with magisterial studies of the collapse of the Weimar Republic and the nature of the Third Reich, remains a board member of the pro-integrationist 'Institut Für Europäische Politik' and has often approvingly labelled the Federal Republic a postnational democracy that should remain committed to maximum integration. Hans-Peter Schwarz, ironically the biographer of Adenauer, the progenitor of Germany's postwar integration policy and Helmut Kohl's guiding star, sees some merit in the traditional European state system and takes a line of argument close to that of the British historian, Alan Milward, which assumes that nation states will always be the key actors in the integration process and envisages a subordinate role for supranational institutions (Schwarz, 1994a; Milward, 1992). Given the preeminence of nation states and his assumption that they will seek to retain key areas of national sovereignty, Schwarz, like Timothy Garton Ash (1994a) recommends for Germany a policy of nationally defined options that nevertheless take account, in a balanced way, of the constraints of the integration framework. This position, sometimes called the 'Frankfurt position' because it appears to correspond to the assumptions of the *Frankfurter Allgemeine Zeitung* and to some extent those of the Frankfurt-based Bundesbank, however commonplace it might be in other member states, differs sharply from the prevailing 'Rhineland' position exemplified by Bracher, in which positions are framed in a multilateral framework.

To the right of Schwarz and others represented in a volume of essays edited by Arnulf Baring (1994) lie a group of scholars, including Rainer Zitelmann, who argue for a much more nationalistic position and for the importance of geopolitical considerations (Zitelmann, 1993).

Neither the sane and balanced revisionism of Hans Peter Schwarz nor the more provocative views of Zitelmann have had any marked impact on the discourse or content of the foreign policy of the Federal Republic, with the possible exception of former Yugoslavia (discussed below), however much they may have excited disapproving comment in the liberal weekly *Die Zeit* or approbation in the *Frankfurter Allgemeine Zeitung*, the conservative daily.

The grounds for this lack of impact are fairly easy to discern. Neither school has been able to offer anything useful in choosing between Germany's policy options. Helping resolve the difficult acts of choice is normally held to be a major virtue of the national interest school, but one which both the moderate conservatives and the more explicit nationalists fail. Neither school seriously analyses what constitutes power in a world of nuclear weapons and interdependent economies. Their rediscovery of some of the virtues of the balance of power and their hope that Germany's geographical position (*Mittellage*) and human resources would allow it to play a balancing role is simply vacuous. 'For all the evocation of Germany's new "central position", it can no longer play a balancing role; there is nothing to balance' (Pulzer, 1995b, p. 13). For all of their passion neither group of writers are able to suggest any plausible example of where following a national interest policy would have produced a better outcome for Germany. Apart from the palpable weakness of the arguments, the dominating presence of Chancellor Kohl will ensure that as long as he remains chancellor the discourse will stay firmly Rhineland.

Finally, while individual politicians and indeed political parties need to be able to respond to changes in the public mood and intellectual fashions, the key ministries are more constrained since they possess institutional memories where collective experience is stored and whose deep structures reflect four decades of successful experience in multilateral institution.

The Civilian Power

The discourse of national interest is usually related to a state that focuses on the projection of hard power, but as Hans Maull has argued, postwar Germany has developed as a civilian power with a set of foreign policy responses and style that correspond to its vocation as a *Handelsstaat* (trading state) (Maull and Gordon, 1993).

The civilian power orientation has become more marked in the post-Cold-War situation than in the four preceding decades, when international issues were defined by East–West tension and Germany shared fully in the West's determination to resist any expansionist attempt by the Soviet Union. This bipolar world ended in 1989–90 and the balance between Germany as a civilian power and alliance member has shifted as the alliance has necessarily lost some of its centrality.

Hans Maull has defined civilian power along four dimensions:

- A close entanglement of domestic and external considerations, of strong value orientations and democratic elements.
- A disbelief in the utility of military force and a lack of understanding that others might not share this insight into the changing nature of international relations.
- A preference for diplomatic bargaining, negotiation and compromise, and, if necessary and useful, for chequebook diplomacy.
- An inclination to seek solutions to international problems through multilateral channels and division of labour policies that downplay national pride, concern for sovereignty and the autonomy approach (Maull and Gordon, 1993, p. 8).

Germany's civilian power orientation appeared to many inside Germany to be in tune with the post-Cold-War world about which their civilian power mindset led them to entertain very optimistic assumptions. Outside Germany realists such as John Mearsheimer (1990) expected a dramatic increase in Germany's security role, including a nuclear capacity. Caught between external expectations, especially from the United States, and the civilian power assumptions of public opinion the federal government has inched towards an increased security role, a strategy greatly facilitated by the ruling of the Federal Constitutional Court of 12 July 1994 on 'out of area' operations (see Chapter 10), but constrained by a public opinion that still conforms more closely to the civilian power image.

The key factor in Germany's avoidance of hard-power solutions and its continued adherence to the civilian power model lies in Germany's interaction with its environment. Will Germany, with its considerable soft-power resources, be able to shape its environment in its image, or will the international environment prove to be as threatening as realists suppose and reshape Germany?

> If Germany is to remain a civilian power, it will have to convince others to be 'more like Germany' and to convince them that compromise, multilateralism and civilian solutions are always best. That will be no easy task and if it does not work, Germany may be forced to become more like them! (Maull and Gordon, 1993, p. 26).

Germany and Former Yugoslavia

The harsh pressures of the international environment and the implications for Germany were already apparent in former Yugoslavia. German pressure for what other EC member states perceived as a precipitate and ill-judged recognition of Croatia and Slovenia in December 1991 has often been portrayed, not only as an example of new German self-assertiveness, but as a harbinger of future German policy. There is little doubt that it was an example of self-assertion, but it remains an isolated example and the subsequent developments in that area make it a departure from the path of multilateral virtue that is highly unlikely to be repeated.

At the outbreak of the crisis in what was then Yugoslavia, the Federal Republic followed its conventional multilateral policy line. The Federal Republic supported the visit of the troika of EC foreign ministers, headed by Jacques Poos, to Yugoslavia in April 1991 to offer additional credits and an association agreement with the EC On 19 June 1991 a Bundestag resolution, supported by all parties, argued in favour of maintaining Yugoslavia only through the creation of a confederation. The situation then changed with amazing rapidity.

Slovenia and Croatia declared independence, but while the majority of the EC member states continued to argue for measures designed to keep Yugoslavia intact, Germany moved swiftly to a policy of favouring recognition of Croatia and Slovenia, arguing that it was now too late to hold Yugoslavia together, while ignoring the arguments put by other member states that recognition should be conditional on proper safeguards for ethnic minorities if future disasters were to be avoided.

The CDU called for diplomatic recognition of Croatia and Slovenia on 27 June and by 1 July when the foreign affairs committee of the Bundestag was called together for an extraordinary session at the suggestion of the SPD, foreign minister Genscher found himself isolated (Crawford, 1995, p. 7). By 9 July, Genscher's party, the FDP, had adopted a recognition policy. During the course of the summer public support grew for the new position of the political parties and by November 1991 69 per cent supported full recognition of Slovenia and Croatia (Crawford, 1995, p. 7). The German position was strengthened during the Maastricht conference in early December 1991 when, it has often been argued, German support for a number of British negotiating positions was traded against the British government agreeing to drop its objection to the recognition policy.

On 11 December 1991 the cabinet made public its decision to recognise Croatia and Slovenia. Germany's partners were thus boxed in and on 16 December agreed, under German pressure, to set up a five-member commission that would establish whether Croatia and Slovenia met the criteria for recognition. The outcome was never in doubt and formal EC recognition was granted on 15 January 1992.

A popular explanation outside Germany for this position relates it to Nazi Germany's support for the wartime Croatian Republic. On closer examination this view is unconvincing. Not only would it have been out of character for the foreign policy elites of the Federal Republic, whose defining historical memory is the disaster of the Nazi regime, but more crucially the parties that were most strongly in favour, the SPD and the Greens, were the most postnational, most secular and least likely to be affected by historical ties to the conservative Catholic Croatians. Their support is much more obviously related to support for self-determination.

While the influence of ties to the historical state of Croatia can largely be discounted, the presence of a high proportion of Croats among the 700000 Yugoslav population in Germany did have some impact, especially in moving the CDU–CSU towards recognition through their heavy involvement in the Catholic Church. This pressure was especially marked in Bavaria and on the CSU.

Perhaps more important in explaining why in this case domestic pressures prevailed was the weakness of the multilateral side of the equation.

> They opted to please domestic elites and betray an EC negotiated agreement. They chose this option because, in the absence of clear multilateral sanctions for unilateral action and the underdevelopment of multilateral norms and institutions to guide action in this issue, a spiral of mistrust emerged in EC negotiations. This spiral of mistrust started when Germany threatened to act alone as a negotiating tactic to press its partners to move to the German position. In response, France and Britain then urged a U.N. Security Council resolution to force Germany to cooperate. France and Britain further demanded conditions for multilateral diplomatic recognition that Croatia would most likely not be able to meet. Genscher could not take the political risk of an EC denial of recognition in the face of increasing domestic pressure. Germany thus took unilateral action (Crawford, 1995, p. 3).

Resort to national channels was made only when multilateral ones seemed incapable of action. This episode may well lead one to the general conclusion that German power will become more evident when European institutions prove too weak.

The escalation of the crisis in former Yugoslavia in the years following the recognition decision and the nature of the crisis in Bosnia had a perceptible effect on German policy. Most members of the German foreign-policy-making elite came around to the view that German policy on recognition had been ill-judged and precipitate and had seriously underestimated both the complexity and intensity of intra-ethnic disputes. The further unfolding of the crisis also demonstrated the weakness of German foreign policy in a context in which soft power was insufficient, and the German domestic consensus against the use of force condemned Germany to a very restricted role compared with Britain and France, which both had large peacekeeping contingents in Bosnia, although it was Germany that suffered most through the absence of peace in the area since the overwhelming proportion of refugees washed up in Germany. During the course of the crisis the government was able to extend gradually the nature of German involvement. The change of view was most pronounced in relation to the Greens and the SPD. While the majority in both parties remained opposed to German participation in the use of force in the area, significant minorities in both parties were persuaded by the horror of the crisis that Germany should make a contribution.

Europeanisation

Germany's European vocation has been so profound as to make a change of direction towards a neorealist national interest policy very unlikely. Klaus Goetz has recently pointed to a process of Europeanisation in Germany, which 'makes the search for the national, as opposed to the European interest a fruitless task. The national and the European interest have become fused to a degree which makes their separate consideration increasingly impossible' (Goetz, 1996, p. 40).

At first sight this argument looks less than compelling. Two defining German institutions, the Bundesbank and the Federal Constitutional Court, have been able to distinguish between German and European interests when they have considered it necessary. The Bundesbank has always made it clear that its monetary policy is necessarily determined by German interests, and in its ruling on the constitutionality of the Maastricht Treaty on 11 October 1993 the Court ruled that it rather than the European Court of Justice would determine whether or not the EU institutions were operating within their competence. It defined the European Union as a *Staatenverbund*, a type of association of states falling somewhere between a federation and a confederation, and stressed that member states remained *Herren der Verträge* (masters of the treaties). It also argued that any significant steps towards further unification needed to be legitimised by the Bundestag.

Despite these caveats there is much to agree with in the broad thrust, particularly since Europeanisation is palpably to Germany's advantage, given – as Simon Bulmer has recently and persuasively argued – that the close fit between German and European institutions has empowered Germany by making it 'at home' in institutional terms with the patterns of policy making and institutional interaction in the EU.

Finally, the notion that power can only be viewed in the neorealist national interest mode involves a rather narrow view of power, for the exercise of which German institutions are intentionally rather ill-designed, but this weakness in neorealist power is compensated for, as Simon Bulmer (1995) argued, by three other faces of power. The second face of German power is reflected in its indirect influenc on the structures, norms and policies of the EU. An obvious example here would be the question of standard setting in the Single European Market, where the efforts made by large German companies to influence the relevant committees and the prestige of the DIN system proved a winning combination. The third face of power, what Bulmer calls non-intentional power, derives from the unintended consequences of domestic political and economic power, and the key example here would be the impact of the Bundesbank interest rate decisions. The fourth face, in which Germany is empowered by the correspondence of German and European institutions, has been referred to above.

Germany, the United States and the Gulf War

The foreign policy of the original Federal Republic was set negatively by the Soviet Union and positively by the United States. Both pressures pointed in the same direction and the Federal Republic became the first German state to be unequivocally Western, securely anchored to the developing Western institutions.

German–US relations remained extraordinarily close throughout the history of the Federal Republic despite occasional clashes on policy, especially during Helmut Schmidt's chancellorship, when the federal government felt let down both by the monetary policy of the Carter administration and its espousal and subsequent rejection of the neutron bomb proposal.

Relations were restored to normality under Helmut Kohl, though the issue of short-range nuclear weapons had put some strain on the relationship by 1988. The steadfast support of President Bush for German unity, and indeed his offer of a 'partners in leadershp' in June 1989 even before reunification, meant that relations between the united Germany and the United States got off to a very good start. One of Helmut Kohl's most senior foreign policy advisors, in conversation with the author, analysed the German reunification process in the following terms: 'We [Germany] have only three people to thank – Bush, Gorbachev and Delors. The others can be forgotten'.

However the post-reunification period unexpectedly turned out to be somewhat more problematic, with quite deep policy differences appearing in the years immediately after reunification. The perennial US–German disputes about monetary policy took on a new sharpness after reunification, with the Americans arguing that high German interest rates would put pressure on US interest rates and impede recovery, while the Bundesbank, confronted with high budget deficits and surging consumer demand, felt it had no alternative but to raise interest rates if it were to fulfil its statutorily prescribed role in countering inflation.

A more novel rift opened up in relation to policy towards the Soviet Union, an issue on which Bonn would traditionally have simply followed Washington. Chancellor Kohl and the German government were very strongly committed to trying to maintain Mikhail Gorbachev in power, since his failure and an accelerated break-up of the Soviet Union were likely to have very adverse consequences for European stability and German trade with the USSR, and even might have endangered the agreed withdrawal of Russian troops from Germany by 1994. By 1991 Germany had committed $33 billion to the USSR, while the United States had committed less than a tenth of that amount. Kohl invested a great deal of his political capital in attempting to persuade the United States and the G7 significantly to increase their aid to the Soviet Union. When Kohl gave his Edinburgh speech (Kohl, 1991) he had just returned from failing to persuade Bush to back his policy, and his deep personal commitment to that policy and his disappointment at its rejection by the US leadership was demonstrated by the degree to which he departed from his prepared text on that issue – too far for the officials of the chancellor's office, who insisted that his remarks should be removed from the final text. The Americans, in contrast, confident of their overwhelming military superiority were unwilling to pour money into the Soviet Union in the absence of far-reaching economic and political reforms. The attempted coup in the Soviet Union in August 1991, Gorbachev's later removal and the subsequent break-up of the USSR removed the issue as an area of contention.

US disappointment with Germany was greatest in relation to the Gulf War. The US administration and American opinion more widely was disappointed by the initial lack of readiness of the German government to help the United States after the United States had borne the costs of defending Germany for four decades, and in this case was also defending German oil supplies. The federal government, weighed down by the costs of transforming the five new Länder and support for Eastern Europe, only agreed after a prolonged period of indecision to commit financial aid. The final amount of $11 billion represented about 0.7 per cent of Germany's GNP, but this sizeable contribution was less material than the delay in making the offer.

Those German–US divergences healed rather quickly and the relationship continues, along with the Franco–German relationship, to set the parameters of German foreign policy. Resolution of the Uruguay Round of GATT and increased support for NATO within Germany, as Russia looks increasingly threatening, have also helped keep the relationship in good repair.

Another major contribution to healing the rifts imposed by the Gulf War was the introduction of a significant tightening up of export control procedures. Considerable damage was done to Germany's image, especially in the United States, by the involvement of German nationals and firms in nuclear and chemical weapons projects in Iraq and elsewhere in the Middle East. Reform was effected by a series of measures, including the appointment of over 400 government officials to monitor this area, much heavier penalties for unauthorised exports and the legal obligation for companies to appoint an export executive who will be held personally responsible for any illegal actions by the firm.

There remain, however, divergent visions of Germany's role. The United States finds it increasingly difficult to maintain its global economic and security role and is looking for partners in leadership. Whether or not Germany will play a visibly increased role in economic leadership will depend on the success or failure of the economic and monetary union project. If it is successful then it will be from within a European framework, if it fails it will have to play this role as the home base of the Deutsche-Mark.

On its security role, Germany has inched forward, and the Federal Constitutional Court ruling of July 1994 (see Chapter 10) cleared an obstacle to more extended operation, but Germany remains a very reluctant power and historic memory and budgetary implications would make it very difficult for Germany to transform itself into the kind of military power envisaged among American policy makers.

Germany's attempts to increase its role through the development of Eurocorps and its commitment to building up the Western European Union as a European defence institution is viewed with a certain degree of ambivalence in Washington. At the declaratory level, European self-help is welcomed, but concerns remain about the Europeans drifting too far from the United States.

While the US vision of a normal Germany playing a political and security role at the global level commensurate with its economic strength would find some support among economic elites and conservative political circles in Germany, it remains a much less powerful vision than the European vocation which commands a much wider and deeper consensus, including those who would support a modified version of the US vision. However there is almost no wider enthusiasm in Germany for playing the role of junior global partner to the United States.

Collapse and Change in the Soviet Union

For much of the postwar period the Federal Republic had no need to develop a separate policy towards the Soviet Union. It was unwilling to contemplate reunification with East Germany on the terms offered by the Soviet Union, and the Soviet Union was perceived primarily in terms of the threat it posed to German security. Responsibility for addressing that threat was a matter for NATO rather than for the Federal Republic.

This situation was dramatically altered by the reunification process. The German government, and Chancellor Kohl in particular, were very conscious of the role played by Mikhail Gorbachev in bringing about the change. This sense of indebtedness to Gorbachev was a feature of all Kohl's major speeches after 1989, and his shock at the attempted coup against Gorbachev in August 1991 was palpable.

The grounds for supporting Gorbachev were of course deeper than mere gratitude. Germany had a vital interest in the smooth completion of the Soviet military withdrawal by 1994, a withdrawal that could have been endangered by Gorbachev's replacement by hardliners. In addition the Federal Republic did not want to see total breakdown in the area, followed by mass migration.

Taken together, these factors encouraged the federal government to give Mikhail Gorbachev very strong backing. Conscious that the difficulties of the Soviet economy were too profound to be dealt with by Germany alone, Chancellor Kohl lobbied incessantly for the other Western powers, especially Japan and the United States, to share the burden of the economic transformation of the Soviet Union. The poor state of the US budget made a positive US response extremely unlikely and Japan still had territorial arguments with the Soviet Union. It was Kohl who insisted that Gorbachev make his ill-fated plea at the G7 conference in 1991 for a massive increase in aid. By 1991 Germany had provided over DM60 million in economic aid to the Soviet Union, approximately 56 per cent of all Western aid to date.

> However, in this decisive phase of developments, in this process of the opening of his huge country, we must not sit back as pure spectators saying that what is happening there is something on which we shall keep a watching brief and that later on when decisions have been made we will come in and help them. We must help them help themselves sensibly and feasibly. I am absolutely persuaded that this is vital at this point in time. This will help the Soviet Union to develop in a way that will ensure peace for us all. This is a point I have also made in Washington time and time again, because there are western voices suggesting something different. But I think any policy aimed at bringing about the dissolution of the Soviet Union as a whole is political folly (Kohl, 1991).

Kohl's support for Gorbachev led to major policy incoherence. Whereas German policy generally stressed self-determination, the federal government was very muted in its support for the Baltic republics and little pressure was exerted on the Soviet leadership to move quickly on that issue. 'The Soviet leadership will realise that in the end the right to self-determination will prevail' (Kohl, 1991).

The failed coup in August 1991 and the gradual break up of the Soviet Union occasioned some adjustments in German policy. Support for Gorbachev was reduced and support for Yeltsin increased, a change symbolised by his visit to Germany in November 1991. Hans-Dietrich Genscher announced Germany's recognition of the Baltic States on 28 August and called on the EU to move quickly to conclude association agreements with them.

The German strategy of pouring aid into the Soviet Union now looked even less sensible. In the absence of settled institutional structures, administrative competence and plausible programmes for economic reform, aid would simply disappear into a black hole. In this connection Germany's experience with the rather less daunting terrain of the five new Länder had been a salutary lesson for the federal government.

Germany and Russia in the Post-Gorbachev Era

A 'special relationship' with Russia of the kind that sometimes pertained in the historic past is no longer a possibility. In the nineteenth century Russia and Germany often shared a common interest in controlling Poland. In the Weimar period Germany and Russia, as the two excluded powers, shared a large number of common interests, especially in the area of security cooperation. At the time of reunification, there were some fears in the West that Germany and the Soviet Union would develop too close a relationship, a fear that was reflected in the word used to describe the Gorbachev–Kohl agreement concluded in Stavrapol in July 1990 – *Stavrapallo* – an allusion to the close and to some extent anti-Western Russian–German agreement of the interwar period symbolised by the Rapallo Pact. This was always a mistaken view but the dissolution of the Warsaw Pact and the Soviet Union has robbed it of what little credibility it possessed. Germany remains deeply integrated into the multilateral institutions, indeed the continuing participation of united Germany in NATO was a precondition (the Washington condition) for US support of reunification, while Russia has become largely isolated. Russia has to make the painful adjustment from being a superpower that was also a regional hegemon to a middle-ranking power. Possessed of enormous natural resources, it is nevertheless too poor for membership of the European Union ever to be a possibility. In contrast Germany, with its increased power resources, is becoming a more important international actor. With the collapse of the Soviet Union, the demise of Gorbachev and Russia's increasing economic difficulties the belief that Russia could make a positive contribution to a post-cold-war order has been gravely weakened. German–Russian relations are only rarely seen as an opportunity, it is rather a question of damage limitation and of minimising Russia's destructive potential.

Moreover the Russian factor greatly complicates relations with Central and Eastern Europe, especially in the security area. The difficulty of responding to Central European security worries without inflicting loss of face on Russia and disturbing the delicate balance of democratic forces in Russia in a way that would harm the pro-Western forces has fed into an interministerial dispute typical of the Federal Republic. Defence Minister Volker Rühe, a prominent member of the CDU, has given priority to the eastward expansion of NATO, an institution in which his ministry is securely anchored. The view from the Foreign Ministry gives much more emphasis to Russia. While it has scaled down its support for the Organisation for Security and Co-operation in Europe (OSCE), a favourite vehicle for Genscher and Gorbachev, it is playing down the priority of eastward expansion of NATO in favour of enlargement of the European Union. While the calming of Russian fears is essentially a flanking policy for Rühe, it is central to the perspective of the foreign minister. The resolution of this dilemma was also typical of the Federal Republic in that the coalition agreement of November 1994 deliberately avoided choosing between the alternatives. It was in any case clear that rapid NATO enlargement was not going to be ordained by the United States, the key player in the Atlantic alliance, until after the elections in the United States and Russia. Traditionally, in the area of European security when progress proves impossible, states turn to the Western European Union, and the Central European states were offered special status in the WEU as a result of a Franco–German initiative.

There are three further unresolved problems that continue to preoccupy Russian–German relations. German policy makers – coordinated by Horst Waffenschmidt, the state secretary in the Interior Ministry – saw in the loosening of structures contingent on the break-up of the Soviet Union an opportunity to staunch the flow of ethnic Germans to Germany by encouraging the refounding of the Volga Republic as a homeland for ethnic Germans. This hope quickly foundered on the rocks of local opposition, and despite contributing DM100 million per annum to deal with this issue very little progress has been made and policy makers now accept that the ethnic Germans in Russia are likely to end up, like their Rumanian counterparts, in Germany.

In the postwar settlement Königsberg, situated in the north eastern part of Prussia, was ceded to Russia. Since the collapse of the Soviet Union there have been various attempts by German conservative and refugee circles to raise the Königsberg issue. Ethnic Germans have been encouraged to settle there, a German–Russian House (a cultural/social club) has been opened with help from Germany, and German business circles have suggested the creation of an enterprise zone. These efforts have largely proved a failure. While some ethnic Germans have chosen to move to Kaliningrad, they mainly seem to regard this as a step on the way to the West and the concept of an enterprise zone is unlikely to prosper, given Russia's present chaos.

The German–Russian Partnership Treaty of November 1990 foresaw the return to Russia of all art treasures removed during the Second World War. This commitment was restated during Yeltsin's visit to Bonn in November 1991 and in the cultural agreement concluded in December 1992. Despite this very little progress has been made, and feelings of injured national pride have continued to grow on the Russian side.

A Global Role for Germany?

Drawing up a balance sheet of German power resources half a decade after German reunification, it is difficult to avoid the conclusion that they have increased (Bulmer and Paterson, 1996). Part of this increase can be explained by the decline of other powers, but there has also been an unmistakable increase in economic and diplomatic power resources. This increase has been enough to transform it into a 'European great power' (Schöllgen, 1994, p. 31) and 'Europe's central power' (Schwarz, 1994), but there must be real doubt about whether it yet fulfils the preconditions to play a global role.

Of course some things have changed. Germany has been a member of the Security Council of the United Nations since 1995, and the remaining difficulties in relation to Germany becoming a permanent member of the Security Council of the United Nations are procedural rather than directly political. Yet the barriers to a global role remain profound. In terms of diplomatic resources, not only can Germany obviously not be compared with the United States, but it is also much less well-endowed than Britain, with its Commonwealth connections and global experience, or even France. Its military forces, which are considerable in the European context, have neither the experience nor the equipment and organisation to play a global role and the successive efforts of the federal government to play an expanded role are clearly constrained by an adverse public opinion.

If Germany is to play an enhanced global role it can only really be as the external projection of its role as a trading state. Germany is now the world's most important exporting nation and the Deutsch-Mark is the second most important reserve currency. Germany's position as *economie dominante* in the European Union and its general commitment to multilateralism, however, sets quite narrow limits on German influence. Trade policy is an EU competence, and while Germany clearly has a major impact on EU policy it acts in concert with other members. It played a crucial role in the resolution of the GATT negotiations but, unlike the French government, without ever having to stress in any explicit manner its own particular interests. Germany is, of course, less bound by EU constraints on monetary policy and it normally plays a more obvious role in this issue. During recent years it has been an outspoken critic of budgetary indiscipline by the United States and the burdens this imposes on other states.

The Federal Republic has played a major role in helping shape the response of the West to the North–South problem. Willy Brandt acted as chairman for the North–South Commission whose reports in 1980 and 1983 shaped the debate on North–South issues. The Federal Government has however preferred, in line with its general commitment to a multilateral policy style, not to involve the Bundesbank – except in its role as protector of monetary stability and lender of last resort in the distribution of funds – but to operate through the International Monetary Fund, where its views have carried considerable weight. In recent years the federal government has made some effort to incorporate an ecological dimension into aid policy.

Conclusion

Some of the recent dilemmas facing German foreign policy seem to be mirrored in Kenneth Grahame's recently revived classic *The Wind in the Willows* (1908). The characters who live along the river bank (which could be interpreted as a metaphor for 'the Rhineland position') order their actions through a process of continuous consultation and are especially concerned to keep the economically much more powerful Toad of Toad Hall (who may be identified with Germany) firmly within the multilateral framework. In general, this succeeds but occasionally Mr Toad slips the multilateral leash and essays an *Alleingang* (solo effort). This, like the premature recognition of Slovenia and Croatia, always ends in disaster. In contrast to the river bank, the wild wood is portrayed as a very threatening neo-realist environment for the river folk where their multilateral conceptual maps are largely ineffective and cheque book diplomacy proves completely ineffective against the threat posed by the weasels. This represents a pessimistic reading of the prospects in Eastern Europe. The Wide World by contrast is much alluded to but very rarely encountered. *Wind in the Willows* concludes with Mr Toad, after a number of mishaps and the expenditure of a great deal of money and some use of force firmly restored to the path of multilateral virtue while the tamed inhabitants of the wild wood work as servants in the houses of the people of the river bank.

Half a decade on from the achievement of German unity, German foreign policy is still poised between the river bank and the wild wood. The collapse of the Soviet Union and its external empire has been quicker and more complete than almost anyone envisaged in 1990. France, Germany's most intimate ally, is clearly finding the run-up to economic and monetary union, the core of the Franco–German European project, increasingly difficult to sustain. Far-reaching change has been less pronounced, however, in Germany's relationship with the United States. There has indeed been a dramatic reduction in the number of US forces based in Germany, and the US involvement in the Gulf War was to some extent underwritten by Germany's cheque book, but overall the relationship is still more of a leader-led one than 'the partners in leadership' model first launched by President Bush just prior to reunification. As Russia continues to look less and less like a cooperative and positive shaper of the post-Yalta European order, Germany's predisposition to place increasing priority on a continuing US presence and nuclear protection are likely to be long-term features and there was little governmental enthusiasm about President Chirac's offer of access to the French nuclear deterrent. NATO, which had seemed to be ultimately destined for the institutional elephants' graveyard, remains and is like to continue to be the key German security institution, though flanked now by the Eurocorps

One of the ideas behind the expectation of a greatly increased international role for Germany was a belief that, in the post-Yalta situation, soft-power issues relying on economic muscle would become more central than the security issue that defined power in the Yalta system. However, while the central security issue of defence against the Soviet Union has been superseded, it has been replaced not by a harmonious civilian order but by a multiplicity of security threats of different kinds from zones of instability in Central and Eastern Europe, Northern Africa and the Middle East (see Chapter 10). Germany's capacity to address those issues in a meaningful way has increased, but at a glacial pace. Moreover Germany's continuing budget deficit and persistent economic difficulties have reduced the expectations, often unrealistic, about the way in which German soft power could be used as a widely available sticking plaster.

Despite the symbolic move of the capital from Bonn to Berlin in 1998, neither the German population at large nor the foreign party elites show any readiness to define a specifically German national position and abandon the practice established over four decades of making policy 'in Europe's name'. Within these parameters Germany will gradually assume a greater role, in particular as it will be constrained to lessen the degree to which it remains a strategic free rider, and also to manage the process of EU enlargement, in which Germany has the greatest interest. This gradual process of incremental change could be disturbed in three ways. If the United States were to reduce its international commitments in the very precipitate manner advocated by some congressmen, it would exacerbate tensions in Europe and place Germany in a very difficult position. This is a danger that the US administration continues to be very sensitive to and remains a very unlikely option, though 'burden shedding' by the United States will have an impact in the longer term.

A second shock could come from tensions inside the European Union. If France were to prove unable to sustain its commitment to Economic and Monetary Union and the Franco–German relationship, and the EU were then to develop towards the looser association of the type preferred by the United Kingdom, this could hardly fail to have an impact on Germany's profoundly multilateral policy-making style. While divergence's on the deepening agenda constitute one threat to Germany's foreign policy style and goals, expansion of the EU also presents difficulties. Germany has most to gain from the EU expanding towards the east and most to fear from instability in that area, and considerable bitterness might result if Germany is unable to move its EU partners towards enlargement. As we have already noted in relation to former Yugoslavia, German power will be most evident where European institutions prove too weak.

The final shock might come through deepening economic difficulties. Economic difficulties and continued budgetary deficits might make it impossible for Germany to continue to lubricate the EU mechanism through side payments, to make the contribution it does to stability elsewhere, especially in Eastern Europe through its generous financial transfers, or even to sustain progress towards economic and monetary union.

None of these eventualities can be wholly excluded, and indeed some elements of the third scenario are very likely. Germany's new situation has been summarised well by Timothy Garton Ash: 'The states' external dependencies have been decisively reduced, but the external demands on it have significantly increased, and the resources to meet these demands have not grown commensurately' (Garton Ash, 1994, pp. 72–3). So far the indications are that Germany will continue to maintain both its policy commitments and its policy style, but this could be reversed by policy choices of the United States, Germany's European partners or the performance of the German economy.

9

Germany and the European Union: From Junior to Senior Role

EMIL J. KIRCHNER

The twin goals of European unification and German reunification were, for forty years, not only a central plank of the Federal Republic's constitution but also the beacon of its foreign policy. Having reached one of these goals will Germany automatically pursue the other with the same vigour? The answer might not be clearcut. For a start, the sequence in which these goals were expected to be achieved did not accord with actual events. European unification was intended to come first in order to pave the way for German reunification. The fact that it happened the other way round has been the cause of some anxiety both within Germany and externally. That it should coincide with the disappearance of the Soviet Union as an external threat to the EU, a waning of the United States' commitment to Europe, a power vacuum prevailing in Central Europe, disproportionate German economic strength within the EU and the growing attraction of Germany for Central and Eastern European economies has given rise to further concern. Fears are also expressed about the new generation of Germans, who are less guilt-ridden by Germany's past, more self-assertive and used to economic success, especially as it is symbolised by the stature of the Deutsche Mark. Joining this new generation is an East German population that is more inclined to obtain economic benefits than to share them with other European partners. Put succinctly, with Germany as a successful and wealthy economy without an external threat, with the prospect of Germany becoming the prime trading partner of Central and Eastern Europe, and American overtures to become a 'partnership in leadership' in international affairs, why should Germany maintain its commitment to a unified Europe, which would first require a politically integrated European Union?

The case for a continued German commitment to European unification rests mostly on fears of the past, a view that Germany has done well, both economically and politically, out of EU membership, and a recognition that no European state can ensure its security either at home or abroad by fulfilling the classical tasks associated with national sovereignty. These views find particular resonance with Chancellor Kohl, who sees German reunification as the seizing of an historic opportunity for achieving European integration. They are also held by a significant proportion of German elites. The fear of repeating old mistakes, particularly with regard to the disastrous interwar attempt to play 'power politics' (*Schaukelpolitik*) with both its Western and Eastern neighbours, is deeply engrained in the perceptions of the German elite, as is the acknowledgement of gratitude to the EU for helping Germany's reintegration into the family of nations, for securing peace and stability and for promoting Germany's economic success. There is also a recognition among elites that existing levels of economic interdependence constrain state actions and require multilateral action, especially through the medium of the EU. In addition to elite consensus on European unification, there is a large degree of cultivated 'Europeanness' in the German population. The virtues of being 'good Europeans' were, and are, socialised via schools, churches and the media as being equal to or of greater importance than being German, and this has taken root in German value systems.

Doubts about the European Union

However, how deep these roots are and how far EU citizens, including Germans, are prepared to forego important national features in favour of European ones, such as in the monetary field, remains uncertain. There is therefore no guarantee that, even if governments are willing to pursue European unification on a larger scale, the public will conform. Within Germany, the EU and Europe as a whole circumstances have changed since 1990. With the completion of the internal market programme at the end of 1992, the EU may have reached a glass ceiling beyond which it cannot go, or if it does, it will not be as a cohesive unit or a stable enterprise. Clearly the introduction of economic and monetary union (EMU) raises more difficult and sensitive issues within the EU than did the Common Agricultural Policy, the Customs Union and the internal market. There is no indication that sufficient trust has yet developed among member states and their populations after nearly forty years of EU existence to support or reinforce such a big leap forward as EMU. Much of the EU's construction reflects the notion of *Gesellschaft* (society) rather than *Gemeinschaft* (community). Market operations are the main vehicle of Europeanisation but their contribution to political unification is subject to adequate levels of economic growth, if not economic prosperity. In the absence of such economic performance, and without any European symbols to compensate, there is a danger that nationalism will reemerge, and with it the threat of EU disintegration.

Whilst the German public, together with the Bundesbank and Bundestag, is insisting on stringent EMU convergence and maintenance conditions, and favours a linkage between EMU and political union, Germany's neighbours are finding these conditions a bitter pill to swallow. The Maastricht convergence conditions require national economic adjustments through cuts in public expenditure, some of which involve economic hardship, at least in the short term. Such hardship could spill over into political disruption at the national level and might also affect the European integration process generally. For Germany the success or failure of EMU would entail significant consequences. If it is introduced the German government will have to win public support and might also have to pay a financial price for bringing certain EU members into EMU, either via pressure on the Bundesbank on interest rate policy or greater EU budgetary contributions. The latter two could in turn have negative consequences for the German economy. Alternatively, failure to introduce the single currency might, by default, make the Deutsche Mark the strongest or dominant currency in Europe by the beginning of the twenty-first century, which, it is feared by some Germans, would create jealousy, competition and the reemergence of political confrontation among the European countries. Such a development could result in a decline of the single market, and a return of protectionism, nationalism and fragmentation.

Whilst there are still uncertainties over such issues as EMU, political union and EU enlargement to the east, the potential impact of these developments is beginning to become clearer within the EU. The aims and role of Germany in these developments will be the central focus of this chapter.

A Unified Germany Within the EU

The impact of German reunification on the EU can be described as a silent revolution. Rather than producing immediate visible alterations to EU institutions, decision making and policies, it has set in motion a process of change that, in a gradual way, is affecting relations between EU members and future EU development. The relatively unobtrusive element of German reunification reflects the speedy way in which the GDR was absorbed and the absence of any major EU institutional change to accompany this process. The increase in seat allocations in the European Parliament in December 1992 reflected a general redistribution in terms of size rather than a specific concession to Germany. German demands for a greater share of EU structural funds and a reduction in Germany's budgetary contributions, coupled with resentment at having to provide the lion's share of aid to Central and Eastern Europe, as well as having to absorb a disproportionate number of refugees from former Yugoslavia, were either expressed moderately or remained rhetorical. Germany has continued to be the largest net EU contributor, which meant that by 1996 the EU was costing the average German twice as much as a Netherlander and four times as much as a Briton. (*Economist*, 15 December, 1995, p. 46). It should be mentioned, however, that revisions within the European Regional Fund in 1993 meant that greater financial contributions could be, and were, made to the five new Länder.

Where the unified Germany did start to have a more marked impact was, on the one hand, Germany's insistence on EU recognition of Bosnia, Croatia and Slovenia in 1992, and on the other, the 'fall-out' of German reunification measures on the economies of its partners. Though Germany received strong criticism with regard to the recognition issue (see Chapter 8), partly because of the style in which it pushed recognition and partly because it refused to send combat troops to either the Gulf or Bosnia, the second factor had a greater impact. To finance reunification, large-scale borrowing and publicly financed projects took place. This fuelled domestic inflation in Germany that could only be controlled by increases in interest rates. Given the anchoring role of the Deutsche Mark within the ERM, this forced other members to keep their interest rates higher than domestic conditions required, and therefore delayed a much needed recovery. When the tension reached breaking point it occurred with much acrimony; Britain accused Germany of 'selfishness and uncommunitarian behaviour'. Undoubtedly this acrimony strengthened the position of 'Eurosceptics' in other EU countries, burdened the Maastricht Treaty ratification and generally soured relations among EU members.

The financial repercussions, together with the recognition incident, began to set the tone for growing changes in relations between EU members, especially the larger ones, and a reopening of old rivalries, particularly between Britain and Germany. Though it can be said that the latter was already visible in the initial reactions towards German reunification by leading EU figures, particularly Margaret Thatcher, Ruud Lubers and François Mitterrand, Mitterrand subsequently welcomed the event and saw it as an opportunity to pursue further European integration.

Germany's self-assumed 'watchdog' function after 1993, over strict adherence to the entrance and maintenance requirements of EMU, became another instance of Germany signalling that it had broken with its past habit of playing 'junior partner' in the launching of major EU initiatives; as it had, for example with the EMS initiative in 1979. This new tone again provoked accusations of German dominance of the EU.

There is no doubt that EMU poses difficult choices and that its introduction, due to its deflationary impact, is likely, at least in the short term, to lead to social, economic and political upheavals in many countries, which will put EU integration to a stern test. However, though worries over EMU will be a major concern for most EU countries, further political integration and EU enlargement, both advocated by Germany, will also raise anxieties about sovereignty. It is here that serious questions have been raised with respect to the appropriateness of linking EMU deadlines with progress on political integration and EU enlargement. Not only are the rationale and feasibility of such an undertaking questioned, but also whether Germany will be taking on more than it can cope with, or more than its public and partners will be willing to accept or feel comfortable about. At stake is not only whether Germany can convince its own public about EMU and how much it is prepared to help other EU members to meet the entry criteria, but how German action in the phasing in of EMU will be perceived by its partners. An EMU modelled on German monetary policy and instruments might be associated with greater German influence within the EU. The latter consequence, even if unintended, can be described as 'assumed power by default' and can be differentiated, as Bulmer and Paterson (1996, pp. 9–32) do, from a deliberately sought EU leadership role. It remains to be seen which of the two will become the more important in the process of dealing with EMU, political union and EU enlargement. What is clear, however, is that the more assertive German role is altering relations among EU members.

However the extent to which Germany becomes more assertive in the EU, either with EMU achieved or as a consequence of a failed attempt at EMU, depends as much on internal German factors as on external ones. The issue of EMU, especially with regard to the single currency, is causing serious concern both within Germany and in other EU member states. The fear of losing the Deutsche Mark has resulted in a fierce debate among the German public and has caused a significant amount of resentment; the Deutsche Mark is the only 'real' German national symbol. There is a danger that German public reluctance could persist, especially if this public perceives the 'Euro' to be less stable than the Deutsche Mark. Any concession by the German government on either the convergence or maintenance criteria for a single currency could therefore harden public objections and potentially give opposition parties, such as the SPD, extra leverage.

EMU: To be or not to be?

Germany's tough stand on the EMU convergence criteria is partly necessitated by the Bundesbank's insistence that it will not transfer its authority to a European Central Bank unless similar monetary conditions prevail at the EU level as prevail domestically. In the past the Bundesbank has shown a certain – understandable – reluctance to the idea of submitting its own powerful authority, together with a number of other national banks, to that of the European Central Bank; nor does it wish to collaborate in its own demise. However the criterion of tough adherence to the Maastricht guidelines is also recognised in Germany's ratification of the Maastricht Treaty, and reaffirmed in the Constitutional Court ruling of October 1993, which asks for the Bundestag's affirmation before German entry into a single currency. Partly, it is also dictated by the need to reassure an increasingly disgruntled German public that the Euro will be as strong as the Deutsche Mark, if not stronger. If no tough stand is taken, such dissatisfaction – together with a lack of Bundesbank support – could help the opposition Social Democrats to exploit any apparent weakness or softening of Germany's monetary policy and thus condemn the single currency and EMU as too risky and inflationary.

No doubt member states see virtues in an anti-inflationary policy and admire Germany's economic and monetary success. They are also attracted to the possibility of a zone of currency stability that will cover more than half the trade of its members and thus remove the risk of competitive devaluations. Stable exchange rates, low inflation and low interest rates would produce a boost to trade, which could lead to increased investment, job creation and increased output, quite apart from the substantial savings in transaction costs that a single currency would bring about. Overall, such a currency could improve the efficiency of the single market. But Germany's partners are also wary about the enormous hazards, both economically and politically, that adherence to such a policy would entail. To qualify for EMU a country must demonstrate conservative levels of public debt (60 per cent of GDP), budget deficits of no more than 3 per cent, low inflation and two years of exchange rate stability.

Meeting such conditions will be difficult, but maintaining them beyond entry might raise further problems. The Treaty of Maastricht envisages sanctions, including financial penalties, for countries that threaten to waver from the path of stability. When and how such sanctions should come into operation has been the subject of a proposal by the German finance minister, Theo Waigel. According to this proposal, participating states should make a voluntary pledge that, even during periods of economic difficulty, they will not exceed a maximum deficit of 3 per cent of GDP. In normal economic circumstances, however, the deficit target should be a maximum of 1 per cent of GDP. Sanctions should take effect if a country exceeds the deficit limits laid down in the Treaty of Maastricht. Within its budgetary planning or implementation, the country concerned would have to pay into the EU budget a non-interest-bearing stability deposit of 0.25 per cent of the country's GDP for each percentage point by which it exceeded the limit.

The downside of phasing in such measures is that cuts (for example in welfare programmes) that were not mitigated by higher economic growth could result in higher unemployment. This could lead to stagnation in parts of Europe, as well as heavy migration from these areas to other member countries, with consequent social upheaval. Furthermore, in periods of high unemployment tax revenues are lower, which means budget deficits are harder to cut, especially in the absence of currency devaluations, as foreseen in EMU. In December 1994, 10.5 million people were out of work – that is, one in ten workers in the EU did not have a job.

In situations of rising unemployment and growing cuts to public expenditure it might be expedient for governments to blame Germany for being high-handed or arrogant, too much concerned with its own domestic audience and too insensitive to disruptions of the economic, social and political fabric of other member states. Already *The Herald Tribune* (12 October, 1995) has described Theo Waigel's announcement that Italy was unlikely to meet the initial entry requirements of a single currency as 'German bullying'. Other critics see such attempts as deliberate and purposely intended to set high hurdles in order to prevent Germany's partners from clearing them, and then to blame them for wrecking EMU, when in actual fact it is German reluctance that is the cause.

In this context Helmut Schmidt, the former German chancellor, has delivered a series of warnings. In his opinion 'none of the governments – neither London nor Paris nor Bonn – understands the importance of monetary union' (Marsh, 1994). Unless the Deutsche Mark is replaced by a single European currency the German currency will one day be 'overwhelmingly strong'. This would eventually make the Germans 'masters' of the European Union – a position which, he says, would rebound on Germany by making it vulnerable to 'coalitions' of European states formed to curb its strength (ibid). This could result in the reemergence of competition, nationalism and old-fashioned power politics in Europe. Nationalism, as the enemy within, could replace the external enemy, for a long time the 'red menace' of the former Soviet Union, as the main threat to the existence of the EU.

Similar sentiments are expressed by Helmut Kohl, who argues that if the Deutsche Mark is left to itself and if German industry becomes stronger, Germany might become too powerful by the end of the 1990s. It thus might lose the political will to forgo monetary sovereignty in the process of establishing a single currency and a European Central Bank.

Yet it will be difficult for Germany to strike a balance between creating an EMU rigidly reflecting Bundesbank monetary policy and one loosely in line with such a policy. Too much insistence on the former might cause negative economic, social and political repercussions in other EU member states, as witnessed in the widespread strikes the French government encountered during the winter of 1995 as a consequence of preposals for substantial cuts in social expenditure; mainly to meet the Maastricht convergence criteria. This could substantially weaken the prospects of membership, denying some states the opportunity to become part of the critical mass of EU countries, and might undermine the success of the single market. Such a situation would neither promote the cause of further EU integration nor provide a platform for matching German reunification with European integration. On the other hand a more loosely constructed EMU might work in the short run but break down in the medium term. If the latter were to happen, this could have detrimental consequences for the EU as well as for Germany, where memories of currency bankruptcies of the thirties and forties are still alive.

The success of EMU will ultimately depend on whether the EU can make the idea relevant to its citizens. By 1995 there was little sign that a single currency had caught the public imagination. Instead the citizens of many countries feared for the safety of their welfare systems and the Germans the loss of their currency. Yet the fickle nature of public opinion was once again revealed in 1995, when two thirds of those Germans asked were opposed to the introduction of a single currency, but in the same survey the majority supported the Maastricht Treaty, of which the important component is, of course, irrevocable progress towards a single currency. Whilst this makes observers believe that the Germans do not know what they want, Wolfgang Schäuble, chairman of the CDU–CSU parliamentary party in the Bundestag, suggests that 'the soul of Germany is Europe, it is not the D-Mark' (*Financial Times*, 21 March 1996).

Yet it is not only German public opinion that has caused some anxiety. Further signs of erosion of national consensus on the single currency became apparent when Germany's six leading economic institutions called for a more flexible interpretation of the Maastricht criteria. In addition, leaders of the SPD declared they would make the single currency an election issue. They rejected accusations by the CDU and the FDP of 'cheap populism' by stressing that the SPD supported EMU. However, different motives seemed to prevail within the SPD leadership. Whereas Scharping and Lafontaine insisted that the SPD simply wanted to stress that it would be wrong to give up the Deutsche Mark for a European currency that was less stable, Schröder's call for a delay was more motivated by the potential exclusion of Italy. Schröder, who is on the right wing of the party, is minister–president of a Land that is one of the largest shareholders in Volkswagen, and therefore wants Italy included. His fear is that a loss of competitiveness in some of Germany's most important European export markets would result if a single currency, based on a hard core of five or six member states, were to appreciate against the currencies of those on the outside.

A delay in the introduction of EMU would put enormous pressure on the Deutsche Mark, either to revalue or to help ailing currencies in the ERM to meet the entry requirements. Already the Bundesbank is being seen as having to help prop up the French franc. A revaluation of the Deutsche Mark would be detrimental to German exports, an increase in which is much needed to revitalise the domestic German economy, particularly employment. Revaluation of the Deutsche Mark and subsequent depreciation of other currencies would also cause an

ERM realignment; monetary disorder rather than monetary stability could be the consequence. This would be particularly harmful in the run-up to the 1998 German elections. Given his commitment and dedication to EMU and political union, Kohl will be determined throughout 1998 to avoid monetary disorder, and to have a decision by late spring 1998 (or shortly before the French general elections in the summer of 1998) of those countries able to meet the EU entrance requirements, and to press for more, rather than fewer, political integration measures, given that this will be his last chance to fight for his long-cherished cause. He is of course hoping that France will be ready to join by that time, since an EMU without France or Germany would be unthinkable.

In view of this build-up to both the single currency and the German general elections, but also to counter growing scepticism within Germany towards the single currency, the Bundesbank and the German government called for a political campaign in Germany to improve the image of EMU. At the Madrid European Council, the European Commission was instructed to undertake an extensive publicity campaign in all member states, except Britain and Denmark, to promote the benefits of EMU. It was too early to predict whether such a campaign would succeed or fall victim to other factors such as strains within the governing coalition of CDU–CSU and the FDP. By the beginning of 1996 the FDP had staked its political survival on securing an early cut in income taxes and by insisting on eliminating the 'solidarity surcharge', which adds 7.5 per cent to the income tax bills of individuals and companies to finance the restructuring of the east German economy. Waigel had opposed such demands, fearing that such action could push Germany's budget deficit above the Maastricht ceiling of 3 per cent of GDP. Incidentally all EU countries except Luxembourg failed to meet this criterion in 1995.

The margin of error is therefore small and the potential for conflict great, both within Germany and between Germany and its partners. The potential difficulties between Germany and its partners partly result from Germany's past experience and are also influenced by geographical considerations. They centre on Germany's insistence on coupling EMU with progress on political integration and on pressing for a speedy EU enlargement to the east.

Political Integration: A Dream Too Far or the Price for having EMU?

There are at least three reasons why Germany is pressing for greater political integration. One is because it believes that EMU needs to be linked to federal fiscal measures that can only be secured through greater integration. The second is that a further strengthening of common foreign and security policy requires greater moves towards political unification. The third relates to a long-held German aim, anchored in Article 23 of the Basic Law, to bring about 'the realisation of a united Europe'. Due to their more practical implications, only the first two reasons will be examined here.

The attempt to link EMU to political integration measures can be seen as a compensation for relinquishing control of the Deutsche Mark, the most powerful German economic resource. This price, it is generally assumed, was extracted by France for its agreement to German reunification. Germany has long held the belief that France, whilst committed to fixed exchange rates, is either unwilling or unable to make the necessary economic and fiscal adjustments required for the proper functioning of fixed exchange rates or a European monetary policy. It has similar reservations about some other EU member states. The notion that fiscal discipline is a necessary condition for monetary stability is therefore implicit in Waigel's stability pact, which advocates deposits and fines. For such a system of deposits and fines to work, fiscal policies will have to be jointly supervised and coordinated, which will require a federal polity. The latter could legitimately impose deposits and fines.

This is a radical proposal. Taxation and spending go to the heart of national sovereignty. It is difficult to envisage many EU members, including those that are likely to enter EMU first time round, being willing to make such a commitment. Yet there is considerable insistence and widespread support among German elites to such a linkage. These include the views of Roman Herzog, the German president, for whom EMU is unthinkable without political union. Most importantly, it is also espoused by Hans Tietmeyer, president of the German Bundesbank. He argues that a community sharing a largely common destiny can hold together only if the common currency is embedded in a more broadly based and lasting political community; such a community would include acceptance of limits to national fiscal policy (Tietmeyer, 1996, p. 45). For him 'the destinies of currency and politics are closely intertwined' (ibid., 1996, p. 46). Indications such a linkage make observers fear that Germany will continuously tighten the entry and maintenance conditions for EMU, and therefore bring about a situation where only very few, and possibly an insufficient number of members will be able to fulfil the EMU criteria, which will represent fully fledged Germany monetary conditions, that is, EMU will become a clone of Germany features, policies and habits.

It is in this context that calls by Karl Lamers (1993) and Schäuble and Lamers (1994) for a federal state can be seen, with the European Parliament and the Council of Ministers as equal partners in a two-chamber legislature and the Commission having features of a European government. These attempts were intended to force France into making a clear decision in favour of a federalist and core-oriented EU. The latter would comprise five or six countries that were more willing to commit themselves to far reaching integration in the monetary, fiscal, budgetary, economic and social policy fields than other EU members. But France, under Chirac, seems to prefer the formation of *ad hoc* coalitions varying according to different problem areas and the prevailing circumstances. This would mean agreeing to EU jurisdiction on monetary policy in order to remove German monetary hegemony, but to prefer a system of variable geometry, for example a core of shared activities on other issues. Under the latter type of intergovernmental arrangement, France is prepared to support Germany's demands for the integration of the Western European Union into the EU and the creation of a European army. France also seems willing to change its long-held position on NATO, in that it now appears to share Germany's view that the creation of an independent European defence component should not be seen as an alternative to NATO, but more as a contribution to its strength. France may use this willingness and its offer for concerted nuclear deterrence to subdue Germany's pressure for more majority voting in the Council of Ministers, including the CFSP. Germany stresses, however, that no member state will be forced against its will by majority vote to take part in common military operations. On the other hand no single member state should have the right to block a policy decision that has been judged worthy by the majority. Germany, together with Britain and France, advocates double majorities: the majority of the represented population and a majority of the member states.

Germany would also prefer closer cooperation on common domestic and legal policy and would like EU-wide powers on asylum, visa and external border controls. It sees Europol as an instrument of critical importance for fighting international organised crime. But on these issues, as well as on majority voting and extended powers to the European Parliament, Germany is either opposed or insufficiently supported by other major players such as Britain and France. This has at times caused Kohl and Kinkel to warn that a drift back to intergovernmental cooperation would lead to institutional deadlock, for example allowing the pace to be dictated by the speed of the 'slowest ship in the convoy'. Such statements are partly targeted at the domestic audience. For example the German Constitutional Court, in the ratification of the Maastricht Treaty, stipulates the necessity for greater democratic control. However it is unclear to what extent the Court wants to check and approve of the legality of EU decisions and acts, and ensure that democratic accountability is observed in EU decision making (Ress, 1994, pp. 47–74). It is also uncertain how subsidiarity, the idea that decisions should be taken by bodies as close to the citizens as possible, will underpin German pressure for democracy and decentralisation within the EU.

However, Germany cannot design policy proposals only to suit its domestic audience or to conform to its own practice of federalism and subsidiarity. In line with the progress of EU integration, Germany, like other member states, knows that such proposals are only worth submitting if they have some chance of acceptance by other member states. As pointed out by Werner Link (1996, p. 23) it would be unrealistic of Germany's foreign policy on Europe if it insisted on an exclusive policy of integration. Furthermore it would be risky because it would create high expectations that, if unfulfilled, could give rise to a wave of anti-European sentiment. It might also promote objectives that could rekindle suspicions of 'a Germanisation of her partners' among other European countries. This means that Germany must place less emphasis on a federal Europe, an inner EU-core, increased powers for the European Parliament and the Commission. In other words, it must strike a balance between measures intended to improve the decision making and efficiency of the EU, while preserving the sovereignty and identities of the member states. However, whilst much of the 1996 Intergovernmental Conference negotiations might be characteristic of such a balance, the issue of a more effective common foreign and security policy (CFSP) and the eastward expansion of the EU, both high priorities for Germany, might turn out to be contentious, as will be illustrated below.

Enlargement: A Security Necessity or a German Ploy?

In spite of the fact that Germany provides 55 per cent of all payments by the G-24 nations to the Commonwealth of Independence states, it might be said that Germany's primary interest in its neighbours to the east is not so much economic as political: only 5.6 per cent of German exports go to Central and Eastern Europe (Schwarz, 1994, p. 125). There is a recognition by German elites that its pivotal role between East and West has been troublesome in the past, not only for Germany but for the rest of Europe too. Germany fears that the opening up of Europe may reawaken historical machinations in the Central and Eastern European region, with Germany once more as the pivot of instability between East and West. Germany is therefore primarily interested in extending the zone of Western security to its Eastern neighbours, both through EU and NATO membership. This would help to avoid, according to the Germans, a security vacuum to the east of NATO territory, between Russia, which is still a great power, and the territory of the European Union. In addition, it would diminish perceived risks to Germany's security from potential mass migration from East to West and from cross-border criminality. Interests in enhanced security and EU/NATO membership is, of course, shared by countries in Central and Eastern Europe. However Germany is also keen that Russia is not excluded from the search for a new European security system – and that the EU and NATO must try to find an inclusive arrangement with Russia.

By 1996 there was general support for an eastern enlargement, but it was coupled with anxiety. The Mediterranean countries and Ireland feared a loss of subsidies as a consequence. Britain was apprehensive about enlargement being coupled with greater political integration. France was exercised by exactly opposite considerations. It perceived two potential dangers. First, eastern enlargement might dilute the efforts to deepen the EU and embed Germany into a more integrated EU. Second, it might enable Germany to expand its economic and political interests disproportionately in these countries and to create potential voting allies for Germany in EU decision making.

Massive German aid programmes in Central and Eastern Europe (exceeding £30 billion since 1990) have aroused some suspicion, that is, that it was motivated more by hegemonic ambitions than by altruistic principles; that Germany sought the creation of satellites rather than fostering economic recovery, democratisation and political stability in these countries, or laying the foundation for eventual EU membership (Markovits and Reich, 1991). Similar criticisms had been raised in connection with Germany's insistence that Bosnia, Croatia, Macedonia and Slovenia be recognised in 1992, for example that Germany was encouraging the break-up of Eastern Europe into small states that would then be economically dependent on Germany.

It is precisely for these reasons that Germany is insisting on a linkage between the widening and deepening of the EU, in particular strengthening EU institutions, decision-making processes and improving the efficiency of the common foreign and security policy. However it needs to ensure that enlargement negotiations do not become derailed by rows over such issues as the European budget and the reform of the common agricultural policy. The latter might also involve demands by German farmers for compensation. Other concerns that might arise include the size of Germany's EU budgetary contributions and its aid programmes in Central and Eastern Europe. Whilst the cost of German reunification has made the German public more resentful about the country's relatively high budgetary contributions, future sharing of aid expenditure on Central and Eastern Europe might reduce Germany's costs in this specific area, or provide additional value for German payments. A similar sharing of refugee support costs would also please German taxpayers, who have provided for a particularly large number of Bosnian refugees (400,000).

German Interests: Intended and Unintended Consequences

The German government remains committed to the goals of European unification but it is confronted with internal constraints and external opposition. There is also a greater interaction between these internal and external factors than has been the case hitherto. Internally, there is considerable public scepticism about the single currency, combined with a reluctant Bundesbank, a SPD ready to pounce and a Bundestag with a gate-keeping function over entry to the single currency. These constraints have reinforced the German government's insistence on tough EMU entry and maintenance criteria, with the objective of making the Euro as strong as the Deutsche Mark. However the convergence criteria are causing economic hardship in Germany and other member states, provoking hostility about the price to be paid for a single currency. Germany has a very difficult balancing act to perform. It has to satisfy a sceptical German public and ensure the support of France and at least a minimum number of other member states, whilst avoiding criticism that it is bullying its partners into submission.

There is a danger that Germany might not be fully successful in any one or a combination of these tasks. Introduction of the single currency is scheduled for 1999, and any delay could terminally weaken the future prospects of such a project. This is partly because of the enormous monetary upheavals a postponement would unleash; partly because German industry might be less inclined to forego the Deutsche Mark in the future, especially in the event of the German economy becoming more powerful; and partly because opposition in other member states, especially Britain, to a single currency will probably grow. Such an outcome would undermine the internal market, strengthen the German economy, revive nationalism and reintroduce old-fashioned power politics to Europe. On the other hand the successful introduction of a single currency might force Germany into more of a leadership position than it or its partners feel comfortable with. It might also enhance German influence, either intentionally or unintentionally, if, as seems likely under these circumstances, the EU were to be modelled along German monetarist and federalist lines (Bulmer and Paterson, 1996, p. 31). The intentional element might be Germany's insistence on its own monetary system, and federal fiscal and subsidiarity principles, as well as its preference for an extension of *Ostpolitik* in foreign and security policy. The unintentional element could be member or potential member states attempting to emulate the German model, or, as suggested by Markovits and Reich (1991), being submissive to German interests.

Clearly, since 1990 Germany has both assumed a more assertive role and been given greater recognition by its partners as an influential state. This has resulted in a gradual alteration of power relations within the EU, which has particular relevance for Franco–German relations. Whereas France formerly considered itself in charge of political matters within the EU and Germany in charge of economic matters, increasingly Germany is taking the lead in both. Germany has moved from being a junior or copartner to a senior or lead partner in Franco–German EU initiatives. On the other hand the time has passed when a German government could present the result of policy negotiation within NATO or the EU as identical with German interests (Schwarz, 1996, p. 115). Nonetheless we will probably see an increasing number of unilateral German actions.

But this is not to imply that Germany seeks a neutral status or a *Sonderweg*. As Helmut Kohl (1996) suggests, 'A neutral Germany would isolate itself more and more – to the detriment of itself and its neighbours'. Nor is it an indication that Germany is seeking leading status or dominance. Rather, particularly with Kohl as chancellor, it will continue to promote collective EU action and to stifle the reemergence of national competition and power politics. Kohl consistently warns about the future by declaring that unless the EU constructs a 'stable house' it will drift apart and not get another chance. He also suggests that a new generation of German leaders will not be sufficiently aware of Europe's propensity for chaos. In line with this outlook, Germany has so far pursued a lead role in three respects: tough EMU entry and maintenance conditions; progress on political union and early EU admittance for the Czech Republic, Hungary and

Poland. On each it has to tread a careful line between domestic concerns, the reaction of its EU partners, and the cohesion and progress of the EU enterprise.

Given its demographic strength and economic clout, coupled with a lesser degree of consensus on the EU within Britain and France, Germany's role is likely to grow within the EU. It certainly appeared stronger in the run-up to the 1996 Intergovernmental Conference than it had during the one in 1991, when it had been more concerned with German reunification. Because of its geographic position and historical legacy, Germany sees the EU as a guarantee against repetition of past mistakes, and as an effective framework for peace and stability in Europe. It will therefore continue to support further economic and political integration.

10

'Of Dragons and Snakes': Contemporary German Security Policy

ADRIAN HYDE-PRICE

> We have slain a large dragon, but we now live in a jungle filled with a bewildering variety of poisonous snakes (Mueller, 1994, p. 536).

The demise of the Cold War and the subsequent reunification of Germany has fundamentally and irrevocably changed the nature of European security. For forty years Europe was riven in two by an Iron Curtain that ran through the heart of Germany and Berlin. Then in 1989–90 this bipolar structure unravelled with breathtaking speed as communist regimes imploded and the Soviet Union disengaged from Central and Eastern Europe. All the European states were profoundly affected by this *Zeitenwende* (era of change), and none more so than Germany. For four decades the Federal Republic constituted the front line in a global struggle between two nuclear-armed alliance systems, but today finds itself at the heart of a Europe without antagonistic blocs or deep-seated ideological divides. Indeed, for the first time in the history of the Teutonic peoples, Germany is at peace with its neighbours and no longer has any clear and identifiable enemy.

Contemporary German foreign and security policy is thus evolving in the novel context of a uniquely benign international environment. As former President Richard von Weizsäcker observed, 'For the first time [in history] we Germans are not a point of contention on the European agenda. Our uniting has not been inflicted on anybody: it is the result of peaceful agreement' (Joffe, 1991, p. 84). Yet at the same time new security concerns have appeared, and some long-suppressed problems have reemerged. Although the end of the East–West conflict has removed the threat of a nuclear Armageddon, other sources of tension

– particularly ethnonational conflict – have emerged in Europe. For Germany, therefore, a fearsome 'dragon' has at long last been slain, but the woods remain full of poisonous snakes. In this still troubled world, new demands and expectations have been focused on the German government. Many of Germany's allies and former enemies expect the reunited German state to assume a greater part of the burden for international peace and security. However memories of Nazi aggression linger in the minds of some of Germany's neighbours, and any apparent steps towards the 'renationalisation' of Germany's defence and security policies have been greeted with suspicion and concern. German security policy thus remains an acutely sensitive policy area, both within Germany itself and in the wider international system.

As a consequence of these conflicting pressures, German *Sicherheitspolitik* (security policy) since reunification in 1990 has exhibited elements of both continuity and change. The government of Chancellor Helmut Kohl has sought to respond to the changed international environment whilst at the same time reaffirming Germany's postwar alliance commitments. In the new post-Cold-War era, German security policy continues to confront many of the dilemmas it faced during the Cold War. These dilemmas, none of which are amenable to simple solutions or clear-cut choices, revolve around three multilateral organisations: NATO, the Western European Union (WEU) and the Organisation for Security and Cooperation in Europe (OSCE). The purpose of this chapter is thus to identify the elements of continuity and change in contemporary German security policy, and to explore the dilemmas faced by the government.

Germany and the European Balance of Power

Germany has long been the key to the European balance of power. From the 1648 Treaty of Westphalia (when the 'German question' emerged as a wider European issue) to the creation of the Bismarckian Reich in 1871, Germany was a weak and fragmented collection of states. It thus acted as axis around which the other great powers manoeuvred. The creation – through 'war and bloodshed' – of a Prussian-dominated *Kleindeutschland* (small Germany) signalled the emergence of a major new great power and produced a destabilising challenge to the European balance of power (Sheehan, 1996, p. 135). Germany's pivotal role was a consequence of two factors: its size, and its *Mittellage* (central geographical location).

Germany's size has long been perceived as a threat to its neighbours. 'What is wrong with Germany', A. J. P. Taylor once wrote, 'is that there is too much of it' (Taylor, 1967, p. 21). Following its unification in 1871 Germany became the largest state in Central and Western Europe. Only Russia in the East was larger, both geographically and in terms of population. However, in contrast to Russia, since the late nineteenth century the German economy has been arguably the most dynamic and productive in Europe. Industrialisation transformed Germany into the industrial and financial powerhouse of Europe. Germany, in the words of John Maynard Keynes, became the central support around which the rest of the European economy grouped itself, and 'on the prosperity and enterprise of Germany the prosperity of the rest of the continent mainly depended' (Wallace, 1990, p. 15). It also gave the Berlin government the wherewithal to build up a formidable military machine, harnessing Prussian militarism to the productive capacity of the *Ruhrgebiet* (Ruhr industrial area).

Germany's size and economic potency would not have been of such concern to the European great powers had it not also been for Germany's central geographical location. Few countries have as many neighbours as Germany. Situated at the heart of the European continent, straddling its major waterways (the Rhine and the Danube) and standing at the cross-roads between Latins and Slavs, Germany has long been destined to play a central role in European international relations. Its central position gives Germany political, economic and strategic interests in both East and West, and in part explains the nature of the 'German problem'. Indeed whilst some have ascribed the 'German problem' to national character (Thatcher, 1993, p. 791), more perceptive analysts have recognised that the 'Germany problem stems rather from its geography:

> unlike Britain, Russia, or the United States, the Germans lacked the space to work out their abundant vitality. Moreover, because of geography, Germany's vitality was an immediate threat to the rest of Europe. Modern Germany was born encircled. Under the circumstances, whatever the lesson of the wars between Germany and its neighbours, it cannot be found merely by analyzing the faults of the Germans (Calleo, 1978, p. 206).

If Germany's pivotal role in the European balance of power can be ascribed to its size and its geographical location, the threat it has at times posed to its neighbours can be attributed to its internal political complexion. The Germany that Bismarck forged from 'Blood and

Iron', and upon which Hitler constructed his 'Thousand Year Reich', was characterised by a propensity towards authoritarianism, militarism, intolerance and economic protectionism. It was Nazism – that 'unforgettable lesson of the perversion of the German presence in Europe' (Magris, 1990, p. 32) – that made Germany a threat to European civilisation, not simply the country's size or location. Indeed as the Czech President, Vaclav Havel, has acknowledged, 'Germany can be as large as she wants to, as long as she stays democratic' (Hyde-Price, 1996, p. 207).

The Federal Republic and Cold War Europe

The crushing of the Third Reich in May 1945 created a qualitatively new strategic and political environment in Europe. A bipolar structure of power emerged in which Germany became (in the words of a British Foreign Office memorandum of the time) the 'pawn which both sides wished to turn into a queen' (Moreton, 1987, p. 32). Divided Germany became the focus of the East–West conflict in Europe, and each of the two German states were firmly integrated into their respective alliance systems. This fundamentally changed the geopolitics of Germany, and in the eyes of some, seemed to provide a solution to the problem of a too-powerful German state at the heart of the European continent. Rather than being united in one large and vibrant country located at the heart of Europe, pursuing their *Sonderweg* (special path) between East and West, Germans now found themselves divided into two states, each of which constituted the front line in a new global struggle between antagonistic nuclear-armed alliances.

For Germans in the Federal Republic, the Cold War proved a mixed blessing. On the one hand the bipolar division of Europe – with the *Spaltung* (division) of Germany and Berlin at its core – transformed the perception of the Germans in the eyes of their fellow West Europeans: from being perpetrators of the recent war, they became the victims of Soviet aggression. Moreover, by aligning itself with the transatlantic community and committing itself to the process of West European integration, the Federal Republic was able regain much of its sovereignty – albeit in a multilateral context. On the other hand the Cold War violated the national and democratic rights of the German people. It also hung a sword of Damocles over Germany in the shape of the greatest concentration of nuclear and conventional military forces the world has ever seen.

All told the Cold War had a profound and deep-seated impact on German political, military and strategic thinking. It transformed Germany's 'strategic culture' so extensively that postwar German security police bore little if any similarity to the military and security policies of previous German states. Two features of postwar German security policy deserve attention. The first was its multilateralism. From the very start, German security policy – indeed its foreign policy in general – was characterised by a pronounced commitment to multilateralism. The federal government, conscious of the lingering suspicion harboured by its neighbours and former enemies, sought to pursue its own national interests through multilateral cooperation with its new Western allies. Indeed *Westbindung* (anchoring in the West) became part of the very *raison d'être* of the Federal Republic (Juricic, 1995, pp. 111–12). West Germany subsequently became one of firmest supporters of both the European integration process and the Atlantic Alliance. Multilateralism also provided the means of regaining its sovereignty in the postwar period, and has subsequently become deeply internalised in the contemporary German mind. As Jeffrey Anderson and John Goodman have argued, precisely because 'the Federal Republic was a semi-sovereign state operating within a bipolar system, the country was forced to rely almost entirely on international institutions to achieve its objectives' (Anderson and Goodman, 1993, p. 24). Yet despite the instrumental origins of its commitment to multilateralism and institutional cooperation, the Federal Republic has developed 'a reflexive support for institutions' which has become 'one of the principal legacies of the Cold War period':

> Over the course of forty years, West Germany's reliance on a web of international institutions to achieve its foreign policy goals, born of an instrumental choice among painfully few alternatives, became so complete as to cause these institutions to become embedded in the very definition of states' interests and strategies (Anderson and Goodman, 1993, p. 60).

The second distinctive feature of postwar German security policy has been its commitment to deterrence rather than defence, coupled with an emphasis on the political rather than the military dimensions of security. The terrible legacy of Nazism and the trauma of total defeat in war led many Germans to reject militarism and advocate peaceful modes of international intercourse. These feelings were reinforced by the 'civilising' impact of democratic politics, a rising standard of living and a social market economy that tempered economic efficiency with social justice. They also found expression in the Basic Law, which sought to create constitutional safeguards against renewed German aggression. The result has been the creation of very distinctive strategic culture characterised by a 'studied a military, i.e., purely political, understanding of security policy';

> The interpretation of NATO strategy as a political means to avoid war by the threat of nuclear retaliation was portrayed positively in contrast to 'war-fighting strategies', which were declared to be out-of-date in the nuclear age . . . . In the popular version of this argument, the mission of the Bundeswehr would be seen to have failed as soon as the first shot was fired (Stratman, 1988, pp. 97–8).

This a military strategic culture contrasts starkly with Germany's pre-1945 strategic culture, and reflects the far-reaching changes that have taken place in West German society and politics. The influence of this distinctive strategic culture on postwar German security policy has been profound, and continues to colour the political leadership's approach to security issues on the post-Cold-War world.

West German security policy after 1949 was built on three key planks. First, a transatlantic alliance with Washington, and integration into NATO (the Federal Republic joined NATO in 1955, and since then the Alliance has provided the bedrock of West German security; Kaiser 1995). Second, a West European alliance with Paris, and integration into the European Economic Community and the Western European Union (the Franco–German axis was formally institutionalised in the 1963 Treaty of Friendship and Cooperation, and the French and German governments have consistently coordinated their European policy in order to further their shared commitment to European integration). Third, a policy of detente towards the Soviet Union and the Warsaw Pact countries, including East Germany – a policy that became most pronounced with the adoption of *Ostpolitik* in the late 1960s and 1970s, and achieved institutional expression in the Conference on Cooperation and Security in Europe (CSCE) (Garton Ash, 1993).

From the late 1960s the dilemmas at the heart of German security policy became more apparent, as tensions between these three policy orientations became increasingly more pronounced. The policy of close alliance with the United States and commitment to NATO was not wholly compatible with the Franco–German 'tandem' in Europe, given France's aspirations to create a more autonomous West European defence identity. Similarly, tight integration into the Western Alliance made the pursuit of detente with the East more difficult. Nonetheless these underlying tensions were largely suppressed given the overarching security imperatives of the East–West conflict.

Germany and the Post-Cold-War Security Agenda

For four decades West German security policy was dominated by one overriding concern: the perceived threat posed by the concentration of Soviet and Warsaw Pact armoured forces in Eastern Europe. This was the dragon that preoccupied the minds of the West German public and politicians, and provided the rationale for the *Bundeswehr* (federal army) and West Germany's alliance commitments within NATO and the WEU. The slaying of this dragon has thus raised questions concerning the future aims and concerns of German security policy, and indeed the very purpose of Germany's armed forces.

Yet as we have seen, although Germany today enjoys a uniquely benign security environment, violent conflict remains endemic in the wider international system, whilst in Europe new security problems have arisen. The new security agenda is no longer dominated by one single, overriding security 'threat'; rather it is composed of a series of potential 'risks' and 'challenges'. What is more, not only are these new security concerns increasingly diffuse, multifaceted and intangible, they are increasingly concerned with the non-military dimensions of security. They are, in other words, neither military in nature nor amenable to military solutions. Rather they are economic, social, political or environmental in character. As the federal president, Roman Herzog, observed in March 1995, many threatening instabilities are no longer to do with the balance of power or geopolitical concerns:

> Social, ecological and cultural destabilisation present additional security risks, which in the long-term are scarcely less dangerous than military threats. Meanwhile the list of these risks has become well-known: population explosion, climate change, economically-motivated migrants, nuclear smuggling, the drugs trade, fundamentalists of different colours, genocide, the collapse of state authority (Herzog, 1995, p. 161).

Of the various risks and challenges on the new security agenda, one prominent concern is the residual military arsenal of the former Soviet Union. The Russian Federation remains a major military superpower with substantial conventional and military assets. Even though the operational effectiveness of the Russian army has been called into question by the conduct of its campaign in Chechenya, Russia's military strength continues to cast a long and dark geopolitical shadow over the European continent. This, coupled with the continuing political instability of many post-Soviet republics and the danger of nuclear proliferation, will be a major security concern for Germany until well into the twenty-first century.

A second major concern for the federal government is the security implication of the resurgence of ethnonational conflict in much of Eastern Europe and the Balkans. The collapse of communism and the socioeconomic costs of transforming authoritarian communist systems into democratic market-orientated societies, has fuelled long-suppressed historical animosities and kindled new patterns of ethnic, religious and national conflict. As the bitter fighting in former Yugoslavia and around the fringes of the former Soviet Union demonstrates all too vividly, ethnonational conflict has emerged as one of the most pressing concerns on the European security agenda (Hyde-Price, 1991, pp. 55–9). The federal government's worry is not only that the intercommunal conflict could spread across the often arbitrarily delineated borders in the post-communist East, but that such conflict will encourage further waves of refugees seeking security and prosperity in Germany's social market economy.

Thirdly, there are security concerns arising from developments in the wider international system. Germany is a major trading nation and cannot but be concerned about potential threats to supplies of vital raw materials, markets and maritime trade routes. Technological developments also mean that the international system is increasingly subject to global security concerns, above all the spread of ballistic missile technology coupled with the proliferation of chemical, biological and nuclear weapons. On top of this Germany remains concerned about the problems of international terrorism (especially state-sponsored terrorism), economically motivated immigration from North Africa, the eastern Mediterranean and Asia, and the instability generated by the appalling levels of poverty and underdevelopment in many countries in the South. Many of these international security concerns are focused on the emerging southern 'arc of crisis', which stretches from the Balkans and the Eastern Mediterranean, through the Middle East and the Persian Gulf, to the Mahgreb and the North African littoral (Federal Ministry of Defence, 1994).

Germany therefore faces a radically changed security environment. The Cold War was indisputably unjust and morally indefensible, but the bipolarity it engendered was at least predictable and stable. The collapse of communism has undoubtedly opened up the prospect of a further spread of democratisation and market economics throughout Europe and beyond, but it also threatens to lead to renewed multipolar instability, greater uncertainty and a proliferation of small-scale 'low-intensity' conflicts. Thus, as Karl Kaiser has written

> A united Germany free of the East–West confrontation on its soil and now one of the world's wealthiest democracies, must face a novel and difficult task: to reconcile its foreign policy traditions with the new responsibilities that inevitably accompany its enhanced position and require the – sometimes unpopular – use of its political, economic and military resources in partnership with others to preserve peace on an unstable globe (Kaiser, 1991, p. 205).

NATO: The Bedrock of German Security

Multilateralism, as we have already seen, is one of the distinctive features of German security policy. As the German government seeks to respond to the changing demands and challenges placed upon it by the post-Cold-War security agenda, it is doing so within a firmly multilateral context. Although its foreign and security policy is being conducted within a dense institutional framework composed of a series of regional, European and international organisations, three institutions stand out in importance. These are NATO, the European Union/WEU and the OSCE (formerly the Conference on Security and Cooperation in Europe, CSCE). In contrast to many of its allies and partners who wish to privilege one or other of these organisations, the German government advocates an interlocking network of institutions without any pronounced or overarching hierarchy between them. Yet postwar FRG security policy was based first and foremost upon NATO.

From its very first hours, the fledgling Federal Republic was reliant on the transatlantic alliance for its security and territorial integrity. After becoming a member of NATO in 1955, the the Federal Republic played an increasingly important role in the Alliance, both as a base for forward-deployed NATO forces, and as a major contributor to the conventional military strength of the sixteen-nation alliance. Although the German government has collaborated with France in seeking to develop a European defence and security identity, and has also been keen to see the development of a more cooperative European security system based on the CSCE/OSCE, this has not yet resulted in any significant weakening of Germany's commitment to NATO. Even with the end of Cold War, therefore, the NATO alliance remains the bedrock of German security policy.

There are four main reasons why the German government remains so resolutely committed to NATO. First, the alliance provides an invaluable security guarantee against a resurgent and revanchist Russia. It also offers an insurance policy in the event of instability in the former Soviet Union generating large-scale military conflict in the East. Second, German participation in NATO's integrated military command provides a very visible demonstration of its continuing integration with the West and its commitment to multilateral defence cooperation. Third, the German government enjoys a close relationship with the United States (as 'partners in leadership'), and remains convinced that a strong US military commitment to Europe is essential for the peace and security of the continent. Finally, NATO is seen as a tried and tested alliance based on democratic principles, and one that makes a vital contribution to the security and stability of the wider European continent. Although there are some Germans who favour the development of a common European defence and security policy, or an OSCE-based collective security system, most are unwilling to risk giving up an established bulwark of security until a more viable security structure has been created.

Yet whilst NATO remains the bedrock of German security policy, a broad consensus has developed since reunification that the alliance must significantly reform its structure and functions if it is to remain relevant to the changed security environment of post-Cold-War Europe. To begin with, there is broad agreement in Germany that NATO must become a more *European* organisation. The belief that the Europeans need to assume a greater responsibility for their own defence is widely held on both sides of the Atlantic. The German government has therefore supported the idea of a stronger 'European pillar' within the alliance, based primarily on the WEU. The problem with this, however, is that building a more cohesive 'European pillar' risks undermining the United States' self-styled 'leadership role' NATO. The worry is that by strengthening the political cohesion and operational effectiveness of the WEU – which also serves as the 'defence arm' of the European Union – Washington may increasingly feel marginalised within the North Atlantic Council, and may therefore lose interest in maintaining a substantial commitment to European security. Managing the tension between the transatlantic alliance and the development of a common European security and defence policy has been a major concern of the German government in recent years, and is an issue to which we will return below.

The second set of changes to NATO championed by the Germans concerns the alliance's relationship with the countries of the former communist East (Hyde-Price, 1996, pp. 243–53). The German government was a prime mover behind NATO's 'London Declaration' of July 1990, which, amongst other important changes, offered to extend 'the hand of friendship' to its former enemies in the Warsaw Pact. Since then Germany has actively encouraged the development of a more complex network of bilateral diplomatic and political links between NATO on the one hand, and the new democracies of the former Soviet Union and Eastern Europe on the other. For example, in October 1991 Hans-Dietrich Genscher, in a joint initiative with his US counterpart, James Baker, proposed the creation of an institutionalised forum for regular high-level consultation and discussion between the NATO sixteen, the USSR, the three Baltic states and the countries of Eastern Europe. This US–German initiative was formally endorsed by the Rome NATO summit in November 1991, which agreed to establish a 'North Atlantic Cooperation Council' along the lines of the Baker–Genscher plan. By strengthening political dialogue across the former East–West divide the German government hopes that greater mutual understanding and tolerance can be fostered. This is something very much in the interests of Germany, given its geographical proximity to potentially unstable countries in the former communist East (Rühe, 1993, p. 135).

In the spring and summer of 1993, influential voices from within the ruling coalition could be heard arguing for the selective eastward expansion of NATO. In particular it was suggested that the countries of East Central Europe should be offered early membership of the alliance in order to bring greater security and stability to the region. This caused growing anxiety in Moscow (thereby undermining Germany's other security interest, namely the construction of an OSCE-based pan-European system of cooperative security), and was coolly received in a number of other NATO capitals. Instead of offering the East Central Europeans either firm security guarantees or the promise of early membership of the alliance, a new initiative was launched. This was the 'Partnership for Peace' scheme, which was formally inaugurated in January 1994 and offered individual countries from the former communist East tailor-made packages of bilateral military cooperation with NATO. It was designed to prepare some of the new democracies for membership of NATO, and to consolidate the emerging patterns of functional military cooperation and security dialogue the alliance had been advocating since the end of the Cold War. The Partnership for Peace scheme was warmly embraced by Germany, which had been fully involved in a series of joint military exercises with the cooperation partners from the East.

The third set of changes sought by Germany within NATO have been to the organisation's military strategy and force structure. Germany played an important role in shaping NATO's far-reaching 'Strategic Review', a review made necessary by the withdrawal of Soviet troops from Central and Eastern Europe and the disbandment of the Warsaw Pact. The Strategic Review was completed in late 1991, and subsequently NATO's 'New Strategic Concept' was adopted at the November 1991 Rome summit. This advocated a greater reliance on reinforcements in the event of war, and smaller, more mobile stationed forces configured in multinational corps (Weisser, 1992). The subsequent creation of a Rapid Reaction Corps was welcomed by the German government, although the leading role assigned to British forces within it was the source of some contention. Of considerable importance for German domestic opinion was the statement in the London Declaration of July 1990 defining nuclear weapons as 'weapons of last resort', and the call for the negotiated limination of all short-range, ground-launched nuclear weapons. The new strategic concept also reduced the emphasis on maintaining a robust ladder of nuclear escalation. This removed what had been a major bone of contention between Germany and some of its NATO allies (particularly France and the United States), and helped diffuse one of the most divisive aspects of NATO's military strategy and force posture. Today the issue of most concern to both German public opinion and German policy makers is not NATO's nuclear strategy, but rather the risks of nuclear proliferation arising from the disintegration of the former Soviet Union.

Towards a European Defence and Security Identity?

Whilst NATO remains the bedrock of German security policy, the German government is also an enthusiastic proponent of a more pronounced 'European defence and security identity'. The precise meaning of this phrase remains institutionally ambiguous and politically contentious. Nonetheless, for the ruling coalition it means the fostering of a more consistently multilateral approach to foreign and security policy issues by EU members, and the gradual development of an operational European military capability. Chancellor Kohl has consistently pursued this line since late 1989. He joined with former President Mitterrand to advocate an accelerated transition to political union within the European Community (in joint initiatives issued on 18 April and 6 December 1990), and has called repeatedly for the development of a common European defence and security policy. This was reflected in the Maastricht Treaty, which announced the formation of a 'Common Foreign and Security Policy', which 'may in time include defence'. The Treaty also recognised the WEU as 'an integral part of the development of the European Union', which may ask the WEU 'to elaborate and implement [the EU's] decisions and actions . . . which have defence implications'. A declaration on the WEU attached to the Treaty also noted the member states' intention to 'build up the WEU in stages as the defence component of the Union'. As the 1996 Inter-Governmental Conference drew nearer the German government made it clear that it would like to see a further strengthening of the EU's common foreign and security policy, 'of which a common European defense policy and defense force must form an integral part' (Seiters, 1995, p. 6). Germany, in tandem with France, is also the driving force behind the 'Eurocorps', a multinational force of 35 000 that became operational in 1995.

The German government recognises that these 'Europeanist' initiatives have caused unease in Washington, London and other more 'pro-Atlanticist' capitals. Bonn has had to work particularly hard to convince the Americans, British and Dutch that the Eurocorps is not a threat or rival to NATO. Chancellor Kohl believes that the tension between these two seemingly contradictory approaches to European security – Atlanticist and Europeanist – can be resolved through the medium of the WEU, which he envisages as the bridge between NATO and the EU. For this reason the Germans have welcomed the NATO decision of January 1994 to create 'combined joint task forces' (CJTF). These will be command and control structures within NATO's integrated military command structure, which will be 'separable but not separate'. It is planned that the CJTFs could then be placed under a WEU operational command in order to allow the WEU to conduct humanitarian and peace-keeping operations (the so-called 'Petersberg Tasks' defined by the June 1992 WEU Petersberg Declaration).

The German government thus hopes that by formulating ambiguous statements on the role of the WEU and encouraging the formation of the CJTFs (a development that is proving very difficult to realise in practice) it can overcome the tension between its commitment to NATO and its desire to see a more coherent and effective European defence and security entity. But this position may well prove increasingly hard to sustain in the medium to long term. As the United States has pointed out, the decisive issue is where security decisions are taken: in the Atlantic Alliance (which would leave the United States as *primus inter pares*), or in the EU/WEU(which would exclude the United States, along with non-EU NATO members such as Norway and Turkey, whilst including non-NATO countries such as Sweden, Austria and Finland). At some stage in its development, therefore, a robust security and defence dimension within the EU would inevitably undermine the current centrality of NATO to German security.

For some in Germany this would be a very welcome development. Although the dominant school of thought within the German security community has been Atlanticist, a significant minority of German 'Gaullists' have advocated an unambiguously Europeanist approach. Europeanists can be found on both sides of the political spectrum, from anti-Americans in the SPD to conservative nationalists in the CDU. They would like to see NATO replaced by an autonomous European security organisation, analogous to the failed European Defence Community (EDC) of the early 1950s.

Although there is undoubtedly broad support for a robust common European foreign and security policy (including defence) in Germany, such overtly Europeanist perspectives remain marginal to the security debate. The central aim of the current German government is to manage the dilemmas of its security policy, which aspires to be both Atlanticist and Europeanist at the same time. Whilst NATO remains the only tried and tested collective defence alliance, and the role of the WEU continues to be shrouded in a studied ambiguity, these dilemmas will be easy to manage. But if transatlantic relations were seriously to deteriorate, or if European integration were to result in an effective common foreign and security policy, including defence, then the dilemmas at the heart of German security would become virtually impossible to conceal. At that point, Germany would be forced to make some tough decisions concerning the very foundations of its security policy.

The OSCE and a Cooperative Security System?

The OSCE (Organisation for Security and Cooperation in Europe) began life in 1975 as the CSCE (Conference on Security and Cooperation in Europe). Since its formation in Helsinki at a time of blossoming detente in Europe, the Federal Republic has been one of the staunchest supporters of the CSCE process. From Germany's perspective, the CSCE provided an ideal pan-European framework for regulating the East–West conflict and provided a welcome multilateral forum for pursuing its Ostpolitik.

With the end of the Cold War the CSCE acquired a new lease of life. In Germany there was a widespread feeling that, freed from the debilitating effects of the East–West conflict, the CSCE would finally be able to fulfil its promise as the institutional setting for new forms of pan-European cooperation and interaction. Hans-Dietrich Genscher, the long-serving foreign minister of the time, was a determined advocate of the CSCE, and strongly believed that the CSCE could provide an invaluable framework for integrating the former communist states into a new, more cooperative security structure. Genscher therefore played an important role in outlining ideas for the 'institutionalisation' of the CSCE following the end of the East–West conflict. This was achieved at the Paris Summit of CSCE Heads of State and Government in November 1990. As well as providing the CSCE with a number of permanent institutional structures, the grandly named 'Paris Charter for a New Europe' also codified a series of principles for the conduct of interstate relations and human rights.

The Paris Charter reflected the mood of tremendous optimism that swept Europe in the wake of the collapse of communism. However, as ethnonationalist conflicts erupted in the Balkans and around the fringes of the former Soviet Union, this mood of optimism gave way to a deepening sense of angst and foreboding. This was reflected at the CSCE summit in Helsinki in the summer of 1992, which issued a more sober-sounding document called 'The Challenges of Change'. From then onwards the CSCE focused primarily on early warning, preventive diplomacy and crisis management. The established place of the CSCE in Europe's post-Cold-War security architecture was acknowledged in December 1994 at the Budapest Summit, when the CSCE was renamed the Organisation for Security and Cooperation in Europe.

Throughout the years since the end of the Cold War the German government has been a consistent supporter of the CSCE process, and has encouraged the institutionalisation of the CSCE/OSCE. For Germany, the OSCE provides a forum for developing new forms of cooperative security, and offers an institutional framework for addressing the legitimate security concerns of Russia. Germany is unwilling to countenance Russia's plans for the establishment of a collective security regime that would subject NATO and the WEU to OSCE decisions, but it does believe that the OSCE fulfils five key functions. First, it provides a forum for promoting and codifying common standards, values and norms of behaviour, particularly in the sphere of human rights and the peaceful resolution of conflicts. Second, it offers a series of mechanisms for the continuous monitoring of human rights, both for individuals and for national minorities. Third, it acts as a forum for promoting military transparency, arms controls and confidence- and security-building measures, thereby 'reducing dangers of armed conflict and of misunderstanding of miscalculation of military activities which could give rise to apprehension'. Fourth, it provides a framework for pan-European multilateral diplomacy across a comprehensive range of issues. Finally, it is developing instruments for preventive diplomacy, conflict avoidance and crisis management (Höynck, 1994).

Thus the mainstream German view of the OSCE is that it constitutes an important supplement to NATO and the EU/WEU, within a pluralist, non-hierarchical and multidimensional European security system. There is, however, a minority school of thought that finds its adherents primarily amongst radicals on the political left. This minority envisages a much more ambitious role for the OSCE as the institutional basis of a pan-European system of collective security, replacing the Atlantic Alliance and making a European defence and security entity superfluous. Thus, for example, Egon Bahr has called for the transformation of the OSCE into a regional equivalent of the United Nations, with a European 'security council' (capable of taking decisions on the basis of qualified majority voting) and European peace-keeping forces to intervene when necessary (Rotfeld and Stützle, 1991, p. 79).

Such a far-reaching transformation of the nature and purpose of the OSCE is unlikely in the foreseeable future, given the vested national interests involved. This leaves the OSCE without the necessary decision-making procedures or enforcement mechanisms that a robust and viable system of collective security would need. The dominant German view is therefore to support the further institutionalisation and development of the OSCE as a forum for cooperative, rather than collective, security, within a multifaceted and non-hierarchical European security architecture. This approach was embodied in the German–Dutch proposal for the agenda of the then CSCE Summit in Budapest, which called for the further institutionalisation of the CSCE with the aim of creating a common CSCE security area.

The Bundeswehr and Out-of-Area Operations

One of the most contentious issues on the German security agenda today is the future role and operational tasks of the federal army (*Bundeswehr*). Whilst there is no significant domestic political constituency for an autonomous national force-projection capability, there is a growing feeling that Germany needs to be able to participate in multinational crisis management by military means when necessary (Schlör, 1993, p. 53). The Gulf War proved a rude shock to many Germans. Constrained legally and politically from deploying federal forces outside the NATO area, Germany was left in the secondary role of paymaster and diplomatic cheerleader for the Allied coalition in the Gulf. This was a role that did not sit easily with Germany's self-professed desire to share with its allies the responsibilities of maintaining international peace and stability. Since then Germany has faced increasing domestic and international calls to face up to the issue of using the federal army for multilateral peacekeeping and crisis management operations outside the NATO area.

Given its desire both to be seen as an active and responsible member of the international community, and to bolster its claim to a permanent seat on the UN Security Council, the government of Chancellor Kohl has been keen to expand the federal army's out-of-area activities to include UN-mandated peacekeeping operations. However this has been resisted by the opposition Social Democrats, who have been able to prevent a constitutional amendment to the Basic Law. The government has therefore adopted an 'inch-by-inch' approach, committing the forces to constitutionally less contentious and operationally safe 'humanitarian missions'. German military forces have consequently been involved in UN-sanctioned operations in places as far apart as Kuwait, Cambodia, Croatia, Kenya, Somalia and in the Adriatic (Kamp, 1993).

The lingering constitutional Ambiguity concerning the issue of the federal army's out-of-area role was finally clarified in mid 1994. The ruling CDU's coalition partner, the FDP, decided to test the legality of the government's 2 April 1993 decision to authorise the participation of German crews in AWACs (airborne warning and control systems) deployed to enforce the UN-mandated 'no-fly' zone over Bosnia. The Federal Constitutional Court in Karlsruhe ruled on 12 July 1994 that the deployment of AWACs was permissible because failure to participate would have jeopardised the confidence of other NATO members. However, although there is now no constitutional impediment to federal army participation in UN, NATO and WEU missions (subject to parliamentary approval), the issue remains politically sensitive. Whilst most Germans accept the need for the army to participate in peacekeeping operations, there is much less support for combat missions, even if they are sanctioned by the UN or the OSCE. For this reason Germany has continued with its 'inch-by-inch' approach towards an out-of-area role for the army whilst hoping for a new political compromise to emerge around this sensitive political issue.

A European 'Peace Order'

The end of the Cold War has given united Germany the opportunity to define a new role and identity for itself in the international system. This search for a new role and identity has clearly affected German security policy, which exhibits elements of both continuity and change. The elements of continuity are most apparent in Germany's continuing commitment to multilateralism, and in Chancellor Kohl's concern to manage the deepening policy dilemmas brought about by simultaneously maintaining the NATO alliance, developing a common European foreign and security policy, and building a cooperative security regime based on the OSCE. As Germany grapples with a changing security agenda and seeks to define a new international role for itself, it could be that a new security policy dilemma will emerge. The government's to play a more active role, in cooperation with its allies, in preserving international peace and security through multilateral organisations could come into conflict with Germany's anti-military strategic culture. As Schöl notes:

> Multilateral organizations are becoming increasingly associated with military commitments, which Germans are reluctant to undertake. The German public's aversion to military involvement might lead it to reject the multilateralization of German security policy as well. Thus, the feared nationalization of German security policy may take a quite different form from what many observers expect: rather than returning to power politics, Germany may abdicate its ambitions to play a role in international security matters, concentrating instead on solving its domestic problems and avoiding the divisive debate on a greater security role (Schlör, 1993, p. 65).

Whether or not this new security policy dilemma does emerge, the many and positive changes that have taken place in Germany's security since 1990 should not be overlooked. Germany today enjoys a uniquely benign security environment, and no longer constitutes a threat to its neighbours or to the peace and stability of Europe. Indeed Germany is part of the 'pluralist security community' that has developed in the transatlantic area in the postwar period. Within this security community, war and the threat of war no longer plays significant part in interstate relations. This is a development of tremendous import, and signifies the emergence of the sort of 'Pacific Union' first outlined by Immanual Kant in his 1795 essay 'Perpetual Peace'. On the eve of the twenty-first century, the historic task facing Germany – in cooperation with its allies and partners – is to preserve and expand this Kantian Pacific Union in order to lay the foundations for a *europäische Friedensordnung* (European peace order) throughout the continent. If Germany lacks the vision, the commitment or the courage to work towards this end, the losers will be not only the Germans themselves, but also the wider international community.

PART THREE

The Economy and Social Policy

11

The Economic Order – Still *Modell Deutschland*?

KENNETH DYSON

Analysis of Germany as a world and European actor has conventionally focused on the paradox of the country as an economic giant but at the same time a political dwarf. In the process attention has been drawn to the reasons why Germany punches below its weight in international bargaining and to the implications of this situation. In a parallel manner, a similar central paradox needs to be brought into the foreground in analysis of the contemporary German political economy: between an economy whose actors, notably in manufacturing, are used to being active in world markets and traditions of economic thought and practice that are strongly national, even provincial, in character. This paradox is highlighted in the entrustment of the management of the Deutsche Mark – the second most important currency in world foreign exchange markets – to the Bundesbank, on whose council the majority of members are drawn from the state (Land) central banks.

In fact both paradoxes are crucial to an understanding of why the postwar German political economy emerged as a model. Between them they identified the cluster of factors that accounted for the strengths of *Modell Deutschland* (German model). The low-profile international political role of the German state freed the German economy from the burden of external commitments and the threat of overcommitment. Political objectives were European-centred (and thereby limited) and submerged in the European Community and NATO (and thereby shared). With the process of 'normalisation' consequent on German reunification the German state of the 1990s found itself confronted with new debates focused on the problem of the level of international commitment appropriate to its economic capability and potential.

Should it shoulder a new role as a world policeman; where does its responsibility *vis-à-vis* eastern Europe end; and how far should it bear the costs of enlarging and 'deepening' the European Union? The political agenda of the 1990s will be increasingly shaped by the problems of increasing international commitments and their implications for the German economy, at a time when that economy is facing new challenges from globalisation and reunification.

Similarly, it is possible to see how national traditions of economic thought and practice have underpinned Germany's success in world markets. Together, as we shall see below, a combination of old and new factors have provided a framework of long-term stability for German industry: notably, the 'insider' system of corporate governance, in which cross-shareholdings amongst leading firms and representation of banks on the supervisory boards of firms create a degree of corporate solidarity that is not evident in the Anglo-Saxon economies; the aversion to an equity culture and a preference of firms to rely on bank financing of investment; the pronounced regulatory culture in which the 'public-interest' obligations of firms are emphasised; the ideas of social partnership between employers and workers and of sectoral solidarity in wage bargaining; the dedication to a 'stability culture' in monetary policy, leading to prioritisation of the goal of price stability and to the power and status that accrue to the Bundesbank as the institution with statutory responsibility for this goal; and the doctrine of 'ordoliberalism', with its idea of the state being limited to providing a framework of order for the economy and pursuing intervention that conforms with the principle of market competition. These ideas and institutional arrangements are in effect the constituent elements of the German model, providing German actors with a substantial capability to control the terms of economic development. But since the 1970s indicators of challenge and threat to the model have mounted, being thrown into bolder relief by each successive down-side of the economic cycle. These indicators were of structural challenge and crisis, represented by radical changes in the international political economy (globalisation, as multinational firms escaped national political control, and 'post-Fordism', as economies became characterised by flexible consumption patterns, production processes and labour markets), by developments in the European Community (the single European market and economic and monetary union), and by post-1989 German reunification and the opening up of Eastern Europe. The cumulative nature of these challenges suggests a second direction of development in the political agenda of the 1990s, additional to the debate on problems of external commitments: the problem of diminishing control. Before exploring these challenges in detail and their cumulative effects it is necessary to identify the basic characteristics of the German model.

The Character of the German Model

Postwar capitalism has offered three main models of economic thought and practice associated with superior economic performance: the US model (with, since Thatcherism, increased reference to an Anglo–American model of 'enterprise culture', deregulation and privatisation); the Asia–Pacific models (with Japan as the now traditional model, and with their work-centred cultures and ethos of group values and discipline); and the German model. As the German model finds itself increasingly challenged by the others two, German policy makers face a dilemma: whether to adapt by importing the best features of these models (for instance an 'equity culture') or to focus on the EU (perhaps a 'hard core' of EU members) as an arena in which to consolidate the German model by transferring its features to that level.

The national and international prestige of the German model derives from its brilliant balancing trick. At one and the same time it has provided an outstanding economic performance and done so in terms that strongly accord with traditional German values and the values that have been reinforced by German experience and memories of the 1920s and 1930s. The superior economic performance was exemplified in economic growth, external balance, price stability and employment (see Giersch *et al.*, 1992, ch. 1). Germany's 'economic miracle' was apparent in average annual increases of real GDP of 8.2 per cent between 1950 and 1960 and 4.4 per cent between 1960 and 1973. Between 1949 and 1990 the economy suffered a current account deficit in only seven years; indeed the trade surplus showed a tendency to rise over time as a percentage of GDP. Exports were clearly a major driving force of economic growth.

Despite the occasional inflationary threats consequent on the Korean boom, the oil crises and German reunification, the Bundesbank's record on price stability has been exemplary in international comparisons – in the 1–4 per cent per annum range. Not only did manufacturing industry's share in total employment begin to decline late by international standards (from the early 1970s), it also remained unusually high. The fact that by the 1960s the only major economic problem was the size of the external surplus was testament to the economic miracle, which in turn was crucial to the achievement of a consensus on economic policy principles (the 'social market economy') between the major political parties and, more fundamentally, to the stabilisation of the new state as a functioning liberal-democratic regime.

Not least, the economic miracle was consistent with a deeprooted cultural attachment to values of stability and order that had been nourished by the profound dislocations of the 1920s, 1930s and 1940s: the experiences of the ravages of hyperinflation, the suppression of trade union activity, the contempt for law and the subordination of the economy to political ideas and exigencies that overburdened the economy. The practice of monetary stability by the Bundesbank, of social partnership by both sides of industry and of regulation by the state received powerful support from German culture. In effect the economic order was rooted in specific national cultural patterns that in turn reflected Germany's distinctive path of historical development. 'Sound' money, order and consensus in industrial change, a long-term approach to managing corporate government, and the notion of a limited state that frames general rules but refrains from intervention (ordoliberalism) became integral features of the German model.

A key new postwar ideological element was provided by 'ordoliberalism' with its commitment to a competitive order protected by the state from the dangers of a concentration of private economic power, liberated from central planning and harnessed to a sense of social responsibility. It has dominated the academic economics profession and the Council of Economic Experts (*Sachverständigenrat*), which since 1963 has delivered annual and special reports on the economy to the federal government. Advocated in the writings of Böhm, Eucken and Röpke, ordoliberalism offered a diagnosis and remedy against any return to totalitarian dictatorship. The remedy involved a strong state (in contrast to the *laissez-faire* state it was to stand apart from and referee sectional interests) but one that limited itself to designing an 'economic constitution' of general rules (for example for the conduct of monetary policy) and avoided detailed meddling in economic processes. Ordoliberalism was translated politically into the social market economy. For the principal ordoliberals, 'social' was restricted mainly to a rigorous state competition policy, designed to avoid the oligopolies and cartels of prewar Germany and the consequent concentration of economic power and to open up opportunities (Nicholls, 1994). The basic task was to maintain a well-functioning price mechanism based on the highest possible degree of competition, with only limited redistribution via progressive taxation and some basic social welfare provisions.

Given that this ordoliberalism was in tension with other main strands in postwar German culture, notably associated with a regulatory culture, social partnership and sectoral solidarity, its advocates continued to represent a powerful critical force: from their attacks on the weaknesses of the Cartel Law of 1957 to their advocacy of deregulation and privatisation in the 1980s and 1990s. In practice the social market economy was interpreted politically to make it compatible with these other traditions of thought by making its social dimension incorporate partnership in industrial relations, sectoral solidarity in wage bargaining, detailed regulation and substantial redistribution by means of a highly organised social security system.

For ordoliberals the most substantial achievement of the German economic order was the depoliticisation of monetary policy with the creation of an independent Bundesbank. If the Cartel Law of 1957 was a mark of their failure to halt the concentration of economic power, the Bundesbank Act of 1957 was their main political victory. Charged with safeguarding the currency, the Bundesbank has demonstrated the credibility of German anti-inflation policy by establishing a reputation for a tough, proactive approach (Marsh, 1992). As a consequence of this price stability, and buttressed by the fact that it has never been devalued, the Deutsche Mark has emerged as a strong international currency. Indeed by 1992 it had become easily the second most important world currency, accounting for some 38 per cent of daily foreign exchange market turnover (Dyson, 1994, p. 273). The European Monetary System (EMS) had *de facto* emerged as a 'Deutsche Mark zone' in which the Deutsche Mark had become the 'anchor currency' of the exchange rate mechanism (ERM). The result of this combination of policy credibility with the anchor role in the ERM was that the Bundesbank was able to maintain German short-term and long-term interest rates at a lower level than its EU neighbours and major trading partners, to the benefit of German industry (Dyson, 1994). Domestically, the great beneficiary was the Bundesbank, whose bargaining power was augmented by widespread political support. The Deutsche Mark was perhaps the paramount domestic symbol of national pride in the new Germany, uniting ordoliberals and Bundesbank officials in a powerful constituency of support for the virtues of price stability. But at the same time German industry could – as in 1995 – find the effects of an appreciating Deutsche Mark (which the Bundesbank welcomed as a means of preventing imported inflation) a painful pill to swallow. Though united in the constituency of support for the Bundesbank, they could be more critical of its exchange-rate operations.

Much more problematic for ordoliberals were the other three dimensions of German economic tradition: the regulatory culture, the 'insider' system of corporate governance, and social partnership and sectoral solidarity. The pervasive regulatory culture involves a major element of continuity, notably in the energy, haulage and insurance industries and the craft trades, as well as the organisation of training (Dyson, 1992). In the postwar period regulation actually proliferated with, for instance, tight restrictions on the liberal professions, strict closing hours in the retail sector, mandatory minimum wages, tough protection of workers against dismissal and, particularly since the 1970s, the proliferation of environmental regulation. Notably the Cartel Law of 1957 exempted agriculture, banking, coalmining, insurance, iron and steel, public utilities, telecommunications and transport. Donges and Schatz (1986) concluded that only half of the West German economy operated according to market principles. This firm framework of regulatory culture has deep roots in the German state tradition (Dyson, 1992, pp. 259–60). Associated with the state tradition is the value placed on order, consistency, predictability and integration, ensured through legal regulation based on public-interest arguments and seen as the application of constitutional principles. Lawyers, a powerful elite group in German society, have ideologically and professionally a strong interest in this regulatory tradition and tend to be well-represented at the official ministerial level in German government.

The insider system of corporate government also has its roots in tradition, in this case spawned by the specific characteristics of German industrialisation. Being relatively late, this industrialisation encountered higher entry costs than earlier industrialisers such as Britain. Germany's success in establishing a strong position in new capital-intensive sectors depended on a capacity for substantial capital mobilisation. The search for this capacity led nineteenth-century German industrialists to attempt to exploit economies of scale, to establish intercorporate linkages (cartels being an instance) and to rely on bank finance and participation (Dyson, 1982).

As a consequence, in German industrial culture the firm was seen as enmeshed with outside interests, and the notion of 'stakeholder' capitalism took root, enshrined in company law. This notion of various interests having an interest in the firm was associated with the distinction between two levels of corporate decision: the supervisory board and the management board, with the former having a representational and strategic function and the latter being responsible for the day-to-day management of the firm. Debate focused on who should be recognised as stakeholders (is the postwar period employees joined banks and suppliers) and on what restrictions should be placed on individual stakeholders. From the outset, in companies such as Siemens, AEG and Mannesmann the big commercial banks assumed a key role in supervisory boards, sometimes with substantial direct shareholdings, more often wielding their power via proxy shareholder votes exercised on behalf of their customers. The result was a tradition of bank rather than equity financing of industry; of building up long-term relationships between banks and key firms (the tradition of a firm having a 'house bank') and amongst key firms; of secretiveness surrounding financial reporting; and of hostility to takeover bids as a means of engineering corporate change. The lack of an equity culture is reflected in the following facts in 1993: only 6 per cent of German households owned shares (compared with more than 20 per cent in Britain and the United States); there were only about 665 quoted companies in Germany compared with more than 2000 in Britain; and the market capitalisation of the German stock market amounted to 25 per cent of GDP, against 127 per cent in Britain.

Though the overall role of banks within this framework can be exaggerated (Edwards and Fischer, 1994), the stakeholder system of corporate governance has given a strongly national and stable character to German industrial structure and management. Companies have attached importance to retaining their German identity, to promoting cross-holdings of shares so that there is a stable core of owners, and to fending off threats of external takeover. They have also drawn on German managers with technical qualifications and corporate loyalty rather than on more mobile generalists of the Anglo–American type. The result is that the German model has become associated with a technological corporate culture enshrined in the term *Vorsprung durch Technik* (leading by technology).

With the postwar period social partnership has come to be linked to the insider system of corporate governance. In Germany the key focus of social partnership has been the firm rather than, as in Austria, the level of macroeconomic management (Crouch, 1993). The supervisory board and the works councils have been institutional mechanisms for developing and sustaining a notion and practice of collaboration between management and employees around the theme of common interest at the level of the firm. This means that the aim has been to reconcile the management of industrial change with the maintenance of social peace. In addition to cementing the insider system of corporate governance, social partnership rests on a system of juridification (*Verrechtlichung*) of industrial relations in the spirit of Germany's regulatory culture (Dyson, 1992). Legislation, labour court decisions and legally recognised national and regional collective agreements define and constrain the practice of industrial relations. One aspect of this is the strong emphasis on consultation and consent within German management, with work rationalisation measures requiring the involvement of works councils and being constrained by dismissal legislation. Sectoral solidarity takes the form of centralised wage bargaining to hammer out unified agreements for each sector, involving peak negotiations between the industry-wide trade union and the employer organisation. Such bargaining can be extended to cover working hours and new technologies.

The Challenge to the German Model

This inherited German model of political economy, with its different constituent elements, sometimes mutually supportive, and sometimes in conflict, has been put under mounting and cumulative pressure during the 1990s. Partly this pressure stems from the prospect of rising international commitments on the part of the German state, prompted by a political (and economic) interest in stabilising Eastern Europe, by the implications of European political, economic and monetary union, and by Germany's search to play a constructive role in the UN and NATO. Partly it derives from the huge problem of managing German reunification. And partly it has resulted from Germany's exposure to profound changes in the nature of the international political economy. It is not at all clear that the German model provides German actors in the public and private sectors with the means to deal effectively with this pressure. The result is a serious policy dilemma for the Federal Republic that will have to be worked out by the end of the decade.

In fact the challenge predates the 1990s, but in the 1990s it has taken a more complex and virulent form. Ominously, the symptoms of relative decline and structural problems have been evident for two decades (for the figures below see OECD, 1995). Relative decline was apparent in the growth of real GDP by the 1960s. Already eclipsed by the French, Italian and Japanese rates during the 1960s and again in the 1970s, Germany achieved an annual growth of real GDP of only 1.9 per cent during the period 1980–89, behind Britain, France, Italy, Japan and the United States. The economic miracle had, in short, been failing for some time (Giersch *et al.*, 1992).

A second key indicator has been unemployment, which since 1975 has mounted with each recession, succeeding booms failing to reverse prior increases. Structural unemployment had become an ever more severe problem before the shock of German reunification. By 1995 only between a third and a half of the 3.59 million unemployment total was of a cyclical nature that could be helped by economic growth. An indicator of labour market problems was the fact that the level of West German unemployment at which wage inflation stabilises rose from less than 1 per cent in the early 1970s to some 7 per cent by 1994. By the end of 1995 unemployment stood at 9.7 per cent (up from 6.3 per cent in 1991), approaching the four million level.

A further indicator of relative decline is that over the last twenty years Germany's share of international patent registrations has fallen continuously. In electronics and biotechnology Japan is now four times more inventive than Germany. Another indicator is labour productivity growth, which declined steadily from an annual growth of 7.3 per cent (1950–60) to 2.2 per cent (1980–89). There were even heavy clouds on the horizon of German exports. Its export success remained heavily concentrated in traditional manufacturing areas, such as capital goods. In high-technology exports it fell far behind the United States and Japan. In the big global picture, reunited Germany's share of world output in 1993 was about 7.5 per cent, compared with 9 per cent for West Germany in 1970, and contrasting with a 27 per cent share for the United States and 16 per cent share for Japan in 1993.

Globalisation and 'Post-Fordism'

Over the last two decades two challenges from the international political economy have accelerated in pace and grown in scale: globalisation and post-Fordism. Globalisation involves a qualitative change in the terms of engagement of economic actors in the international economy: from the idea of exporting from a home base (Germany) to the idea of companies such as Volkswagen and Bayer as production centres, being simultaneously present in many different countries and organising production and distribution on a transnational basis. This phenomenon has affected such strategic and fast-growing sectors as financial services and telecommunications, where it has been accompanied and facilitated by US-initiated deregulation. With its mixture of insider corporate governance and regulatory culture in these sectors, Germany has defensively confronted rather than actively shared in and shaped globalisation. Post-Fordism refers to the shift from mass production to flexible specialisation in both products and production processes as a consequence of accelerating technological change. This shift is coterminous with the displacement of employment prospects from manufacturing to services (so-called 'de-industrialisation') and, within manufacturing, to a core of high-technology, extremely capital-intensive sectors.

Both these developments raise serious questions about the continuing effectiveness and viability of the German model. They place a premium on speed of decision, reduction of costs, flexibility of employment and working practices, more innovative methods of raising capital for new ventures and more internationally experienced managers. Globalisation and post-Fordism have mobilised ordoliberals around a new domestic agenda of deregulation to open up market and employment opportunities, from the liberalisation of retail opening hours to the creation of new financial instruments, from the reduction of barriers to market entry in financial services and telecommunications to more flexible employment practices. In the German case such measures are made difficult by federalist structures and neocorporatist practices at the sectoral level, which give enormous scope to vested interests to block reform (see Dyson, 1992, for case studies). A second theme for resurgent ordoliberalism has been a reduction of the costs of employment by reducing social security contributions, which by 1995 amounted to 41.3 per cent of wages.

Deepening and Widening the European Union

Germany's role within the European Union has had an ambivalent effect. On the one hand it has provided Germany with an opportunity to shape EU legislation in the form of Germany 'writ large', for instance to Europeanise the social dimension of its political economy. Its capacity to act effectively in this arena was apparent in the provisions of the Treaty on European Union dealing with economic and monetary union (EMU). In effect an independent European central bank with a single mandate – to pursue price stability – was the Bundesbank 'writ large'. But on the other hand German support in principle for a total programme – such as the single European market – could not translate, into control of the new European regulatory framework particularly in conditions of qualified majority voting in the Council of Ministers. In fact by April 1995 Germany had the worst record after Greece and Ireland for transposing EU single market directives into national law. The most troublesome areas were public procurement, banking, securities, company law and intellectual property. In areas such as financial services, telecommunications and road and air transport the German government found itself on the defensive, caught between EU pressures and powerful domestic vested interests (Bulmer, 1992). The EU dimension was ultimately important in forcing the hand of the federal government to act and provide that action with legitimation.

A more enduring problem has been the EU budget, given Germany's role as the largest net contributor. One aspect of the problem is that, following German reunification, that role became questionable. In purchasing power terms, reunification transformed Germany from the second (after Luxembourg) to the sixth most prosperous EU state. With gross German transfers to the EU set to grow at an annual rate of 8 per cent there was a heightened sense of caution, expressed by the Bundesbank in its monthly report of November 1993. Two aspects of increased EU budget demands were a source of concern: the financial transfers that might be demanded in a monetary union embracing EU states with problems of structural adjustment, and the financial transfers that would follow EU enlargement towards Eastern Europe. The problem for German policy was how to limit the role of the EU as a demander of German budget contributions for these purposes whilst not being seen as undermining them. In the case of EMU the solution was found in strict convergence criteria on inflation, budget deficits, public debt, interest rates and exchange rate stability as a precondition of entry (a solution that remains politically difficult to apply). In the case of EU enlargement to the east a solution has yet to be found. One attraction of the idea of a 'hard core' within the EU is that it would reduce the demand for transfers as a condition of a speedy move towards political and economic and monetary union.

German Unification and the Opening to the East

In 1989–90 the West German federal government underestimated the scale of the challenge presented by German reunification and its long-term implications, despite warnings from the Bundesbank, from many economists and from within industry. Quite simply, the divergence between the two economies was enormous. The exchange rate selected for monetary union (against the advice of the Bundesbank) meant an effective revaluation of more than 300 per cent for the area of the GDR; economic union meant immediate access to cheaper, high-quality Western goods; whilst measures supporting trade with the Eastern bloc came to an end. As a consequence eastern Germany was plunged into deep economic crisis. The index of manufacturing production in the former GDR slumped by nearly 40 per cent between 1990 and 1992; the number of economically active dropped from nearly 10 million to under six million; and the unemployed, including those on government schemes, rose to 37 per cent of the working population (Hoffmann, 1993). A core problem was unit labour costs (see Bundesbank monthly report, July 1995). In the context of a productivity level of only 54 per cent of that in western Germany in 1994 (against 26 per cent in 1990) and of a wage explosion taking wages to some 70 per cent of those in the west (against 34 per cent in 1990), unit labour costs far exceeded those in the west. The so-called wage quota (the amount of national income devoted to wages) stood at more than 100 per cent in 1993. In effect no profits were being earned, and all investment was being financed by transfers from the west.

These developments provided the background to net transfers to the east amounting to the equivalent of 5 per cent of western Germany's GDP and 40 per cent of the value-added component of the east German economy (Bundesbank monthly report, July 1995). The result was that the budget deficit rose from 1 per cent of west German GDP to 6.2 per cent in 1993; a temporary 'solidarity' surcharge on income tax of 7.5 per cent was imposed (and then reintroduced); successive spending cuts were agreed; state and local authorities in the west were faced by the prospect of harsh funding cuts, with major implications for service provision; and privatisation gained attractiveness as a means of generating revenue. In the (successful) effort to choke off inflationary pressures the Bundesbank hiked interest rates to unprecedented levels. Not least, developments in the east opened debate about the appropriateness of extending the German model to the east as a means of regeneration; about whether the imposition of the west's regulatory culture on the east and centralised collective bargaining at the sectoral level were compatible with the requirements of rapid job creation there. As the former GDR was threatened with a 'subsidy mentality', in the words of the Bundesbank, west German industry was attracted not so much to eastern in Germany as the vastly lower unit labour costs in the Czech Republic and Hungary. The opening up of the East provided a major challenge to eastern Germany, given its proximity to the German and major European markets.

The Response to the Challenge to the German Model

The combination of these mounting structural challenges with the shock of the deep 1993 recession and the appreciation of the Deutsche

Mark in 1994–95 (up 10 per cent against the US dollar in a year) prompted both an agonised debate about Germany's future as a location for investment (the so-called *Standort Deutschland* debate) and a flurry of initiatives in both public and private sectors. Problems inherent in the German model were harshly exposed by corporate crises: in 1994 at Mannesmann and the Schneider property group, and then in 1995–96 at Daimler-Benz. A common factor was the weakness of internal control within the system of German corporate governance, and in each case the Deutsche Bank's performance as 'house bank' was put into question. In contrast attention was focused on the merits of the Anglo–American 'equity culture' and the mechanism of takeovers as a spur to company efficiency. Additionally, the tradition of solidarity in collective bargaining was brought into question: by the employer organisation's cancellation of the wage equalisation accord (between west and east) in the metals sector as ruinous to competitiveness; by the same organisation's threat to dissolve itself if sectoral agreement could not be reached on work-time flexibility in 1995; and by the success of companies such as Opel and BMW in doing plant-level deals on flexible working patterns. Flexibility was the new keyword, including demands to treat Saturday as an ordinary working day, and irregular shifts.

The pressure to reconsider elements of the German model was increased by clear evidence that traditional German companies were beginning to redefine themselves as global players: Daimler-Benz took the historic step of seeking the listing of its shares on the New York Stock Exchange in 1993, thereby opening up financial reporting requirements; Deutsche Bank moved its investment banking activities to London in 1995, sending shock waves through the German financial establishment; whilst Siemens, BMW, Volkswagen and Hoechst pursued major foreign acquisitions and investments. In addition they began to seek out non-German managers with international experience. This development towards globalised companies can in fact be dated to the 1980s and preceded the more recent Deutsche Mark appreciation. At the same time Deutsche Mark appreciation acted as a force for industrial restructuring, for taking painful decisions that might otherwise have been postponed. More alarming was evidence that global players' inward investment to the EU, notably Japan, was shunning Germany for other locations, such as Britain, closing the door to a major means of importing new technological and managerial skills.

The result has been to put domestic political structures under new pressure – notably in sectors such as financial services and telecommunications – to introduce market liberalisation. Here, strikingly, Germany has lagged behind other major EU states, and indeed has been stimulated to act by EU deadlines to implement single market legislation. Thus it was not till 1994 that financial market legislation introduced a new regulatory structure (the Federal Supervisory Office for Securities Trading) to ensure conformity with international standards on shareholder disclosure, publication of price-sensitive information and the outlawing of insider trading. It also introduced money market funds to give savers access to higher short-term interest rates (which the Bundesbank had strongly opposed as threatening its control of the money supply). But even these measures to strengthen *Finanzplatz Deutschland* (Germany as a leading financial centre) did not deter the Deutsche Bank from relocating its investment banking to London. Indeed the pursuit of the new opportunities offered by financial market liberalisation, whether at home or abroad, threatened to shift the behaviour of German commerce away from long-term support for German companies and their role as the policemen of corporate problems within German capitalism.

In the case of measures to promote new financial instruments such as money market funds, the Bundesbank found itself on the defensive. In part at least, the promotion of *Finanzplatz Deutschland* threatened its capacity to monitor and control monetary developments. Already the restrictions of the German financial market had led German banks to shift a substantial part of their operations to the much more deregulated environment of Luxembourg. This factor, along with the emergence of the Deutsche Mark as a major world currency and a wider Deutsche Mark zone in Europe, cast long-term doubts over the mechanisms available to the Bundesbank to meet its objective of monetary stability. With wider and larger Deutsche Mark holdings outside Germany the Bundesbank was given an added incentive to act to retain the currency's credibility. But with a single European financial area and new financial instruments the future adequacy of its tools of control was in question, perhaps then offering an actual gain for the Bundesbank in being part of a European system of central banks (as long as the European central bank was the 'Bundesbank writ large'). Insofar as national central banks were no longer able to control their own money supplies, a shift of monetary policy responsibility to the European level opened up new prospects for reestablishing control.

Another key sector in which change was relatively late, consequent on domestic institutional obstacles to reform, was telecommunications. Following the liberalisation of specialised business services, the federal government pushed for the liberalisation of basic network services by 1998. The result was the emergence of four alliances to challenge

Deutsche Telecom, one of which was joined by AT and T in 1995, another by Cable and Wireless and another by British Telecom. Meanwhile Deutsche Telecom sought out international alliances to service global business customers. German telecommunications was clearly on the threshold of globalisation.

The themes of deregulation, privatisation and reform of the social security system took on a new centrality with the publication in September 1993 of the Economics Ministry's report on 'safeguarding Germany's future as an industrial location'. In fact these themes were presented within the context of a celebration of traditional German values rather than of the need to import foreign models and practices. The ordoliberal component of the German model, celebrated by the Council of Economic Advisers, was being appealed to for inspiration. The greatest scope for privatisation was clearly at the state and local levels where governments had holdings in utilities, savings banks and occasionally stock-market listed companies (for example Lower Saxony in Volkswagen). One signal here was the Bavarian state government's decision of 1993 to sell its holding in Deutsche Aerospace. At the federal level four main companies have been identified as candidates for privatisation: Lufthansa, the Postdienst (postal service), Deutsche Telecom, and the Deutsche Eisenbahn (railways). In the case of Lufthansa and Deutsche Eisenbahn there are problems of operating losses and debts to resolve; and in all cases substantial opposition and the problem of negotiating change through a Bundesrat in which the SPD has a majority. Deregulation has focused on financial markets, telecommunications, working hours and employment practices. Here again the institutional interests of trade unions and bodies such as the Bundesbank and Deutsche Telecom, in conjunction with the problem of negotiating change with the SPD in the Bundesrat, have slowed the pace of reform.

Tasks for the Political Actors

The impact of the structural challenges to the German model, the 1993 recession and the Deutsche Mark appreciation of 1994–95 has to be put into perspective. Most strikingly, the German political economy has absorbed the challenges in a way that demonstrates its extraordinary versatility and resilience. Notably, excessive budget deficits and inflationary pressures have been kept under control, with the Bundesbank playing a key role in sending early, tough signals to the government and both sides of industry about its determination to act to control their mistakes of judgement following reunification. The resulting credibility of the German economy was reflected in the strength of the Deutsche Mark within the ERM and in world currency markets and in its relatively good performance in approximating towards the strict convergence criteria required for entry into the final stage of EMU (though recessionary trends pushed the budget deficit to 3.6 per cent in 1995).

At the same time these laudable and important achievements relate to nominal rather than 'real' factors in the economy (such as productivity, investment and unemployment rates). As far as financial performance is concerned Germany's achievements, especially post-reunification, seem impressive. But at the level of the 'real' economy there remain grounds for substantial concern: structural unemployment is rising; the divergence between the economies of the west and east is profound; average growth rates have undergone a secular decline; and high-technology inventiveness and exports are lagging seriously behind major rivals. The effects of these problems will continue to feed through to the political arena. The best that can be said (and it is saying a lot) is that problems with nominal economic performance will not compound problems in the 'real' economy. Indeed phenomena such as the appreciating Deutsche Mark act as forces for structural change in industry; whilst stable and relatively low long-term interest rates support industrial investment. But they cannot replace more far-reaching changes to the way in which the German model functions. Sound financial indicators alone will not reverse the declining attraction of the German model *vis-à-vis* the Anglo–American and Asia–Pacific models. Moreover they will not remain sound – or the costs of keeping them sound will rise – unless reforms tackle the structural problems of the real economy, notably in labour markets.

For such changes to be feasible, actors in the political arena will need to muster the will and capability to resist mounting external political pressures (notably from within the EU and from Eastern Europe) for Germany to take on greater international commitments in relation to Germany's economic performance and potential. Overcommitment could cripple the German economy; and German politicians and diplomats, sensitive for historical reasons to a policy of good neighbourliness, do not like to say no. Political actors will also have to operate in a policy environment in which globalisation and Europeanisation offer fewer instruments of national economic and monetary control. For instance the German commercial banks, given the new incentives provided by financial market deregulation, are losing interest in acting as 'house banks' to specific firms and policing the corporate problems of German capitalism. Above all, political actors will have to negotiate deregulation, privatisation and reforms of the social security system through a political system in which, as we have seen elsewhere in this volume (see also Dyson, 1992), institutional requirements of consensus building place formidable hurdles in the path of policy innovation. What is clear is that with the 1990s policy initiative has shifted to the ordoliberals, as their long-standing criticisms of the development of the German political economy seem to be born out by the mounting evidence of underlying structural crisis.

12

Economic Management and the Challenge of Reunification

CHRISTOPHER FLOCKTON

The speed and depth of the economic downturn at the beginning of 1996, with its threat to employment and public finances, leads one to believe that Germany has been delaying difficult decisions on the reform of its social market order. The collapse of industrial firms with household names has furthermore led to a pervasive feeling that the German economic constitution is under threat. Of course the higher growth of the late 1980s in West Germany, and the reunification-induced boom there in the early 1990s, disguised the need for improved competitiveness and led to undue confidence that Europe's strongest economy could absorb the costs of reunification with its eastern half. Economic growth, so long as it continued, could support the transformation of the collapsing eastern economy and could perhaps sustain the huge deficits and debt accumulation in the public finances. In a recession, however, the problem is that the debt burden becomes more onerous and policy makers cast around to discover new sources of growth to sustain activity. At the turn of 1995–96 the federal government issued a '50 Point Plan for Growth and Employment', which replayed old tunes of 'supply-side' economic improvements, which had been proposed at repeated intervals since the first Kohl government in 1982. The large IG Metall trade union had meanwhile proposed an 'Alliance for Jobs', which sought to sustain the trade unions' alternative approach to the defence of employment. In Germany, as in neighbouring countries, there are opposing approaches, but also a certain sense of helplessness as to how to promote reforms to meet the challenge of world competition, global industry and capital movements.

Competitiveness and Economic Transformation

The *Standortfrage*, namely the question of Germany's external competitiveness as a production location, has come once again to dominate public discussion, together with fears of *Sozialabbau*, of the erosion of employment rights and a loosening of the welfare safety net. A liberal market approach would be to attack labour market rigidities, so as to raise productivity and to reduce employers' non-wage labour costs (which had risen to equal 82 per cent of direct pay in 1995 from 48 per cent in 1972). This would strengthen the competitiveness of German exports on foreign markets, but would clearly involve some weakening of labour protection and the social security net, which are held to be a fundamental part, even if increasingly disputed, of the social market order. Of course, market liberals have long criticised the rigidities of the institutional system of collective wage bargaining in the Federal Republic, since the late 1970s and they have drawn attention to the inexorable rise of subsidies to industry, together with the attendant increases in taxation and the state's share of national expenditure. However, reunification has escalated the concern that German economic institutions lack flexibility and do not promote adjustment and innovation (Giersch *et al.*, 1992; Schlesinger *et al.*, 1993; Siebert, 1992). Thus the extension of the West German wage bargaining system to eastern Germany (which resulted in the rapid equalisation of eastern with western wages), the scale of subsidies to maintain and sell off obsolescent industry, and the level of state assistance to the labour market to ameliorate mass unemployment were seen by market liberals as signs of the pervasive regulation and lack of spontaneous adjustment inherent in the German economic model. Such criticisms may seem heartless given the traumas of deindustrialisation in eastern Germany, but they served to underline the agenda of the policy debate.

The absorption of the collapsing, centrally planned economy tested the German economic constitution in every way, but overall the robust economic strength of the west appears to have been adequate to cover the huge, unexpected costs of transformation, and the large-scale transfers to support living standards and investment there. The 'dual economy' evolution of slump in the east and boom in the west (which was later reversed to make eastern Germany into Europe's fastest-growing region), has nevertheless imposed an exceptional burden on public finances. The debt-financed transfers to the east have pushed up tax and social security burdens to historic highs (of 45 per cent of income compared with 40.5 per cent in 1990) and have doubled state debt in five years. In the gathering recession of early 1996, these burdens are making it difficult for Germany to meet one of the Maastricht Treaty criteria for membership of the EU monetary union: of a maximum deficit of 3 per cent of GDP.

The *Standort* debate focuses on Germany as a high-cost, highly regulated location. At hourly average pay rates in manufacturing of DM45 at the end of 1994 in western Germany, Germany has unit labour costs (per unit produced) that are 25 per cent higher than those of the average of its OECD competitors. It also has the shortest working hours and machine-running times, while employers also criticise the high corporation tax levels and the restrictive environmental regulations.

In view of the rising value of the Deutsche Mark (by 6 per cent trade-weighted during 1994 to mid 1995) and wage settlements well above inflation for 1995 and 1996, it is unsurprising that German foreign direct investment (FDI) abroad has been accelerating. There is daily news of production being transferred to lower-cost locations, sometimes to Central Europe, where unit labour costs are 40 per cent lower. The net outflow of FDI in the period 1992–94 amounted to DM79 billion, while in the first eight months of 1995 alone it reached DM33 billion. The German Confederation of Industry (BDI) estimates that 300 000 jobs were transferred abroad from 1990–94. The fear of course is that this represents an accelerating 'export of jobs' to escape German costs and regulations. Since it has paralleled a phase of rapid labour-shedding in German industry, and of low overall growth performance, this is a matter of singular concern. Overall German GDP rose only 5.4 per cent between spring 1991 and the final quarter of 1995, with manufacturing output 7 per cent lower in January 1996 than five years previously. The manufacturing workforce has fallen from 11.1 million to 8.8 million.

In connection with the question of the flexibility of the German social market system, the federal government has returned several times to the more liberal market approaches it embraced under the first Kohl government of September 1992. The '*Standort* Report' of 1993 listed 147 measures for liberalisation, and a number were included in the 1994 *Standortsicherungsgesetz* (Law to secure the productive competitiveness of Germany). Many more were reincluded in the January 1996 '50 Point Plan for Growth and Employment'. This recurrence points to the fact that in practice very little has been achieved from coalition politics, lobbying and the checks and balances between upper and lower houses of parliament. As will be seen, the *Bündnis für Arbeit* (Alliance for Jobs) proposals favoured by the trade unions press for further job sharing, and cuts in working time and overtime as a way of spreading the available work for the unemployed, but their fatal flaw is that they do not address costs appropriately, and therefore do not reduce the price of labour.

In the following discussion we address first the challenge to and responses of economic policy making at the federal level, with some stress on the reunification context. A critical discussion of the transformation strategies in eastern Germany is then followed by an assessment of the liberalisation and deregulation strategies adopted to date.

Economic Policy and the Dual Economy

As is well known, reunification between the highly developed West Germany economy and the far less productive, centrally planned East German economy produced overnight a dual structure, with boom in the west and slump in the east. This divergent evolution, which continued later with reversed roles as the eastern economy experienced recovery, is evident in Table 12.1. The causes of the eastern slump have been extensively discussed (Flockton, 1992; Padgett, 1993; Sinn and Sinn, 1992; Ghanie-Ghaussy and Schäfer, 1993) and lie in the perhaps fourfold overvaluation of the rate of exchange at the time of currency union, the technological obsolescence or highly polluting character of much of East German industry, the collapse of COMECON and the unresolved position of property claims by dispossessed owners. Also critical was the rapid wage harmonisation in line with western collective wage rates, which, because of the very low productivity in eastern Germany, led to unit wage costs of 70 per cent above those in the west. This is termed the 'Mezzogiorno effect', in analogy with a similar

TABLE 12.1 *Macroeconomic evolution in the FRG, 1990–94*

	West Germany					
	1990	*1991*	*1992*	*1993*	*1994*	*1995**
GDP change (%)	4.5	4.9	1.2	−2.3	1.6	–
Gainfully employed						
(1000s; EG 1990 and 1991 estimated)	28479	29190	29452	28994	28650	28491
Unemployed (1000s)	1883	1689	1808	2270	2556	2538
Unemployment rate (%)	6.4	5.7	5.9	7.3	8.2	8.2
Consumer prices (% change)	2.7	3.5	4.0	4.2	3.0	2.0

* First half.

situation in Southern Italy, and it resulted in mass redundancies and financial transfers from the west of a previously unimagined scale. Industrial output in the east slumped quickly to 60 per cent of pre-reunification levels and reached only 68 per cent by July 1993 (MRDB, 7/1993). The total labour force shrank from 10 million to around 6.4 million (with 350 000 commuting daily to the west), and industrial employment proper shrank from 3.5 million to only 622 000. In February 1996 the unemployment rate reached 17 per cent (1.3 million) in the east and a further 800 000 are benefiting from 'second labour market' measures such as retraining, job creation projects or early retirement.

In contrast the west experienced a reunification-induced boom, a 'straw fire' overheating of demand that faded quickly in late 1992, particularly under the impact of high Bundesbank interest rates to curb the 4.5 per cent inflation rate. The western recessions of 1993 and 1995–96 have been mirrored by a continuing upturn in the east, which, even if it has failed to reduce unemployment, has nevertheless produced growth rates that make it Europe's fastest growing region, expanding at 8 per cent per year since 1992. Brutal restructuring and labour-shedding, combined with inward investment and small-firm creation, have doubled relative productivity there to perhaps 55 per cent of that which prevails in the west. However, with wage rates due for equalisation with west Germany's in July 1996, it is apparent that the region remains a high cost location and will continue to be dependent on large-scale public and private transfers of perhaps DM200 billion annually until well into the next decade. Living standards and productivity will not equalise until at least the year 2005. As a final point, these improvements remain dependent on western Germany's ability to continue its support, which the deepening current recession is undermining.

East Germany						*FRG*					
1990	*1991*	*1992*	*1993*	*1994*	*1995**	*1990*	*1991*	*1992*	*1993*	*1994*	*1995**
−14	−28	10	7	9	–	–	3.7	2.2	−1.2	2.9	2.6
8855	7179	6387	6208	6303	6387	–	–	35839	35202	34953	34878
240	913	1170	1149	1142	1029	2123	2602	2978	3419	3698	3567
–	10.4	14.6	15.1	15.2	13.7	–	–	7.7	8.8	9.6	9.5
–	8.3	13.5	10.5	3.7	1.8	–	–	4.6	3.9	2.6	2.0

The successive coalition governments under Chancellor Kohl in the 1990s, then, were faced with three large-scale policy concerns. The transformation of eastern Germany and its adoption of the economic constitution of western Germany had to be supported by the full panoply of policy instruments, without however forcing the degree of intervention and control so far as to undermine the social market economy model. As will be seen, the degree of intervention was such that many liberal market economists and politicians were deeply concerned by these market distortions in the east. Secondly, the scale of financial transfers required for investment and income support in the new Länder had to be managed, even though for growth reasons the successive Kohl governments sought to rein back the state's share of national expenditure in an effort to secure supply-side efficiency improvements. Lastly, structural economic changes in the form of deregulation and privatisation remained firmly on this supply-side agenda, in order to raise Germany to a higher growth path in the context of intensifying world competition. Before we turn to a more detailed discussion of these policy directions, the macroeconomic context of the post-reunification period requires analysis.

The shock to the East German system of its overnight exposure to world competition at probably a fourfold overvaluation of the exchange rate, and the requirement for a root and branch restructuring of its economy, would in almost all circumstances have produced a deep slump requiring large-scale financial support for the purchasing power of its inhabitants. In addition the scale of its investment needs was enormous. This alone would place a significant strain on the federal budget, and would absorb much of the pool of savings into the future. However the politically motivated refusal by Chancellor Kohl's government to raise taxes before the December 1990 election meant that a huge funding gap in public finances appeared, which could only be closed by borrowing. The costs of public transfers to the east provided for in the Unification Treaty were DM22 billion for 1990 and DM35 billion for 1991, the remaining costs to be covered by *Treuhand* (Trustee Institution) asset sales, but in practice the transfers have averaged DM200 billion gross per annum over the intervening period.

The fact that production in the new Länder has met only one half of consumption over several years indicates the scale of the problem of borrowing to finance consumption. In addition only 25 per cent of western German transfers actually funded new investment, the remainder supported incomes and consumption. State deficits and debt mounted, even as western Germany experienced a reunification-induced boom by supplying this eastern demand. Western Germany experienced overheating and inflation at 4.5 per cent in 1991–92. Apart from a more balanced budget through tax increases, a real rise in the value of the Deutsch Mark (this is, an appreciation) would have greatly facilitated the adjustment. It would have cooled the western German economy and would have painlessly attracted in foreign capital flows to fund the east. It would also have transformed the previous record current account surplus (DM106 billion for West Germany in 1989) into a deficit, so as to supply the goods to meet eastern demand. The failure to revalue the Deutsche Mark, (since concurrently with German monetary union the EU was entering the first stage of its own monetary union), represented a further highly damaging policy error.

In the period 1990–92, therefore, budgetary laxity and overheating prevailed, forcing a highly critical Bundesbank to step in and pursue an interest rate *Kraftakt* (demonstration of strength) by forcing up the cost of money in late 1992 to stifle the inflation. This high interest rate policy contributed substantially to the tensions in the European Monetary System (Schäfer, 1993; Kurz, 1993) and helped tip western Germany into recession by 1993. Meanwhile Germany's huge trade and current account surpluses melted away and the country moved from being the world's largest exporter to having a current account deficit of 1 per cent of GDP. These were the counterparts to the large public finance deficits.

Market Distortions in Policy for the East?

If we look at the economic policies adopted by the Kohl governments in the first half of the 1990s, it is clear that the policy for rejuvenating the east caused many of the most acute problems. At the outset in 1990, the liberal FDP economics minister, Haussmann, expressed great confidence that renewal in the east would be rapid, just like the 'economic miracle' in West Germany following the 1948 Currency Reform. At that stage, therefore, six public sector funds were put in place to support and foster rapid structural change. The German Unity Fund, with its DM115 billion endowment, pump-primed the new pension, social insurance and health insurance funds in the east, as well as funding infrastructure and renovation projects by local authorities. The regional development assistance programmes granted the highest priority assistance to the east, covering more than one half of the investment costs of projects in their first year. The Federal Labour Office guaranteed short-time working pay over a period of 18 months to support those in the labour force affected by the profound transformation of the productive structures, and it offered early retirement and retraining assistance, covering 1.28 million persons in 1993 at an annual cost of DM35 billion. The *Treuhand* (Public Trustee Office) offered liquidity credits and investment injections to the former state industries until they were privatised or closed. On average to support loss-makers pending privatisation it spent DM38 billion a year to the end of 1994. Finally, the federal railways and post and telecommunications funded thorough-going, long-term infrastructure replacement programmes of approxiamtely DM1 billion each. This policy of extending the western German programmes eastwards, however, came to be severely tested in 1991, when the full scale of the collapse in activity was becoming apparent, and when the closure of once-famous East German enterprises were giving rise to street demonstrations in Berlin.

Demands became louder for a far more interventionist strategy to protect production and employment in the new Länder by long-term subsidisation of labour and industry, and the restructuring of the old, monopoly 'combines' of East Germany while still in state hands. This contradicted the clearly defined policy of 'privatisation first' (as enshrined in the Unification Treaty), as well as threatening serious distortions in the social market economy order. Where, in short, the chosen policy orientation was one of rapidly privatising eastern state assets, and of providing transitional assistance and capital investment subsidies for new industry, political opponents in the SPD and PDS were demanding the maintenance of a huge state sector, directed investment and the longer-term subsidisation of jobs. Already the rapid and highly damaging harmonisation of eastern wages with those in the west was regarded by market liberals as key evidence that labour market rigidities would induce mass unemployment over many years of transition. In addition, further critical distortions to market behaviour, this time as part of government policy, were to be found in the establishment of energy supply monopolies in the east (the result of their having been taken over by the member companies of the West German electricitiy and gas cartel), in the distortions induced by the process of privatising farm land and housing, and, above all, in the massive injections to loss-making, obsolescent state firms to make them attractive to purchasers.

Budgetary Crises and State Deficits

This highly unbalanced macroeconomic policy stance of budgetary laxity and relatively tight monetary policy began to be addressed with the 'temporary' tax increases of 1991, when, following the federal elections, an exceptional solidarity surcharge of 7.5 per cent on income tax payable for 1991–92, together with VAT and petrol tax increases, was imposed. The ballooning costs of transfers to the east, which were leading to a rapid accumulation of deficits and debt, had to be addressed. Gross public transfers of an average DM205 billion annually (net transfers equalled DM140 billion) were unsustainable without large tax increases.

The evolution of the fiscal position of the public sector is shown in Table 12.2 and the scale of transfers to eastern Germany over time is presented in Table 12.3. The deterioration of general government finances in 1993, and of broader public sector finances in aggregate, is apparent in Table 12.2 Only with the first serious attempt to reign back state deficits – the opening of 'Solidarity Pact' talks between government, industry and unions in September 1993 – do we begin to see an improvement. Since January 1995 the *Treuhand* and east German housing system debts, previously off-budget, have been absorbed

TABLE 12.2 *Public sector revenue, expenditure and balances (DM billions)*

	1992	*1993*	*1994*
Central government and local authority revenue	956.0	934.5	1042.5
of which federal	399.5	401.0	439.0
Expenditure	1066.0	1117.5	1148.5
of which federal	431.0	462.0	478.5
government balances	−110.0	−133.0	−106.5
Special Funds balances			
Unity Fund	−22.5	−13.5	−3.0
Debt Processing Fund	+0.5	–	–
ERP Fund	−6.5	−1.5	−2.0
Railways Fund			−5.5
Social Security Fund Balances	−7	+4.0	−2.0
Public sector total	−117.0	−129.5	−108.0
Memorandum: deficit of *Treuhand* agency	−30.0	−38.0	−37.0
Total debt: central, regional, local authorities		1509.1	1654.5
Memorandum			
Treuhand Agency		168.3	204.5
Railways		66.0	–
Federal Post Office		104.5	124.0

Note: Indebtedness of the total public sector may reach DM2000 bn, or 57 per cent of GDP at the end of 1995. This is double the level of 1989. The national accounts definition of the public deficit excludes the *Treuhand*, and so the ratio of deficit to GDP in 1994 was 2.5 per cent (Maastricht limit: 3 per cent).
Source: DBbk Annual Report, 1994.

TABLE 12.3 *Public financial transfers to eastern Germany (DM billions)*

	1992	*1993*	*1994*	*1995*
Transfers by territorial authorities:	121.9	138.5	132.4	163.5
German Unity Fund	36.1	36.4	35.8	–
Net federal transfers	74.4	90.7	85.7	114.5
VAT *equalis*, by Länder	11.5	11.4	10.8	–
New financial equalisation	–	–	–	49.0
Financial transfers by social security funds	29.1	23.9	33.2	32.0
Public transfers total	151.0	162.4	165.6	195.5
Memorandum item: *Treuhand* deficit	29.6	38.1	37.1	–

Source: Five Economics institutes; Vesper, 1995.

into the federal government's account in the form of the *Erblastentilgungsfonds* (Debt Redemption Fund – total debt DM260 billion), upon which interest must be paid. The tax increases introduced in January 1995 (7.5 per cent solidarity surcharge on income tax payable, together with a rise in wealth tax and tax on insurance premia) will help redress the public deficit. Evidence supports the view that the costs of reunification may be coming under control (MRDB, 6/1995). With small real expenditure cuts annually in the future, a federal deficit of only DM29 billion is programmed for 1999 (DM60 billion in 1995). However the recession in early 1996 is threatening this more favourable outcome and a large overshooting of the federal budget is forecast.

Table 12.3 shows the scale of net public transfers to the east (Vesper, 1995). In gross terms, federal support per inhabitant in the east stood at DM8500 in 1994, compared with DM5500 for the west. With respect to transfers, 1 January 1995 saw the extension to the east for the first time of the *Länderfinanzausgleich* (states' financial equalisation), which serves to reduce tax-raising disparities between rich and poor states. The exceptional arrangements contained in the German Unity Fund therefore came to an end. The *Länderfinanzausgleich*, as recast from January 1995, encompasses an overall transfer of DM55 billion between federation and Länder and between eastern and western states, thus guaranteeing to the new Länder an average per capita tax revenue of 95 per cent of the federal average (Vesper, 1995).

For its part, the Bundesbank's fight against inflationary overheating aggravated the recession in Germany, attracting sharp criticism. In particular it refused to take account of 'special factors' associated with reunification that subsequently lost their inflationary force. The policy of monetary targeting began to lose credibility, requiring repeated Bundesbank statements of purpose (MRDB, 7/1995).

The Welfare State and the Labour Market

The twin prime objectives of the government's '50 Point Programme for Growth and Employment', produced hurriedly in January 1996 in response to the sharp downturn in activity, were to (1) cut unemployment by half by the year 2000, and (2) reduce the state's share of GDP from 50 per cent to the 46 per cent it had been in the west at the time of reunification. Clearly reductions in welfare coverage are dictated in the short term by budgetary exigencies, but the supply-side linkage of budgetary consolidation, growth and employment is made via the need to reduce the non-wage labour costs levied on employers, and to cut the tax 'wedge' (the gap between gross and take-home pay) for employees. In Germany, social security charges levied on firms on behalf of their employees make up 41 per cent of the total wage bill, while the tax and social security contributions make up 45 per cent of income, compared with 40.5 per cent in 1990. It is held that a reduction in such charges will lower the cost of labour and increase its supply, thus aiding employment creation. The 'pulling up by the bootstraps' character of this argument is clear however, in that a part of the rise in costs is generated by the very spread of unemployment itself.

The '50 Point Programme' included a few new policy proposals, but many stretch back to 1992 and 1993 in the form of the Council of Economic Advisors' recommendations for liberalisation, or were contained in the September 1993 *Standortbericht* (report on Germany as a production location). Aside from the recurring issue of reducing direct business taxation (reduction of the 51 per cent corporation tax on retained profit and abolition of the *Gewerbeertragsteuer*, a local tax on trading capital), one may divide the changes in welfare support between (1) the reform of health-care and nursing provision, and (2) reduction in financial support to the unemployed and welfare benefits.

Health-care reform stretches back at least ten years to the introduction in 1988 of quantity controls to reduce the number of hospital beds. Since 1993–94, however, a further three-stage reform has been put in place, which first sought to control doctors' remuneration and then to bring drug prescription costs under control. The extended political discussion in 1995 and 1996 in the closer control of hospital expenditure (by favouring day surgeries and home care) must find some resolution, since hospital budgets represent one-third of the total health-care expenditure. Partly to relieve the cost of geriatic care in an ageing German population, the Nursing Care Reform imposed further social charges on employer and employee alike (of 1 per cent rising to 1.7 per cent of the wage bill in 1996) to meet the mounting cost of caring for the elderly.

In 1995–96 there were a number of attempts to rein back expenditure on unemployment benefit and social assistance, with the claim that to do so would increase the incentive to work. The changes were not insubstantial, but they have nevertheless left the bulk of the social safety net intact. They include, for instance, a cut in unemployment benefit by reducing the reference wage, against which the benefit is calculated, by 5 per cent per year of unemployment. Other changes limited the access of asylum seekers to the dole, as well as cutting the access of those Germans whose social insurance entitlement had not been established because they had spent an insufficiently long periods in work. In the case of social assistance, cuts in benefit have been introduced for those who refuse the offer of an acceptable job; and benefits, which are paid for three years after the expiry of unemployment pay, are now linked to the increase in the net collective wage rate. Finally, and directly linked to the '50 Point Programme', the government is seeking to discourage the practice of using early retirement as a way of 'painless' labour shedding. The 300 000 taking early retirement in 1995 alone will force up pension contribution rates to 20 per cent of gross remuneration by 1997 (it was 17.7 per cent in 1992), and so the government is seeking to promote half-time employment as an alternative to early retirement.

These adjustments are not seriously undermining welfare provision, but it is evident that financial constraints and the ideological pressure to cut welfare 'scrounging' are driving the reform agenda. In the area of labour market reforms, there are clear differences between the government and much of the economic establishment on the one hand, and the trade unions on the other, over the question of employment creation, the absorption of unemployment and the challenge to Germany's competitiveness. Nevertheless the federal government gave a warm welcome to the proposal in November 1995 by Klaus Zwickel, head of the huge IG Metall union, for an 'Alliance for Jobs'. From the government's standpoint the explicit link it made between a real wage standstill and job creation was an example to the broader union movement. The government's and (largely) the economics profession's view has long been that the rise in unemployment in western Germany is only in part recession-induced, and that a substantial proportion of total unemployment is structural, and not amenable to demand management solutions. More than one half of western Germany's 2.96 million unemployed (9.6 per cent) in February 1996 had been unemployed for more than a year, and this pointed to the existence of a level of unemployment of perhaps 7 per cent, below which it would be unsafe to let unemployment fall as it might accelerate inflation (Bundesbank Annual Report, 1994). The traditional recommendation of market liberals such as the Bundesbank, the Council of Economic Advisors (SBGE, 1994) and the Deregulation Commission in their Reports I and II of 1990–91, has been to favour far greater flexibility in German collective bargaining, which would produce much greater wage differentiation by plant, branch and region, to match relative productivities. Of course the total absence of any link between the low productivity in the eastern Länder and the harmonisation of wages there with those in the west has meant that unit wage costs in the east, even in early 1996, remained 23 per cent higher than in the west, a 'job killer' strategy that substantially explains the rise in unemployment there.

The federal government's approach has consistently stressed wage moderation, whereby 'cost-neutral' salary increases would be justified by productivity gains. Given the constitutional requirement that the government should leave collective bargaining to the 'social partners', the federal government has sought by labour market measures to improve the supply of skills, and by incremental legislative changes to foster job-sharing, part-time employment and fixed-contract working. The trade union federations, in contrast, since 1984 have sought to reduce the working week to 35 hours (to be finally achieved in mid 1996) as a method of sharing the available work. Few economists are persuaded by this approach, particularly since no *pro rata* pay cuts have been made in line with the reduction of the working week. However, in practice far greater flexibility in working methods and working times has raised the machine running times in factories, and so productivity gains have paid for the fewer hours worked. The 1994 chemical industry settlement broke new ground in that it set a working time 'corridor' of maximum and minimum hours to be worked: this allows employees to build up 'overtime hours accounts', which they can draw upon when business is slack. In the 1995 wage negotiations in Opel and Volkswagen, for example, employers were determined to achieve such flexibility, matching the variation in the working week with the pattern of demand, and thus helping to counter high costs.

The 'Alliance for Jobs' proposal sought to trade flat real wages in the period 1997–99 for the creation by employers of 300 000 new jobs, and a 5 per cent rise in apprentice intake. The calculation was that the productivity gains obtained by employers would pay for the creation of employment. The marked rise in German unemployment to a postwar high of four million, however, changed the focus of union discussion to a trade-off between the number of overtime hours worked (three billion in 1995) for the creation of posts. However these approaches remain rooted in the fallacy that there is a fixed volume of work to be divided. The fact is that unit labour costs, taking into account the external value of the Deutsche Mark, are a decisive factor in such a heavily export-dependent economy. The course of unemployment in the future will continue to reflect this, as Germany's international competitiveness remains under stress, though measures such as deregulation in utilities and services would be employment-generating, a question that will be returned to in the final section.

Economic Restructuring in the East

Table 12.1 presented the macroeconomic data for the region since 1990. It is clear that after the traumatic impact of reunification on production and employment, the ensuing fundamental transformation has brought about a marked improvement since 1992, albeit from a much reduced productive base. With GDP growth rates in the region averaging 8 per cent over this period, and industrial output growing by 20 per cent in 1994 and an estimated 15 per cent in 1995, eastern Germany is Europe's fastest growing region. Productive investment per head in the east is now one third higher than in the older Länder. The upturn was first experienced in the construction and fitting-out sectors, together with supply sectors such as bricks and quarrying, and sectors sheltered from interregional competition, such as food processing and printing. From late 1993, however, orders and output statistics displayed a much broader-based recovery.

A nuanced assessment is needed of the economic evolution in the east. The shrinkage of the industrial base has meant that only 622 000 workers remained in industrial employment at the end of 1994, and that production is very skewed towards branches of the industry that are less subject to extraregional competition. The region's foreign exports represent only 1.8 per cent of Germany's total merchandise exports. Yet the strong upturn has been accompanied by a boom in enterprise formation, with 500 000 – generally small – private firms created there, alongside the 10 000 private firms established by the *Treuhand* and the 25 000 restructured by it. Much new employment has been created in the artisan craft sector (167 000 employees at the end of 1994). This has been particularly favoured by regional aid policy, and it is to this that we now turn.

The *Gemeinschaftswerk Aufschwung Ost* (joint task for recovery in the East) regional development assistance programme was introduced in March 1991 as an emergency supplement to the generous regional aid provisions that already existed. In addition EU structural assistance of DM6 billion was paid during the years 1991–93. Federal regional aid offered in aggregate a 50 per cent subsidy on investment projects in the first year, but the *Aufschwung Ost* programme offered an additional DM24 billion over two years for the establishment of new firms, infrastructural improvement and support for local authority capital investment. For the period 1996–98 further aid, focusing on the *Mittelstand* (small and medium-sized enterprises) is available, as well as loans to consolidate their capital base. Total public support of DM200 billion to end 1994 (excluding *Treuhand* expenditure of DM295 billion) has stimulated a total public and private investment level of more than DM750 billion since 1991 (MRDB, 7/1995; Eckart, 1995).

The *Treuhand* and Privatisation

The *Treuhand* (Public Trustee Office) was replaced by four successor organisations on 1 January 1995, and with the subsequent sale of much of the heavy industry that remained, a large part of the privatisation of east German state assets has been completed. Yet the debate on the wisdom of the priority given to privatisation continues. Was a sale at knock-down prices inevitable, or did this represent a straight handover of east German wealth to west German opportunists? Would a careful restructuring in state hands have avoided the liquidation of productive assets, with such destructive consequences for employment, incomes and regional wealth? The productive state assets with which the *Treuhand* was endowed in March 1990 were then valued at DM1000 billion, revised downwards at the end of 1991 by *Treuhandanstalt* President Rohwedder to DM600 billion, and finally on 31 December 1994 these assets had dissolved away to a loss of DM275 billion. Asset sale revenues amounted to only DM74 billion. The debate continues as to whether economically productive assets were squandered and handed over to the west, or whether they were engulfed in a sea of red ink.

Table 12.4 shows the final balance of the *Treuhandanstalt* in late November 1994: 8389 enterprises were either fully or partially privatised, and although 3713 were scheduled for liquidation, approximately 6000 productive units from them were to be sold, thereby preserving 30 per cent of those jobs. As indicated, the employment and investment guarantees contained in sales contracts amounted to almost 1.5 million jobs and DM207 billion in investment commitments. Remaining at the end of 1994 were four management limited partnerships, comprising 66 firms and five companies (primarily in the 'industrial core') in which the *Treuhand* retained a minority shareholding. While many of the 'small' privatisations (management buyouts, hotels, restaurants, repair shops) had been offered to eastern Germans, the bulk (80 per cent) of the assets were sold to western German investors. The scale and rate of disposal is impressive, but it has to be borne in mind that the number employed in enterprises in the *Treuhand*'s remit shrank from 3.5 million in 1990 to fewer than 1.5 million, with only 600 000 employed in industry proper at the end of 1994.

The priority given to rapid privatisation was enshrined in both the early 1990 East German legislation and in the Unification Treaty, but it is clear that it gained greater weight with time. The president of the *Treuhandanstalt*, Detlev Rohwedder, spoke of the 'triad', of 'rapid privatisation, decisive restructuring and cautious liquidation', while his successor, Birgit Breuel, saw privatisation as the best form of restructuring. The transformation process began with the break-up of the 126 giant industrial combines into 12 000 firms (joint stock or limited liability). Non-core activities such as crèches and other welfare support were separated out, and on 1 July 1990 all enterprises were required to draw up an asset evaluation and prepare a corporate plan. Only after the plan had been approved (when it was judged *sanierungsfähig*, capable of being restructured) could investment credits be given. Until that point only liquidity credits to cover running costs were afforded. Much criticism focuses on the supposed reluctance of the *Treuhand* to invest and pursue an active restructuring policy rather than to seek rapid asset disposals, and to this point we will return. The privatisation policy itself comprised a number of elements:

TABLE 12.4 *Treuhand balance sheet, November 1995*

1. Of 12 370 firms
   - 7 853 fully privatised
   - 3 713 closed
   - 536 transferred to municipalities or majority private shareholding
   - 268 remain

2. Investment guarantees of DM206.5 billion Employment guarantees of 1 487 280 jobs

3. July 1990–1994:
   - Income DM 41.7 billion
   - Expenditure DM 171.1 billion

- Enterprises that had been expropriated in the years 1933–45 or in the last nationalisation wave in 1972, and those expropriations up to June 1953 (on the orders of the East German authorities) were all returned to their previous owners. In respect of the 14 100 applications for restitution in April 1994, 4200 firms had been returned to previous owners plus 1842 other items of real estate.
- In order to develop a *Mittelstand* (small and medium-sized firms) in the east, to be the seedbed of entrepreneurship and innovation, management buy-in and management buy-out were the favoured mechanisms for selling productive capacity to east German managers. One fifth of all privatisations, involving 137 700 employees, took this route.
- Management limited partnerships were set up, each as a mini-conglomerate, grouping a disparate range of difficult-to-sell firms with the objective that the partnerships would restructure and then sell the enterprises in their portfolios, with payment by results.
- Foreign investors were courted, and of the 702 investors in May 1994, one half came from Switzerland, Britain and Austria.

Clearly the experience of the *Treuhand* was that firms serving the regional market could be readily disposed of. However those in sectors subject to Third World competition, and in particular those in the heavy industry sector (heavily polluting and with obsolescent technology) were almost unsaleable. The latter were termed the 'industrial core'.

Criticism of the *Treuhand*'s supposed ideological blindness to any approach other than privatisation focus on the lack of political control, the absurdly low selling prices and the unwillingness to pursue an effective industrial policy that would restructure capacity while in state hands, and thus help adjustment to the new competitive market conditions. In a sense, lack of political control underlies the other two criticisms.

It is doubtful whether close political control would have avoided the scandals of the early period, when ex-communist managers sold to party friends, when asset-stripping and the filleting-out of prime real estate was rife, or when the Halle region of the *Treuhand* indulged systematically in illegal activities. In the early days, when few trained staff were available and reliable data non-existent, well-founded asset valuation was impossible to achieve.

Sales revenues amounted to a meagre DM74 billion, and many transactions were accompanied by 'sweeteners' of hundreds of millions of marks. For example a 50 per cent share of the Carl Zeiss plant in

Jena was sold to its West German sister, Carl Zeiss Oberkochen, for DM1, after the *Treuhandanstalt* and the Land Thüringen had invested DM1 billion. The formal sales method was as follows. Management buy-outs and the sale of small pieces of real estate in the service sector were at fixed prices, but larger assets were sold by tender. The *Treuhand* started from the book valuation of 1 July 1990 and deducted inherited debt, plus the cost of commitments to protect the workforce and environmental clean-up. Given the scale of these liabilities, it was inevitable that very large discounts would have to be offered (DIW Wochenbericht, 1992a). However it is also the case that the initial valuations were grossly optimistic: they were distorted by the GDR asset pricing system, by the old hard currency exchange rates used, and by the long period adopted for historic depreciation of asset values. Equally, credits to other enterprises and socialist brother countries were fully accounted for when there was little hope of their being repaid in full. Much criticism (Nick, 1995) focuses on rushed privatisation in the manner of a forced sale: potential purchasers could insist on low prices. Had the original valuations prevailed, this would have absorbed three years' worth of total German investment, which was not possible. As Nick (1995), Sinn and Sinn (1992) and Kurz (1993) point out, a large asset value loss was preordained if valuations reflected a future profit stream: at reunification this was negative, and high real interest rates depressed forecast returns even more. In reality, as will be seen below, the economic terms and conditions of reunification, including rapid wage catch-up, implied a haemorraging of enterprise finances, and the scale of operating losses was overwhelming.

Should the *Treuhand* have pursued an active industrial policy? It is held that the *Treuhand* starved its enterprises of investment funds, devoting all its energy to finding private buyers. It is true that the investment rate in its enterprises was only one half that of privatised companies, for example in 1992 investment and capital injections into *Treuhand* firms amounted to only DM2.8 billion, while liquidity credits totalled DM8 billion. Yet the *Treuhand* judged that 80 per cent of its enterprises were capable of being restructured: the evidence points again to the scale of current losses, which absorbed most funds. Proponents of alternative and more active approaches vary from those in the liberal market tradition to those with a markedly protectionist viewpoint (DIW Wochenbericht, 1992a; Meyer, 1991; Arbeitsgruppe, 1992).

As a separate policy strand, the federal government began to speak of the preservation of 'industrial cores' in the east for regional employment reasons. The chancellor's working group on 'Structural Changes in the East', reporting in spring 1992, first proposed longer-term support. Finance Minister Waigel and Chancellor Kohl then used such support as a bargaining counter in the Solidarity Pact negotiations in September 1993, seeking union wage restraint while directing state expenditure to the east. For a group of these essentially unsaleable, obsolescent industrial monoliths, Waigel allocated DM45 billion for their support and restructuring to the year 2000. The concept of an 'industrial core', is wholly vague (Breuel *et al.*, 1993; DIW Wochenbericht 13/1993) and the motivation is political. In practice most were sold in 1994 and 1995 with previously unimaginable injections of public funds. Examples are the Baltic coast shipyards, where each surviving job has been saved at a cost of DM1 million, and the Buna–Leuna–Bitterfeld chemicals triangle, where only 2700 jobs remain in chemicals and DM30 billion in public funds has been spent since 1990.

On 1 January 1995 three successor companies began operation, and a fourth will commence on 1 January 1997. By far the largest continuing activity will be that of supervising the *Treuhand*'s 75 000 privatisation contracts to ensure that contractual requirements, including investment and employment guarantees, are adhered to: 2300 of the current 4300 *Treuhandanstalt* employees were transferred for this task to the BVS (Federal Institute for Unification-Induced Tasks).

Investment and Liberalisation

As we have seen, in order to address the competitiveness problem and meet the costs of the east, the policy agenda, certainly for western Germany, shows considerable resemblance to that of the first Kohl government of 1982–83, of privatisation, supply-side reforms by liberalisation, including labour market reform, and the elimination of 'structural' (non-cyclically-induced) budget deficits. Since the tax burden will still be high, sources of growth must be found other than reliance on domestic consumption. The *Standort Deutschland* question – whether Germany has fundamentally lost its competitiveness as a production location – is at the forefront of debate. This is at least the third time the issue has been debated since the mid 1980s, and it tends to move to the fore of public discussion when appreciations (rises) of the Deutsche Mark occur. The normal pattern in the past has been that the issue fades under the effect of further currency movements and good cost control in Germany. Thus, typically, the overvalued

Deutsche Mark falls back, while concurrently German industry reduces its unit labour costs by productivity gains and wage moderation (DIW Wochenbericht, 1992b, 1993b), such that export competitiveness is reestablished. Good control of costs is a German feature, such that in the period 1966–91 German unit wage costs rose faster than those of its competitors in only two years. Overall, in national currency terms, unit wage costs remained stable in the two decades to 1994, but the Deutsche Mark appreciation more than offset these cost gains.

Notwithstanding the above, the recent higher wage settlements of 4 per cent for 1995 and 1996, coupled with a 4 per cent trade-weighted rise in the Deutsche Mark in the first half of 1995, have fuelled the debate, and are certainly given as the reason for sustained job cuts and the transfer of production abroad. Over the period 1991–94, for example, manufacturing in western Germany shed 1.13 million jobs (OECD, 1995), and the car industry, chemicals and aerospace all plan significant employment reductions, accompanied by investment outside Germany. In a questionnaire survey of February 1995 by the Munich IFO Institut, of companies representing 25 per cent of German manufacturing, 56 per cent planned to raise their share of investment abroad compared with that in Germany. The most obvious cases are DASA Aerospace, which has incurred losses of hundreds of millions of Deutsche Marks due to the weak dollar, and Mercedes-Benz, which plans to out-source 30 per cent of its components.

Liberalisation is a foundation stone of the FDP junior coalition partner's ideology, and Economics Minister Rexrodt published a report in September 1993 entitled the *Zukunftssicherung des Standorts Deutschland.* It proposed 147 measures for deregulation and a small number of changes, such as a reduction in corporation tax and the promotion of part-time working in the civil service, were enacted in the *Standortsicherungsgesetz* (Law to secure the production competitiveness of Germany) of 1993. Reform in Germany is painstaking, legalistic and consensual, particularly if it requires constitutional change, since this requires agreement in the SPD-dominated Bundesrat.

The federal government took the decision in mid 1992 either to privatise or to 'corporatise' (create a joint-stock company status) utilities such as post and telecommunications, the Lufthansa airline and the railways. Concerning the latter, the Deutsche Bahn AG was created in December 1993, thereby uniting the western and eastern railway companies. It was organised into three subsidiaries covering the rail network (which charges for its use), passenger transport and freight, thereby granting much greater managerial freedom and offering the possibility of private railway operating concessions, as well as private capital injections. The intercity services are expected to earn a positive return, while the matter of subsidising local and regional services has been devolved to lower tiers of government (SBGE, 1995). In the case of Lufthansa, privatisation has begun in three stages, with federal participation falling from 51.4 per cent to 38 per cent in 1995, and in subsequent years to zero.

The liberalisation of the postal and telecommunications services offers a fascinating insight into the political economy of abolition of monopoly. In 1993 the monolithic Bundespost was broken up into three joint-stock companies: Telekom, Postdienst (Postal services) and Postbank. According to Single Market directives, the voice transmission monopoly must be liberalised by 1998, while terminal equipment and value-added network services have already been liberalised to varying degrees. Postal Minister Bötsch published proposals in June 1995 for the fundamental liberalisation of telecommunications and the postal service. In telecommunications the key principle has been established that an unlimited number of licensees may offer telecom services from 1998 subject to performance criteria. Only firms with more than 25 per cent of the market, such as Deutsche Telekom, will be required to operate a universal service throughout Germany. Other operations with more than a 5 per cent market share must contribute to a universal service fund, which will compensate for the costs of providing such a service. It is planned that Deutsche Telekom will be partially privatised in 1996, raising DM50–70 billion in a complete sale before the year 2000. However, of considerable concern from a competition policy standpoint is the fact that Deutsche Telekom retains the world's largest and densest optical fibre cable network, and that it has recently forged a highly oligopolistic alliance with the French telecom monopolist, France Télécom and with the third largest US telecom operater, Sprint.

The Slowness of Reform

Fundamental changes such as these have been slow to achieve, partly because of due deliberation, and partly because changes affecting the status of civil servants (pensions, job tenure) are highly costly and require lengthy negotiation. In the postwar era the German social market order, with its mix of corporatism together with open markets in manufacturing and its emphasis on consensual negotiation, has proved its strength. However there are now more fundamental doubts as to whether this German model of regulation, with its 'stakeholder' capitalism (where banks, suppliers and key customers may sit on the supervisory board of the company), its high levels of training, its specialisation in producing goods of medium to high value-added, can survive the intensifying world competition. It is commonly said that Germany has further refined its specialisation in investment goods, but has failed to gain a comparative advantage in high-technology goods. Tight regulation of genetic engineering and biotechnology is one example.

The slowness of change is very much a function of the consensual mode of management at company level, and of the need in the capital to forge agreements within the ruling coalition, and with the SPD-dominated Bundesrat. In spite of the many successes in the absorption of eastern Germany, including the fiscal management of huge transfers to the east, one may register considerable doubts as to whether the much-admired strengths of the German model will suffice to sustain growth and employment into the next decade.

13

Interest Groups in the Five New Länder

STEPHEN PADGETT

Interest groups play a vital role in pluralist political systems. Representing the interests of major social groups and mediating between their members and government, they provide the institutional linkage between state and society. As intermediary organisations they help to establish order amongst the myriad of private interests in society, weaving these into the broader fabric of the public interest. Effective systems of interest representation promote social cohesion, overcoming the clash of competing interests and resolving conflicts between the private and public spheres.

Organised interests have a key role to play in the democratic transformnation of post-communist societies, contributing to the formation of the new socioeconomic order and countering the social fragmentation accompanying economic upheaval. In Germany they also have a role in bridging the divisions between east and west, articulating eastern interests and ensuring that easterners have a voice in the new German polity. Whilst interest groups have been slow to form in most of the post-communist states of Eastern Europe, their emergence in the new German Länder was rapid. Reunification was accompanied by the institutional transfer of a 'ready-made' system of organised interest representation from western Germany.

Although institutional transfer endowed the new German Länder with a functioning system of interest representation, a number of questions remained unanswered. The questions clustered around the ability of the (western) German model of interest organisation to take root in a differently structured society in the east. First, in the absence of a culture of voluntary organisation, it was uncertain whether interest groups would be able to recruit effectively. A second question related to the ability of interest groups based in western Germany to adapt to a different configuration of interests in post-communist society. Third, how quickly would easterners learn the behavioural and procedural conventions of interest group activity? Finally, could we expect to see the emergence of a network of relations between interest groups and government in the new Länder, on the lines of the German model? Before turning to these questions, however, we shall examine the origins of interest organisations in the reunification process.

The Rise of Interest Organisations in the East

With the progressive disintegration of the GDR, the previously closed sphere of civil society was opened up. Organisational initiatives, however, were characterised by hesitancy and disorientation. The GDR oposition was made up of an amorphous popular movement centred on the churches and dissident intellectuals. In contrast to Poland, the trade unions remained tied to the regime. Unlike some other Eastern European countries, there was no emerging private sector to nurture a business class. Professional groups were subordinated to the party and state. In short there was no foundation for launching economic or professional interest groups. Organisational initiatives emerged amongst managers in state enterprises, would-be entrepreneurs pressing claims for the restitution of businesseses confiscated in the 1950s, and in the medical profession. These early initiatives, however, remained largely informal, the participants unsure of the future. Driven by an ill-defined 'reform euphoria', they were overtaken by the acceleration of reunification. With but a few exceptions, indigenous organisational activity was incorporated into the structures of interest representation in the Federal Republic.

As reunification gathered momentum, the tempo of organisation building was stepped up in a headlong dash to keep pace. Attempts to reform GDR institutions were abandoned, and indigenous initiatives lost ground, their adherents increasingly attracted by the organisational strength of their western counterparts. Western interests intensified their activity in the east, either consolidating partnership arrangements with GDR initiatives or establishing organisational networks of their own. Thus organisational activity was decisively marked by the logic of reunification, as the institutional blueprint of the Federal Republic was superimposed upon indigenous initiatives.

In the absence of an entrepreneurial middle class, the organisation of business interests emerged out of an alliance between the GDR managerial elite and business associations in the Federal Republic. The first tentative steps were taken by managers in the metals and electricals sectors. From the outset their initiative was oriented towards cooperation with Gesamtmetall, their counterpart in western Germany. (Ettl and Wiesenthal 1994, p. 7). A cooperation agreement was quickly concluded, committing the partners to working together in wage bargaining (Gesamtmetall, 1992, pp. 4–5). For both employer associations and trade unions, organisational building was a race for competitive advantage in the forthcoming wage bargaining rounds. By September 1990, with massive logistical support from Gesamtmetall, there was a Verband der Metall- und Elektroindustrie (VME) in each of the new Länder. Subsequently the VME played the vanguard role in promoting employer organisations in the other industrial sectors.

Organisational activity also emerged at the level of the local economy, in the form of *Industrie und Handelskammern* (IHK, Chambers of Industry and Commerce). Organisational activity began in November 1989, with initiatives aimed at reform of the GDR *Handels und Gewerberkammern* (Chambers of Trade and Commerce). Consisting of an alliance of small retailers and managers in local state enterprises, the reconstituted chambers immediately sought the cooperation of their counterparts in the west. The new chambers quickly affiliated to the Deutscher Industrie and Handelstag (DIHT – German Chamber of Industry and Commerce); formation of an autonomous confederation of chambers in the new Länder was never seriously considered.

Organisation building in the trade unions initially centred on the reform of GDR labour organisations. Reform was problematical, however, due to the inseparability of the old structures from the GDR regime. Democratic statutes and a new leadership failed to establish popular legitimacy, and the unions continued to lose members (Schmid and Thiemann, 1992, p. 139; Thiemann, Schmid and Löber, 1993, p. 42). With the acceleration of reunification, the reform strategy was fatally undermined. Bolstered by polls indicating huge public support, the western German unions adopted a more assertive role (Fichter and Kubjuhn, 1992, p. 162), taking control of the reform process and assimilating new structures into their own organisation. The largest member of the Federation of German Trade Unions, IG Metall, made a complete legal break with the past, winding up its GDR counterpart and simply extending their own organisation eastward (Fichter, 1993, pp. 29–31). For western German trade unions the organisational decrepitude and legitimacy deficit of their eastern counterparts made them unattractive partners as they sought to establish a strong presence in the collective bargaining arena.

In professional life the direction of organisational activity varied from one group to another. In the medical profession, indigenous organisational initiatives such as the Rudolf-Virchow-Bund (RVB) were quickly left behind by the gravitation of doctors to the powerful western German associations. Again the logic of reunification was decisive. Once the decision was taken to assimilate eastern Germany into the Federal Republic's health care system, a separate doctors' association in the new Länder appeared anachronistic (Erdmann, 1992, p. 327). Already overburdened by the demands of establishing themselves in private practice, doctors had little time for independent associational activity, and were attracted by the organisational strength of the doctors associations based in the west. Exclusively eastern German organisations survived only where their western counterparts failed to respond to the interests of easterners. Amongst engineers, for instance, the Kammer der Technik (Chamber of Technology) represented a large number of semiqualified engineers who were initially denied professional status in the Federal Republic. With engineers associations in the west unresponsive to their claims, the Ingenieurtechnische Verband retained a role as the advocate of eastern interests. For most occupational groups, however, integration into the professional life of the Federal Republic meant a parallel assimilation into associational structures in western Germany.

Organisational Structure

The associational order in post-communist Germany reflects its origins in institutional transfer from the Federal Republic, corresponding broadly to 'the German model'. Germany provides the role model of organised capitalism, a strong and effective system of organised interests being the key to 'an orderly relationship between the economic and political systems' (Edinger, 1993, pp. 177, 187). The model is rooted in intensive networks of organised interest activity.

Business organisation rests on three pillars. Employers' interests are represented by the Bundesvereinigung der Deutschen Arbeitgeberverbände, (BDA Federation of German Employer's Association), consisting of specialist associations covering all the main economic sectors, and with a primary function of wage bargaining. The wider interests of German industry are served by the Bundesverband der deutschen Industrie (BDI, a confederation of trade associations spanning the range of industrial branches). The third pillar of business organisation consists of the *Industrie und Handelskammer* (Chambers of Industry and Commerce). There are chambers in every major city, regulating and representing local commerce.

Employers' interests are quite well entrenched in eastern Germany, thanks mainly to the strong presence of the Verband der Metall- und Elektroindustrie (VME, a federation representing employers in the metals and electricals sectors). Across eastern Germany the VME has a staff of around 150, and provides the personnel, financial backing and office premises for the 'peak' confederations of employers' associations in the Länder. With the exception of Brandenburg, which is merged with Berlin, there is an employers' confederation in each of the new Länder. Although they are affiliated to the BDA, they exercise considerable autonomy, representing a regional coalition of employers' interests. At times the Land confederations have combined to articulate specifically eastern employer interests when they have felt that these interests were being neglected by BDA headquarters in Cologne. In contrast organised industry is virtually absent. More centralised than the BDA, the BDI is correspondingly weaker at the regional level, with only one small bureau in eastern Germany.

Competing with the BDA affiliates are the independent eastern German *Unternehmerverbände* (entrepreneurs' associations). One of the very few specifically eastern interest organisations to survive the unification, *Unternehmerverbände* are present (though with uneven strength) in all the new Länder. Their membership is composed for the most part of small and medium-sized firms that consider themselves poorly represented by employers' associations dominated by large-scale business. The latter regard the *Unternehmerverbände* as unwelcome intruders in the associational order, attempting (without success) to drive them into extinction through competitive recruitment.

The organisational structure of the Chambers of Industry and Commerce reflects their primary purpose of ordering the local and regional economy, with 14 chambers in the main cities across the new Länder. With legally enforced membership and performing a range of quasi-public functions, the chambers of commerce are well resourced and have a staff establishment of between 50 and 200. The chambers have complete territorial sovereignty and financial autonomy. The functions of the DIHT in Bonn are limited to coordination and political representation with the federal government.

Like organised business, trade union organisation embodies the sectoral principle, with 16 industrial unions. All maintain a presence in eastern Germany, although the presence of the smaller unions is tenuous. IG Metall has the strongest presence in the new Länder. Its regional organisation is based on four 'mixed' *Bezirke* (regions) in which the new Länder are assimilated into their neighbouring western regions. Only Sachsen remains independent (*Bezirk* Dresden), and there are moves to merge this with Berlin–Brandenburg. 'Mixed' regions are seen as a way of avoiding the institutionalisation of east–west divisions, and have also served to harness the strength of established structures in western Germany to organisational activity in the new Länder. Regional structures based in the west are inevitably remote, but this is offset by an extensive 'on the ground' organisation, with 35 *Verwaltungsstellen* (district offices) across the new Länder. Of the other industrial unions, only ÖTV comes close to matching the intensity of IG Metall's district organisation. Smaller unions are too weak to maintain an extensive apparatus.

Collectively the industrial unions constitute the *Deutscher Gewerkschaftsbund* (DGB, Federation of German Trade Unions), a 'peak' confederation responsible for representing the 'political will' of organised labour. The DGB speaks for the trade unions in relations with Land government, and has a strong organisational presence at this level, with *Landesbezirke* for each of the new Länder (Brandenburg is combined with Berlin). It also has an extensive infrastructure at the *Kreis* (district) level. The trade unions have an army of staff in the new Länder. IG Metall employs almost 200 officials, whilst the DGB has a staff of over 300. Given the weakness of the east German economy it is questionable whether these staffing levels can be maintained, and with the decline in trade union membership organisational rationalisation is on the agenda.

Profesional associations are less oriented than employers and trade unions towards regional issues, and their centre of gravity is located nearer to federal government. Activity is more centralised, and regional and local organisation correspondingly less intensive. In the medical profession, even the larger associations such as the doctors' associations based in the West maintain little more than a skeletal organisation in the new Länder. Amongst engineers, organisational activity is even weaker. One of the few GDR organisations to survive reunification, the Kammer der Technik (KdT), ran into financial trouble and went into bankruptcy in 1994. Successor organisations were established, but with their assets subject to liquidation proceedings and their membership decimated, the new groups face an uncertain future. With the collapse of independent organisational activity amongst eastern German engineers, the Düsseldorf-based Verein Deutscher Ingenieure (VDI – Association of German Engineers), mounted an aggressive campaign to establish itself. The VDI, however, remains an essentially western association with only a few field staff in its branches in eastern Germany.

Interest Group Membership

Given the absence of an organisational tradition, and without social foundations, interest group membership in the new Länder is surprisingly high. In the DGB trade unions, organisational density (membership as a percentage of the total labour force) stands at around 50 per cent compared with about 32 per cent in western Germany. The organisational density of IG Metall is higher than average at around 60 per cent of the labour force, against 46 per cent in the west. Amongst employer associations membership is surprisingly close to western German levels. The VME in Sachsen, for instance, has a membership of around 330 in a sector employing a labour force of 115 000, against about 350 in Schleswig-Holstein and Hamburg, where the sector is of similar size.

High membership levels reflect strong recruitment in the immediate aftermath of reunification. Since then there has been a sharp decline in membership across the spectrum of interest organisations. Falling membership stemmed from deindustrialisation and the corresponding decline in the economically active population from which business groups and trade unions draw their members. Membership decline in the trade unions coincided with the rapid escalation in unemployment from late 1991 onwards. DGB membership fell by 18 per cent during 1992, with a further decline of around 15 per cent the following year. IG Metall was amongst the hardest hit, losing over 40 per cent of its 1991 members (see Table 13.1). Although the rate of decline continued to slow in 1994–95, it was clear that membership had not yet stabilised.

TABLE 13.1 *IG Metall membership, 1991–94*
(decline over previous year [%] in parentheses)

	31.12.91	*31.12.92*	*31.12.93*	*31.8.94**
Mecklenburg Vorpommern	64 715	51 018 (21.1)	44 643 (−12.5)	39 719 (−16.5)
Thüringen	187 020	146 002 (−21.9)	117 646 (−19.4)	107 309 (−13.0)
Sachsen	344 751 (−18.0)	282 069 (−17.9)	231 682 (−13.0)	211 234
Sachsen Anhalt	157 464	126 736 (−19.8)	107 655 (−15.1)	94 853 (−17.9)
Berlin (E) Brandenburg	196 954	157 095 (−20.2)	124 295 (−20.9)	110 249 (−17.0)
Total	950 904	762 920 (−19.8)	625 921 (−17.6)	563 364 (−15.0)

* Based on interim figures at 31.8.94; percentage decline annualised.

Business groups have suffered a similar decline, with company liquidations leading to a steady loss of member firms. Corporate restructuring and the accompanying boardroom instability has also broken up group membership, requiring business associations to re-recruit members. Companies often take the opportunity of restructuring to leave the employers' association. Amongst new business start-ups, employers' associations have an acute recruitment problem. The reluctance of new companies to join employers' associations has been seen as an attempt to escape from a centralised system of wage bargaining. With labour markets shifting sharply in their favour, many employers find collective bargaining an encumberance. By remaining outside the associations they are free to negotiate their own terms with their employees. Employers' associations are particularly weak amongst small and medium-sized firms (the so-called *Mittelstand* sector) which are struggling to meet pay agreements geared to convergence with the west (Ettl and Heikenroth, 1995). In the *Mittelstand* sector the large employers' associations are facing competition from the independent eastern German entrepreneurs' associations (Ettl, 1995, pp. 46–52), and the Bonn-based Bundesverband mittelständische Wirtschaft (BVMW, Federal Association of the Mittelstand Economy). Outside the system of collective wage bargaining, and with a focus on the problems of the small and medium-sized firms, these organisations can appear more 'user friendly' than employers' associations based in western Germany.

Professional associations in the new Länder remain weak. Around 35–40 per cent of doctors in the new Länder are members of a profesional association, compared with around 60 per cent in western Germany. All the doctors' associations have suffered a loss of members since they were established. Hartmannbund membership fell by almost 20 per cent between 1991 and 1994, and the Marburger Bund also suffered significant losses. In engineering, professional group membership is even lower. The collapse of the Kammer der Technik, left engineers largely unorganised. Its successor organisations were able to rerecruit only 4500 of the 65 000 affiliated to the KdT at the time of its bankruptcy. Despite the collapse of its main rival and a vigorous recruitment campaign, the VDI finds recruitment difficult with a membership of only around 8500 in the new Länder against 120 000 in western Germany. Low membership in professional associations can be ascribed to the absence of an organisational tradition. Lacking a professional ethos, group ties are weak and association membership is often subject to pragmatic, cost–benefit calculations.

Problems of Interest Representation

In the German model, both business associations and trade unions have a relatively well-developed organisational capacity for generating broadly based interest positions and for reconciling interest differences. In post-communist Germany, however, the spectrum of interests is more heterogeneous than in a mature capitalist economy, making interest representation correspondingly more difficult.

The representation of business interests in post-communist society is particularly problematical. The dynamics of economic transformation mean that the composition of the business class is highly diverse, with cross-cutting cleavages based on company size, structure of corporate ownership and sectoral differences (Ettl and Wiesenthal, 1994, pp. 9–13). A number of company types can be identified: undertakings remaining under *Treuhand* administration; concerns privatised as subsidiaries of parent companies in the west; management buy-outs; reprivatised companies (expropriated under the GDR regime and now returned to their former owners) and newly established firms. Management buy-outs, reprivatisations and newly established firms constitute the *Mittelstand* of privately owned, small to medium-scale undertakings. Reconciling the divergent interests of *Treuhand* companies, the subsidiaries of large western German firms, and the indigenous *Mittelstand* is the central problem of business interest representation in post-communist Germany. The roots of business associations in large-scale industry mean that the interests of smaller firms are often marginalised. Consequently organised business finds it difficult to recruit amongst *Mittelstand* companies. Barely 50 per cent of these firms are members of employers' associations, as against over 80 per cent of large firms with ownership in the west (Ettl and Heikenroth, 1995, pp. 20–1).

Trade unions are confronted with a similar diversity of interests, arising out of the dynamics of the post-communist economic transformation. Threatened by corporate restructuring and mass redundancies, workers' interests are tightly bound to the survival of the individual company, posing a challenge to industrial unions geared to the representation of broad sectoral interests. This problem is reflected in wage bargaining. The traditional model of uniform industry-wide pay agrements (*Flächentarifverträge*)) is insensitive to sharp variations between companies in productivity, commercial performance and security of employment characteristic of the post-communist economy. The unions' response is to defend the *principle* of industry-wide agreements whilst at the same time negotiating company-level settlements (*Haustarifverträge*). Whilst this strategy enables the unions to accommodate the divergent interests of its members, it risks undermining the principle of sectoral pay settlements and relinquishing control of the wage-bargaining arena to local actors. Trade unions also face a conflict of interests between wage earners and the unemployed. They have successfully defused this conflict by combining strong wage claims with demands for proactive industry and employment policies on the part of the state. Their success in integrating the interests of the unemployed is underlined by the failure of rival organisations seeking to represent this clientele.

Internal Organisational Life

Although most interest groups in Western democracies have elaborate structures of internal democracy, participation tends to be low. A close relationship between economic interest groups and the state has led to a more technical style of interest representation, with professional specialists playing the leading role. Organisations have become increasingly complex, remote and subject to the domination of salaried officials. Members act more like clients of the organisation than participants in its internal life. Membership passivity is exacerbated by an individualistic preoccupation with private concerns, which has been identified as a hallmark of post-communist society. Economic and social transformation makes heavy demands upon the individual. Material insecurity and the need to adapt to new economic structures leads to a syndrome of 'lifeboat economics', in which everybody is looking for an individual way to escape. In the initial stages of reunification, organisational activity was buoyant. With the emergence of market structures, activism quickly gave way to private responses: either the exploitation of market opportunities through engagement in individual economic activity, or perceiving economic change as a threat, leading to withdrawal and a sense of powerlessness. Both of these responses are antithetical to participation in organisational activity.

For the most part, the formal structures of internal democracy remain lifeless. Contests for elected office tend to be low key, and some organisations find it hard to find willing incumbents. Voting rates in elections are correspondingly low. Group activity is heavily dominated by salaried officials. In the employers' associations and chambers of commerce, elected office holders are usually managers or business people heavily committed to running their own firms, with little time to engage in associational activity. They rely heavily on the chief executive (*Hauptgeschäftsführer*), who assumes a pivotal role in the internal life of the organisation, and its external representation.

Similar tendencies are evident in the trade unions. In IG Metall's district organisation, for example, the *Ortsverwaltung* (management committee) is dominated by its two salaried officials, with the lay members generally passive. The latter are normally works councillors in local companies, and whilst they are often highly committed, they lack the organisational skills to play a major role in managing union business. Formally the management committee is accountable to the *Vertreterversammlung* (membership assembly), but in practice the latter rarely exercises its democratic sovereignty. Thus the apparatus of rank and file democracy in IG Metall is rarely brought to life, and organisational activity depends heavily on salaried officials.

Reliance on salaried officials is part of the institutional inheritance from the Federal Republic, where the associational order is highly professionalised. This tendency is accentuated by the dominance of western Germans in organisational life. Although the balance has been redressed somewhat since reunification, western Germans continue to occupy key salaried posts. The imbalance in organisational skills and experience between easterners and westerners inevitably accentuates elite domination and mass passivity.

Passivity is combined with very high expectations of the capacity of organised interests for realising their demands. This syndrome is prevalent across the associational order, but is particularly pronounced in the trade unions. Eighty-four per cent of easterners expect trade unions to realise 'optimal' results 'despite all the difficulties', against 57 per cent of westerners. The corollary of exaggerated expectations is dissatisfaction. Only 56 per cent of union members find their expectations 'fully' or 'mostly' fulfilled, against 70 per cent in the Federal Republic overall. High expectations and the satisfaction deficit are compounded by the relative weakness of ties between unions and their members. Membership commitment is significantly lower in eastern Germany than in the west. Survey data shows that only 44 per cent of union members are unable to conceive of leaving the union, against 56 per cent in the west (IfEP, 1994).

Theories of collective action have identified a 'free-rider' syndrome (Olson, 1965) in which individuals can benefit from the lobbying efforts of 'their' organisation without subscribing to membership. To discourage free-riding, interest groups have to offer selective services that are available exclusively to their members. The weakness of membership loyalty in eastern Germany means that interest groups have to place particular emphasis on their role as service providers. In addition to their wage bargaining role, trade unions offer their members a range of vocational and legal advice. Employers' organisations offer many of the services associated with business consultancy. Professional groups provide technical back-up and advice on the financial problems facing members newly established in private practice. Interest groups thus tend to resemble quasicommercial tertiary sector organisations servicing a clientele that judges the value of membership on the basis of pragmatic cost–benefit calculations. The client relationship between groups and their members is a very pronounced feature of interest organisation in eastern Germany, reflecting the weak social foundations of organisational activity.

Organisation without a Social Base

Interest organisation is rooted in the social structure of capitalist society. The division of labour intrinsic to capitalism generates social groups bound together by shared interests, a common status and a distinctive cultural identity. The introduction of a capitalist economy in the new German Länder has led to the emergence of market-based social structures – an entrepreneurial middle class, and the variegated strata of salaried white-collar staff and manual wage earners. However these social groups lack the cohesion of their counterparts in mature capitalist societies. The predominant characteristics of post-communist society are fragmentation, individualisation and absence of the broadly based social formations that underpin the associational order in the West (Offe, 1991, pp. 876–7).

Organised business suffers from the weakness of the entrepreneurial middle class, and from the absence of business networks. In western Germany, business organisation takes place against the background of well-established commercial relations between firms in a particular sector or in the local economy. The 'insider system' of corporate governance (see Chapter 11) generates a strong sense of shared identity amongst a 'business class' in which competition is combined with a sense of belonging to a group. In the emerging capitalist economy in the new Länder, business people and managers were isolated. The initial task of the employers' associations was to bring them together through activities such as seminars and 'entrepreneur evenings' designed to establish their social foundations. The emergence of a business class has been retarded, however, by the corporate instability accompanying economic transformation. A rapid turnover of managers and boardroom personnel has disrupted the formation of business networks. In the face of this instability, group interests and identities have been slow to form.

Organised labour also lacks a stable social foundation. The differentiated labour market exhibits sharp variations in earnings and employment between sectors and regions. The service sector, and the 'islands' of high-technology industry (such as that around the new Opel plant at Eisenach), stand out from the general picture of deindustrialisation. The result is social fragmentation, between a minority of high wage workers with secure employment in the sunrise sectors, the marginally employed and low paid in the industrial 'rust belt', and the unemployed (Bialas and Ettl, 1992, p. 34). With the post-communist economy undergoing profound structural change, labour-movement solidarity is acutely difficult to sustain.

Regional Corporatism

Organised interests perform the function of mediating relations between the state and the economy. The more interventionist the state, the more it relies on the 'mediation' of interest groups. In the post-communist economic transformation of eastern Germany the state is inevitably being drawn into a central role (Bullmann and Schwanengel, 1995, p. 194), setting out the ground rules of the new order and ameliorating the social problems brought about by rapid economic change. State intervention is reflected in a dense network of neocorporatist relations between government, organised business and the trade unions. Relations are focused on the extensive apparatus of industry and labour-market policy in the Länder.

Corporatist trends in the new Länder emerged in 1991 in response to the deepening crisis of deindustrialisation and a growing consensus amongst trade unions, employers and Land governments about the need for a more activist industrial policy. The first meeting of the social partners and Land government in Saxony-Anhalt, for instance, took place in October 1991. Early in 1992, the Sachsen government pioneered the 'Atlas model' of cooperation between IG Metall, business, Land government and the *Treuhand* in securing the future of key firms in the regional economy. The Atlas model received a significant boost from the *Treuhand* policy shift of mid 1992, giving increased priority to employment considerations in the process of industrial restructuring. In November the new industrrial policy orientation was adopted by the Chancellor; 'firms that have not yet been restructured should not be allowed to go under' (*Der Spiegel*, 23 November 1992). Saxony's Atlas experiment was subsequently replicated across the new Länder.

Industrial policy activism has greatly strengthened corporatist relations, with business and trade unions represented across the extensive apparatus of industry and labour-market policy. Relations between organised interests and Land government occur at a number of different levels. The most intensive interaction takes place at 'the working level' of routine contact (on a weekly or even daily basis) between organised interest officials and civil servants in Land ministries. At the political level there are quarterly *Spitzengespräche* (summit talks) between the government and the leaders of economic interest organisations. In some of the Länder these multilateral talks are augmented by annual bilateral discussions between government and the Land level leadership of the DGB and the employers' confederation. In between these set-piece summits, interest-group chief executives meet ministers and leading officials on a fairly regular, informal basis.

The quality and intensity of corporatist relations is subject to considerable variation across the new Länder. Saxony remains the primary example, with a CDU-led government engaged in a creative dialogue with trade unions and business groups. Elsewhere corporatist relations have taken longer to emerge, and are more dependent on partisan alliances. Trade unions find access easier under an SPD administration or grand coalition; employers' associations find CDU governments more congenial. Nevertheless partisanship is less ingrained than in western Germany. Institutions are less formalised and ideology less ingrained. Both interest groups and government are open to a wider range of contacts and dialogue.

The exception to the corporatist pattern was Thüringia, where industry policy under the CDU government was limited in extent and private sector in orientation. Relations between government and economic interests were strained, with trade unions and business groups united in their criticism of government passivity in the face of deindustrialisation. With this exception, however, corporatist interest mediation has taken root in industrial and labour-market policy. The social tensions arising from rapid economic change have been contained and moderated within the system of interest representation, indicating that the system is adaptable to the rigours of post-communist economic transformation.

A Post-Modernist Model?

There can be no doubt that a functioning system of interest representation contibuted to the stability of democratic transformation in the new Länder. As shown in Chapter 11, social partnership is intrinsic to economic life in the Federal Republic. Interest groups provide the institutional apparatus of the partnership, ordering the wage bargaining arena and industrial relations, participating in corporate governance and contributing to public policy through dialogue with the government. Integration of the new Länder into the German economy would have been inconceivable without this supportive institutional framework. Trade unions and business associations have taken much of the social strain of economic transformation, mediating industrial restructuring and the popular backlash against deindustrialisation.

Initially, some observers suggested that interest groups in the new Länder lacked the organisational strength to perform their function as agents of social integration (Boll, 1994, p. 114). Others argued that interest groups based in western Germany would be unable to respond to a differently constituted spectrum of interests in post-communist Germany (Wiesenthal, 1993, pp. 5–10). Five years after reunification it is clear that these fears were exaggerated. Although resource constraints are reflected in a 'leaner' organisation than in the west, trade unions and employers' associations are now established in the political economy of eastern Germany. Interest groups reflect the German federal system. Their organisational presence in the Land capitals makes them a focus for regional interest formation. The emergence of 'regional corporatism' is indicative of their capacity to respond to specifically eastern interests.

Whilst organised interests are implanted in eastern Germany, however, they display a number of weaknesses. In the absence of broad based and cohesive social formations, group interests and identities are only partially formed. The social infrastructures that support collective action in western Germany are weakly developed. Relations between interest groups and their members remain remote, mediated by salaried officials. Participation rates are low and membership loyalties are weak. The prevalence of the 'free-rider' syndrome means that interest groups must combine their lobbying activities with the provision of more tangible benefits for their members. Thus they display some of the characteristics of tertiary sector organisations providing quasicommercial services for a loosely constituted and pragmatic clientele – the post-modernist model of interest representation.

PART FOUR
Current Issues

14

German Welfare and Social Citizenship

STEEN MANGEN

Reunification exacerbated – but did not create – the institutional and fiscal problems inherent in contemporary German welfare. Yet, after the inevitable distractions that this process provoked, social policy has now entered a new phase, with the return to a search for resolution of chronic concerns that have centred on the modernisation of the system. It is argued here that the ultimate outcome will be a revised understanding of social citizenship within an evolving post-Fordist welfare state.

Prior to reunion the two Germanies maintained distinct welfare systems. Whilst the western model was characterised by pluralism, corporatism and decentralisation, the eastern one had pronounced centralised and universalist elements, with greater emphasis on equity of treatment and marked not so much by lack of coverage, as partial deficiencies of quality. In concluding the details of reunification it was the western model that prevailed: vested political and welfare supplier interests in the old Länder, combined with those of certain emerging elites in the east, ensured that no serious energy was expended on preserving positive aspects of the GDR's '*soziale Errungenschaft*' (social achievement).

Although organisational uniformity was imposed, in terms of social entitlements dual welfare arrangements were to operate, at least in the short run. Thus key elements of welfare remain partitioned. For example, although western social insurance was introduced and benefits were converted at parity rate, eastern entitlements are calculated on the basis of eastern, not national income trends; furthermore, open access to western health facilities is denied to easterners.

Patton (1993) has examined how in the intense speed of reunification, interest coalitions shifted ground on the priority to be afforded to 'national' as opposed to 'social' dimensions. Ultimately the day was won by those arguing that equity of access to welfare would be more soundly ensured by rapid introduction of the 'social market economy': this would do for the east what it had done for the west and stimulate an economic miracle to fund future welfare gains. (Further discussion of social policy in the transition phase is provided in Mangen, 1992, 1994.)

German Welfare Pluralism

Table 14.1 summaries of the principal characteristics of (west) German welfare pluralism. Its cornerstone is the *soziale Rechtsstaat* (social state guaranteed by law) specified in the 1949 Constitution, a compromise reflecting a christian democratic approach to state responsibilities whilst upholding broad liberal preferences for self-help and the family, and social democratic notions of social justice manifested in a commitment to full employment (Freeman and Clasen, 1994). The competences of the federal government in most areas of social policy are constitutionally limited, but there are several important coordinating mechanisms (see Chapter 5). Nonetheless, in many areas of social provision considerable differences persist among the Länder.

Germany is the archetype of what Esping-Anderson (1990) has broadly defined as a 'conservative corporatist' welfare regime, for what has primarily evolved within the constitutional guarantees of social equality and uniformity of living standards is a tradition of 'corporate solidarity' among various occupational groups, as opposed to a more universal solidarity predicated on a wider interpretation of the welfare rights of individuals as citizens. Thus the Germans negotiated a 'social security state' with an emphasis on the preservation of income status of occupational groupings through the twin principles that benefits are (1) determined by prior insurance contributions (2) earnings-related (Leibfried and Ostner, 1991).

In comparative terms German claimants enjoy entitlements with high replacement values in relation to former earnings (see Table 13.1), but there have been growing criticisms of social inequities: the inequalities of income derived from the labour market are faithfully reproduced by social security; the stress on prior activity in the labour market to establish a contribution record disadvantages the young and women, who, because of the conservative pro-family bias of the system,

TABLE 14.1 *The German Welfare System*

The German welfare state is a plural, neo-corporatist and decentralised system faithfully reflecting the federal division of responsibilities enshrined in the constitution. Thus German notions of welfare are inextricably linked to the principles of a social state guaranteed in law. Moreover it is guided by the objectives of the social market economy, which in turn has been critically affected by social catholic teaching: the principle of subsidiarity determines that the lowest level of actor possible should determine policy and deliver services, many of which are organisationally based on the principle of self administration by independent citizens' groupings (such as employees and employers via the social partnership in the operation of social insurance, the welfare professions and other service suppliers, and independent or voluntary agencies (*freie Träger*) in health and social services). In terms of policy the federal level retains largely residual powers, except in the regulation of social security entitlements and the enactment of outline social legislation. Elsewhere in social policy (for example health, social services and education) the key policy-making actors are the Länder, although certain competences are the reserve of local authorities (see below). Many policy-making arenas routinely involve public authorities, the social partners and service suppliers (for example medical associations) and funders (for example sickness schemes) and other interested parties in corporatist consultative and decision-making structures.

Social Insurance

Contemporary German social insurance is largely cognate with Bismarck's formula enacted over one hundred years ago as the world's first national system. It functions as a semi-autonomous organisation administered by the social partners (employer and trade union representatives) under the supervision of the federal government. There are separate schemes for each of five contingencies or 'pillars':

Sickness: over one thousand funds are in operation. There is a locally based general scheme, funds organised for specific occupational groupings and special *Ersatz* 'contracted out' schemes. Insurance pays for sickness benefit and health treatment. Until 1993 there was no cross-subsidisation among schemes.

Unemployment is the only risk for which a unified, federally organised fund exists. This is administered by the Federal Labour Office but controlled by the social partners and public authorities. Insurance-based benefits generally last for one year (but under certain conditions can last up to three years) and amount to 63 per cent of former income for those with children (60 per cent without). Thereafter the FLO administers a federally funded, means-tested unemployment assistance which represents 57 per cent of former income for those with children (53 per cent without). In 1992, 46 per cent of the unemployed received insurance benefits, 23 per cent unemployment assistance and about 25 per cent relied on social assistance; the remainder being explained by ineligibility or non take-up.

Industrial accidents schemes are administered by the social partners but are the only element of social insurance funded entirely by employers.

Old age, survivors and invalidity separate blue-collar and white-collar schemes. Civil servants enjoy non-contributory benefits that amount to 1.5 per cent of GDP. The funds pay for pensions and rehabilitation of the disabled. The average old-age pension in the late 1980s was 40 per cent of former income for blue-collar workers and 60 per cent for white-collar employees and the low-wage earner.

Long-term care the new scheme administered by the sickness funds is, in most Länder, financed by the employee and employer with interim contributions from the public purse.

Social Assistance

Local authorities fund means-tested subsistence benefits for those without resort to social insurance and the Länder fund the care of those in residential or health institutions without other entitlements. Until the federal government assumed responsibility for subsistence benefits for refugees, local authority funding comprised over 75 per cent of the total. Taking all allied benefits into consideration, it offers up to 50 per cent replacement value.

Social Housing and Personal Social Services

A large number of voluntary and, in the case of housing, cooperative agencies are active, with certain reserve functions for local authorities. Social services are for the most part organised into five national organisations under the control of the German Red Cross, the trade union Workers' Welfare Agency (*Arbeiterwohlfahrt*), the Lutheran 'Diaconate' services; the Roman Catholic 'Caritas' agency; and an association of small, locally based agencies (*Paritätische Wohlfahrt*).

Health Services

A large number of hospitals are provided by some of the peak organisations cited above. There is also a large private hospital sector. Local authorities also operate hospitals and are responsible for public health measures. Until very recently, doctors in independent practices had a near monopoly on the provision of specialist outpatient care and also offered general primary care. The total expenditure on health in 1993 amounted to 8.6 per cent of GDP (in the EU this ranges from 5.7 per cent in Greece to 9.8 per cent in France).

Social Protection Budget

In 1993, 27.1 per cent of GDP was consumed by this budget (EU average = 27.8 per cent). Two thirds of the budget comprises monetary transfers, the remainder are services in kind. Seventy per cent is raised via social insurance contributions, which account for 21 per cent of labour costs. The employer pays 40 per cent, the protected person 30 per cent and 26 per cent comes from general taxation. German social protection benefits per person (in purchasing power standards) are ECU 5380 per person (EU average = ECU 4327).

Source: Eurostat (1995); Evans (1996); Statistisches Bundesamt (1995)

are seen as doubly handicapped (see Chapter 15); 'insider–outsider' effects are pronounced – the system operates by means of complex bargaining, which has ensured high levels of expenditure and, despite budgetary retrenchments, substantial preservation of rights for those well placed in the labour market, but which historically has been comparatively weak in innovation, particularly for those outside the world of work; the principle of 'subsidiarity' means that strict assessment of social assistance has acted as a deterrent to claim; on the other hand German social security perpetuates privileged niches, for example the large cadre of civil servants who enjoy non-contributory benefits.

In common with all major EU states, welfare budgets for much of the past fifty years have risen faster than economic growth, as political parties competed for votes among a growing welfare constituency by extending coverage and granting new entitlements. Social expenditure in Germany accounted for 47 per cent of total public outlays in 1994; in 1950 it had been just over a quarter. In the 1990s, of course, it has been the cost of extending the welfare system to the east, and especially of introducing western social insurance, albeit at lower rates of entitlement, that has demanded high funding requirements. The consequence is that, merely to prevent the budget from rising further would require an annual GDP growth of about 3 per cent for the rest of the decade, which is above current performance (the wider budgetary issues were discussed in Chapter 12).

The recession in western Germany, where in 1993 GDP contracted by almost 2 per cent (OECD, 1994), resurrected worries about *Standort Deutschland* – the position and prospects for Germany that were aggravated by concern about the ability of Germany to meet the Maastricht convergence criteria. For Smith (1994) the *Standort* argument has tended to be interpreted in terms of the deleterious impact on economic competitiveness of high social expenditure, especially the high non-wage labour costs, which in 1995 amounted to about 40 per cent of the total wages bill.

Unification and Welfare

The agenda for completing institutional transformation was deliberately tightly drawn: the initial intention was that transitional welfare arrangements should be phased out by 1995 at the latest. In this haste, organisational problems and requirements were seriously underestimated. Matters were not helped by the fact that the administrative task was made more daunting by the abolition of even those elements of the eastern welfare system that were functioning adequately and whose goals were broadly consonant with those in western Germany.

Empirical studies of the situation in the east reveal an ever expanding litany of implementation constraints. Among them are eastern administrators' resistance to speeding up the necessary structural changes, such as land release (Hüther and Petersen, 1993); the pressures arising from raised expectations of welfare reform in the east; tight budgetary deadlines combined with the urgency of the tasks in hand; extended remits of public authorities for areas such as economic regeneration and acceptance of responsibility for a range of social services being shed by GDR enterprises for which no other underwriter has been found, such as kindergartens; the need to master the complex legalism of federal processes; and the inadequacy of external monitoring controls. All these have raised doubts about planning and administrative capacities in the east.

Much has been written about the lack of civil society in the GDR. At root, eastern actors were ill-prepared for effective engagement in *Politikverflechtung* (interactive nexus of policy making). Within welfare they were naive to one of its central manifestations, *Verbändedemokratie* (the incorporation of non-governmental organisations into democratic decision-making): the passivity of the 'niche society' in the GDR meant that the few large voluntary organisations that did exist were essentially compliant; yet the whole structure of the west German third sector was to be imposed almost *de novo* on the east in the very short term. Moreover, unlike their western counterparts, eastern local authorities were better understood as providing field services of the central state rather than as constitutionally independent actors. The impoverished fiscal position of the new Länder and their constituent local authorities reinforced their weak position as bargaining agents, creating what some have seen as a German version of the Mezzogiorno syndrome, where chronic dependence on high expenditure transfers reinforces economic peripheralisation and fosters clientelistic relations. Balme *et al.* (1994) judge that the new Länder and other local actors have been less jealous to conserve their autonomy, and in practice the federal government has unavoidably assumed a more dirigiste role. Moreover public administration in eastern Germany has been dependent on guidance from western counterparts and western voluntary organisations have varyingly engaged in colonising competences.

The fiscal burdens of reunification (see Chapter 12) had an immediate impact on the social budget due to the exigencies of extending coverage from 65 million to 81 million inhabitants. Transfers from western Germany have ranged from 5–7 per cent of GDP and virtually wiped out the fiscal consolidation gains achieved through Kohl's *Wendepolitik* (politics of change) in the social budget, which declined by almost 3 per cent to 29.4 per cent in 1990, although it must be admitted that expenditure levels have been contained in the west.

Reunification required an immediate transfer to the eastern social security budget of a sum amounting to about one third of all transfers in 1991 (Smith, 1994). Social security upgrading was the immediate task: three quarters of allocations were for income transfers and consumption. Investment expenditure requirements scarcely offered a more propitious scenario, for much of the eastern social infrastructure was in need of major upgrading, if not replacement. Local authority debts there rose almost 300 per cent in the first four years of union and were set to increase in the mid 1990s, when liabilities for general and housing debt were transferred. Per capita outlays by local authorities began to outpace western levels in 1992. Social expenditure by eastern local authorities between 1991 and 1994 increased fourfold to reach 70 per cent of expenditure levels in the west, as opposed to 22 per cent in 1991 (Bohley, 1995).

The cumulative effect was to bring forward what might have been an inevitable, albeit belated fiscal crisis of German welfare. Yet, critically, one solution adopted elsewhere was not available, namely rolling back the state (Wilson, 1993). The task of rebuilding eastern Germany demands considerable dirigiste effort on the part of the federal government. In any case, a major contraction of the welfare state is scarcely an option for a broad-church *Volkspartei* (people's party) with an influential 'SoPo' wing (social policy advocates) and electorally competing for the middle ground. Public sector borrowing has been the favoured strategy. Despite earlier promises, a supplementary policy has been *ad hoc* tax and extensive social insurance increases, although these are negatively impacting on non-wage labour costs and provoking recriminations both about international competitiveness (see Chapter 11) and the lack of social equity, given that insurance levies do not fall heavily on the better off and do not touch civil servants.

A further element has been welfare retrenchment. There have been curbs on social assistance, reductions in unemployment benefit and renewed effort to check tax and social security fraud (OECD, 1994). However the opportunity has been grasped to make renewed attempts to tackle long-contentious issues in health, pensions and social assistance policy; and, acceding to the demands of various political actors, a further partial socialisation of welfare costs has been effected through the extensive assumption of fiscal liabilities on the part of the federal government. These issues form the basis of the rest of this chapter.

The year 1995 was somewhat of a watershed, for several key measures were implemented to stabilise funding over time. One source of additional revenue, as in 1991, was the raising of a 'solidarity' tax surcharge of 7.5 per cent, but this time of indefinite duration. More importantly for the long term, a new inter-Länder financial equalisation scheme aims to ensure adequate funding without the need for *ad hoc* supplements, and a fairer distribution of the fiscal burden among all parties, albeit through increased dependency on federal sources (for further discussion, see Chapter 12).

Social Security

In common with most continental systems, German social insurance budgets were routinely in balance until the 1970s. The recessions of that decade introduced a new phenomenon: dependence on *ad hoc* federal subsidies to counter growing deficits arising from the ageing population and rapidly rising unemployment. In the 1980s deficits were a recurrent problem, and in common with governments elsewhere, Kohl attempted to stabilise revenue by raising levies and, importantly, institutionalising partial fiscalisation so that in 1989 nearly 30 per cent of the social budget was derived from the public purse (see Table 14.1). This strategy has continued, not only for fiscal reasons but also to stimulate a modernisation of the principles of social security in line with the demands of an increasingly post-Fordist economy. One consequence is that the federal government is progressively moving centre stage to guarantee a degree of 'social symmetry' by extending limited 'universal', as opposed to traditional 'corporate', solidarity for those elements of the population excluded from the first labour market.

Hüther and Petersen (1993) identify in these changes the rapid destruction of the contributory insurance principle, one of the keystones of postwar German social policy. Indeed political positions on the longer-term future of social security have been changing. The employers' organisations and elements within the CDU–CSU and the FDP have highlighted what they regard as the moral hazards of the present system, with its comparatively high net replacement ratios and opportunities for claimant abuse. Their preferred solutions are for further modernisation, incorporating more techniques of 'new public management', a reduction in statutory entitlements to foster privately contracted, personal provisions and greater deregulation. In the 1980s the SPD and the Greens supported the creation of a tax-funded minimum social benefit to act as a front-line income-maintenance guarantee. The Greens have developed their ideas further and currently argue that the benefit should be extended as a minimum reward for those in the population who provide unpaid housework and care. In comparison the SPD has moderated its line. In the 1994 election campaign its chancellor candidate, Schärping, acknowledged the deleterious effect of high non-wage costs on economic competitiveness and the perpetuation of long-term unemployment. Lafontaine and influential elements within the SPD accept that high non-wage costs must be reduced, inevitably through a programme of retrenchment and the incorporation of positive aspects of modernisation, but within a wider strategy of more efficient targeting of benefits to reduce the risk of social exclusion. For them, further partial fiscalisation of social insurance funding should proceed through the raising of eco-taxes. These views are broadly in sympathy with those of the social policy advocates in the CDU, including Blüm who, in a recent interview in *Der Spiegel* (1995) reaffirmed his commitment to first-tier statutory insurance and the fundamental traditions of the German model.

Pensions Reform

Two fundamental assumptions determined postwar pensions policy: life-long full employment to fulfil the contribution principle and a relatively short period of retirement. Neither condition pertains for a growing section of the population. Reunification brought these problems and other long-standing inequities of West German pensions into sharp relief. The intergenerational contract has been reneged on on several counts: high unemployment, together with increasing patterns of discontinous part-time and short-term work will exclude many from future welfare benefits, and those currently in full-time work must shoulder the current expenditure demands of an ageing population with little expectation of reciprocity in their old age. Overall, pensioners now live longer. Since 1960 female life expectancy has increased by almost four years. Some have been relatively sheltered from the full rigours of welfare cuts in comparision with other claimants: eastern German pensioners, for example, have been among the 'gainers' in united Germany – by 1995 full pensions there had increased almost threefold, to reach almost 80 per cent of the western equivalent.

The 'demographic timebomb' has been well charted. OECD data unambiguously indicate that after the year 2030 there will be mounting public sector debts because of the 'burden' of pensions. If nothing is done, over 60 per cent of total wage costs will be consumed by social security contributions, much of it directed to pensions funding (OECD, 1994).

The 1992 reform package had the objective of reducing by half the projected increase in the insurance levy to 26 per cent of the wage bill by 2030. There will be a gradual increase in the contribution rate up to 2010, but it was conceded that insurance levies alone could not bear the brunt of rising pensions expenditure, because higher non-wage costs would further endanger international competitiveness. Thus there was a redistribution of liabilities among recipients, contributors and the public purse. Government subsidies, which by 1992 already amounted to 20 per cent of total pension expenditure, are henceforth to be linked to contributions so that the public purse will shoulder part of the burden of increasing levies over time. This partial fiscalisation is an important step towards a limited but clear acceptance of a degree of socialisation of welfare costs that, at least temporarily, was evidenced in the new Länder with the introduction there of a minimum means-tested 'social supplement' pension, funded by tax. Although Blüm has reiterated his opposition to a minimum social pension as a long-term solution for Germany as a whole, the supplement was an important innovation, but one that contravened the principles agreed by political consensus in the 1989 reforms (see Mangen, 1992). About one third of eastern pensioners receive the supplement, which was phased out at the end of 1996.

For the rest, pension reform has relied on a familiar list of measures tailored to reduce liabilities: indexation based on net rather than gross wage levels; the phasing out of very early retirement and the provision of incentives for people to work until the age of 65; and abolition of the flexible retirement age by the year 2001 – progress towards equal age for full pension entitlement between the sexes will be completed by 2012 (Smith, 1994)

However for many, including the OECD, the reform was based on worryingly insecure foundations. Stimulating people to stay longer in the labour market could conflict with policies to reduce unemployment. Gender inequities were not adequately addressed – women's marginal position in the labour market will continue to dictate their inferior pensions profile – although 'baby year' pension credits for mothers were raised to three years (see Chapter 15). Winkler (1994) argues that the 1992 reform actually increased gender discrimination by replacing the independent treatment of married women in the GDR pensions system by western legislation that primarily regards women as dependent spouses. Finally, there have been accusations of clientelism on the part of the federal government, since it has consistently failed to support plans to reduce inequities by tightening up or abolishing non-contributory civil service pensions.

The 1992 reform, in Blüm's judgement, will secure the pensions system until at least 2010. In his preference for continuing to fund statutory pensions from current contributions (as opposed to investment income) he has pointed out that, historically, pension fund budgets have been more closely related to economic growth and productivity than to crude indicators such as the number of contributors. Nonetheless there is clearly a significantly long way to go in policy evolution. For one thing, little has been said about the rapidly increasing funding problems that may occur immediately after 2010 – and not, as is the government's view, in 2020. These, together with the decline in the faith of the German electorate in their future pension entitlements (over half of respondents in a recent survey believed these are not secure) might act as a stimulus to the contracting of personal pensions to make good the shortfall in statutory benefits (Biedenkopf, 1994). In this regard the German government is several paces behind some other EU states in promoting this development. Not that such a policy is without risks. Walter (1993a), whilst acknowledging the increase in investment sources this could provide has speculated that it could negate family policies if, as a result, the generations who have to save for their old age may be less willing to have children.

Consolidating Health Reform

German health care is delivered through a plural system in which there is a separation of funders and suppliers (see Table 14.1). In EU terms it is an above-average spender with average performance in terms of health status indicators. Inevitably, reunification added additional dimension to health policy. Organisational reform took precedence over infrastructural investment, which necessarily will have to be long term. New investment needs in the five Länder are estimated to be in the order of DM30 billion to approach the standards of western Germany, over half of which will be needed for new construction. To this must be added the immediate costs of emergency upgrading of the eastern health facilities. These pressures will to exacerbate the long-term problem that Germany has experienced in devising effective measures to contain health costs in anything but the short run.

In the German health-care system, with unequal power between suppliers and purchasers, lack of effective cost control might appear an inevitable consequence: there are just too many areas where there are incentives to oversupply treatment and the patient has no incentive not to comply. The *Lobby im Weiss* (Lobby in white) and the pharmaceutical companies have enjoyed considerable success in staving off major intrusion into their privileges. Changes, where effected, have tended to be marginal and all too often of short-term impact. On the other hand the funders – the *Krankenkassen* (sickness funds) – have historically been the weak link in the chain of negotiation. When attempts failed to achieve cost containment through non-binding corporatist 'concerted action' by health suppliers and funders, major health reform was imposed by the federal government in 1987. It, too, suffer the short-termism of its predecessors. Thus during the 1980s and the early 1990s annual health budgets in the old FRG increased by almost 10 per cent and, critically, total expenditure on inpatients almost doubled (*Der Spiegel*, 1995).

Pressures of reunification and the severity of problems have led to redoubled efforts. The current health minister, Seehofer, has had more success than his predecessors, at least in terms of concluding wider-ranging budgetary control policy, agreed among competing interests in the health system. The package of largely supply-side measures announced in 1993 and being phased in until 1997, are directed towards the overarching aim of aligning budgetary increases in the health sector with basic income trends. Most significantly, a form of global budgeting was introduced whereby hospitals' annual expenditure is limited to revenues from insurance contributions. Equally crucial – and after decades of resistance on their part – cross-subsidisation among the schemes was imposed to restore a degree of equity for those schemes bearing a heavier risk profile, although at least in the short run the new policy will operate separately in the old and new Länder. Greater competition among the sickness funds' was stimulated by permitting more consumer choice in membership. Various measures were adopted to prioritise outpatient rather than inpatient treatment, and stricter controls were imposed on prescribing and pharmaceutical pricing.

Yet there have been accusations that the reforms could lead to two-tier medicine in that the new budgeting mechanisms will provide incentives for health facilities to offload high-cost patients or withold appropriate but expensive treatment. Since specialists in office practice also face stricter policing, the same cost-cutting tactics may be adopted with similar effects.

The stimulation of competition among insurance schemes was further advanced by legislative amendments in 1994 that prevented private schemes from imposing more expensive premiums on their elderly contributors than on the young. This innovation reinforces the effect of the prohibition in 1989 of the practice of permitting the transfer of subscribers to statutory funds when private scheme levies become unattractive.

The 1993 package, together with the introduction of care insurance discussed below, are among the most significant reforms of postwar German welfare. At least in the short term, its effect has been to return western German schemes to profit in 1994 and has permitted reductions in insurance levies in 1995. Crucially, there have been substantial reductions in the pharmaceutical bill.

The measures were intended as but one stage in reforming the health system and a new strategy is to be developed from 1996, although there are arguments within the coalition of how much further to proceed with wider deregulation. Key elements will rely on the reinforcment of self-regulation of the system by suppliers and funders, with the aim further to guarantee longer term stability in contribution levies. In particular Seehofer is anxious to strengthen the position of funders *vis-à-vis* suppliers by negotiating more flexibility in medical fees to eradicate wasteful repetition of inpatient and outpatient procedures, and to privilege primary care interventions wherever appropriate. Moreover health facilities are to be encouraged to compete by offering extra services, the costs falling on individual patients electing them.

Resolving the Crisis of Care

In order to consolidate both health and local authority financial reform, resolution has been achieved of the long-debated problem of funding long-term care. Chancellor Kohl was at pains to arrive at a solution prior to the 1994 general election, given the influence of the so-called 'grey vote' of retired people. The chosen policy combines a conservative funding mechanism with modernising attempts to promote effective consumerism: a 'fifth pillar' of statutory social insurance has been enacted and the new scheme aims to give recipients and their families a real choice between financial compensation for informal care and payment for residential and other professional care. It is designed to replace means- tested funding via social assistance provided by local authorities, which will ultimately relieve them of a budgetary commitment of at least DM5 billion. In most Länder the insurance levy is shared equally by employer and employee, with additional interim subventions from public authorities, sickness insurance and health suppliers. In addition, and despite fierce opposition from the unions, one public holiday has been cancelled in these Länder, whereas in those states choosing to retain the holiday the levy is paid by the employee alone to help offset the costs of the insurance to the employer.

A Welfare Impasse: Long-Term Unemployment

Unemployment and its age, gender and regional implications are treated more fully in Chapters 11 and 12. Growth-led job creation has been modest and government training and employment measures have been no match for the scale of the problem. During the 1990s a twin policy has evolved of more extensive subsidies for labour-market reentry, combined with stricter social assistance criteria for unemployed claimants and the introduction of penalties for long-term claimants.

Several authors have indicted the various impasses in German 'conservative corporatism'. Wage bargaining, too, has often operated in the interest of protecting the jobs of 'insiders', including the low paid, rather than being geared to extending opportunities to those excluded from the labour market (OECD, 1994). Clasen (1994) argues that these broad 'insider' coalitions also act to maintain relatively high replacement rates for insurance-based unemployment benefit (see Table 14.1). But this is at the cost of perpetuating status differentials among the unemployed; since there are significant cleavages in access to and quality of entitlement in the tripartite system of insurance, means-tested unemployment assistance and last-resort social assistance (see Table 14.1). Apart from the differences in replacement values, the emphasis on means testing beyond the initial year of unemployment acts as a deterrent to claim, particularly on the part of married women and the young. The OECD data for 1992 contained in Table 14.1 indicate that 6 per cent of the unemployed were either ineligible or did not claim benefit (Evans, 1996).

The tripartite system also provides supplier incentives to offload liabilities between unemployment benefit (substantially paid for by insurance contributions), unemployment assistance (paid by the federal taxpayer) and social assistance (funded by local authorities). For example it is in the interests of local authorities to provide jobs for social assistance recipients in order that they can reestablish their insurance entitlements. In 1995 minsters Waigel and Blüm unveiled a plan to save DM700 million in federally funded unemployment assistance expenditure by increasing the number of long-term unemployed on training schemes, which are paid for by the unemployment insurance fund.

The slower than expected fall in the unemployment rate together with the budgetary constraints imposed by the Maastricht convergence criteria, prompted the government to impose significant cuts in 1994 in replacement values of insurance benefits. Stricter regulations are currently being proposed elsewhere in the tripartite system. They include a 25 per cent reduction in benefit for claimants who decline job offers. In addition the 1996 draft budget proposed a three-yearly reduction of 5 per cent in unemployment assistance to encourage the long-term unemployed to return to the labour market, the argument being that as the period of unemployment increases, so the skills base of the recipient erodes, and hence the level of compensation should be reduced accordingly. Now relieved of the costs of long-term care, local authorities are charged with extending their job-creation programmes for social assistance claimants in order that at least entitlement to insurance benefits can be reestablished.

The series of inroads into unemployment compensation have been opposed by trade unions and the SPD, who proposed debt financing as an alternative. Yet that party's position is compromised by the fact that it is in government in the majority of the Länder and in large cities where social assistance expenditure has been rapidly rising. This has prompted the party to support the long-term containment of benefit increases and a fixed gap between compensation levels and statutory minimum wages to maintain incentives for labour market participation.

The Last Resort: Social Assistance

Despite the strict rules that are applied when assessing entitlement to social expenditure, the number of recipients has been rapidly growing, thus swelling local authority expenditure (the main funders). For example, between 1994 and 1996 it is projected that increased fiscal commitments in western Germany will be 11 per cent, principally because of the long-term unemployed, who have replaced pensioners as the largest category of recipients. In western Germany the unemployed now comprise one third of all claimants; in the east it is two thirds. In recent years claims by asylum seekers and refugees have also inflated budgets: in 1993 one in three recipients was a non-German, half of whom fell into these categories (DIW, 1994a).

Overall expenditure, which accounted for 5 per cent of the total social budget in 1994, had grown threefold during the previous ten years, and understandably has been a dominant concern in local politics. Again, a combination of socialisation of costs, tighter eligibility criteria and reduced benefits has been the strategy adopted. Confronted by a relentless local funding crisis, the federal government extended the right to unemployment benefit for the older recipient. The Länder have also been allocated extra resources for job creation. In 1995 a package of measures was announced to subsidise younger claimants to take up low-paid work. And finally, the federal government assumed liability for social assistance for asylum seekers and refugees, a contested proposal being that benefits be set at 25 per cent below the prevailing rates.

The basic legislation, dating from 1961, assumed that social assistance would be a small-scale residual benefit: it was never intended as mainline funding for the variety of contingencies now included. Wide-ranging amendments are to be introduced, including changes to the entitlement criteria, in the wake of growing concern with the problem of 'welfare dependency' and the 'poverty trap'.

Insiders–Outsiders: The Welfare State in the Twenty-First Century

Internationally, based on the combined impact of taxation and social welfare, Germany achieves an average performance in terms of redistributing net income from rich to poor (Mitchell, 1991). Nevertheless poverty has been increasing in recent years (DIW, 1994b): according to EU criteria about 8 per cent of western and 15 per cent of eastern German households have disposable incomes that are below half the national average. The issue of growing inequality in the east has been investigated by Hauser *et al.* (1994), who examined the welfare gainers and losers from unification. Eastern pensioners have been among the principal gainers, but critically families there, especially one-parent families, have been relatively disadvantaged by reunification, primarily due to loss of employment by women. In general reunification boosted income inequality in the east due to high levels of unemployment, although these inequalities are not as acute as in the west.

The comparatively good performance of the German system for the majority consolidates the 'insider' welfare constituency whose representatives, aided by welfare suppliers, mobilise to preserve as many as possible of their entitlements within the plural system. These interests reinforce corporate notions of solidarity, but they now coexist with *ad hoc* and incremental socialised solidarity, as the federal government assumes liability for increasing numbers of 'outsiders' through pensioner 'social supplements', funds social assistance for refugees and asylum seekers, raises 'social solidarity' taxation supplements, and affords itself a more central role in subsidising the inter-Länder financial equalisation scheme. The objectives to be served are diverse. Fiscal stabilisation has been a primary concern, rapid upgrading of welfare in eastern Germany another. To a degree, government policy has been influenced by the sensibilities of its social policy advocates. Thus the rhetoric of social exclusion and the danger of a 'two-thirds' society have been well aired. Hence the high profile given to job-creation measures and the socialising of welfare costs, which has also been exploited as an opportunity for tighter regulations and stricter policing. Thus, while action on subsidising social insurance from the public purse has been occurring in other EU states, these added dimensions give the German solution a certain uniqueness. Nonetheless, in rapidly developing dual labour markets policies need to be ever more innovative, since increasingly differentiated welfare statuses are unfolding for those in precarious positions, for those with formal employee status and those in the growing labyrinth of the submerged economy, (i.e. work contracted outside statutory regulation and evading tax and social security liabilities).

15

Women in the New Germany

EVA KOLINSKY

Before reunification the two Germanies pursued distinctly different policies towards women. Although both were pledged to women's equality, the West German model left the conflict between employment and family roles unresolved, while the East German model was based on the full integration of women into the labour market and social policies to support motherhood and child care. This chapter explores the different patterns of disadvantage and opportunities in West and East Germany, and argues that after reunification the hidden inequalities of pay, occupational fields and qualifications of the GDR era turned into low incomes, employment uncertainties and even a risk of poverty for women in the new Länder, in particular for women with children.

New Germanies and the Emergence of Equality

There have been several 'new' Germanies in the course of modern German history, each adopting a different view on the place of women in society and the meaning of equality. The 'new Germany' of 1871 ranked women as second-class citizens without political, economic or social rights of their own, but opened some access to higher education, professional employment and political participation. Active and passive voting rights followed in 1918, prior to laying the constitutional foundations for democratic government. Although the Weimar years extended educational and employment opportunities, women remained second-class citizens before the law in all areas except politics. The 'new' Germany of 1933 rejected equality and its liberal heritage. Subjected to the purposes of the Nazi state, women found themselves typecast as mothers and homemakers, and from the mid-1930s onwards they were increasingly conscripted into compulsory labour programmes and war industries. The 'new' Germany between 1945 and 1949 restored the rights of political participation of the Weimar years. Most women, however, were preoccupied with survival and stayed aloof from the political renewal around them.

The Federal Republic, the 'new' Germany in the West, granted full equality in its Basic Law with the unequivocal wording ' men and women are equal'. Yet full equality has remained an unmet promise (Kolinsky, 1993a) It took until the mid-1970s to replace the 'housewife' model of marriage with a model of 'partnership', and until the 1980s to focus on equal opportunities in employment and on using legislation to modify the conflict between motherhood and employment (Berghahn and Fritzsche, 1991). By that time policy makers were responding to EC directives, and especially to the expectations of younger women that their opportunities in society and politics should match their own motivations and qualifications, and not pander to traditional views about women's supporting roles in a social and political order devised and commanded by men.

The German Democratic Republic, the 'new' Germany in the East, also commenced with a constitutional promise that all citizens should be equal. Equality depended, above all, on employment (Gysi and Meyer, 1993). With employment a right and a duty, women's equality seemed to involve no more and no less than their full integration into the world of work. As will be shown below, financial and institutional support for mothers and their children diminished the conflict between employment and family roles that had persisted in the West and most East German women thought their constitutional promise of equality had been met.

Unification Treaty Agendas

The Unification Treaty for the 'new' Germany of 1990 made two exceptions to its general approach of discarding the East German model and adopting that of West Germany. Both pertained to women and seemed designed to advance matters of equality by learning from practices in the East. In both instances West German priorities ultimately prevailed. Article 31.4 announced improved legislation on abortion while Article 31.1 placed the further development and implementation of equal opportunities on the agenda of the new Germany (Verträge, 1990, pp. 29–30).

Abortion had been legal in East Germany since 1972 but remained a criminal offence in the West Germany (Thietz, 1992). In reality, West German women could apply for special permission on a variety of medical and social grounds and were almost as likely as East German women to have an abortion if they so wished. In both Germanies, however, abortion had come to symbolise a woman's right to self-determination that had no place in existing West German law. In East Germany a majority of the population endorsed the right to abortion, and the issue was not contentious. In West Germany, the issue had become contentious by 1990. Conservative and church circles wanted abortion curtailed and women placed under a legal obligation to protect the unborn life, while forces of the centre and the left objected to the criminalisation of abortion and advocated a system based on self-determination and mandatory counselling (Prützel-Thomas, 1993). In June 1992, the *Bundestag* agreed to the moderated formula. This liberalisation of the law was, however, reversed in May 1993 when the Federal Constitutional Court reaffirmed the 'right to life' and the status of abortion as a criminal offence, albeit a non-punishable one during the first twelve weeks of pregnancy (*Informationsmaterial*, 1993). Future legislation will have to implement this ruling.

With regard to equal opportunities, a replica of the East German model was never considered. In the autumn of 1994 the Bundestag resolved to supplement the Basic Law. While the original article had promised equality in principle, the new one admonished policy makers to act upon it: 'The state promotes the actual implementation of equal rights for women and men and pursues the abolition of existing disadvantages' (Zahn, 1995, p. 1). As will be shown in this chapter, the constitutional pledge to counteract discrimination cannot resolve the unresolved conflict between family roles and employment in Germany nor can it undo what the new rules of engagement have inflicted on women in eastern Germany since reunification.

Equality between Promise and Reality: Developments in West Germany

In the 1950s the normal life of women differed little from what it would have been in the 1920s: some 80 per cent left school at the age of 14, half would complete an apprenticeship before employment, the others take on unskilled or semiskilled labour. About 2 per cent of young women attended grammar school and qualified to go to university, while one in five completed intermediate education in preparation for commercial or administrative functions. Education and employment, however, were deemed secondary in a woman's life compared with marriage, motherhood and homemaking. Most women were married before they were 21 and gave up their employment to become housewives. Nine out of ten women had at least one child, and few returned to the labour market in later life. Although one in ten marriages ended in divorce, the nuclear family of a couple and their children constituted the social norm, while living together before marriage or other forms of sharing a household were rare exceptions (Meyer and Schulze, 1992).

However the 1950s also saw the emergence of the career woman, since the war had left many single or widowed and in need of earned income. These women did not retreat into family roles but worked until their retirment. Some rose to public prominence as members of parliament, ministers or journalists, others gained leadership positions at their place of work. Since the mid-1950s, governments and public bodies have tended to comply with equal opportunities legislation by including a proportion of women. As levels of affluence improved and mellowed class distinctions, traditional social norms also began to recede. Women found themselves increasingly free to make choices. Initially these extended no further than going on holiday or eating at a restaurant unaccompanied; over time they consolidated into an emphasis on self-realisation and a new sense of equality.

Education, Employment and Family Roles

Education played a key role in recasting women's lifestyles and opportunities. When educational reforms set out to broaden access to higher education, young women emerged as the main beneficiaries. Soon, over half of A-level students and over 40 per cent of university students were women while the proportion obtaining advanced education rose from one in twenty to one in three (Kolinsky, 1995a, pp. 33–8). As women remained longer in full-time education, marriage occurred later, families were smaller and became more pluralistic in structure. On the eve of unification, women in West Germany married at an average age of 24; one in five marriages remained childless; and two out of three families with children had just one child. For many women with children, marriage continued to be the norm, but many lived in other relationships, alone or in one-parent households (Meyer, 1992, p. 264; Hettlage, 1992) With one in three marriages ending in divorce, family roles and structures had taken on a new unpredictability.

A more explicit employment motivation followed in the wake of educational qualifications. The majority of young women now expected to combine employment and family duties, not choose between them. University graduates were less likely to accept the role of housewife than women with little formal education. At all levels, however, more women than ever before obtained vocational or professional qualifications. In the mid-1980s, 60 per cent of women over the age of 45, 25 per cent of women under 35 and 12 per cent of women under 25 possessed no vocational qualifications (*Quintessenzen*, vol. 4, 1994: p. 12; Datenreport, 1994, p. 54).

Access to employment remained more elusive. Discrimination at the point of recruitment made it difficult for women to enter their chosen fields, and many were employed at the lower end of the occupational hierarchy. Despite legislation on equal pay, women's average pay has been one third lower that of men. This could be linked to the fact that women tend to concentrate in a narrow band of occupational and professional fields. More important, however, has been the unresolved conflict between motherhood and employment. On the one hand employers have hesitated to employ and promote women. On the other hand family duties have forced women to interrupt or give up their employment. In the mid 1980s, eight out of ten women had taken one or more career breaks, in most cases to look after family members. Many found it impossible to return to the labour market, others took on part-time employment with few prospects of promotion, or worked beneath their formal qualifications. Unemployment has always hit women harder than men. Nearly one in ten women compared with one in twelve men were unemployed in the early 1990s. The female unemployment figures would stand at twice that level if the 'silent reserve' were included: women who are out of work but do not appear in the statistics since they are not entitled to claim benefit.

Women's participation in the labour market appears to have been remarkably constant throughout the twentieth century, amounting to just over one third of the total labour force. Since the 1980s a slight increase has occurred. In 1990 women made up 38 per cent of the labour force, in 1995, 41 per cent. The apparent continuity, however, hides a momentous shift from single to married women and from the young to the middle-age groups. Women today remain longer in full-time education and training and enter the labour market later than in the past. At the opposite end, most retire before they reach the age of 60. Thus the majority of working women are aged between their early twenties and late fifties. Family phase and working lives are no longer consecutive but increasingly interwoven. These developments have intensified the challenge of combining employment with the role of wife, mother and carer. In 1993 just 29 per cent of women in western Germany gave their profession as 'housewife' (Datenreport, 1994; see also Table 15.2 below). All others were actual or prospective participants in the labour market and were faced with the need to balance the various female roles and alleviate the conflicts between them.

Conflicts between family roles and employment are multifaceted. Men in western Germany contribute significantly less to household tasks and family duties than women (Ipos, 1992, pp. 27–31). In fact working women with children appear to receive less support from their husbands or partners than working women without children. In addition, less than 1 per cent of preschool children in the old Länder attend full-time child-care facilities, partly because none exist and partly because this type of care is not readily accepted by western German parents. Provisions for preschool children tend to be restricted to two or three hours per day, while schools close before lunch, leaving a major part of child care to the family, usually the mother.

In the 1980s the West German government introduced a series of measures designed to ease the conflict between family duties and employment. Women who had given up their employment to raise their children won some pension rights in recognition of their mothering role and either parent could apply for up to three years' part-paid leave after the birth of a child, with a guarantee of reemployment at the same level of seniority and pay. Financial provisions during this period of leave were improved in 1993 (synopsis in Kolinsky, 1995a, pp. 256–8). Although devised by the CDU in an unsuccessful attempt to attract the electoral support of younger women, these legislative steps have taken some of the sting out of the conflict between motherhood and employment in German society.

Decree and Perception: Equality in the Former GDR

In the former GDR women constituted a vital labour resource in a polity built on employment, an *Arbeitsgesellschaft*. The dream of German socialists that ordinary working men should earn a good enough wage to keep their wives at home did not fit into the socialist model derived from the Soviet Union and implemented in the GDR. Initially the labour-market integration of women was hampered by their lower skills and the lack of child-care facilities outside the family. From the mid 1960s onwards, both shortcomings disappeared. When the GDR collapsed, virtually all East German women held vocational qualifications and the dead-end of remaining unskilled had become a thing of the past (full details in Winkler, 1990). For nine out of ten young East Germans, women as well as men, the so-called Polytechnic High School provided compulsory full-time education up to the age of 16. Although access to advanced education was restricted compared with the situation in West Germany, men and women were represented in equal numbers at all but the most advanced levels that led to top leadership positions.

From the mid 1960s onwards the East German state also offered child-care provisions for all children from birth up to the age of ten. Employers, including universities and colleges, were obligated to run child-care facilities, including during vacation periods. This comprehensive network of child care allowed the maximum integration of women into employment (Geissler, 1992).

Women as Working Mothers: Hidden Inequalities

The conflict between motherhood and commitments outside the family to employment or educational participation that has challenged women in West Germany to find their individual solutions and balances, was effectively diffused in the East as the state took on the responsibility to ensure that commitments could be balanced and roles combined. East German women and men accepted without evident reservations that their children should be cared for outside the home. They even believed that such care encouraged desirable traits in their children, such as solidarity and a sense of egality. On the eve of reunification over 80 per cent of children under three and well over 90 per cent of preschool and school-age children attended full-time day-care centres from seven o'clock in the morning or earlier to the end of the parental working day. Women in particular valued this level of child-care support (Winkler, 1992, pp. 142–3).

Women in the GDR were earlier to reach landmarks of adult life, such as full-time employment, marriage and motherhood, and were financially independent at a younger age than in the West (based on *Jugend '92*, pp. 207–12). By the age of 17, most had firm career plans and prospects of employment (85 per cent). At 19, seven out of ten were in full-time employment and financially independent of their parents. By 21, the average East German woman would be married, and one in five had children before they were 22 years old. The ideal family in the East was held to consist of a couple and their two children, and 70 per cent of women in East Germany had two children. One in three children were born to unmarried mothers. Many chose to remain unmarried and perceived single parenthood as a viable alternative to married life. In 1989 one in five East German households with children was headed by a single parent, almost always a woman (Hölzler and Mächler, 1993, pp. 34–5). Despite their traditional path into early marriage and motherhood, over 90 per cent were employed or in work-related full-time training. From the 1960s women constituted half the East German labour force; after the mass exodus in 1989 and 1990, when more men than women fled to the West, they occupied a majority position of 52 per cent (Kolinsky, 1995b, p. 184).

Numerically, the GDR provided equal opportunities for women in education, training and employment. At the more complex level of choice of occupational field, degree of advancement and the route to leadership and managerial positions, gender disadvantages remained endemic and hidden. Increasingly women were directed into *Frauenberufe* (female career tracks). Some sectors of employment, such as banking, retailing, health care, child care and textiles, employed mostly women, although men dominated the managerial level in all except primary school teaching. Women held one in four management positions at the intermediate level but only about 2 per cent in the top bracket in all areas of the economy (Winkler, 1992, pp. 90–4).

The hidden inequalities in East German employment even extended to pay. Although the promise of equal pay was central to the GDR constitution, women's average earnings were one third below those of men. At all levels of seniority women's pay was in the lower bracket of the relevant wage band. Even women who made it to the top tended to earn less than their male colleagues (Kolinsky, 1993a, p. 276).

The proliferation of women's occupational fields served to obscure their poorer earning capacity, although wages for all ordinary East Germans were kept low and in a narrow band. Since housing, energy, basic foodstuffs and other essentials were subsidised, even the lowest-income groups could get by and poverty, homelessness and dependence on benefit were unknown. In addition the state rewarded motherhood with a 'second wage package'. Taking child benefit, the low cost of child-care and other allowances together, a woman with two children could increase her monthly income from employment by 50 per cent. Although badly paid for her employment, her actual income matched that of men and may often have been higher.

Women faced no uncertainties about going out to work. After the birth of a child, women could take up to twelve months' paid leave at 90 per cent of their earnings and a further two years at 65 per cent for each child. Since most East German women interrupted their employment for at least one year after the birth of a child, the pattern of moving in and out of the labour market was none too different from that in West Germany. In the latter, however, guaranteed return to employment was only introduced in the mid 1980s. In financial terms, the West German pattern of parental leave has never been able to rival the generous provisions in the East, but in both Germanies the likelihood that a woman might interrupt her employment left her disadvantaged. In the West women found it more difficult to be taken on until equal opportunities legislation rendered it an offence to discriminate on the ground of gender, and recommended that employers should appoint women in preference to men in those cases where candidates were equally well qualified. In the East such positive discrimination was unknown (Belwe, 1989, p. 138). In fact women faced disadvantages since their role as mother and their family duties left them less time for the political activism upon which professional advancement depended.

Women's Place and State Policy

East German women's policy was, above all, mothers' policy (*Muttipolitik*). It failed to address issues of equal opportunities, equal pay and representation at all levels of seniority. Instead it cosseted women with material bonuses and a sense of security. In the absence of an equal opportunities policy, structures of inequality remained. The East German labour market was segmented by gender and not designed to break gender barriers. In addition the dominance of material shortages and concerns about day-to-day provisions impeded the change from materialist to post-materialist values that occurred in advanced Western industrial societies. Thus traditional views, attitudes and behavioural patterns remained relatively unaltered in East German everyday and family life despite the transformation of the political and social system to a socialist format. At home, East German women performed all the domestic duties of the traditional housewife, although none regarded themselves as a housewife by profession and most were in full-time employment. During the first year of marriage East German husbands seem to have been more helpful than in the later years of marriage (Kolinsky, 1995a, pp. 263–4). As in West Germany, after the birth of children the contribution of men to domestic duties declined and women's domestic roles became more traditional. The high divorce rate in East Germany – 40 per cent of marriages ended in divorce – and the preference for single motherhood suggest that women rejected traditional role expectations and tried to find their own personal solution or liberty.

By the time the East Germany state collapsed, East German women had accumulated a good deal of private discontent. Some articulated it in calls for a better form of socialism or became involved in citizens' action groups. Others, notably women with less education and fewer chances to gain a stake in the more privileged society of GDR society, left for the West. Studies of resettlers show that the majority of women who moved to the West were less skilled and educated than average and felt by-passed in a society where the link between employment and achievement had been severed and ordinary working people were prevented from achieving the living standards of the political and intellectual elites (Integrationsprobleme, 1991).

The majority of East German women, however, expressed their discontent not by migrating to the West but by embarking on a kind of inner migration. Taking employment for granted, they focused on their private sphere as the core of their daily lives. In a society where confidence was undermined by surveillance and the ubiquitous *Stasi* informers, the close circle of family and friends became a niche, a shelter from state intrusion and a haven for individual activities and personal indulgences. Retreat into the private sphere might involve tending an allotment, turning a garden shed into a *Datscha* (holiday cottage) or furnishing the home as lavishly and expensively as possible. Women had a major part in turning East Germany into a niche society of citizens whose discontent with their government and leadership simmered for several years before finding the political voice of exodus and the demonstrations that toppled them.

Between Opportunities and Exclusion: Women in the New Germany

The reunification of Germany held two main promises for the inhabitants of the GDR: the promise of Western-style living conditions and the promise of personal and political freedom. Both kindled hope that a sudden leap in affluence would follow the introduction of the Deutsche Mark and hope that freedom to travel, freedom of speech, freedom of individual development and choice of life-style would exist and could be enjoyed by all. The transformation that turned the former GDR into new German Länder put an end to the socialist shortage society and marked the onset of consumerism and a free market; it also put an end to restrictions and afforded the opportunity to travel, to articulate political preferences and to voice any views. Transformation, however, was accompanied by the collapse of employment security, which rocked the very foundations of everyday life by making employment open to competition and uncertainty. For women this was doubly momentous as it also entailed the destruction of the social policy network that had underpinned their place in the GDR.

The policy decisions taken after the elections of March 1990 to model the East German economy on the West German one put an end to socialist planning and state ownership. The decisions were implemented within months by establishing the *Treuhand* and the currency union. Political unification followed in October 1990, several months after economic unification. Unification was truly sealed only after the first all-German election in December 1990 generated a parliament and government for the whole of the new Germany (Merkl, 1993). For East Germans the end of the GDR was quickly manifest in unrestricted access to Western goods. Less visible but almost as rapid was the collapse of internal and external markets for East German manufacturing output, agricultural produce and services. East Germans themselves rejected domestic products as inferior in quality, while the democratisation of Eastern Europe and political upheavals in the Third World closed markets that had traditionally been supplied by the GDR. Indeed the GDR had aimed much of its production at specific markets in compliance with state contracts, not in response to demand or competition. As the rules changed from state planning to market principles, all areas of economic activity in the former GDR proved outmoded, hampered by obsolete technology and a degree of overmanning that has been described as hidden unemployment of around 15 per cent.

Although the economy in the new Länder ground to a virtual standstill in 1991, the social consequences were obscured by government-funded programmes to delay the onset of unemployment. In 1990 some 400 000 east Germans (4.9 per cent of the population) were unemployed. By 1994 unemployment had risen to 15 per cent and affected 1.15 million people (Schramm, 1994). Women constituted over 60 per cent of the unemployed; in regions with a high concentration of textile production or in former *Frauenberufe*, female unemployment was even higher (Nickel and Schenk, 1994, pp. 264–5). In 1994 one in five women in the new Länder were unemployed compared with one in ten men.

Among the government's measures to alleviate unemployment, the introduction of shorter working weeks and special reemployment measures (*Arbeitsbeschaffungsmaßnahmen*) were of great importance. In 1991 for instance, close to half the labour force in the Leipzig region were working fewer hours and the number of people employed on this basis was nearly twice as high (1.62 million) as those out of work (913 000). By 1993 the situation had 'normalised' and the number working fewer hours had been scaled down to 181 000 while unemployment now stood at about 1.2 million (Kolinsky, 1995b, p. 27). As in western Germany, the practice constituted an instrument of employment policy alongside government-funded schemes and retraining, and was not the main device to sustain employment.

From the outset men outnumbered women by two to one in short-time work and government funded-employment (ABM) in the new Länder, while women were more likely to move directly from employment to unemployment. Moreover the main device to ease unemployment stipulated in the Treaty on German Unity – early retirement above the age of 55 – should have pertained equally to men and women but was brought in more speedily for women than for men. By 1993 over 70 per cent of women and less than 50 per cent of men in the relevant age bracket had been forced to retire and enter the expanding non-employed sector in the new Länder (Kolinsky, 1995b, p. 187).

Within five years of reunification, active participation in the labour market in the former GDR had been halved. Unemployment and non-employment still constitute a formidable problem for all those conditioned to live in the East German employment society, unused to competition, the need for personal career development, changing jobs, and the financial and status problems of unemployment. Women have been hit harder than men by the collapse of the former employment society. They have been less successful in retaining or regaining employment and more likely to have been pushed into long-term unemployment. In the mid 1990s most east German women had experienced unemployment at some point since reunification. Twenty per cent were unemployed, many of them since the early years of reunification, while most others had moved in and out of employment and retraining programmes several times.

Employment has lost the predictability it once had and has emerged as a major area of social and material uncertainty for women. East German women see unemployment and non-employment through early retirement in terms of social exclusion. Having retained their psychological need to work, only about 2 per cent see homemaking and life as a housewife as an alternative role for women. Instead they continue to look for employment, retrain, take on temporary jobs and use any opportunity that presents itself to retain their place in the labour market. Although an estimated 50 per cent of unemployed women in the old Länder are no longer identified in the statistics as unemployed, east German women have refused to retreat into the 'silent reserve' and continue to claim that employment constitutes a core part of their lives.

Since reunification recast the economy from central planning to market principles, women in the new Länder have lost their numerical equality with men in the workforce, but labour-market participation still remains much higher for women in eastern than in western Germany across all age groups (Table 15.1). In the age groups 30–50 over 95 per cent of women in eastern Germany are in employment, 25 per cent more than in the west. However, for women over 55 but below the normal retirement age, labour-market participation plummeted by 70 per cent and was less than in western Germany. At the younger end of the labour market, the decrease in employment points to increased participation in further and higher education, not to accelerated unemployment.

With participation levels at 97 per cent in the middle age groups, employment can be said to constitute as normal a dimension in a woman's life in the new Länder as it had done in the GDR, although continuing employment has become more uncertain. Most women perceive their prospects in the labour market as bleak. Women older than 45 fear they will never find another job if they become unemployed, while many young women doubt that their educational and vocational qualifications are good enough to withstand the new competitive pressures of the labour market. There is evidence that women (and men) are working more than the statutory hours in an

TABLE 15.1 *Labour-market participation of women by age groups in the old and new Länder (%)*

Age Group	*Old Länder*		*New Länder*	
	1992	*1993*	*1992*	*1993*
15–20	34	33	43	37
20–25	73	71	85	83
25–30	73	72	95	94
30–35	68	68	97	96
35–40	70	70	97	97
40–45	73	73	97	96
45–50	69	70	96	95
50–55	61	62	90	91
55–60	46	47	27	27
60–65	12	12	3	3
65–70	4	4	*	*

Note: Percentage figures are rounded and may not add up to 100.
Source: *Datenreport*, 1994, p. 80.

attempt to be kept on. From a normal area of life that women took for granted, employment has turned into a key area of anxiety and concern.

Family Roles: Continuity and Transformation

In the GDR women's employment had been assured by a state policy that alleviated the conflict between motherhood and participation in the labour force. Reunification put an end to this, although transitional arrangements for the funding of child care and the entitlement to parental leave and child allowances ensured that family support collapsed less drastically than employment opportunities. Within two years of reunification, however, the West German model had been adopted. Benefits did not amount to the 'second wage package' they had been in the GDR and were perceived as inadequate. Child-care facilities at the workplace had long been closed or taken over by local authorities. As subsidies from the federal government ran dry, these facilities had to raise 20 per cent of their operating cost through charges, while regional and local government took care of 80 per cent between them. Most crèches and nurseries charged around DM3 per day for full-time care, including meals. Compared with West Germany, these prices were low; but compared with the DM0.35 it had cost in the GDR, the new rates appeared exorbitant.

Early fears, however, proved unfounded that child-care facilities would close in the wake of economic restructuring or that charges would prevent women from using them. Although in some areas provisions have deteriorated significantly since reunification, generally speaking the new Länder can offer a full-time day-care place for every child between birth and school age. Moreover the majority of women continue to use full-time care as they have always done. Although some children under the age of three are cared for at home or by relatives, nine out of ten preschool children attend a day-care institution. Yet neither the provision of day care nor its accessibility can be taken for granted, exacerbating women's sense of disorientation and uncertainty.

In the GDR provisions were based on location, that is, the workplace. In united Germany they are based on administrative guidelines and a set ratio of nursery staff per number of children. By these standards East German nurseries were overstaffed and costly to run and the adjustment to FRG standards entailed closures in order to increase overall efficiency. Then, unexpectedly, the number of children in the youngest age groups declined sharply and changed the pattern of demand beyond recognition. Post-reunification East German women no longer married in their early 20s, and they no longer had their first child at that age. Immediately after reunification the number of marriages declined to an all-time low and the number of births dropped by 50 per cent within one year and by a further 60 per cent in 1992. This trend has since slowed, but the eastern German birth rate in the mid 1990s remains significantly lower than that in the west (Statistisches Bundesant, 1995; Kolinsky, 1995b, p. 179). Half of the children born in the new Länder are born to unmarried mothers, that is, a detachment from traditional family structures and later parenthood go hand in hand.

The massive drop in the birth-rate can be interpreted as women's personal adjustment to the new uncertainties by postponing family duties and reducing family size in order to secure their place in the labour market. The decline in the number of babies and small children drastically reduced the demand for day-care places and contributed to a process of closure, relocation and reorganisation. This meant that from one week to the next women did not know whether their children would have to transfer to an institution in a different district and with a different nursery staff. No longer tied to the workplace, child-care facilities could be situated anywhere in the local authority that operated them and transport emerged as a new and unfamiliar problem. Although the number of day-care facilities seemed to remain more than adequate, women saw the situation as one of deterioration and an additional source of dissatisfaction with conditions in the new Germany.

Incomes and Poverty

Reunification also dismantled the web of state subsidies that had kept rents at their prewar levels, energy prices unchanged since the 1940s and essential goods, the so-called *Grundbedarf,* very cheap. Luxury goods included accessories of modern living such as televisions, washing machines, refrigerators and cars and absorbed a huge proportion of earnings (Voigt *et al.*, 1987, pp. 212–31). Yet poverty in the Western sense of individuals being unable to afford housing, food, clothing and day-to-day essentials had not existed in the GDR. Within three years of reunification, rents and the cost of domestic energy trebled, while the cost of living index rose by 38 per cent (Kolinsky, 1995b, p. 188). Incomes from employment were pitched at 65 per cent of those in the old Länder, and while post-reunification incomes were higher for all social groups, the rises did not offset the increased costs in other areas. Income surveys for the city of Leipzig have shown that in 1992, 56 per cent of women and 28 per cent of men earned less than DM1000, less than one third of average incomes in western Germany at the time. Nine out of ten women earned less than DM1500, the poverty level of the West. In 1993 one in ten in the east had fallen into poverty and earned less than DM600 (Datenreport, 1994, p. 104). Over two thirds of the new poor were women.

In the GDR female pensioners had lived in conditions that came close to those endured by the poor. After reunification, widows received a windfall since they became entitled to a share of their former husband's pension, a provision that had not been available in the GDR. Widows, then, were reunification winners. The losers were single mothers or one in three women with children in the GDR. Since reunification, most have ended up at the bottom of the pay scale without the bonus of the 'second wage package' described earlier. Single mothers also lost their entitlement to extended maternity leave, found child-care less accessible and often found the competitive pressures of the market economy too difficult to endure. Many were dismissed in the first throes of economic renewal before any 'problems' could appear. As unemployment spread, single mothers were particularly vulnerable.

Unemployment perpetuated women's earlier disadvantages since benefit reflected the level of pay at the point when employment was discontinued. Since their pay was lower, their benefit was lower. Moreover, after 1993 incomes in the new Länder began to lose their former uniformity – the salaries of administrative, managerial and civil service employees nearly doubled within one year, leaving the earnings of blue-collar and low-skilled white-collar workers far behind. Those unemployed who had lost their jobs in the first two years after reunification, those phased out into early retirement, and those who had to move from job to job in order to remain in the labour market, were in no position to benefit from the new mobilisation of incomes and opportunities (Nickel and Schenk, 1994). Again, most of those thus excluded were women.

For women above the age of 21, reunification turned their commitment to the family and motherhood into the risk of unemployment. As discussed earlier, older women and single women faced exclusion from the labour market earlier and for longer than other groups. However even those in employment were subject to social exclusion. As in the GDR years, women predominated in the lower income brackets. In

1993 one in ten women in the new Länder lived in poverty, with incomes below 40 per cent of the eastern average (Kolinsky, 1995b, p. 190). Single mothers in particular encountered poverty. In 1995 they constituted the largest group on income support in the new Länder. Having been unemployed for too long to qualify for benefit or receiving unemployment pay beneath the subsistence threshold, these unmarried and divorced mothers found themselves without the support of a social net (let alone a *Muttipolitk*) and in a poverty trap.

The New Employment Society

Five years after reunification, one in two eastern Germans thought that living standards had improved and would improve further for them personally and for their region during the next five years (Politbarometer). Women, however, were less confident about their personal prospects than about the economic fortunes of the new Länder generally. Women who had been turned into housewives were more dissatisfied than other groups. One in three of these reluctant housewives expressed dissatisfaction with their circumstances, although even in this group one in four were positive about their situation since it allowed them to spend more time with their families than when they had been at work (Schlegel, 1992, pp. 26–7). Of women without employment and below retirement age, 8 per cent in the new Länder and 60 per cent in western Germany gave their status as 'housewife' (Datenreport, 1994, p. 481). While the majority of housewives in the West had no immediate plans to find work and were not actively looking, most in the East were (Table 15.2).

TABLE 15.2 *Non-employed women and the labour market in the new and old Länder*

Labour-market orientation	*Aged 18–63*		*Aged 18–34*		*Aged 34–49*		*Aged 50–63*	
	New L.	*Old L.*	*New L.*	*Old L.*	*New L.*	*Old L.*	*New L.*	*Old L.*
General wish to work	76	23	73	29	97	29	68	12
Wish to work within 3 years	89	31	95	58	97	44	79	8
Looked for work in previous year	67	10	60	14	84	11	77	12
Finding work would not be difficult	15	33	29	51	4	45	5	22

Source: Wohlfahrtssurvey, 1993, in *Datenreport 1994*, p. 481.

Reunification dismantled the East German employment-centred society but did not remove the centrality of employment in people's lives. On the contrary the threat of unemployment even strengthened the emphasis on employment, forcing people to work longer hours and invest more effort into work than they had done in the GDR. In post-reunification Germany, employment emerged as the dividing line between social and material inclusion and exclusion. Those without work faced poverty in an environment without the state administered safety net of the 'second wage package' and housing and other subsidies.

Its very uncertainty made employment into the most important aspect of everyday life in the new Länder and placed unemployment at the top of the list of vital issues. Not dissimilar from West Germans in the immediate aftermath of the Second World War, East Germans have tended to focus on survival to the detriment of political renewal. In the 1940s, most people in the western zones ignored the work of the Parliamentary Council and took no interest in the new constitution. In 1990, when democratic politics had only just begun, one in four East Germans were dissatisfied with it (Datenreport, 1994, p. 432). While this initial dissatisfaction may have echoed experiences from the GDR years that neither parties nor politicians could be trusted, or may have resulted from a sense of disorientation at a time of rapid change, the same dissatisfaction three years on pertained to post-reunification democracy, not its predecessor. In 1993 disappointment with democracy increased in the new Länder to 48 per cent of the adult population, and nearly the same percentage did not want to participate in politics or found none of the political parties worth supporting. If the stability of democratic government is founded on the acceptance of democratic processes in the political culture, the new employment society in the east constitutes a source of political unpredictability.

Women in the new Länder have remained more passive and detached from democracy than men. The GDR, of course, had operated a women's quota of representation in its parties, parliament and committees, and women had constituted up to 40 per cent of the membership of these bodies. This type of participation, however, had nothing to do with political power and contributing to decision making, but rather reflected the state-prescribed view of how groups of the population should be represented in public life in order to acclaim the state, not influence it. While East German women had been drafted into political activities in large numbers, the activity demonstrated conformity rather than political involvement. Reunification removed the reasons for this compliance. The mass memberships of the remodelled bloc parties in the new Länder first sank into passivity and then gradually fell apart (Jesse, 1995, pp. 231–6). This drift away from active politics went hand in hand with a ground swell of disenchantment in the arduous economic transformation, the social dislocations and the persistent hiatus between the everyday living conditions on either side of the former East–West border.

In the old Länder women had focused their demands for equality on equal rights to party and parliamentary positions (Kolinsky, 1993b). Since the mid 1980s all political parties except the CSU have introduced mandatory or recommended women's quotas, transforming the gender balance of political organisations and parliaments. This concern to secure a political voice for women meant nothing to women in the east. They even mistook the demand for quotas as a repetition of the GDR practice of allocating meaningless functions to predetermined groups and felt alienated by it. In western Germany the introduction of a quota for women was the result of ten or more years' frustration at persistent inequality. However women in the East continue to be more preoccupied with the material organisation of their lives, their employment prospects, income potential and education in order to find their individual solutions to managing the conflict between employment and family roles that has arisen since reunification.

For women in the East, the new Germany is above all a society with unfamiliar employment uncertainties. Perhaps the post-reunification generations of young women who have curtailed their family commitments, and optimised their educational and professional qualifications in response to the challenges and opportunities of achievement and advancement in the new Germany, will welcome the challenges of democracy and the opportunity to shape its agenda once their own place in the world of employment has been secured.

16

Crime and Policing in Germany in the 1990s

PETER CULLEN

The 1990s have seen crime issues rise to the top of the political agenda in Germany. Polls suggest that since reunification the German public, especially in the new Länder, has become increasingly concerned about the increase in crime. Government politicians and senior policemen, to some extent playing on these fears, comment in dramatic terms about the threat to German democracy posed by the 'new' phenomenon of organised crime (*Organisierte Kriminalität*). The crime debate has become conflated with the controversial reform of Germany's asylum laws and with public attitudes to foreigners. This chapter will discuss the principal policy developments in the criminal justice field since reunification, including the constitutional and legal dimensions of the internal security debate. There have been significant changes in German criminal law in recent years and these reforms have certainly impinged upon the constitutional values expressed by the Basic Rights (*Grundrechte*) of Germany's constitution. There is also increased discussion of the proper role for the police in the next century, in the light of changing political, social and economic conditions. Some important aspects of the evolution of policing and crime-control strategies will be highlighted. Finally, the chapter will briefly examine Germany's role in European police cooperation.

Developments in Criminal Policy since Reunification

Crime and Policing in the Former GDR

Reunification in 1990 required a radical overhaul of the criminal justice and policing systems of the former GDR to bring them into line with

West German practice. Adaptation to the standards of the Basic Law has posed a wide range of difficult legal, political and organisational problems. Those trying to make the necessary adjustments have found their task made all the more difficult by the grave crime problems that have afflicted the eastern Länder since reunification. Many of these, including crimes against property, had been deliberately concealed by the communist authorities (Rupprecht, 1993, p. 392). The violence against foreigners reflects a more general rise in violent crime in the east, which may have its roots in the social dislocation caused by reunification (Kube and Dörmann, 1993).

The Unification Treaty of 1990 provides for rehabilitation of victims of criminal court judgments made in the GDR, in cases where they were based on political or ideological factors, and for retrospective appeal against such judgments. Such provisions, and prosecutions in respect of decisions of the GDR authorities that were taken lawfully under GDR law, are difficult to reconcile with the constitutional prohibition of retroactive criminal law (Article 103.2 of the Basic Law). Political as well as legal problems bedevil the delicate process of review of past wrongs in which the courts and other legal authorities of the Federal Republic are engaged. The important objectives of national integration and reconcilation with past enemies would be endangered by overzealous prosecution of loyal supporters of the former GDR regime. On the other hand there is an expectation among the many victims of communist oppression that their oppressors will be brought to justice. If these expectations are not fulfilled, it will not be easy to convince the majority of eastern Germans not involved in the activities of the *Stasi* (*Staatssicherheitsdienst*, or secret police), that the Federal Republic is genuinely committed to the rule of law and human rights (cf. Gauck, 1994).

The reform of the policing system in the eastern Länder directly confronts the GDR's totalitarian past. The police in the GDR were part of the state apparatus controlled by the ruling SED. The statutory mission of the ironically named *Volkspolizei* (people's police) was to participate in the 'construction of socialism' by enforcing 'socialist law'. Initially the *Volkspolizei* closely resembled a military force; it continued to have access to and train its members in the use of heavy weaponry until its demise (the police forces of West Germany have also, however, found it difficult to rid themselves of such weaponry: Busch *et al.*, 1988, p. 183). More sinister were the activities of the much-despised *Stasi*, whose job it was to act as the 'Sword and Shield of the Party' in spying and reporting on dissidents. Thousands of files were passed on to the Ministry for State Security, which would then act to stifle the critics of the regime. The ministry ensured that the *Stasi* and the *Volkspolizei* cooperated closely; *Stasi* members were active in the police and the ministry secured the appointment of loyal supporters of the regime to senior police jobs (Gill and Schröter, 1991, p. 75).

The first freely elected government of the GDR committed itself to the establishment of a democratic police force organised on a provincial basis. This promise was made good by a law of the People's Assembly of 13 September 1990, which set out the basic tasks and powers of the police forces of the new Länder, pending the adoption of separate police laws. These important reforms in policing went hand in hand with fundamental reform of the whole system of criminal justice in the former GDR: the Basic Law required the setting up of a system of state prosecution independent of the police and the establishment of an independent judiciary. These new systems were installed according to the West German model, by lawyers trained in the Federal Republic.

The *Stasi* was speedily dismantled after the fall of the Berlin Wall. Following reunification a law of 20 December 1991 ordered that the *Stasi* files be opened up to those on whom files had been kept, in order to enable them to discover what influence the *Stasi* may have had on their lives. The 'Gauck' authority (named after the keeper of the records) maintains the files and supervises access to them. They contain appalling revelations of abuses of power, betrayal of trust and breaches of privacy by *Stasi* agents, leaving a 'poisonous legacy' (Jarausch and Gransow, 1994, p. 245). The police–society relationship in the new *Länder* is heavily burdened by this history, which also constitutes an obstacle to acceptance of 'secret police' tactics such as those being contemplated to combat organised crime (see below). The widespread use by the *Stasi* of persons sympathetic to the regime as informants or 'unofficial helpers' (*inoffizielle Mitarbeiter*) probably also makes it more difficult for police there to enlist the support of local communities to combat crime in the new political circumstances. There has, however, been a cleansing of the police of persons, especially high-ranking officers, implicated in the 'political policing' of the GDR regime.

A great deal of western German financial and technical assistance has been forthcoming to help reorganise and modernise the eastern German police. Almost all of this has been coordinated by one or more western Länder, which have also supplied personnel to run the new police and criminal investigation departments. There have been godparentships (*Patenschaften*) between particular western and eastern Länder for this purpose (for example between Baden-Württemberg and Bavaria in the west and Saxony in the east). The German Police Leadership Academy (*Polizei-Führungsakademie*) at Münster-Hiltrup, which is jointly run by the federal government and the Länder, has been busy educating future police leaders in the east in the ways of democratic policing. It is, however, evident that it will take much longer to educate the eastern German police in western laws and practices than it has taken to reequip them to western standards. Interviews in *Der Spiegel* of police officers in eastern Germany, conducted four years after reunification, tell of their sense of 'helplessness' faced with massive operational adjustments and substantial new crime problems (*Der Spiegel*, 5 September, 1994, p. 62ff.).

Countering Right-Wing Violence

The federal government has generally been content not to interfere in the establishment of new police structures in the former GDR. It has tended to become involved only when public-order crises of nationwide interest have arisen, for example the anti-foreigner riots in Rostock-Lichtenhagen in 1992 and Magdeburg in 1994, when east German policemen stood by as foreigners and their property were attacked (*Der Spiegel*, 5 September, 1994, p. 62). After the Rostock incident the federal minister of the interior, Rudolf Seiters, rushed forward with an idea for joint 'rapid reaction squads' – *Polizei-Alarmtruppen*, consisting of officers from the federal police (including the Federal Border Guard, or *Bundesgrenzschutz*) and the Länder – to quell such disturbances. This suggestion was swiftly rejected by the Länder police, who perceived it as an intrusion into their sovereignty in police matters and pointed to existing provisions of the constitution allowing the Border Guard to be called upon to assist a Land force. Seiters did, however, ban a number of neo-Nazi organisations thought to be involved in these and other incidents of racist violence (Marshall, 1995, p. 197).

Hans-Ludwig Zachert, the president of the *Bundeskriminalamt* (BKA, Federal Criminal Police Office), has conceded that German police and judicial authorities failed to predict and then adequately react to the resurgence of violent right-wing extremism in Germany after reunification (*Frankfurter Allgentinf Zeitung*, 18 April 1993, p. 3). There were similar shortcomings on the part of the central government and the federal and Länder Offices for the Protection of the Constitution (Marshall, 1995, p. 197). Zachert accounts for such failure by referring to the fixation of law-enforcement authorities on the activities of left-wing extremists associated with the terrorist groups of the 1970s. The criticism of bias in criminal law enforcement against left-wingers is now less easy to sustain. Since the publication of the 1992 report of the Federal Office for Protection of the Constitution which revealed a huge

(74 per cent) increase in crimes against foreigners perpetrated by right-wing groups compared with the previous year, policy makers and courts at federal and Land level have begun to adopt tougher measures to counter the right-wing threat. As Zachert's remarks demonstrate, senior figures in the law-enforcement community are now more conscious of the need to eradicate violence directed at foreigners. The Bundestag responded with important debates condemning racial attacks and, in 1994, with a law that heavily penalises incitement to racial hatred and denial of Nazi crimes.

Police attitudes and behaviour towards foreigners in Germany was, nevertheless, severely criticised in an Amnesty International report in 1995 (*Independent*, 17 May 1995). The report's claims of a 'pattern' of racist abuse were strongly rejected by the Standing Conference of Interior Ministers of the Länder (*Innenministerkonferenz*) at its meeting of May 1995. Politicians and senior police officers can help create a climate of opinion in which human rights abuses will not be tolerated. Their task is made more difficult by possible policy conflict. Foreigners are associated with the *commission* of crime in the political debates concerning organised crime and asylum. Fighting between different foreign groups has become a serious problem in recent years; tension between immigrant Kurdish groups and Turks, in particular, has resulted in outbreaks of violence. There is also growing concern about the presence of militant Islamic groups in Germany. Police crime statistics isolate crime by foreigners; *prima facie* the statistics may be interpreted as evidencing a greater propensity on the part of non-Germans than Germans to commit certain crimes. This topic is very hotly debated (Wassermann, 1995; cf. Geißler, 1995). Right-wing extremist groups responsible for perpetrating acts of violence against foreigners fed on public fears about the asylum 'crisis' in the early 1990s, taking full advantage of politicians' vacillation on the issue. The immigration and criminal policy debates in Germany now overlap. Put more concretely, controlling immigration has become a facet of criminal policy (Busch, 1995, p. 155).

Organised Crime

Apart from asylum, the allegedly 'new' phenomenon of organised crime has been the dominant subject on Germany's internal security agenda since reunification. It has been taken to justify a number of recent policy and legislative initiatives in the criminal justice sphere and is often the main item raised for discussion by German representatives in international police and security fora. Criminal policy under Chancellor Kohl's government has in recent years tended to focus on 'high profile' areas such as drug trafficking (including money laundering), organised crime and public order offences. The first two of these are closely linked. Ministerial policy statements on criminal matters in the post-reunification era have almost invariably highlighted the threat to society posed by organised crime. Similar sentiments are expressed by the BKA. The important *Programm Innere Sicherheit* of 1994 (Programme for Internal Security), issued jointly by the interior ministers of the Länder and the federal minister of the interior (building upon a similar programme of 1974) identifies the fight against organised crime as a 'special priority' of criminal policy.

Organised crime continues to defy clear definition. There is no legislative definition and instead the police and judicial authorities work according to an informal text agreed by a joint working party in 1990. According to this text, the distinguishing features of organised crime are:

> the pursuit of profit or power by the planned commission of crimes, which, when taken singly or together, are of a serious nature, involving cooperation by more than two persons working as a team over a long or indefinite period, where such cooperation involves: a) the use of commercial or quasi-commercial structures, b) the use of violence or other methods of intimidation or c) the exercise of influence on the political process, the media, judicial authorities or the functioning of the economy (Zachert, 1995, p. 13).

In 1994, 789 organised crime investigations were opened. They concerned approximately 100 000 individual crimes, almost one third of which were drugs-related (Police Crime Statistics, 1994, p. 533). Over half of those implicated in these crimes were foreigners – Turks, former Yugoslavs and nationals of the states of Central and Eastern Europe being the principal groups involved. Since the fall of the Berlin Wall many hierarchically organised criminal gangs have been operating from Russia, though they have not yet attained the level of 'sophistication' of the Italian mafia (Raith, 1995).

While mostly active in drug-smuggling and dealing, organised gangsters are also heavily involved in prostitution, traffic in people (including smuggling illegal immigrants across borders) bribery, car theft, illegal dealing in weapons and explosives and fraud, among other crimes. The economic damage caused by their activities is immense, reckoned in hundreds of millions of Deutsche Mark each year. There is substantial 'laundering' of money in the lawful economy. In light of the

Italian experience, there is serious concern in Germany about the potential of organised criminals to corrupt public institutions; the funds that they have at their disposal to bribe officials, bankers or politicians are clearly considerable. 'Home-made' corruption of public officials has already proved grave enough for the Bundesrat to propose the creation of specific criminal offences in this sphere.

That there is potential for exaggerating the scale of organised crime however, should also be recognised. Politicians across Western Europe, not only in Germany, are greatly skilled in scaremongering about crime for electoral advantage. The police have an obvious institutional interest in painting the picture blacker than the reality. With organised crime in particular, owing to the difficulties of definition it is not easy to gauge how much of the 'boom' is really 'new' – the claim that political and economic collapse in the countries of Central and Eastern Europe has led to a significant increase in such crime is not usually substantiated (Police Crime Statistics, 1994, p. 543; cf. den Boer, 1994, p. 187). Damage is done to the police case by controversial practices such as organising 'stings': at the time of writing a Committee of Enquiry of the Bundestag is investigating allegations that the German Federal Intelligence Agency (the *Bundesnachrichtendienst*) stage-managed the smuggling of a quantity of plutonium from Moscow to Munich in August 1994.

There is concern among civil libertarians that the federal legislator has rushed into passing draconian legislation to combat organised crime without any clear justification (Hassemer, 1993). Their recent fire has been aimed at the *Verbrechensbekämpfungsgesetz* (Crime-Fighting Law) of 28 October 1994, which *inter alia* extends the powers of the intelligence agencies to tap international telephone calls and preserves the *Kronzeugenregelung* ('Turning Queen's Evidence Rule'), developed in the context of terrorist crime, for crimes committed by organised groups. The reforms regarding the intelligence services are feared partly because they are thought to be the thin end of the wedge; since the war the Federal Republic has observed a strict separation of the functions – and powers – of the police and the intelligence services. The functions of the Federal Office for the Protection of the Constitution (*Bundesamt für Verfassungsschutz*), for example, and those of its counterparts in the Länder, have been limited to gathering intelligence on political extremists and may not include the conduct of criminal investigations or the exercise of police powers. There are pressures for these agencies to extend their observational activities to organised criminals; in 1994 Bavaria changed its Law on Constitutional Protection to enable this to happen. Perhaps not surprisingly, some senior German policemen are doubtful about the intelligence services' competence in this field (Raith, 1995, p. 107). The Bavarian move will anger civil libertarians, who are already unhappy with provisions of Länder police laws which allow police investigations to be carried out before a concrete suspicion of crime is present (*im Vorfeld*).

The use of police undercover agents (*Verdeckte Ermittler*) was endorsed by the federal Law against Money Laundering and Organised Crime of 15 July 1992, and there are similar provisions in provincial laws. Their use is dangerous and, therefore, not in fact a popular police tactic. There are also a number of important legal restrictions that operate as a disincentive. Under present legal arrangements, for example, while working undercover officers may not themselves commit crimes and there are problems about their giving evidence as witnesses in criminal trials (Raith, 1995, p. 101). Even more controversial is the use by police of underworld criminals as *Vertrauensmänner*, or *V-Männer* (police moles), to infiltrate and report back on criminal gangs. But the greatest controversy surrounding the extension of police powers presently concerns the proposal (not yet clothed in draft legislation) to give the police the authority to indulge in the electronic bugging of private homes as a measure to help catch drug dealers and others involved in forms of organised crime (*großer Lauschangriff*). This would require legislation to amend Article 13 of the Basic Law. Opponents regard the privacy of the home as sacrosanct, and among some of them the idea has provoked similar outrage to that stirred up by the asylum controversy. Her party's approval of the proposal was enough to prompt the resignation of Germany's FDP federal minister of justice, Mrs Leutheusser-Schnarrenberger, in December 1995.

It can plausibly be argued that the Basic Law is being 'stretched' to enable the police and intelligence services to intensify their fight against organised crime, though the scale of the threat to civil liberties has probably not yet reached the dimensions achieved during the 1970s by antiterrorist legislation and accompanying police measures (Cullen, 1992, pp. 55–57). Constitutional theorists on the side of greater repression argue that a *Recht auf Sicherheit*, an individual's right to the provision of security *by the state* in the face of crime, is implicit in the Basic Law. The Federal Constitutional Court has not embraced such a 'security' or 'state-oriented' approach to the constitution. Rather its jurisprudence has emphasised the duty of the state not to interfere with an individual's autonomy, for example in the famous 'Census' decision of 1983, which developed the law to give the individual control over the use by public authorities of personal data, subject to very strict exceptions. This has proved a very important precedent for the police laws at both federal and *Land* level. The police complain bitterly about how the Court's decision has made their job harder.

A storm of protest from police and conservative politicians was also unleashed by the Constitutional Court's decision of 10 January 1995 to limit the scope for police interference in demonstrations that take the form of 'sit-down protests' (*Sitzblockaden*), for example outside military bases. Controversy was also provoked by the Court's decision of 9 March 1994 that the possession of small amounts of cannabis for personal use should not be prosecuted. This decision was justified by reference to federal drug control legislation of 1992, which signalled a move away from a purely repressive strategy on drug abuse. In the same case the Court rejected a claim to a broad constitutional 'right to intoxication' by drugs or alcohol (*Recht auf Rausch*).

Policing and Crime Control Strategies for the 1990s

It is not possible to discuss policing strategies in Germany without taking account of the diversity of police agencies at federal and Land level. Under Germany's constitutional arrangements the police function of *Gefahrenabwehr*, (averting dangers to public order), is the responsibility of the Länder. The sixteen Länder police forces are constituted by and operate in the precriminal phase of investigations according to police laws (*Polizeigesetze*) enacted by their respective legislatures. In operational matters, for example the policing of demonstrations, the police act under the instructions of *Polizeipräsidenten* (chief constables), who are often civilian appointees. Ultimate political responsibility lies with the interior minister of each Land. Federal law, in the form of the Codes of Criminal Law and Procedure, governs criminal investigations by the police. Whereas the Länder police laws can and do vary, these codes apply uniformly across the country. In addition the Basic Law prevails in the case of conflict with Land law, with the result that all police action must be in conformity with the Basic Rights as interpreted by the Federal Constitutional Court.

The BKA and the *Bundesgrenzschutz* are Germany's two federal police agencies. Their existence reduces Länder autonomy in police matters, but their powers are carefully circumscribed by statute. The Federal Border Guard is a fully operational force around 30 000 strong. Formerly entrusted with the policing of the inner-German border, since the tightening of Germany's asylum laws it has assumed the unenviable task of enforcing Germany's immigration laws, for example detaining and expelling from German soil asylum seekers from so-called 'safe countries' (Walter, 1994, p. 50). The BKA has around 4000 staff. It is responsible for 'servicing' the Länder police forces, by collecting, analysing and distributing of criminal data, which is held in a central computer network (INPOL) in Wiesbaden that is accessible by Land forces.

The BKA has grown significantly in power and influence thanks to its acquisition of investigatory powers in respect of international crime, including drug trafficking, illegal trade in weapons, counterfeiting and terrorism (the latter is not an original competence but a delegated one). It also oversees cooperation with foreign police forces and acts as the National Central Bureau for Interpol. The BKA would obviously like to assert jurisdiction over the whole field of organised crime (Zachert, 1995, p. 18). To bolster this claim, a sympathetic federal government brought forward proposals for clarification and extension of the BKA's jurisdiction in February 1995; the draft law has so far been resisted by the Länder, who do not wish to see any more of their sovereign powers over police matters being transferred to the federation.

Given this dispersal of power, the coordination of police strategy and operations among the various actors is not easy. This was amply demonstrated by the tragic incident in Bad Kleinen in 1993, when an antiterrorist operation involving joint action by the BKA, the Border Guard and the Länder authorities was bungled, with one suspected terrorist and one member of the Border Guard being killed. The then federal minister of the interior, Rudolf Seiters, took responsibility for the incident and resigned. Controlling criminal activities that extend beyond the borders of one Land, and combating international crime in particular, obviously require close collaboration between agencies. There are instances of American-style 'task forces' (*Sonderkommissionen*), consisting of officers from the various levels and agencies working together, but these are usually of an *ad hoc* nature. The federal government is particularly keen to encourage better cooperation between the police and intelligence agencies. To facilitate interministerial coordination in relation to policy on drugs, the federal government has established a new position – that of 'Drugs Coordinator' (*Drogenbeauftragter*) – within the Ministry of the Interior (Lintner, 1995). Drugs control has thus been recognised as a cross-departmental responsibility, reflecting the abovementioned move away from an exclusively criminal-law-centred strategy. The 1990 'National Plan to combat Drugs' (*Nationaler Rauschgiftbekämpfungsplan*) provided the basis for this development (Albrecht, 1995, pp. 192–3).

In general terms, the federal government and the BKA favour the continuation of a criminal-law-centred approach to combatting organised crime. As we have seen, more laws are being prepared to deal with such crime. The interior minister has confidently stated that such measures have brought about 'more internal security' (Kanther, 1995). A similar strategy is favoured by the Kohl administration with regard to public order crimes: in 1989, as part of a package of legislative measures, the wearing of masks at demonstrations was criminalised and some police powers were extended (Cullen, 1992, p. 30). There is, however, widespread recognition that this approach has not succeeded in addressing the much larger problem of mass or ordinary crime, and that criminal policy in this area must try to achieve a better balance between prevention and repression. Preventive strategies have often been espoused in governmental programmes but German criminologists complain that far too little emphasis has been placed on prevention in ordinary police work (Zimmermann, 1992).

The Programme for Internal Security of 1994 (p. 6) refers to the vital role of non-police agencies in creating 'social conditions' that are conducive to a reduction in crime. Youth crime has ballooned dramatically in the past decade, and much of it is violent. Here the 1994 Programme endorses an holistic approach, stressing the part of local authorities in improved leisure provision, for example sports facilities, especially in areas that are potential trouble spots; town planning development should take particular account of youth requirements; and the media are prevailed upon to act responsibly in their portrayal of violence (Programme for Internal Security, 1993, p. 18). In an 'Action Programme against Aggression and Violence', some DM65 million has been invested by the federal government in youth crime prevention programmes in the eastern Länder, where youth unemployment is high: these programmes will be implemented in cooperation with church, police and youth groups (Kanther, 1995, p. 114). The limits of what the police alone can do to stop youth crime are expressly recognised in the Programme for Internal Security, which favours better targeting of police resources (1993, pp. 17–18).

The German police are becoming increasingly interested in developing strategies of 'community policing' that have scored some successes in other countries, including the United Kingdom and the United States (Dölling and Feltes, 1993). Several Länder forces are now experimenting with models drawn from neighbouring countries: in Frankfurt, where crime in some areas has reached epidemic proportions, the police have established crime prevention councils involving citizens' groups and other agencies (Bauer and Blaesing, 1992). North-Rhine Westphalia is distinctive among Länder police forces in having incorporated 'Police Advisory Councils' (*Polizeibeiräte*), elected by local councillors, as part of the police administrative structure. Apart from advising the police on community issues, they have the right to be consulted on police reorganisation and in the appointment of chief constables.

Nevertheless, there are a number of obstacles in the way of a better relationship between police and citizens in Germany. The special historical circumstances of the GDR have already been mentioned. More generally, it is argued that the police have so far failed appropriately to react to the negative effects on relations with local communities of the trends towards more bureaucratisation and centralisation of policing. These were side-effects of the modernising and streamlining reforms of the 1970s, being also closely related to the police's increased reliance on information technology (Busch *et al.*, 1988, p. 227 ff.) Reversing the 'remoteness effect' created by these changes will not be easy, given that some of these trends are irreversible. One way to make the police appear closer to the citizen is to put more officers on street patrol. Interior ministers at Land and federal level are agreed that the presence of more police on the streets and in public places is desirable in order to instill a heightened sense of security in the public (Programme for Internal Security, 1993, p. 7). It is obviously important for the police's image that they are seen to be helping the citizen in a visible way, though this strategy will require more manpower.

There are significant financial constraints on all public authorities in Germany at present, which makes the provision of extra police resources unlikely. It is therefore quite probable that the burgeoning of Germany's private security industry that has been observed over the last decade will continue apace. The federal government has expressed support for private policing in principle, hoping it will release more police for essential tasks; it accepts, however, that the industry needs to be better regulated. Constitutional obstacles may block the delegation of mainstream policing tasks to private undertakings, but such considerations have not prevented the police and private security firms from joining forces to patrol public places such as underground stations.

A further obstacle to more community-oriented police strategies may be mentioned. For some years now police morale has been at a low ebb, owing to poor pay and conditions compared with other professions. Police pay, whether for federal or Land officers, is linked to a career structure that keeps a disproportionate number of officers on low salaries (Cullen, 1992, pp. 21–2). The average German policeman does not enjoy the relatively high social status of his British counterpart. Demonstrations by police for improved conditions are not uncommon sights on German streets. Finally, an over-reliance on formal legal methods of accountability – an historical product of the positioning of the police within the wider executive arm of government and subject to the jurisdiction of the Administrative Courts – militates against closer community control, for example through independent complaints procedures.

European Police Cooperation

In the 1970s the Federal Republic found common cause with the governments of other Western democracies in its antiterrorist strategies. Together with the United Kingdom, it was the driving force behind the creation, in 1976, of the TREVI group, a standing conference of European Community interior ministers focused on coordinating governments' antiterrorist strategies. Since the 1980s German policy on police cooperation has been intertwined with its stance on border and immigration issues. The year 1985 saw the adoption of the first Schengen Agreement, initially signed by France, Germany and the Benelux states. The objective of Schengen was to facilitate unhindered commercial traffic and the free movement of persons between the contracting states, especially France and Germany (Schengen's main promoters) by abolishing border controls. There was some mention in the agreement of eventual implementation of 'compensatory measures' to offset any loss of security that resulted from doing away with border controls, but that was a secondary consideration.

The second Schengen Agreement of 1990 is almost unrecognisable from its predecessor, which it purports to implement, in the way in which it emphasises security considerations and control of immigration over the free movement of persons. The dramatic collapse of communism has thrown the Schengen policy into confusion; the massive movement of eastern Germans to West Germany after the fall of the Berlin Wall was seen by many as only a foretaste of things to come from further east. The German government came increasingly to emphasise the importance of securing Schengen's external borders, certainly against criminals but more importantly against illegal immigrants, as 'compensation' for the opening of internal borders (Busch, 1995, p. 76ff.)

The policing of Germany's eastern border by the Border Guard is now indeed primarily aimed at stopping illegal immigrants, not criminals (Busch, 1995, p. 76ff). It is a delicate operation, given historical and political sensitivities; excessive 'militarisation' of Germany's borders would create a damaging image of a 'fortress mentality', so soon after the fall of the Berlin Wall. Forty-five thousand illegal immigrants were caught by the Border Guard in 1992 (Walter, 1994, pp. 48, 51). Asylum seekers arriving in Germany from one of the 'safe countries' determined by law – including all countries bordering upon Germany – may be immediately returned to those countries by the Border Guard. Asylum is effectively being denied to these people. Although the constitutional changes made in 1993 have more than halved the number of asylum applications (when compared with 1992), the figures for 1995 still show that nearly 120 000 formal applications were lodged (*Bulletin des Presse- und Informationsamts der Bundesregierung*, 1995, no. 103, pp. 1015–16). Migration to Germany is obviously continuing at high levels; the figures also suggest that frustrated asylum seekers are now trying their luck as illegal immigrants.

There has been a sense of great urgency about German policy on police cooperation with Central and Eastern European countries since reunification, in view of the migration pressures. Bilateral agreements have been concluded by Germany with a number of these states, covering immigration and policing matters. They usually entail, or are accompanied by, substantial financial aid by Germany for policing modernisation in the country concerned and the posting to it of BKA liaison officers (Lintner, 1993). The relationship with Poland is particularly important. Large sums have been paid to Poland in return for its agreeing to take back illegal immigrants who have entered Germany via Polish territory; specific sums have also been earmarked for Poland's eastern border security precautions (Walter, 1994, pp. 49–50). Germany is clearly anxious that Poland should be fully geared up to strict external border controls of its own before it is admitted to the European Union.

The provisions on police cooperation in the 1990 Schengen Agreement are supplemented by developments within the European Union (Title VI or the 'Third Pillar' of the Maastricht Treaty). The German federal government has strongly promoted the creation of a distinctive European police agency, 'Europol', an idea that has already come to partial fruition in the shape of the Europol Drugs Unit in the Hague, headed by Jürgen Storbeck, a leading BKA policeman. A detailed convention establishing Europol, signed by all European Union Member States on 26 July 1995, currently awaits ratification. This provides for advanced institutionalised police cooperation, involving the exchange of criminal data concerning ongoing international investigations between police liaison officers from EU member states. Europol will also advise on strategic planning. It is envisaged that the remit of the Hague agency will in time extend beyond the field of drug trafficking to terrorism and other forms of organised crime. Europol will not, however, be an executive agency, capable of exercising police powers across frontiers, as Chancellor Kohl would have liked. Many legal obstacles currently stand in the way of his more far-reaching idea of a 'European FBI' (Storbeck, 1995, p. 26).

Constraints, Concerns and Innovation

Germany's policy response to crime is conditioned by a number of factors. History weighs heavily on German policing. The country has a legacy of oppressive secret policing. In the Federal Republic, after the war the Nazi experience was addressed by ensuring that the police were placed under Land authority, with a clear distinction being drawn between policing and intelligence functions. Federal policing remains the exception, though there has been control from the centre in relation to some of the most serious crime problems the Federal Republic has encountered since 1949, notably terrorism. The constitutional framework, especially the need to respect the Basic Rights, constrains police action. The Federal Constitutional Court has often interpreted these rights to favour individual freedom of action over police interference. Two generations of German policemen and women in the west have been trained in the democratic tradition; there is no hard evidence to suggest that any substantial number of them have rejected the values espoused by the Basic Law. Experience of secret police tactics in the eastern Länder is of course much more recent than in the west. Both police and population there are having to adapt to wholly 'foreign' legal and administrative practices. This process of reckoning with the *Stasi* inheritance has been hampered by an atmosphere of considerable public insecurity about rising crime.

Since reunification there have been deplorable attacks by right-wing extremists on foreigners in both eastern and western Germany, forcing the police and policy makers to turn their attention away from the traditional focus on left-wing extremism. A number of important measures have now been taken to address this problem, involving a sensible mix of prevention and repression. There has also been a wave of public sympathy for the victims of the most serious attacks. Public tolerance of foreigners has, however, been strained by the asylum debate, as well as by the undeniable association of foreign criminal gangs with organised crime.

While 'organised' and 'ordinary' criminal activities may overlap, and are not treated wholly separately by the authorities, one can nevertheless, in general terms, isolate distinctive policy approaches to these categories of crime. With regard to fighting organised crime, a repressive strategy has held sway under Chancellor Kohl's government. The BKA's push for greater powers cannot be dissociated from its endorsement of this approach. There may be important constitutional changes in the offing to allow for electronic surveillance of private property thought to be used by organised criminal groups. The political path for such legislation was cleared in late 1995 by the resignation of the federal justice minister, who vehemently opposed the idea. Drug control strategies in the 1990s have, however, moved away somewhat from overreliance on the use of the criminal law, at least in relation to 'low-risk categories' of drug users. Recent legislation has been targeted at drugs dealers and money launderers.

In policing terms, more undercover police work is taking place in organised crime circles. The intelligence services are manoeuvring for a role here too. The police claim that they are hamstrung by strict rules on data protection and tight criminal law procedures. While their calls for greater investigatory powers have to some extent been met in recent years, increases in manpower and other resources have not been forthcoming on the level they consider necessary, leading to low morale and a larger role for private security firms. In trying to reduce the incidence of mass crimes such as theft, and to stem the rapid rise in youth crime, the police are seeking to work more openly with local communities and to cooperate more effectively with non-law-enforcement agencies. This approach, which recognises the limitations of the police in crime fighting, has been strongly encouraged by the Programme for Internal Security of 1994. Some German forces have experimented with community policing models borrowed from other countries.

In the context of European policing, Germany has taken the lead in developing new forms of cooperation. It is testimony to the successful postwar rehabilitation of the German police that Chancellor Kohl's ideas on Europol have been received so readily by the majority of EU member states. The setting up of Europol and the Schengen provisions on police cooperation do, however, draw attention to the need – both on effectiveness and on human rights grounds – for proper democratic and legal controls at the European level (cf. Anderson *et al.*, 1995).

Germany's postwar constitutional traditions offer it the chance to have a constructive input here.

Finally, legitimate concerns about civil liberties should not blind one to the fact that Germany faces a serious crime problem. The scale of economic damage and, more importantly, personal distress behind the crime statistics must be immense. Most Western societies are, however, coming to realise that the causes of crime are manifold and complex and that it cannot be 'fought' with repression alone. Similar considerations should apply with regard to the West's immigration 'problem', which will obviously not be solved by the German Border Police.

Note

The author is indebted to Professor Heike Jung of the Department of Criminal Law of the University of the Saarland, Saarbrücken, for his advice and for making available research facilities. Some of the research for this chapter was conducted in the course of an ESRC-sponsored project on European Police Cooperation, in which the author was involved along with colleagues from the University of Edinburgh (ESRC R000 23 2639).

17

Model or Exception – Germany as a Normal State?

PETER PULZER

Was the unification of the two German republics on 3 October 1989 yet another episode in the unceasing German search for a satisfactory form of state, or has the great German question, which has disturbed the spirit of Europe for the best part of two centuries, finally come to rest? Have we been witnessing yet another turbulence, or the belated German arrival in the family of stable European nation-states?

State Formation and the National Question

The German state has undergone five fundamental changes of form since the 1860s – an average of one per generation. We therefore need to ask of this latest transformation, as of all its predecessors, what is new about it and what is not, what is conventional about it and what is exceptional? The old question of continuity in German history, which became salient in the historical evaluation of the Third Reich, remains valid, even if its context has now shifted. What is old and what is new about post-1990 Germany is worth investigating not only for its policy implications, not only because Germany's neighbours, friends and partners – and enemies, if it has any – need to know the answers, but also because it is inherently interesting. The question of old and new, of continuity and interruption is central because of the fractured nature of German history and the fractured relationship of Germans to this history; because of the uncertain relationship between state and nation in the German context throughout modern times; and because of the uncertain – indeed increasingly uncertain – relationship between nationality and citizenship.

All attempts at German state formation since 1848 have been attempts to solve the German national question, that is, what political form best expresses German nationhood. The attempt by the Frankfurt Parliament of 1848–49 to draw up an all-German constitution ended in failure, but bequeathed a number of legacies. It discredited parliamentary institutions, both as a form of government and as a solution to the national question, but the black, red and gold flag that it eventually adopted became the national flag, hotly contested in the Weimar Republic, but uncontroversially shared between East and West after 1949. As experiments in nation building the various state creations after 1848 were in one way or another seriously defective. A successful, stable nation-state needs to satisfy a number of conditions. The first is that political and ethnocultural borders should coincide: in other words, the external definition of the state should correspond with the ideal elaborated in the nineteenth century, that of national self-determination. The second is a reasonable level of social homogeneity: society should not be so fragmented by customs, religion or geographical barriers as to neutralise the unifying thrust of a common language and a shared literature. The third is a constitutional consensus: a sense that the form of government is legitimate, whether or not based on popular sovereignty, and is suited to the task of turning an ethnically cohesive territory into a viable political reality. To mention these conditions, and they are not meant to be exhaustive, is to demonstrate what was missing, to different degrees and in differing proportions, in the German Empire, the Weimar Republic and the Third Reich.

The empire of 1871–1918 was incomplete as a nation-state in a number of ways. Its constitutional basis was dynastic. It was an 'eternal union' of the rulers of the 25 constituent states; it was created by the military victory of one of those states – Prussia – over the majority of the others. It had none of the basic trappings of a nation-state: no single army (except in time of war), no national flag, no national anthem, no equivalent of Empire Day, the Fourth of July or Bastille Day. Nor did the creation of the empire solve the German question. On the one hand it inherited Prussia's non-German minorities – Poles and Danes – and acquired a new minority of doubtful allegiance through the annexation of Alsace and Lorraine. On the other hand the Prussian-based empire made sense only if it excluded Austria and its sizeable German-speaking population, a decision that was to lead to a great deal of trouble in the course of the twentieth century. The empire was therefore a political unit based partly on Hegelian principles –

positing the primacy of the state – and partly on Herderian – positing the primacy of culture. For the entire duration of the empire the tension between the concept of Germans as citizens of a territorial state and members of a *Volk* remained unresolved. Much as it had suited Bismarck to declare the settlement of 1866–71 as final, the increasing pressure on the German populations of the Habsburg monarchy and in the more scattered settlements of the Russian Empire, as well as the growth of the ideology of pan-Germanism, more vigorous initially outside Germany than inside it, made the fate of the German *Volk*, wherever its members might live, a constant political irritant. The pan-German League (*Alldeutscher Verband*) was founded in 1893 on the premise that German national unification had not been completed in 1871. Its declared purpose was 'the cultivation and support of *deutsch-national* endeavours in all countries in which members of our people have to fight for the assertion of their own kind, and the mobilisation of all members of the German people on the earth for this purpose'. Aggressive chauvinism of this kind remained a minority cause, but it served as a reminder of unanswered questions.

Above all the empire lacked a constitutional consensus. Conservatives, especially Prussian Conservatives, supported it only because it was dominated by an unreformed Prussia; left-wing Liberals were alienated because the 1871 settlement aborted further constitutional development; the one-third Catholic population was alienated because the empire was a denial of the greater German solution, including Austria, that had been their ideal. Despite these defects the empire became accepted by imperceptible steps as 'Deutschland', the equivalent in nation-state terms to its French, Italian or British analogues. This development applied even to the Social Democrats who, despite the revolutionary rhetoric of their programme, were well on their way to becoming just another parliamentary party. Not only custom but economic and cultural change encouraged the emergence of a political national sentiment – urbanisation, better communications, the influence of education and military service. In this respect the German experience probably differed little from that of other European nations in the last quarter of the nineteenth century. Governments deliberately encouraged the population's affective identification with the state by exploiting the possibilities offered by monuments, public buildings, parades and festivals. Here, too, a realisation of the opportunities offered by the aesthetic side of politics parallelled a general European trend.

The fragility of the imperial regime was shown by its collapse after the defeat of 1918, but its successor was no more able to establish its normality. True, the Weimar constitution was democratic and proclaimed equality before the law. It was a state based on citizenship in the manner of the republican France. No one was excluded from its rights, no one enjoyed privileges. Yet it was not only burdened with the stigma of defeat, lost territory and reparations, it also inherited many unanswered questions from the empire. Parliamentary democracy was a contested form of government, opposed by nostalgic monarchists, *völkisch* extremists and communists. Social conflicts were exacerbated by the hardships of the interwar years. Above all, the German question had not been solved. Most of the Polish minority of Prussia was now incorporated in the newly independent Poland, but so was a sizeable German minority. Union with German-speaking Austria was vetoed at Versailles. The German minorities of Eastern Europe were under greater pressure than before.

Yet there were other respects in which the Weimar Republic represented a consolidation. It was not a unitary state, but its constituent units had lost their dynastic appeal and some of their powers. Politics were increasingly nationalised, thanks partly to proportional representation, which encouraged nation-wide party organisation. Above all, all those factors that had been homogenising society in the latter decades of the empire continued and even accelerated. The republic was more of a nation-state than the empire had been; what was in dispute was the form of government, not the extent to which the republic was 'Deutschland'. Whether, given better luck, the Weimar Republic would still have yielded to the Third Reich is not a matter that should distract us here. What is relevant is the extent to which the experiences of both Weimar and the Third Reich affected post-1945 German politics, especially that of the Federal Republic, for one of the questions to be asked of the now unified Germany is how far it is an extension and a continuation of the old Federal Republic.

The Third Reich discredited dictatorship and all-knowing ideologies, and if the Third Reich did not finish that job completely the example of single-party rule in the Soviet zone of occupation/GDR certainly helped it along. Dictatorship and authoritarianism were not totally discredited in one fell swoop. Too many people had done well out of the Third Reich, too many had grown up in the years of falling unemployment and of Hitler's diplomatic triumphs, too many had happy memories of Hitler Youth camps or ill memories of Weimar to be cured overnight of their suspicions of democracy. As opinion poll evidence shows, nostalgia for the Third Reich diminished only gradually and confidence in pluralist democracy grew step by step.

From National Chauvinism to Constitutional Patriotism

What was discredited more quickly and more thoroughly was nationalism. With Germany's defeat in the Second World War the German people did not abandon national sentiment or national identity; they did say goodbye to the aggressive, militaristic chauvinism that had characterised German policy making for the two preceding generations – a goodbye that was, one is tempted to say, irrevocable. Friedrich Meinecke, the veteran historian of liberal nationalism, who had once argued that the emergence of the Prussian–German nation-state marked a normal, desirable and irreversible form of progress (Meinecke, 1919, pp. 11–13), now conceded that the work of Bismarck had been destroyed and that Germany had only one future, namely in a 'federation, voluntarily concluded, of the Central and Western European states' (Meinecke, 1949, pp. 161, 168). It was the disavowal of nationalism, rather than the renewed experiment with democracy, that marked the true discontinuity in German politics in 1945–49. In contrast with that, drawing up a new democratic constitution meant, in a sense, taking up where parliamentary politicians had left off in 1933. Lessons would be learned from past mistakes, measures taken to stabilise government, power decentralised and judicial review established to protect civil rights, but there was nothing revolutionary in any of this. In any case, even if West Germany's post-1945 founding fathers had not wanted to construct the new order along these lines, the victorious Allies would have insisted on it. A democratic constitution was therefore preprogrammed; a change in mentality was not.

In various ways, then, the Federal Republic Westernised itself – economically, constitutionally, diplomatically, ideologically. An increasing number of historians began to see the long-term German past in terms of a special path (*Sonderweg*) and saw the roots of the disasters of the twentieth century in Germany's failure to adopt the liberal–democratic society that they assumed to be the normal concomitant of capitalist industrial development. Somewhere between the late 1940s and early 1960s the Federal Republic ceased to be characterised by the 'anticapitalist nostalgia' that had been such a dominant feature of the interwar period. For the first time a competitive enterprise culture that encouraged individual ambition and mobility took over. The forces released by the currency reform of 1948 directed German economic activity from then onwards, turning Germany into a formidable export machine and an integrated member of an open world economy. True, compared with, say, the United States or Japan, aspects of German economic life remained fairly heavily regulated; true also that some of the strongest pressures for liberalisation came from outside, in particular in the form of the conditions attached to Marshall Aid. But, as in the case of the constitutional changes, German aspirations and Allied demands were not too far apart. Those who shaped West German economic thinking after 1945, such as Ludwig Erhard and Alfred Müller-Armack, had already prepared themselves for a decisive move towards the market (Grosser, 1988, ch. 1; Nicholls, 1994, ch. 7).

The Federal Republic's internationalisation, however, was formal as well as informal. It was a founder member of the European Coal and Steel Community and of the European Economic Community; it would have been a founder member of the European Defence Community had the French National Assembly not defeated that project in 1954. Following the failure of the EDC proposal, the Federal Republic became a member of NATO in 1955. These were not contingent or incidental episodes. West German participation was crucial to the creation of all these bodies except NATO, and became crucial to the success of NATO once the Federal Republic had joined. They were designed to incorporate Germany for two interconnected reasons. Without German participation they would have constituted an inadequate defence against the Soviet Union, whether in military capability or economic prosperity. But they were also designed to bind Germany with supranational fetters, not least in order to reassure France that there was no further danger to be feared from that quarter.

But once more the aims of the victorious powers and those of the dominant West German policy makers coincided. The rhetoric of national unity notwithstanding, the creation of a single German state, as envisaged by the four power Potsdam Agreement of 1945, remained an aim for the very long term; the establishment of security, even if only in a part of Germany, emerged as an immediate necessity. There was no unanimity about this in 1949, either within Konrad Adenauer's party or among his allies or opponents, but there was at all times majority electoral support for it. Adenauer had another agenda, however, one that had more in common with his European partners' sentiments than his fellow citizens'. He saw it as his mission to liberate Europe from 'obsolete' nationalism, and in particular his fellow-Germans 'from their past nationalistic thinking'. German reunification, if it came, had to be compatible with the reunification of Europe (Adenauer, 1965, pp. 235, 467; 1967, p. 252). Indeed the Basic Law of the Federal Republic not only permitted, but enjoined the new state to submerge its sovereignty in supranational bodies (Article 24). There is little doubt that this reorientation of West German public sentiment was the most significant change to follow from the Cold War division of Germany, even more important than acceptance of a liberal economic order and steady reconciliation within a party-based parliamentary democracy. In any case, these two profound changes were not independent of the denationalisation of the German political culture. Those who had deplored the *Sonderweg* of previous generations could note with satisfaction that West Germans were joining – or rejoining – the European mainstream.

What, then, replaced the old nationalism? It had two successor sentiments. The first was a new cosmopolitanism. Germans travelled, partly because they could afford to, but also out of a spirit of exploration. They travelled, not as the *Wandervogel* did before the First World War, to contemplate scattered relics of old German *Kultur*, but to embrace the brave new world of a frontierless society. Gradually the traditional German sphere of influence to the East lost its significance; unless there were family links the same was beginning to happen even with regard to the German Democratic Republic. A generation grew up that felt more at home in Paris and London, or even New York and Los Angeles, than in Dresden or Leipzig, a generation for whom English as the language of advertising, popular culture and information technology was second nature.

That did not mean that German national pride disappeared; it did mean that patriotism was largely depoliticised. Few Germans wanted to restore a *Machtstaat* of the kind taken for granted during the empire; nothing underlined the distaste for military glory more than the high rate of options for civilian duty among conscripts. Instead the objects of pride were those of 'soft' power: the speed of postwar reconstruction, the achievements of German technology and industry, the strength of the Deutsche Mark, sporting triumphs and German efficiency, reliability and punctuality (Scheuch, 1991, p. 86). That integration into the West coincided with the Federal Republic's political and economic interests no doubt helped to make that integration widely acceptable, but that was not the only reason for the acceptance. The ethos of the Federal Republic was non-Prussian, in many ways a reversion to the Germany that preceded the formation of the empire. So detached from the past had West German political consciousness become by the 1980s, so casually did many citizens of the Federal Republic take the permanence of the division of their country for granted, that many conservatively minded scholars and publicists were concerned that German national consciousness would disappear altogether, and the German past would be perceived as nothing more than a 'negative myth' (Nolte, 1985, pp. 17–35). This was the basis of the so-called *Historikerstreit*, the public dispute between liberal and conservative historians about the meaning of national history. It polarised intellectual opinion not only in the interpretation of the Third Reich's place in German history, but in the consequences these interpretations had for the political identity of present-day Germans.

There was indeed an alternative agenda to a patriotism based on identification with a seamless past. This is what the Liberal political theorist Dolf Sternberger termed 'constitutional patriotism' (*Verfassungspatriotismus*), a concept popularised by Jürgen Habermas during the historians' dispute. As early as 1979 Sternberger had discerned 'a clear consciousness of the beneficence of this Basic Law . . . . To the extent that we ourselves used the liberties that it guaranteed and we learnt to bear ourselves within and towards this state, a new, second patriotism has imperceptibly evolved' (Sternberger, 1990, p. 13). His colleague Rainer Lepsius complemented this notion with that of the 'citizens' nation' (*Staatsbürgernation*) in which a 'legitimation . . . derived from democratic civil rights and free self-determination on the basis of popular sovereignty' relegated cultural or ethnic determinants of nationality to subordinate status. The relatively easy acceptance of the division of Germany and of the loss of territories proved that the idea of the 'citizens' nation' had defined 'the construction of identity through the civil rights and the constitutional order of the Federal Republic' (Lepsius, 1990, pp. 244–5).

The truth was, not surprisingly, a little more complicated than that. There was undoubtedly greater pride in the Basic Law as a guarantor of liberties than in any previous German constitution and a greater equation of civil liberties with the German political culture than ever before. How far the economic achievements of the years 1949–89 contributed to the reconciliation of most Germans to the new order is impossible to quantify; those who thought it a major factor expressed the fear that German democracy was a fair-weather phenomenon only. Equally the social component of the social market economy must have played a part. The new German political culture combined old etatist and new libertarian elements. There was, however, nothing peculiarly German about that synthesis when we consider the part that the welfare state has played in political integration elsewhere, in countries as different as Sweden, Austria and Britain. What synthesised state and constitution rather more, and symbolised the final acceptance of Federal Republic as a legitimate German state, was the tendency to equate the Western state as 'Germany', *pars pro toto*. Increasingly in common parlance – outside as well as inside the Federal Republic – the West German economy was the German economy, West German sporting teams the German teams, West German interests German interests. The Federal Republic had become the new 'Deutschland'. The constitutional consensus, so manifestly lacking under all previous political orders, was in place, the geopolitical uncertainty of whether Germany belonged to the East or the West was finally resolved, a liberal political and economic order was firmly rooted, the association of national interest with military prowess finally buried. Even the tendency to assume that the Federal Republic was 'Germany' – that is, that this liberal, internationally integrated state satisfied national aspirations – was a sign of normalisation.

These developments could not have been in greater contrast with those in the German Democratic Republic. Because its claim to rule was never put to the test of popular consent, it lacked legitimacy for the whole of its lifetime. This does not mean there was never an East German political identity. Many GDR citizens took – and take – pride in their contribution to postwar reconstruction, however meagre its ultimate outcome. There was an Eastern as well as a Western economic patriotism. As the regime moved away from its line of revolutionary confrontationism it incorporated all kinds of non-revolutionary figures – Luther, Frederick the Great, Scharnhorst – into its national pantheon, accepting and even emphasising continuity with the past.

The popular reactions, however, were not those the regime had hoped for. Those who felt the strongest GDR identity were not the regime's supporters but its opponents: they derived their identity from its proclaimed ideals, not from the practice of 'real existing socialism'. Whatever else the GDR was for them, it was not a normal state. For the non-dissident bulk of the population it was even less of a normal state. Normality was *drüben* ('over there'), then visible on television every night. Insofar as they were constitutional patriots, the object of their loyalty was the Basic Law. For them, as for most West Germans, it was the Federal Republic that was the real Germany. The different forms of political identity developed by the last-ditch supporters of the GDR, by its dissident opponents and by the politically detached majority were all to compound the difficulty of creating a common loyalty after 1989.

Nationality and Citizenship in the New Germany

All these experiences raise problems for the categorisation of post-reunification Germany. It is both an old and a new state. Formally it is no more than an enlarged Federal Republic. The five reconstituted Länder and East Berlin acceded under Article 23 of the Basic Law. The currency is the Deutsche Mark, the main political parties are extensions of those in the West, the significant political leaders are, with few exceptions, from the West. Monetary policy is controlled, as before, from Frankfurt; the Basic Law is interpreted, as before, in Karlsruhe; the federal ministries and the houses of parliament remain, for the time being, in Bonn. The administrative and legal structures and the industrial relations and social security systems of the Federal Republic were transferred wholesale, except where specifically exempted in the Unification Treaty. There was no other solution, since the GDR lacked almost all of the relevant structures. To have invented a new Germany, forty years after the invention of the Federal Republic, would have meant discarding the loyalties, the authority, the internal and external legitimacy of the Federal Republic, not to mention its numerous international obligations. Every treaty would have needed resigning, with the risk of pressures for renegotiation. In all these respects the new Germany is but the old Federal Republic writ large.

But there are just as many respects in which it is not so. The two postwar Germanies were not nation-states. They were the two states of a divided nation, though in other respects the Federal Republic came to satisfy the remaining preconditions listed at the beginning for successful nation-state status. Post-1990 Germany is a nation-state; not only that, it is the first true nation-state in German history, free of the defects of the empire, the Weimar Republic and the Third Reich. But all victories have their price. The peaceful upheaval of 1989–90, swiftly and skilfully brought to a conclusion, concealed, by the very elegance of its settlement, what a deep change it presaged. The creation of unified Germany, for all the smooth transfer of institutions that constituted its formal side, was yet another discontinuity and the tremors it sent out are only now being registered. Above all, one old dilemma of German nation-building has reappeared in a way that has at times almost dominated German domestic politics and Germany's image abroad: the old disjunction between nationality and citizenship, between *ius soli*, which determines nationality by place of birth, and *ius sanguinis*, which determines it by descent. The German Nationality Law of 1913 – and it is characteristic of the empire that there was no uniform legislation on nationality until that year – rested on *ius sanguinis*, as opposed to French or Anglo–American *ius soli*.

The ideological roots of this definition lie in the romantic notion of the *Volk*, of nationality as a cultural as opposed to a legal category. In post-1990 Germany it has led to problems that may not be new in kind, but are unprecedented in extent. The *ius sanguinis* that the Federal Republic and, after it, united Germany, inherited and enshrined in

Article 116 of the Basic Law, made possible the admission, absorption and integration of millions of refugees from the GDR, of expellees from the states of Eastern Europe and, more recently, of ethnic German resettlers from Poland, Romania and Russia. There has been a huge ingathering of the German diaspora. At the same time the West German economy demanded the recruitment of foreign labour, mainly from Mediterranean countries. They were classified as migrant workers (*Gastarbeiter*), even if they settled with their families. Their children and grandchildren, even if born in Germany, remain aliens, though naturalisation on an individual basis is becoming easier. Parallel with the large-scale settlement of *Gastarbeiter* there has been the increasing inflow of asylum seekers, attracted by the ultrapermissive Article 16 of the Basic Law which, until it was amended, gave an unrestricted right to claim political asylum and culminated in the record-breaking number of applicants in 1992 and 1993.

Unified Germany is therefore in a paradoxical situation. On the one hand, for the first time in history the political and linguistic frontiers coincide, especially if we assume that Swiss-Germans and Austrians no longer think of themselves as Germans. But while there are no more than two or three million ethnic Germans left in Eastern Europe and no irredentist provinces populated by non-Germans, as there were during the empire, there is a large non-German population scattered through Germany, which renders redundant the debate on whether Germany ought to be a country of immigration. Thus at the very moment when Germany achieved the normality of being a classically defined nation-state, it found itself obliged to face the challenge of multiculturalism. While the anomalies of Germany's nationality law can hardly be considered the main cause of Germany's ethnic problems – states that have adopted *ius soli* also experience racial tensions – it may well be that the law exacerbates them by giving a legal sanction to a cultural divide.

Nation State and National Interest

One respect in which the new Germany has changed less than many observers expected is in its international alignment. The Western integration of the old Federal Republic has been passed on almost intact to the new state. No doubt this was facilitated by the way that the Conservative government was able to manage reunification, so that its twin ideals of the nation-state and Western orientation could be married. Whether a government of a different potential colour would have pursued a different line is improbable, however much Germany's neighbours might have feared it. Visions of a 'Fourth Reich . . . and possibly a Hohenzollern Kaiser to go with it', as dreamed up by Conor Cruise O'Brien (O'Brien, 1989), or even Margaret Thatcher's 'over-mighty bull in a china shop' (Thatcher, 1993, p. 814) were no doubt exaggerated. The 'Two-plus-four' Treaty, which formed the basis of German reunification, actually put a limit on German conventional forces below that of the old Federal Republic's contribution to NATO and reinforced the ban on atomic, bacteriological and chemical weapons. The Preamble of the Unification Treaty of 1990 contained a specific commitment to 'contribute to the reunification of Europe'.

When Peter Katzenstein in the 1980s defined the German Federal Republic as a 'semi-sovereign state', he had the domestic constraints on policy making chiefly in mind (Katzenstein, 1987). But there were external constraints as well, including the vulnerability of West Berlin and West German dependence on the strategic planning of NATO, of which it was a not-quite-equal partner. The Unification Treaty and the 'Two-plus-Four Treaty', despite the conditions noted above, restored German sovereignty, a transformation completed by the final withdrawal of all occupation troops in September 1994. Yet the Western alignment, which was a defining feature of the old Federal Republic, remains in place. As long as over half of Germany's foreign trade is with the rest of the EU, and much of the rest with other OECD states; as long as the threat of chaos in the former Soviet Union underlines the need for a continued NATO umbrella; as long as the Franco–German axis, however unevenly weighted, remains the *sine qua non* of any European order, Germany cannot revert to its traditional balancing act between Occident and Orient. The fear of a second Rapallo – a repeat of the German–Soviet Treaty of 1922, that so stunned western statesmen – is negated by the absence of an Eastern partner. Unification has not restored a German 'realm of the middle' (*Reich der Mitte*). It has brought an Eastward extension of the West.

Nevertheless some things have changed. Germany is no longer merely first among equals in Europe. As a result the debate has revived about the place of the Federal Republic in German history and whether there is a German national interest. The thesis of the *Sonderweg* is once more a question. In the years between 1949 and 1989 this thesis became the 'founding myth' of the Federal Republic: the justification for the new, Westernised state was that it had renounced continuity with a ruinous past. Above all the Federal Republic reemphasised that there was no necessary connection between state and nation in Germany: the attempt to merge the two had not only led to disaster, it had turned out to be no more than an interlude in the history of the German people. With reunification, however, this pre-1989 consensus is once more being questioned. Was the creation of the Federal Republic really a decisive breach with the past, or only the 'step-child of the times' (Naumann, 1994, p. 75)? The 'new right' publicist Rainer Zitelmann and his colleagues distinguish between 'those who saw in the Western alignment of the Federal Republic a proven antidote to the re-emergence of a nation-state' and 'those who saw in it a means of overcoming the division' (Zitelmann *et al.*, 1993, p. 16) – the implication being that reunification made the Western alignment redundant.

Zitelmann's arguments are not widely shared. A greater number of scholars and publicists, however, feel that within the Western alignment German interests have been neglected, and indeed that their existence has been ignored. The upsets of 1989 have had their effect on the public debate. 'Germany is back', the Erlangen historian Gregor Schöllgen has proclaimed (Baring, 1994, p. 35) and the Berlin historian Arnulf Baring has echoed that 'we are back in the Germany Bismarck created in 1871' (Baring, 1994, p. 9). These assertions, if true, have implications for the *Sonderweg* thesis and the concept of normality. If Schöllgen and Baring are right, if we can agree with the Bonn political scientist Hans-Peter Schwarz that Germany is now 'the central power in Europe' (Schwarz, 1994a), then the *Sonderweg* of the Federal Republic – 'a breathing-space in world history for us Germans' (Baring, 1991, p. 125) – has come to an end and the new German nation-state has become a normal sovereign player like Britain and France. This in turn means that Germany has – potentially at least – state interests that are separate from those of the supranational institutions to which it belongs. This is a theme that has received added emphasis from reunification, but it is not new. Already ten years earlier Schwarz had complained of 'the tamed Germans' who had moved 'from obsession with power to an oblivion of power' (Schwarz, 1985).

The trouble with these formulations is that the nature of power has changed since Germany was last a sovereign player. The instruments of the 1990s are not those that Bismarck would have recognised. Germany's largely untried conventional forces have taken only minor roles in the world's security missions, even after the Federal Constitutional Court's ruling of July 1994 permitted 'out-of-area' participation. Germany has become, in the words of the Trier political scientist Hanns Maull, a 'civilian power' (Maull, 1992). Its principal institution for exercising this power is the Bundesbank and its principal weapon the Deutsche Mark. It is with these that Germany wields its influence in determining the shape of European institutions and the development of integration, but it can do this only within the multilateral framework it has helped to construct over the past decades. In other words, it will safeguard and advance its interests only by continuing to Europeanise itself. Schwarz and those who think like him would not disagree (Schwarz, 1994a, pp. 173, 238; Hacke, 1993, p. 547). Such a project depends on the agreement of others. If Germany's EU partners will not or cannot follow the German agenda, Germany's supranational commitment will in turn be called into question.

What, then, has reunification done for the German quest for normality? That 'unconditional opening of the Federal Republic to the political culture of the West' that Jürgen Habermas evoked as 'the great intellectual achievement of our postwar epoch' (Habermas, 1987, p. 135) is as strongly in place as ever. Outbursts of violence against foreigners and votes for the ex-Communist Party of the eastern Länder do not seriously qualify this claim. The reemergence of a German nation-state – a new normality – has not cancelled out the inherited normality of Westernisation. As for the civilian nature of German power: is it a model or an exception? The old Federal Republic was a civilian power, partly on the insistence of the victorious Allies, partly out of conscious choice. In this respect it was an exception among the major states of Europe, an exception easily explained by the legacy of the Third Reich. This legacy still affects the status of post-1989 Germany, but in the post-Cold-War world, in which the stand-off between the nuclear superpowers no longer defines the lines of conflict, the civilian components of power are likely to become more prominent. If that is so, the German civilianisation of power may yet become a model.

Guide to Further Reading

Chapter 2 Government and Political Order

For the post-1945 history of Germany, refer to Bark and Gress, 2 volumes (1993) and the concise treatment by Pulzer (1995a). In German there is a standard edited work (Weidenfeld and Zimmermann, 1989). There are numerous texts on the political system, for instance Conradt (1989), Dalton (1989) and Hancock (1989), and in German there is Hesse and Ellwein (1992). On German reunification, its causes and consequences, see Glaeßner and Wallace (1992), Glaeßner (1992), Merkl (1993), Hancock and Welsh (1994), as well as the predecessor to this present volume, Smith *et al.* (1992).

Chapter 3 A Divided Electorate?

Kendall Baker and his colleagues (1981) provide a comprehensive overview of the evolution of public opinion and voting behaviour from the early 1950s to the late 1970s; Franklin *et al.* (1992) and Dalton (1996a) update this research in a comparative framework. The German-language literature on public opinion and voting behaviour is exceptionally rich and sophisticated. For an introduction to this research see Bürklin (1988), Bürklin and Roth (1994), and the edited volumes prepared by Klingemann and Kaase (1990) and Kaase and Klingemann (1994). Finally, a series of books tracks the actions of the parties and the voters through the 1990 and 1994 *Bundestagswahlen* (Dalton, 1993; 1996b).

Chapter 4 The Party System at the Crossroads

For the earlier development of the parties in the Federal Republic, Braunthal (1996) is a useful introductory text. The post-reunification party system is examined from a number of perspectives in the collection edited by Padgett (1993). Kitschelt (1991) is recommended for an analysis of the changing bases of party competition. On the 1994 elections, see Conradt (1995) and Roberts (1995). Specifically for eastern Germany and the PDS, Bastian (1995), Betz and Welsh (1995) and Niedermeyer (1995) should be consulted. *Das Parlament* (1996) provides an assessment of the individual parties. In addition, on the Greens, refer to Poguntke (1993) and Scharf (1994).

Chapter 5 The Territorial Dimension

The twin challenges of reunification and deepening European integration have produced a welter of studies in the German language, of which Hesse and Renzsch (1990) is one of the earliest and best overviews. Peffekoven (1994) is excellent on financial equalisation, and Borkenhagen *et al.* (1992) is an indispensable insider account from Länder civil servants on the Maastricht negotiations. In English, Jeffery and Sturm (1993) provides a wide-ranging review of the problems facing the federal system since 1990. Shorter accounts of problems of domestic and European policy adaptation are provided in Jeffery (1996) and Goetz (1995a) respectively.

Chapter 6 The Federal Constitutional Court

Germany's constitutional history is survey in Koch (1984). The constitutions of 1849, 1871 and the Weimar Constitution are reproduced in Hucko (1987). Up-to-date English translations of the Basic Law are regularly published by the Federal Press and Information Office and are available from German embassies. Böckenförde (1991), a former judge on the Court, provides many insights into the historical evolution of German conceptions of state, society and law, which underpin much current constitutional thinking. The edited collection by Wellenreuther (1990) also makes a number of interesting points on this subject. The main principles of the Basic Law are set out in detail by Currie (1994). This can be read together with the edited collections by Starck (1983), 1991), Karpen (1988) and Kirchhof and Kommers (1993). Constitutional development since reunification is covered in Goetz and Cullen (1994). The best introduction to the Court and its judicature is Kommers (1989), which provides useful excerpts of key judgements. This complements and partly updates Kommer's earlier monograph (1976) on judicial politics in Germany. The Court's important role in shaping intergovernmental relations is explored in Blair (1981). A collection of major decisions relating to international law and the European Communities has been published by the Federal Constitutional Court (1992).

Chapter 7 Continuity and Change in the Policy Process

There is no post-reunification literature on all aspects of policy making in Germany. Still, a very good introduction is Bulmer (1989). In Germany, too, studies of policy-making in the united Germany have yet to be written. For a few policy fields new studies are available. The role of the banks in industrial policy-making is debated by Edwards and Fischer (1994), the problem of poverty is the topic of Hanesch (1994), and Döring and Hauser (1995) have edited a volume on the related topic of social policies. The effect of reunification in the health sector has been investigated by Manow-Borgwardt (1995).

Chapter 8 Beyond Bipolarity: German Foreign Policy in a Post-Cold War World

There is no satisfactory overview of post-unity German foreign policy. The most reflective piece is the Maull and Gordon paper (1993) referred to in this chapter. The Baring collection (1994) is rather indifferent and its major authors, for example Schwarz, have written much better pieces elsewhere. Bulmer and Paterson (1996) is wider ranging than the title indicates, and there is a very good piece by Josef Janning (1996) in the same issue of *International Affairs*. For German speakers the Deutsche Gesellschaft für Auswärtige Politik has published two solid volumes (Kaiser and Maull, 1994, 1995).

Chapter 9 Germany and the European Union: From Junior to Senior Role

The early period of West German involvement in integration is covered in Willis (1965). The period 1969–86 is examined in Bulmer and Paterson (1987), with particular emphasis on the origins of the sectorised, and occasionally contradictory, nature of European policy. The essays in Morgan and Bray (1986) examine both the Franco–German relationship and the Anglo–German one in the triangle of contracts between Bonn, Paris and London on European matters. Saeter (1980) explores the wider European context, including *Ostpolitik* and defence. Kirchner (1989, 1992 and 1995) offers an interpretation of 40 and 45 years of the Federal Republic and European integration and on the nature of German–EU relations. The implications of German reunification on EU–German relations are analysed by Bulmer and Paterson (1996), Campbell (1993), Cerny (1993), Huelshoff (1993), Jeffery and Sturm (1992) and Kirchner (1994). The possibility of a reunified Germany becoming hegemonic is explored by Markovits and Reich (1991). The edited collection by Schweitzer and Karsten (1990) attempts a cost–benefit analysis of German membership of the EU. Of the German-language material, Hrbek and Wessels (1984) consider West German interests in most of the key areas of European cooperation and integration, while May (1985) attempts to evaluate the costs and benefits of German membership of the EU.

Chapter 10 'Of Dragons and Snakes': Contemporary German Security Policy

For recent English-language studies of German security policy, see Schlör (1993), Druffield (1994), Linnenkamp (1992) and Szabo (1990). Those who read German should consult Heydrich (1991), Weidenfeld (1990) and Haftendorn (1983). For those interest in German security during the Cold War, see Larrabee (1989) and Garton Ash (1993). Public attitudes towards security policy are analysed in Asmus (1993). On Germany and nuclear weapons, see Boutwell (1990). On the issue of an out-of-area role for the *Bundeswehr*, see Clemens (1993) and Kamp (1993). Germany's grand strategy is discussed by Joffe (1994), whilst Germany's relations with its allies, neighbours and former enemies is addressed by Verheyen and Søe (1993). For the broader European context of German security policy, see Hyde-Price (1991).

Chapter 11 The Economic Order – Still Modell Deutschland?

A useful introduction for readers of German to the domestic debate about the challenges to *Modell Deutschland* is Henzler and Späth (1993), Späth having been head of government in Germany's most dynamic state, Baden-Württemberg. For an account of the West German economy before reunification and an initial assessment of the economic implications of reunification, see Giersch *et al.* (1992) and Smyser (1992). On the implications of German reunification see also Marsh (1994) and, for readers of German, Hoffmann (1993). Useful accounts of the Bundesbank are to be found in Marsh (1992); of 'ordoliberalism' in Nicholls (1994); of Germany's regulatory culture in Dyson (1992); of social partnership in Crouch (1993); and of the 'insider' system of corporate governance in Edwards and Fischer (1994). Germany and European economic and monetary union is dealt with in Dyson and Featherstone (1996). The case for privatisation is spelt out by the chief economist of the Deutsche Bank in Walter (1993). The most valuable German sources of information on economic and monetary developments remain the monthly reports of the Deutsche Bundesbank: the *Wirtschaftswoche* and the *Handelsblatt*. For a good general overview of key economic policy sectors, see Smith (1994). Useful comparisons between the German and Japanese models on a sectoral basis are contained in Fukui *et al.* (1993).

Chapter 12 Economic Management and the Challenge of Unification

The monthly reports and annual reports of the Deutsche Bundesbank give excellent English-language reviews of the state of the German economy. The *Financial Times* offers the best up-to-date commentary of events in English. As a reader, E. Owen Smith (1994), *The German Economy*, remains by far the best and most comprehensive text in recent years, though W. R. Smyser (1992), *Colossus at the Crossroads*, offers a good, accessible introduction.

Chapter 13 Interest Groups in the Five New Länder

English-language material on interest groups in the transformation of the new German Länder is limited to Boll (1993) and Wiesenthal (1995). Edinger (1993) provides a standard account of the (West) German model of interest representation. There is, however, an extensive and growing literature on the subject in German. The two volume work edited by Eichener *et al.* (1992) provides a theoretical perspective on the emergence of organised interests in the east, as well as a wealth of empirical studies of particular sectors. Wiesenthal (1995) provides an excellent and wide-ranging analysis of interest politics in the transformation process, combining sectoral studies with an evaluation of the dynamics of interest representation in post-communist Germany. Some of the contributions to this volume are drawn from the extensive list of working papers produced by the Max-Planck-Gesellschaft, Berlin, which offer the advanced student invaluable source material. Particular attention is drawn to Bialas (1994) on trade unions, Ettl (1995) on employer associations, Bialas and Ettl (1992) on the social foundations of interest representation, and Ettl and Heikenroth (1995) on trends in interest group membership.

Chapter 14 German Welfare and Social Citizenship

The most comprehensive English-language work on the evolution of social policy in Germany since reunification is the collection edited by Clasen and

Freeman (1994). The chapters by Landua (1993) and Wilson (1993) and the article by Ganssmann (1993) are valuable additions to the growing literature in English. Schmidt's (1995) analysis of party politics includes treatment of welfare issues. The OECD Economic Surveys of Germany have extensive coverage of social policy. Finally, a regular review of social policy developments is provided in 'Labour and Social Affairs', a monthly bulletin issued free by German Embassies.

Chapter 15 Women in the New Germany

Geissler (1992, in German) compares the contrasting social developments in West and East Germany from 1949 to the present while Helwig and Nickel (1992, in German) and Kolinsky (1993a) focus specifically on the position of women. The volume edited by Nickel, Kühl and Schenk (1994, in German) concentrates on the transformation of employment since reunification and presents empirically well-founded analyses of the changing gender balance in key sectors of the economy, the impact of unemployment on women and other aspects of labour-market exclusion. In the context of a case study of Leipzig, Kolinsky (1995b) shows that low incomes in the GDR and the disappearance of the 'second wage package' of child-related benefits exposed women and single mothers in particular to the risk of poverty. *Datenreport* (1994, in German) provides an excellent range of data on social change and also incorporates a useful section on the personal perceptions and social expectations of women and men in the new and old Länder.

Chapter 16 Crime and Policing in the New Germany in the 1990s

The most comprehensive account, in English, of West Germany's internal security policy is Katzenstein (1990). It also contains a very clear description of the police services in Germany, though Fairchild (1988) goes into more depth on this subject. The substantive focus of these works is anti-terrorist or public order policing. On the legal dimension, Kommers (1989) has compiled an invaluable English-language casebook of Constitutional Court judgments covering important civil liberties cases. Raith (1995) provides an excellent and balanced discussion of the phenomenon of organised crime in Germany. Most German commentaries on crime and policing are written from the standpoint of the lawyer or the criminologist, with the result that there is a dearth of social science literature on policing theory and strategies, police–society relationships or accountability questions. The work of the Berlin-based *Arbeitsgruppe für Bürgerrechte* forms a notable exception (e.g. Busch *et al.* 1988); this group's journal '*Bürgerrechte und Polizei*' is well-known for its highly critical stance on policing issues. Braunthal's detailed analysis of the 1972 'decree on radicals' also asserts the paramount nature of civil liberties in criminal policy (Braunthal, 1990). Contrasting perspectives may be found in some of the research undertaken by the BKA or by the *Polizei-Führungsakademie*; their work does not, however, invariably endorse official policy (Zimmermann, 1992). Recent empirical German research on police attitudes and strategies, including community policing – to some extent filling the gap referred to above – includes Feltes and Rebscher (1990). English language literature on these themes remains thin on the ground (cf. Dölling and Feltes 1993). European police cooperation, in contrast, is the subject of a growing literature in English (Anderson *et al.*, 1995). For an account of West German involvement in European police cooperation, as well as developments since reunification, see Cullen (1992).

Chapter 17 Model or Exception – Germany as a Normal State?

There is an immense amount of ephemeral literature on the 'new' German question, but relatively little of lasting merit. The most useful summaries of the agenda for the 1990s are Huelshoff *et al.* (1993), Conradt *et al.* (1995), Baring (1994) and Merkl (1996). There is stimulating historical background in Craig (1991) and James (1994). Among the many German-language contributions, Goetz (1994) and Schwarz (1994b) provide valuable insights.

Bibliography

Abromeit, H. (1992) *Der verkappte Einheitsstaat*, Opladen: Leske und Budrich.

Adenauer, K. (1965) *Erinnerungen, 1945–1953*, Stuttgart: Deutsche Verlags-Anstalt.

Adenauer, K. (1967) *Erinnerungen, 1955–1959*, Stuttgart: Deutsche Verlags-Anstalt.

Akerlof, G. A. *et al.* (1991) 'East Germany in from the cold. The economic aftermath of currency union', paper presented to the Conference of the Brookings Panel on Economic Activity, Washington DC, 4–5 April 1991.

Albrecht, H.-J. (1995) 'Drug Policies and National Plans to Combat Drug Trafficking and Drug Abuse. A Comparative Analysis of Policies of Co-ordination and Co-operation', in G. Estievenart (ed.), *Policies and Strategies to Combat Drugs in Europe. The Treaty on European Union: Framework for a New European Strategy to Combat Drugs?* Dordrecht/Boston/London: Martinus Niihoff, pp. 182–96.

Anderson, C. and Zelle, C. (1995) 'Helmut Kohl and the CDU Victory', *German Politics*, vol. 12, pp. 12–35.

Anderson, J. and Goodman, J. (1993) 'Mars or Minerva? A United Germany in a Post-Cold War Europe', in Robert Keohane, Joseph Nye and Stanley Hoffman (eds), *After the Cold War; International Institutions and State Strategies in Europe, 1989–1991*, London: Harvard University Press, pp. 23–62.

Anderson, M., den Boer, M., Cullen, P. J., Gilmore, W. C., Raab, C., and Walker, N., (1995), *Policing the European Union. Theory, Law and Practice*, Oxford: Oxford University Press.

Arbeitsgruppe Alternative Wirtschaftspolitik (1992) *Memorandum '92-Gegen den ökonomischen Niedergang-Industriepolitik in Ostdeutschland*', Cologne: Pappyrossa.

Ash, T. G. (1994) 'Germany's Choice', *Foreign Affairs*, vol. 73, no. 4, pp. 65–81.

Asmus, R. (1993) *Germany's Geopolitical Maturation: Strategy and Public Opinion After the Wall*, Santa Monica, CA: RAND Corporation.

Baker, K., Dalton, R. and Hildebrandt, K. (1981) *Germany Transformed*, Cambridge: Harvard University Press.

Balme, R., Garrard, P., Hoffman-Martinot, V., Le May, S. and Ritaine, E. (1994) 'Analysing Territorial Policies in Western Europe', *European Journal of Political Research*, vol. 25, pp. 389–411.

Baring, A. (1991) *Deutschland, was nun?*, Berlin: Siedler.

Baring, A. (ed.) (1994) *Germany's New Position in Europe: Problems and Perspectives*, Oxford and Providence, RI: Berg.

Bark, D. and Gress, D. (1993) *A History of West Germany*, 2 vols, Oxford: 'Blackwell.

Bastian, J. (1995) 'The *Enfant Terrible* of German Politics: The PDS between GDR Nostalgia and Democratic Socialism', *German Politics*, vol. 4, no. 3 (December), pp. 95–110.

Bauer, M., and Blaesing, K. (1992) 'Kommune und Prävention – Sachstand Frankfurt am Main in Schriftenreihe der Polizei-Führungsakademie, in *Kriminalprävention – Neue Wege in der Kriminalitätskontrolle*, Lübeck: Schmidt-Römhild, pp. 107–16.

Bauer-Kaase, P. (1994) 'German Unification', in W. Hancock and H. Welsh (eds), *German Unification: Processes and Outcomes*, Boulder: Westview Press.

Belwe, Katharina (1989) 'Sozialstruktur und gesellschaftlicher Wandel in der DDR', in Werner Weidenfeld and Hartmut Zimmermann (eds), *Deutschland Handbuch*, Munich, Hanser.

Benz, A. (1991) 'Perspektiven des Föderalismus in Deutschland', *Die Öffentliche Verwaltung*, vol. 14 (July), pp. 586–98.

Benz, A., (1989) 'Intergovernmental Relations in the 1980s', *Publius. The Journal of Federalism*, vol. 19 (Fall), pp. 203–20.

Berghahn, Sabine and Andrea Fritzsche (1991) *Frauenrecht in Ost und West*, Berlin: Basis Druck.

Bertram, Barbara (1989) *Typisch weiblich – typisch männlich*, Berlin (Ost): Dietz.

Betz, H.-G. (1995) 'Alliance '90/Greens: From Fundamental Opposition to Black-Green', in D. Conradt *et al.* (eds), *Germany's New Politics: Parties and Issues in the 1990s*, Providence, RI, and Oxford: Berghahn.

Betz, H.-G. and Welsh, H. (1995) 'The PDS in the New German Party System', *German Politics*, vol. 4, no. 3 (December), pp. 95–111.

Bialas, C. (1994) *Gewerkschaftlicher Organisationsaufbau und Transformation der Lohnpolitik im Prozess der deutschen Einheit: Die IG Metall in den neuen Bundesländern 1990–93*, Arbeitspaiere, Berlin: Max-Planck-Gesellschaft.

Bialas, C. and Ettl, W. (1992) *Wirtschaftliche Lage und soziale Differenzierung im Transformations-prozess*, Arbeitspapiere, Berlin: Max-Planck-Gesellschaft.

Biedenkopf, K. (1994) *Einheit und Erneuerung: Deutschland nach dem Umbruch in Europa*, Stuttgart: Deutsche Verlags-Anstalt.

Biehler, G. (1990) *Sozialliberale Reformgesetzgebung und Bundesverfassungsgericht*, Baden-Baden: Nomos Verlagsgesellschaft.

Blair, P. (1981) *Federalism and Judicial Review in Germany*, Oxford: Clarendon Press.

Blair, P. (1991) 'Federalism, Legalism and Political Reality: The Record of the Federal Constitutional Court', in C. Jeffery and P. Savigear (eds), *German Federalism Today*, Leicester: Leicester University Press, pp. 63–83.

Blair, P. and Cullen, P. (1996) 'Federalism, Legalism and Political Reality: The Record of the Federal Constitutional Court', in C. Jeffery (ed.), *The Challenges of Unification. German Federalism in the 1990s*, London: Leicester University Press.

Bleckmann, A. (1995) 'Bundesverfassungsgericht versus Europäischer Gerichtshof für Menschenrechte', *Europäische Grundrechtszeitschrift*, vol. 22, nos 16–17, pp. 387–90.

Böckenförde, E.-W. (1991) *State, Society and Liberty: Studies in Political Theory and Constitutional Law*, Oxford: Berg.

Boer, M. den (1994) 'The Quest for European Policing: Rhetoric and Justification in a Disorderly Debate', in M. Anderson and M. den Boer (eds), *Policing across National Boundaries*, London and New York: Pinter.

Bohley, P. (1995) 'Der Kommunele Finanzausgleich in der neuen Bundesländorn nach der Wiedervereinigung Deutschlands', in A. Oberhauser (ed.), *Finanzierungs-probleme der deutschen Einheit. Schriften der Vereins für Sozialpolitik*, vol. 229/III, Berlin: Duncker and Humblot.

Boll, B. (1994) 'Interest Organisation and Intermediation in the New Länder', *German Politics*, vol. 3, no. 1.

Boll, B. (1995) 'Media Communication and Personality Marketing: The 1994 Election Campaign', *German Politics*, vol. 4, no. 2 (August), pp. 120–140.

Borkenhagen, F. *et al.* (eds) (1992) *Die deutschen Länder in Europa*, Baden-Baden: Nomos.

Boutwell, J. (1990) *The German Nuclear Dilemma*, Ithaca, NY: Cornell University Press.

Braunthal, G. (1990) *Political Loyalty and Public Service in West Germany: the 1972 Decree against Radicals and its Consequences*, Amherst: University of Massachusetts Press.

Braunthal, G. (1996) *Parties and Politics in the New Germany*, Boulder, CO. Westview Press.

Breuel, B. *et al.* (1991) 'Welchen Beitrag können Beschäftigungsgesellschaften leisten? Anforderungen aus gewerkschaftlicher Sicht', *Wirtschaftsdienst*, VIII/1991, pp. 385–8.

Breuel, B. *et al.* (1993) 'Erhaltung industrieller Kerne in Ostdeutschland?', *Wirtschaftsdienst* II/1993, pp. 59–70.

Bullman, U. and Schwanengel, W. (1995) 'Zur Transformation territorialer Politikstrukturen; Landes- und Kommunalverwaltungen in der neuen Bundesländern', in S. Benzler, U. Bullman and D. Eissel (eds), *Deutschland-Ost vor Ort; Anfänge der lokalen Politik in den neuen Bundesländern*, Opladen: Leske und Budrich.

Bulmer, S. (ed.) (1989) *The Changing Agenda of West German Public Policy*, Aldershot: Dartmouth.

Bulmer, S. (1992) 'Completing the European Community's Internal Market: The Regulatory Implications for the Federal Republic of Germany', in K. Dyson (ed.), *The Politics of German Regulation*, Aldershot: Dartmouth.

Bulmer, S. (1995) 'European Integration and Germany; The Constitutive Politics of the European Union and the Institutional Mediation of German Power', paper presented at ASGP annual conference, Birmingham, April 1995.

Bulmer, S. and Humphreys, P. (1989), 'Kohl, Corporatism and Congruence: the West German Model under Challenge', in S. Bulmer (ed.), *The Changing Agenda of West German Public Policy*, Aldershot: Dartmouth, pp. 177–97.

Bulmer, S. and Paterson, W. E. (1987), *The Federal Republic of Germany and the European Community*, London: Allen & Unwin.

Bulmer, S. and Paterson, W. E. (1996) 'Germany in the European Union: Gentle Giant or Emergent Leader?', *International Affairs*, vol. 72, no. 1, pp. 9–32.

Bundesrat (1993) *Bundesrat-Drucksache*, no. 121, 1993, Bonn: Bundesrat.
Bürklin, W. (1988) *Wählerverhalten und Wertewandel*, Opladen: Leske und Budrich.
Bürklin, W. and Roth, D. (eds), (1994) *Das Superwahljahr*, Köln: Bund Verlag.
Busch, H. (1995), *Grezenlose Polizei? Neue Grenzen und polizeiliche Zusammenarbeit in Europa*, Münster: Westfälisches Dampfboot.
Busch, H., Funk, A., Kauss, U., Narr, W.-D., Werkentin, F. (1988) *Die Polizei in der Bundesrepublik*, Studienausgabe, Frankfurt/New York: Campus.
Calleo, D. (1978) *The German Problem Reconsidered. Germany and the World Order. 1870 to the Present*, Cambridge: Cambridge University Press.
Campbell, E. S. (1993) 'United Germany in a Uniting Europe', in G. L. Geipel (ed.), *Germany in a New Era*, Indianapolis: Hudson Institute.
Cerny, K. H. (1993) 'The Future Role of a United Germany in the European Community', in G. L. Geidel (ed.), *Germany in a New Era*, Indianapolis: Hudson Institute.
Clasen, J. (1994) 'Social Security – the core of German employment-centred social state', in J. Clasen and R. Freeman (eds), *Social Policy in Germany*, London: Harvester Wheatsheaf.
Clasen, J. and Freeman, R. (eds) (1994) *Social Policy in Germany*, London: Harvester Wheatsheaf.
Claussen, H. R. (1995), *Korruption im öffentlichen Dienst*, Cologne: Carl Heymanns.
Clemens, C. (1993) 'Opportunity or Obligation? Redefining Germany's Military Role Outside of NATO', in *Armed Forces and Society*, vol. 19, no. 2, pp. 225–41.
Clemens, C. (1994) 'The Chancellor as Manager: Helmut Kohl, the CDU and Governance in Germany', *West European Politics*, vol. 17, no. 4 (October), pp. 28–51.
Conradt, D. (1980) 'Changing German Political Culture', in G. Almond and S. Verba (eds), *The Civic Culture Revisited*, Boston: Little, Brown.
Conradt, D. (1989) *The German Polity*, New York and London: Longman.
Conradt, D., Kleinfeld, G., Romoser, G. and C. Søe (eds) (1995) *Germany's New Politics: Parties and Issues in the 1990s*, Providence, RI, and Oxford: Berghahn.
Converse, P. (1969) 'Of Time and Partisan Stability', *Comparative Political Studies*, vol. 1, pp. 139–71.
Conzelmann, T. (1995) 'Networking and the Politics of EU Regional Policy. Lessons from North Rhine-Westphalia, Nord-Pas de Calais and North West England', *Regional and Federal Studies*, vol. 5, no. 2, pp. 134–72.
Craig, Gordon A. (1991) *The Germans*, with a new Afterword, London: Penguin.
Crawford, B. (1995) 'German Foreign Policy and European Political Co-operation; The Diplomatic Recognition of Croatia in 1991', *German Politics and Society*, vol. 13, no. 1, pp. 1–34.
Crouch, C. (1993) *Industrial Relations and European State Relations*, Oxford: Oxford University Press.
Cullen, P. J. (1992) *The German Police and European Police Co-operation*, working paper 2 of the series 'A System of European Police Co-operation after 1992', Edinburgh: University of Edinburgh Department of Politics.

Cullen, P. J. (1995) 'Competing Legitimacy at European and National Levels: The Ruling of the Constitutional Court and Parliamentary Scrutiny of European Union Affairs in Germany', in F. Laursen and S. A. Pappas (eds), *The Changing Role of Parliaments in the European Union*, Maastricht: European Institute of Public Administration, pp. 61–93.

Cullen, P. J. (1996) 'Constitutional Change in Germany', in W. E. Paterson and C. Jeffery (eds), *German Unification*, Oxford: Blackwell.

Cullen, P. J. and Goetz, K. H. (1994) 'Concluding Theses on Constitutional Policy in Unified Germany', *German Politics*, vol. 3, no. 3, pp. 162–78.

Currie, D. P. (1994) *The Constitution of the Federal Republic of Germany*, Chicago: University of Chicago Press.

Dalton, R. (1989) *Politics in West Germany*, Boston and London: Scott, Foreman.

Dalton, R. (1992) 'Two German Electorates', in G. Smith *et al.*, *Developments in German Politics*, London: Macmillan.

Dalton, R. (1994) 'Communists and Democrats', *British Journal of Political Science*, vol. 24, pp. 469–93.

Dalton, R. (1996a) *Citizen Politics*, 2nd edn, Chatham NJ: Chatham House Publishers.

Dalton, R. (1996b) *Germans Divided: The 1994 Bundestagswahl and the Evolution of the German Party System*, Oxford and Washington: Berg.

Dalton, R. (ed.) (1993) *The New Germany Votes: Unification and the Creation of the New Party System*, Oxford: Berg.

Dalton, R. and Bürklin, W. (1996) 'Two German Electorates', in R. Dalton (ed.), *Germans Divided*, Oxford: Berg.

Dalton, R. and Rohrschneider, R. (1990) 'Wählerwandel und die Auschwächung der Parteieigungen von 1972 bis 1987', in M. Kaase and M.-D. Klingemann (eds), *Wahlen und Wähler*, Opladen: Westdeutscher Verlag.

Das Parlament (1996) Supplement 'Aus Politik und Zeitgeschichte', vol. 6, 2 February.

Datenreport 1994 (ed.) Statistisches Bundesamt, Bonn, Bundeszentrale für politische Bildung 1994.

Däubler, W. and Küsel, G. (eds) (1979) *Verfassungsgericht und Politik. Krittische Beiträge zu problematischen Urteilen*, Reinbek bei Hamburg: Rowohlt.

Der Spiegel (1994) 'Wer zahlen kann, überlebt', no. 15, pp. 70–86.

Der Spiegel (1995) 'Hol raus, was du kannst', no. 18, pp. 29–32.

Deutsche Bundesbank (1991–4) Monthly Reports, 3/1991, 7/1993, 6/1995, 7/1995; Annual Report, 1994, Frankfurt.

Diederich, N., Cadel, G., Dettmar, H. and Haag, I. (eds) (1990), *Die diskreten Kontrolleure. Eine Wirkungsanalyse des Bundesrechnungshofs*, Opladen: Westdeutscher Verlag.

DIW (1992a) 'Zur Politik der Treuhand-eine Zwischenbilanz', *Wochenbericht*, no. 7, pp. 62–8.

DIW (1992b) 'Industrieller Mittelstand in Ostdeutschland', *Wochenbericht*, no. 11, pp. 103–9.

DIW (1993a) 'Stand der Privatisierung, Achter Bericht', *Wochenbericht*, no. 13, pp. 131–58.

DIW (1993b) 'BRD: Strukturkrise oder konjunktureller Einbruch?', *Wochenbericht*, no. 26–7, pp. 360–368.

DIW (1994a) 'Kommunalhaushalte: Finanzprobleme sind nur mittelfristig zu lösen', *Wochenbericht*, no. 26, pp. 439–48, Deutsches Institut für Wirtschaftsforschung.

DIW (1994b) 'Die Einkommen in Ostdeutschland steigen weiter – auch die Einkommensarmut nimmt wieder zu', *Wochenbericht*, no. 51–2, pp. 867–72, Deutscher Institut für Wirtschaftsforschung.

Döhler, M. (1995) 'The State as Architect of Political Order: Policy Dynamics in German Health Care', *Governance*, vol. 8, no. 3, pp. 380–404.

Dölling, D. and Feltes, T. (1993) *Community Policing – Comparable Aspects of Community Oriented Police Work*, Holzkirchen, Oberbayern: Felix-Verlag.

Donges, J. and Schatz, K.-W. (1986) 'Staatliche Intervention in der Bundesrepublik Deutschland – Umfang, Struktur, Wirkungen', *Kiel Discussion Papers*, nos 119–20.

Döring, D. and Hauser, R. (eds) (1995) *Soziale Sicherheit in Gefahr*, Frankfurt am Main: Suhrkamp.

Duffield, J. (1994) 'German Security Policy after Unification: Sources of Continuity and Restraint', *Contemporary Security Policy*, vol. 15, no. 3, pp. 170–98.

Dyson, K. (1982) 'Cultural, Ideological and Structural Context', in K. Dyson and S. Wilks (eds), *Industrial Crisis*, Oxford: Blackwell.

Dyson, K., (ed.) (1992) *The Politics of German Regulation*, Aldershot: Dartmouth.

Dyson, K. (1994) *Elusive Union: The Process of Economic and Monetary Union in Europe*, Harlow: Longman.

Dyson, K. and Featherstone, K. (eds) (1996) *Rescue or Transformation? The European State and Economic and Monetary Union*, London: Oxford University Press.

Eckart, K. (1995) 'Wirtschaftlicher Umbau in Ostdeutschland', *Deutschland Archiv*, vol. 6, pp. 578–88.

Edinger, L. (1993) 'Pressure Group Politics in West Germany', in Jeremy Richardson (ed.), *Pressure Groups*, Oxford: Oxford University Press, pp. 175–91.

Edwards, J. and Fischer, K. (1994) *Banks, Finance and Investment in Germany*, Cambridge: Cambridge University Press.

Eichener, R. Kleinfeld, D. Pollack *et al.* (eds) (1992) *Probleme der Einheit*, 12, *Organisierte Interessen in Ostdeutchsland*, vol. 2, Marburg: Metropolis.

Engeis, W. (1991) 'Offensiv vertreten. Subventioniert der Staat ein Teil der Löhne im Osten, spart er Geld und macht die Unternehmen wettbewerbsfähig', *Wirtschaftswoche*, vol. 26, pp. 109–14.

Erdmann, Y. (1992) 'Aufbau und Entwicklung von Ärzteverbände in Ostdeutschland', in V. Eichener, R. Kleinfeld, D. Pollack *et al.* (eds) *Probleme der Einheit*, 12, *Organisierte Interessen in Ostdeutschsland*, vol. 2, Marburg, Metropolis.

Esping-Anderson, G. (1990) *The Three Worlds of Welfare Capitalism*, Cambridge, Polity Press.

Ettl, W. (1995) 'Arbeitgeberverbände als Transformationsakteure; Organisationsentwicklung und Tarifpolitik in Dilemma von Funktionalität und Representativität', in H. Wiesenthal (ed.), *Einheit als Interessenpolitik; Studien zur sektoralen Transformation Ostdeutschlands*, Frankfurt/Main: Campus.

Ettl, W. and Heikenroth, A. (1995) *Strukturwandel Verbandsabstinentz Tarifflucht; Zur Lage ostdeutscher Unternehmen und Arbeitgeberverbände*, Arbeitspapiere, Berlin, Max-Planck-Gesellschaft.

Ettl, W. and Wiesenthal, H. (1994) *Tarifautonomie in de-industrialisierten Gelände: Report und Analyse eines Institutiontransfers im Prozess der deutschen Einheit*, Arbeitspapiere, Berlin, Max-Planck-Gesellschaft.

Eurostat (1995) *Basic Statistics of the EU*, 32nd edn, Luxembourg, Eurostat.

Evans, M. (1996) 'Exploring Statistics and National Rules on Social Security', in L. Hantrais and S. Mangen (eds), *Cross-National Research Methods in the Social Sciences*, London: Pinter.

Fairchild, E. S. (1988) *German Police. Ideas and Reality in the Post-War Years*, Springfield, Ill.: Charles C. Thomas.

Faller, H. J. (1995) 'Das Ringen um die Entlastung des Bundesverfassungsgerichts', in E. Klein *et al.* (eds), *Grundrechte, soziale Ordnung und Verfassungsgerichtsbarkeit: Festschrift für Ernst Benda zum 70 Geburtstag*, Heidelberg: C. F. Müller, pp. 43–66.

Federal Constitutional Court (ed.) (1992) *Decisions of the Bundesverfassungsgericht – International Law and European Communities 1952–1989*, 2 vols, Baden-Baden: Nomos Verlagsgesellschaft.

Federal Ministry of Defence (1994) *Weissbuch 1994: Weissbuch zur Sicherheit der BRD und zur Lage und Zukunft der Bundeswehr*, Bonn, Federal Ministry of Defence.

Feltes, T., and Rebscher, E. (eds) (1990) 'Polizei und Bevölkerung: Beiträge zum Verhältnis zwischen Polizei und Bevölkerung und zur gemeindebezogenen Polizeiarbeit', *Community Policing*, Holzkirchen, Oberbayern: Felix-Verlag.

Fichter, M. (1993) 'A House Divided: German Unification and Organised Labour', *German Politics*, vol. 2, no. 1.

Fichter, M. and Kubjuhn, M. (1992) 'Die Gewerkschaften im Einigungsprozess: Ausdehnung mit alten Organisationsstrukturen und neuen Integrationsproblemen', in V. Eichener, R. Kleinfeld, D. Pollack *et al.* (eds), *Probleme der Einheit*, 12; *Organisierte Interessen in Ostdeutschland*, vol. 2, Marburg: Metropolis Verlag.

Flockton, C. H. (1992) 'The German Economy', in D. Dyker (ed.), *The National Economies of Europe*, London: Longman.

Foster, N. (1994) 'The German Constitution and EC Membership', *Public Law*, pp. 392–408.

Franklin, M. *et al.* (1992) *Electoral Change*, Cambridge: Cambridge University Press.

Freeman, R. and Clasen, J. (1994) 'The German Social State: an introduction', in J. Clasen and R. Freeman (eds), *Social Policy in Germany*, London: Harvester Wheatsheaf.

Fukui, H., Merkl, P., Muller-Groeling, H. and Watanabe, A. (1993) *The Politics of Economic Change in Postwar Japan and West Germany*, London: Macmillan.

Ganssman, H. (1993) 'After Unification: Problems Facing the German Welfare State', *Journal of European Social Policy*, vol. 3, pp. 79–90.

Garton Ash, T. (1994) *In Europe's Name: Germany and the Divided Continent*, London: Jonathan Cape.

Garton Ash, T. (1994a) 'Germany's Choice', *Foreign Affairs*, vol. 73, no. 4, pp. 65–82.

Gauck, J. (1994) 'Dealing with a Stasi Past', *Daedalus*, vol. 123, no. 1, *Germany in Transition*, pp. 277–84.

Geißler, R. (1992) *Die Sozialstruktur Deutschlands*, Opladen: Westdeutscher Verlag.

Geißler, R. (1995) 'Das gefährliche Gerücht von der hohen Ausländerkriminalität', *Aus Politik und Zeitgeschichte*, vol. B35/95, pp. 30–9.

Gesamtmetall (1992) *Arbeitgeberverband Gesamtmetall; die Unternehmen der Metall- und Elektro-industrie*, Köln: Gesamtmetall.

Ghanie-Ghaussy, A. and Schäfer, W. (1993) *The Economics of German Unification*, London: Routledge.

Giersch, H., Paque, K.-H. and Schmeiding, H. (1992) *The Fading Miracle: Four Decades of Market Economy in Germany*, Cambridge: Cambridge University Press.

Gill, D., and Schröter, U. (1991) *Das Ministerium für Staatssicherheit. Anatomie des Mielke- Imperiums*, Berlin: Rowohlt.

Glaeßner, G.-J. (1992) *The Unification process in Germany: From Dictatorship to Democracy*, London: Pinter.

Glaeßner, G.-J. and Wallace, I. (eds) (1992) *The German Revolution of 1989: Causes and Consequences*, Oxford and Providence: Berg.

Goetz, K. (1992) *Intergovernmental Relations and State Discretion: The Case of Science and Technology Policy in Germany*, Baden-Baden: Nomos.

Goetz, K. (1993) 'Rebuilding Public Administration in the New German Länder: Transfer and Differentiation', *West European Politics*, vol. 16, no. 4, pp. 447–69.

Goetz, K. (1995a) 'National Governance and European Integration: Intergovernmental Relations in Germany', *Journal of Common Market Studies*, vol. 33, no. 1, pp. 91–116.

Goetz, K. (1995b) 'Kooperation und Verflechtung im Bundesstaat. Zur Leistungsfähigkeit handlungsbasierter Politik', in R. Voigt (ed.), *Der Kooperative Staat. Krisenbewältigung durch Verhandlung?*, Baden-Baden: Nomos.

Goetz, K. and Cullen, P. (1994) 'The Basic Law after Unification: Continued Centrality or Declining Force?', *German Politics*, vol. 3, no. 3, pp. 5–46.

Goetz, K. and Cullen, P. (eds) (1994) *Constitutional Policy in Unified Germany*, special issue of *German Politics*, vol. 3, no. 3.

Goetz, K. (1996) 'Integration Policy in a Europeanized State: Germany and the Intergovernmental Conference', *Journal of European Public Policy*, vol. 3, no. 1, pp. 23–44.

Greiffenhagen, M. and Greiffenhagen, S. (1993) *Ein schwieriges Vaterland. Zur politischen Kultur im vereinigten Deutschland*, München: List.

Grimm, D. (1990) 'Die Zukunft der Verfassung', *Staatswissenschaften und Staatpraxis*, vol. 1, no. 1, pp. 5–33.

Grimm, D. (1995) 'Constitutional Reform in Germany after the Revolution of 1989', in J. J. Hesse and N. Johnson (eds) *Constitutional Policy and Change in Europe*, Oxford: Oxford University Press, pp. 129–51.

Gros, J. (1994) *Entscheiding ohne Alternativen?*, Mainz: Forschungsgruppe Deutschland, Bd 2.

Grosser, D. (ed.) (1988) *Soziale Marktwirtschaft. Geschichte-Konzept-Leistung*, Stuttgart: Kohlhammer.

Gunlicks, A. (1995) 'The New German Party Finance Law', *German Politics*, 4 (April) 101–21.

Gunlicks, A., and Voigt, R. (1991) *Föderalismus in der Bewährungsprobe*, Bochum: Brockmeyer.

Gysi, J. and Meyer, S. (1993) 'Leitbild berufstätige Mutter – DDR-Frauen in Familie, Partnerschaft und Ehe', in G. Helwig and H.-M. Nickel (eds), *Frauen in Deutschland 1945–1992*, Berlin: Akademie Verlag.

Habermas, J. (1987) *Eine Art Schadensabwicklung*, Frankfurt: Suhrkamp.

Hacke, C. (1993) *Weltmacht wider Willen: Die Aussenpolitik der Bundesrepublik Deutschland*, rev. edn, Berlin: Ullstein.

Haftendorn, H. (1983) *Sicherheit und Entspannung: Zur Aussenpolitik der Bundesrepublik Deutschland 1955–1982*, Baden-Baden: Nomos.

Hancock, D. (1989) *West Germany: The Politics of Democratic Corporatism*, Chatham, NJ: Chatham House Publishers.

Hancock, D. and Welsh, H. (eds) (1994) *German Unification: Process and Outcomes*, Boulder and Oxford: Westview Press.

Hanesch, W. (ed.) (1994) *Armut in Deutschland*, Reinbek: Rowohlt.

Hassemer, W. (1993) 'Innere Sicherheit im Rechtsstaat', *Strafverteidiger*, vol. 12, pp. 664–70.

Hauser, R., Frick, J., Mueller, K. and Wagner, G. (1994) 'Inequality in Income: A Comparison of East and West Germans before Reunification', *Journal of European Social Policy*, no. 4, pp. 277–95.

Häussler, R. (1994) *Der Konflikt zwischen Bundesverfassungsgericht und politischer Führung*, Berlin: Duncker & Humblot.

Helwig, G. and Nickel, H.-M. (1992) *Frauen in Deutschland 1945–1992*, Berlin: Akademie Verlag.

Henzler, H. and Spath, L. (1993) *Sind die Deutschen noch zu retten?*, Gutersloh: Bertelsmann Verlag.

Herdegen, M. (1994) 'Maastricht and the German Constitutional Court: Constitutional Restraints for an "Ever Closer Union"', *Common Market Law Review*, vol. 31, pp. 235–62.

Herzog, R. (1995) *Die Globalisierung der deutschen Aussenpolitik ist unvermeidlich*, Bonn: Bulletin, Presse- und Informationsamt der Bundesregierung, vol. 20, pp. 161–5.

Hesse, J. and Ellwein, T. (1992) *Das Regierungssystem der Bundesrepublik Deutschland*, Opladen: Westdeutscher Verlag.

Hesse, J. J. and Renzsch, W. (1990) 'Zehn Thesen zur Entwicklung und Lage des deutschen Föderalismus', *Staatswissenschaften und Staatspraxis*, vol. 4, pp. 562–78.

Hesse, K. (1995) 'Verfassungsrechtsprechung im geschichtlichen Wandel', *Juristen-Zeitung*, vol. 50, no. 6, pp. 265–73.

Hettlage, Robert (1992) *Familienreport. Eine Lebensform im Umbruch*, Munich: Beck.

Heydrich, W. (ed.) (1991) *Stabilität, Gleichgewicht und die Sicherheitsinteressen des Vereinigten Deutschland*, Ebenhausen: Stiftung Wissenschaft und Politik.

Hildebrandt, R. (1994) 'Die Einrichtungen des Gesundheits- und Sozialwesens in der DDR und in den neuen Bundesländern', *Aus Politik und Zeitgeschichte*, vol. 3, pp. 15–25.

Hoffman, L. (1993) *Warten auf den Aufschwung: Eine ostdeutsche Bilanz*, Berlin: Transfer Verlag.

Hölzler, Ingrid and Mächler, Hermann (1993) *Sozialreport 1992. Daten und Fakten zur sozialen Situation in Sachsen-Anhalt*, Magdeburg: Universität Magdeburg.

Hoppe, U. and Schulz, G. (1992) 'Der Ausschuss der Regionen', in F. Borkenhagen *et al.* (eds), *Die deutschen Länder in Europa*, Baden-Baden: Nomos, pp. 26–35.

Höynck, W. (1994) 'CSCE Works to Develop its Conflict Prevention Potential', *NATO Review*, vol. 42, no. 2, pp. 16–22.

Hrbek, R. and Wessels, W. (1984) *EG-Mitgliedschaft: Ein Vitales Interesse der Bundesrepublik Deutschland?*, Bonn: Europa Union Verlag.

Hucko, E.M. (1987) *The Democratic Tradition: Four German Constitutions*, Leamington Spa: Berg.

Huelshoff, M.G. (1993) 'Germany and European Integration: Understanding the Relationship', in M.G. Huelshoff, A.S. Markovits and S. Reich (eds), *From Bundesrepublik to Deutschland: German Politics after Unification*, Ann Arbor: University of Michigan Press.

Huelshoff, Michael G., Markovits, Andrei S. and Reich, Simon (eds) (1993) *From Bundesrepublik to Deutschland. German Politics after Unification*, Ann Arbor: University of Michigan Press.

Huntington, S. (1968) *Political Order in Changing Societies*, New Haven and London: Yale University Press.

Hüther, M. and Petersen, H.-G. (1993) 'Taxes and Transfers: Financing German Unification', in A. Ghanie Ghausdsey and W. Schäfer (eds), *The Economics of German Unification*, London: Routledge.

Hyde-Price, A. (1991) *European Security Beyond the Cold War: Four Scenarios for the Year 2010*, London: Sage.

Hyde-Price, A. (1996) *The International Politics of East Central Europe*, Manchester: Manchester University Press.

IfEP (1994) Trendbarometer '94; *Zusammenfassende Trendanalyse und Presentationsunterlagen*, Köln: Institut für empirische Psychologie.

Informationsmaterial zur 218 StGB' (1993), Bundesministerium für Frauen und Jugend Dokumentation, *Materialien zur Frauenpolitik* vol. 32.

Integrationsprobleme von DDR-Übersiedlerinnen – Perspecktiven, Erfahrungen, Strategien' (1991), Bundesministerium für Frauen und Jugend Dokumentation, *Materialien zur Frauenpolitik*, vol. 12.

Ipos (Institute für praxisorientierte Sozialforschung) (1992) *Gleichberechtigung von Frauen und Männern, Wirklichkeit und Einstellungen in der Bevölkerung*, Stuttgart, Kohlhammer.

James, Harold (1994) *A German Identity. 1770 to the Present Day*, London: Phoenix.

Janning, J. (1996) 'A German Europe, a European Germany? On the debate over Germany's foreign policy', *International Affairs*, vol. 72, no. 1, pp. 33–42.

Jarausch, K.H. and Gransow, V. (1994) *Uniting Germany. Documents and Debates, 1944–1993*, Providence and Oxford: Berghahn.

Jeffery, C. (1994) 'The Länder Strike Back. Structures and Procedures of European Integration Policy-Making in the German Federal System', *University of Leicester Discussion Papers in Federal Studies*, no. FS94/4.

Jeffery, C. (1995a) 'The Non-Reform of the German Federal System after Unification', *West European Politics*, vol. 18, no. 2, pp. 252–72.

Jeffery, C. (1995b) 'The German Länder and the 1996 Intergovernmental Conference', *Regional and Federal Studies*, vol. 5, no. 3, pp. 357–66.

Jeffery, C. (1996) 'Towards a "Third Level" in Europe? The German Länder in the European Union', *Political Studies*, vol. 44, no. 2, pp. 253–266.

Jeffery, C. and Sturm, R. (1992) (eds) 'Federalism, Unification and European Integration', *German Politics*, vol. 1, no. 3.

Jeffery, C. and Sturm, R. (eds) (1993), *Federalism, Unification and European Integration*, London: Frank Cass.

Jeffery, C. and Yates, J. (1993) 'Unification and Maastricht: The Response of the Länder Governments', in C. Jeffery and R. Sturm (eds), *Federalism, Unification and European Integration*, London: Frank Cass, pp. 58–81.

Jesse, E. (1995) 'Die Parteien in den neuen Bundesländern', in Winand Gellner and Hans-Joachim Veen (eds), *Umbruch und Wandel des westeuropäischen Parteiensystems*, Frankfurt: Lang.

Jesse, E. (1996) 'Die CSU im vereinigten Deutschland', *Aus Politik und Zeitgeschichte* (2 February).

Joffe, J. (1991) 'The Security Implications of a United Germany: Paper 1, America's Role in a Changing World', *Adelphi Paper 257*, London: Brassey's for the IISS, pp. 84–91.

Joffe, J. (1994) 'German Grand Strategy After the Cold War', in Baring, A. (ed.) *Germany's New Position in Europe*, Oxford: Berg.

Johnson, N. (1982) 'The Interdependence of Law and Politics: Judges and the Constitution in Western Germany', *West European Politics*, vol. 5, no. 3, pp. 236–52.

Johnson, N. (1994) 'The Federal Constitutional Court: Facing up to the Strains of Law and Politics in the New Germany', *German Politics*, vol. 3, no. 3, pp. 131–48.

Jugend '92, Gesamtdarstellung und biographische Porträts (1992), Jugendstudie der Deutschen Shell, Opladen: Leske und Budrich.

Juricic, M. (1995) 'Perception, Causation and German Foreign Policy', *Review of International Studies*, vol. 21, no. 1, pp. 105–15.

Kaase, M. and Klingemann, H.-D. (1994) 'The Cumbersome Way to Partisan Orientations in a "new" democracy', in M. Jennings and T. Mann (eds), *Elections at Home and Abroad*, Ann Arbor: University of Michigan Press.

Kaase, M. and Klingemann, H.-D. (eds) (1990), *Wahlen und Wähler*, Opladen: Westdeutscher Verlag.

Kaiser, K. (1991) 'Germany's Unification', *Foreign Affairs*, 70 (1), 179–205.

Kaiser, K. (1995) 'Forty Years of German Membership in NATO', *NATO Review*, 43 (4), 3–8.

Kaiser, K. and Maull, H. W. (1994) 'Deutschlands Neue Aussenpolitik', Band 1 Grundlagen, Munich: Oldenburg.

Kaiser, K. and Maull, H. W. (1995) 'Deutschlands Neue Aussenpolitik', Band 2, Herausforderungen, Munich: Oldenbourg.

Kamp, K.-H. (1993) 'The German Bundeswehr in out-of-area operations: to engage or not to engage?', *The World Today*, vol. 49, no. 8, pp. 165–8.

Kanther, M. (1995) 'Wertewandel und Innere Sicherheit', *Bulletin des Presse- und Informationsamts der Bundesregierung*, no. 14, pp. 111–14.

Karpen, U. (ed.) (1988) *The Constitution of the Federal Republic of Germany*, Baden-Baden: Nomos Verlagsgesellschaft.

Katz, R. and Mair, P. (1995) 'Changing Models of Party Organization and Party Democracy: The Emergence of the Cartel Party', *Party Politics*, vol. 1 (January), pp. 5–27.

Katzenstein, P. (1987) *Policy and Politics in West Germany: The Growth of a Semi-Sovereign State*, Philadelphia: Temple University Press.

Katzenstein, P. J. (1990) *West Germany's Internal Security Policy: State and Violence in the 1970s and 1980s*, Cornell Studies in International Affairs, Western Societies Program, Occasional Paper no. 28.

Kirchhof, P. and Kommers, D. P. (eds) (1993) *Germany and its Basic Law*, Baden-Baden: Nomos Verlagsgesellschaft.

Kirchner, E. (1989) 'The Federal Republic of Germany in the European Community', in P. Merkl (ed.), *The Federal Republic of Germany at Forty*, Cambridge: Cambridge University Press.

Kirchner, E. (1992) 'The European Community: Seeds of Ambivalence', in G. Smith, W. E. Paterson, P. H. Merkl and S. Padgett (eds), *Developments in German Politics*, London: Macmillan.

Kirchner, E. (1994) 'The Impact of German Unification on the New European Order', in H. Miall (ed.), *Redefining Europe: New Patterns of Conflict and Cooperation*, London and New York: Pinter.

Kirchner, E. (1995) 'A Federal Republic of Europe?', in P. H. Merkl (ed.), *The Federal Republic of Germany at Forty-five*, London: Macmillan.

Kitschelt, H. (1991) 'The 1990 Election and the National Unification', *West European Politics*, vol. 14, no. 4 (October), pp. 121–48.

Klatt, H. (1991) 'Centralising Trends in the Federal Republic: The Record of the Kohl Chancellorship', in C. Jeffery and P. Savigear (eds), *German Federalism Today*, Leicester: Leicester University Press, pp. 120–37.

Klatt, H. (1993) 'German Unification and the Federal System', in C. Jeffery and R. Sturm (eds), *Federalism, Unification and European Integration*, London: Frank Cass, pp. 1–21.

Klatt, H. (1995) 'Superwahljahr and After: German Länder Elections 1994–95', *Regional and Federal Studies*, vol. 5, no. 2, pp. 230–8.

Koch, H. W. (1984) *A Constitutional History of Germany in the Nineteenth and Twentieth Centuries*, London: Longman.

Koch, H. W. (1985) *Aspects of the Third Reich*, Basingstoke: Macmillan.

Kohl, H. (1991) 'Our Future in Europe', Edinburgh and London: Europa Institute/Konrad Adenauer Foundation.

Kohl, H. (1996) Interview given in *Deutschland Magazine*, No. 1.

Kolinsky, E. (1993a) *Women in Contemporary Germany. Life, Work and Politics*, Oxford: Berg.

Kolinsky, E (1993b) 'Party Change and Women's Representation in Unified Germany', in J. Lovenduski and P. Norris (eds), *Gender and Party Politics*, London; Sage.

Kolinsky, E. (1995a) *Women in 20th-century Germany. A Reader*, Manchester: Manchester University Press.

Kolinsky, E. (ed.) (1995b) *Between Hope and Fear. Everyday Life in Post-Unification East Germany. A Case Study of Leipzig*, Keele: Keele University Press.

Kommers, D. P. (1976) *Judicial Politics in West Germany: A Study of the Federal Constitutional Court*, Beverly Hills: Sage.

Kommers, D. P. (1989) *The Constitutional Jurisprudence of the Federal Republic of Germany*, Durham: Duke University Press.

Kommers, D. P. (1994) 'The Federal Constitutional Court in the German Political System', *Comparative Political Studies*, vol. 26, no. 4, pp. 470–91.

Kress, C. (1995) 'The External Use of German Armed Forces – the 1994 Judgement of the Bundesverfassungsgericht', *International and Comparative Law Quarterly*, vol. 44, no. 2, pp. 414–26.

Kube, E. and Dörmann, V. (1993) 'Zur Kriminalitätslage in Deutschland als Folge des Politischen Wandels', *Die Polizei*, vol. 84, no. 3.

Kuechler, M. (1993) 'Framing Unification', in R. Dalton (ed.), *The New Germany Votes*, Oxford: Berg.

Kurz, H. D. (ed.) (1993) *United Germany and the New Europe*, Aldershot: E. Elgar.

Lamers, K. (1993) 'German Responsibilities and Interest in the Field of Foreign Policy', paper presented to the conference of the CDU/CSU parliamentary party in the Bundestag in Berlin 24 and 25 August, 1993.

Lamprecht, Rolf and Malanowski, Wolfgang (eds) (1979) *Richter machen Politik: Auftrag und Anspruch des Bundesverfassungsgerichts*, Frankfurt a.M.: Fischer.

Landfried, C. (1988) 'Constitutional Review and Legislation in the Federal Republic of Germany', in C. Landfried (ed.), *Constitutional Review and Legislation: An International Comparison*, Baden-Baden: Nomos Verlagsgesellschaft, pp. 147–67.

Landfried, C. (1992) 'Judicial Policy-Making in Germany: The Federal Constitutional Court', *West European Politics*, vol. 15, no. 3, pp. 50–67.

Landua, D. (1993) 'The Social Aspects of German Unification', in A. Ghanie Ghaussy and W Schäfer (eds), *The Economics of German Unification*, London: Routledge.

Larrabee, S. (1989) *The Two German States and European Security*, London: Macmillan.

Lehmbruch, G. (1976) *Parteienwettbewerb im Bundesstaat*, Stuttgart: Kohlhammer.

Leibfried, S. and Ostner, I. (1991) 'The Particularism of West German Welfare Capitalism', in M. Adler, C. Bell, J. Clasen and A. Sinfield (eds), *The Sociology of Social Security*, Edinburgh: Edinburgh University Press.

Leonardy, U. (1991) 'The Working Relationships between Bund and Länder in the Federal Republic of Germany', in C. Jeffery and P. Savigear (eds), German Federalism Today, Leicester: Leicester University Press, pp. 40–62.

Lepsius, R. (1990) *Interessen, Ideen und Institutionen*, Opladen: Westdeutscher Verlag.

Link, W. (1996) 'Integration and Balance', *German Comments*, January, pp. 17–23.

Linnenkamp, H. (1992) 'The Security Policy of the New Germany', in P. Stares (ed.) (1992), pp. 93–125.

Lintner, E. (1993) 'Grenzüberschreitende Kooperation der Sicherheitsbehörden', in *Polizeiliche Zusammenarbeit mit Osteuropa, Dokumentation eines internationalen Fachkongresses*, Potsdam: Geschäftsstelle der Ständigen Konferenz der Innenminister und senatoren der Länder, pp. 35–46.

Lintner, E. (1995) 'Rauschgiftbilanz 1994', Presse- und Informationsamt der Bundesregierung, no. 14, pp. 114–15.

Lipset, S. and Rokkan, S. (eds) (1967) *Party Systems and Voter Alignments*, New York: Free Press.

Lohmann, H.-M. (ed.) (1994) *Extremismus der Mitte. Vom rechten Verständnis deutscher Nation*, Frankfurt: S. Fischer.

Lösche, P. (1996) 'Die SPD nach Mannheim: Strukturprobleme und aktuelle Entwicklungen', *Aus Politik und Zeitgeschichte* (2 February).

Magris, C. (1990) *Danube: A Sentimental Journey. From the Source to the Black Sea*, London: Collins Harvill.

Mair, P. (1993) 'Myths of Electoral Change and the Survival of Traditional Parties', *European Journal of Political Research*, vol. 24/2, pp. 121–33.

Mangen, S. (1992) 'Social Policy: One State, Two-tier Welfare', in G. Smith *et al.* (eds), *Developments in German Politics*, Basingstoke: Macmillan.

Mangen, S. (1994) 'The Impact of Unification', in J. Clasen and R. Freeman (eds), *Social Policy in Germany*, Hemel Hempstead: Harvester Wheatsheaf.

Manow-Borgwardt, P. (1995) *Gesundheitspolitik im Einigungsprozess*, Frankfurt am Main/New York: Campus.

Markovits, A.S. and Reich, S. (1991) 'Should Europe Fear the Germans?', *German Politics and Society*, vol. 23, pp. 1–20.

Marsh, D. (1992) *The Bundesbank: The Bank that Rules Europe*, London: Heinemann.

Marsh, D. (1994) *Germany and Europe: The Crisis of Unity*, London: Heinemann.

Marshall, B. (1995) 'Migration from the East: German perceptions and policy', in C. Bluch, E. Kirchner and J. Sperling (eds), *The Future of European Security*, Aldershot: Dartmouth, pp. 187–204.

Maull, H. (1992) 'Zivilmacht Bundesrepublik Deutschland. 14 Thesen für eine neue deutsche Aussenpolitik', *Europa-Archiv*, October, pp. 269–78.

Maull, H. and Gordon, P. (1993) 'German Foreign Policy and the German National Interest; Government and American Perspectives', Washington AICGS Seminar Paper no. 5.

May, B. (1985) *Kosten und Nutzen der Deutschen EG-Mitgliedschaft*, 2nd edn, Bonn: Europa Union Verlag.

Mearsheimer, J. (1990) 'Back to the Future; Instability in Europe after the Cold War', *International Security*, vol. 15, no. 1.

Meinecke, F. (1919) *Weltbürgertum und Nationalstaat: Studien über die Genesis des deutschen Nationalstaates*, 5th edn, Munich-Berlin: Oldenbourg.

Meinecke, F. (1949) *Die deutsche Katastrophe: Betrachtungen und Erinnerungen*, Wiesbaden: Brockhaus.

Merkl, P. (ed.) (1993) *German Unification in the European Context*, University Park: The Pennsylvania State University Press.

Merkl, P. (ed.) (1996) *The German Federal Republic at Forty-five*, London: Macmillan.

Meyer, S. and Schulz, E. (1992) 'Frauen in der Modernisierungsfalle – Wandel von Ehe, Familie und Partnerschaft in der Bundesrepublik', in Gisela Helwig and Hildegard-Maria Nickel (eds), *Frauen in Deutschland 1945–1992*, Berlin: Akademie Verlag.

Meyer, T. (1992) 'Struktur und Wandel der Familie', in Reiner Geissler, *Die Sozialstruktur Deutschlands*, Opladen: Westdeutscher Verlag.

Meyer, W. (1991) 'Welchen Beitrag Können Beschäftgungsgesellschaften leisten? Anforderungen aus gewerkschaftlicher Sicht', *Wirtschaftsdienst*, VIII, pp. 385–8.

Milward, A. (1992) *The European Rescue of the Nation State*, London: Routledge.

Mitchell, D. (1991) *Income Transfers in Ten Welfare States*, London: Avebury.

Moreton, E. (ed.) (1987) *Germany Between East and West*, Cambridge: Cambridge University Press.

Morgan, R. and Bray, C. (1986) *Partners and Rivals in Western Europe: Britain, France and Germany*, Aldershot: Gower.

MRDB6 (1995) 'Public Finance' (Monthly Report of the Deutsche Bundesbank).

MRDB7 (1995) 'Monetary Developments' (Monthly Report of the Deutsche Bundesbank).

Mueller, J. (1994) 'The Catastrophe Quota', *Journal of Conflict Resolution*, vol. 38, pp. 335–75.

Naumann, M. (1994) '"Neuanfang ohne Tabus": Deutscher Sonderweg und politische Semantik', in Lohmann (1994).

Neuweiler, G. (1994) 'Das gesamtdeutsche Haus für Forschung und Lehre', *Aus Politik und Zeitgeschichte*, vol. 25, pp. 3–11.

Nicholls, A. J. (1994) *Freedom with Responsibility: The Social Market Economy in Germany 1918–1963*, Oxford: Oxford University Press.

Nick, H. (1995) 'An unparalleled destruction and squandering of economic assets', in H. Behrend (ed.), *German Unification: the destruction of an economy*, London: Pluto.

Nickel, H.-M. and Schenk, S. (1994) 'Prozesse geschlechtsspezifischer Differenzierung im Erwerbssystem', in H.-M. Nickel, J. Kühl and S. Schenk (eds), *Erwerbsarbeit und Beschäftigung im Umbruch*, Berlin, Akademie Verlag.

Niedermeyer, O. (1995) 'Party System Change in East Germany', *German Politics*, vol. 4 (December) pp. 75–91.

Niedermeyer, O. and van Beyme, K. (eds) (1994) *Politische Kultur in Ost- und Westdeutschland*, Berlin: Akademie Verlag.

Nolte, E. (1985) 'Between Myth and Revisionism? The Third Reich in the Perspective of the 1980s', in Koch (1985).

Norpoth, H. (1983) 'The Making of a More Partisan Electorate', *British Journal of Political Science*, vol. 14, pp. 53–71.

Norpoth, H. and Roth, D. (1996) 'Timid or Prudent? The German Electorate in 1994', in R. Dalton (ed.), *Germans Divided*, Oxford: Berg.

O'Brien, C. C. (1989) 'Beware a Reich Resurgent', *The Times*, 31 October 1989.

OECD (1990), *Deutschland (Wirtschaftsberichte 1989/90)*, Paris: OECD.

OECD (1994) *Economic Survey: Germany, 1993–4*, Paris: OECD.

OECD (1995) *Germany, 1994/1995*, Paris: OECD.

Offe, C. (1991) 'Capitalism by Democratic Design; Democratic Theory Facing the Triple Transition in East Central Europe', *Social Research*, vol. 51, no. 4.

Olson, M. (1965) *The Logic of Collective Action: Public Goods and the Theory of Groups*, Cambridge, Mass.: Harvard University Press.

Padgett, S. (1989) 'The Party System', in G. Smith, W. Paterson and P. Merkl (eds), *Developments in West German Politics*, Basingstoke: Macmillan.

Padgett, S. (1990) 'Policy Style and Issue Environment: The Electricity Supply Sector in West Germany', *Journal of Public Policy*, vol. 10, no. 2, pp. 165–93.

Padgett, S. (1992) 'The New German Economy', in G. Smith *et al.* (eds), *Developments in German Politics*, London: Macmillan.

Padgett, S. (ed.) (1993) *Parties and Party Systems in the New Germany*, Aldershot and Brookfield: Dartmouth.

Pappi, F.-U. (1984) 'The West German Party System', *West European Politics*, vol. 74 (October), pp. 7–26.

Paterson, W. (1992) 'Gulliver Unbound, the Changing Context of Foreign Policy', in G. Smith, W. Paterson, P. Merkl and S. Padgett (eds), *Developments in German Politics*, London: Macmillan, pp. 137–52.

Patton, D. (1993) 'Social Coalitions, Political Strategies and German Unification, 1990–1993', *West European Politics*, vol. 16, no. 4, pp. 470–91.

Peffekoven, R. (1994) 'Reform des Finanzausgleichs – eine vertane Chance', *Finanzarchiv*, vol. 51, no. 3, pp. 281–311.

Pfeiffer, H. (1993) *Die Macht der Banken. Die personelle Verflechtung der Commerzbank, der Deutschen Bank und der Dresdner Bank mit Unternehmen*, Frankfurt am Main/New York: Campus.

Pilz, F. and Ortwein, H. (1992) *Das vereinte Deutschland*, Stuttgart/Jena: Gustav Fischer.

Poguntke, T. (1993) *Alternative Politics: The German Green Party*, Edinburgh: Edinburgh University Press.

Poguntke, T. (1994) 'Parties in a Legalistic Culture: The Case of Germany', in R. Katz and P. Mair (eds), *How Parties Organize*, London and Thousand Oaks: Sage.

Politbarometer, Monthly Publication of Survey Data, Forschungsgruppe Wahlen, University of Mannheim.

Polizeiliche Kriminalstatistik 1994 (Police Crime Statistics 1994) (1995), *Bulletin des Presse- und Informationsamts der Bundesregierung*, no. 56, pp. 517–56.

Programm Innere Sicherheit (Programme for Internal Security) (1993) *Fortschreibung 1994 durch die Innenminister/-senatoren der Länder und den Bundesminister des Innern*, Potsdam: Geschäftsstelle der Ständigen Konferenz der Innenminister und -senatoren der Länder.

Prützel-Thomas, M. (1993) 'The Abortion Issue and the Federal Constitutional Court', *German Politics*, vol. 2, no. 3, pp. 467–84.

Pulzer, P. (1994) 'Unified Germany: A Normal State?', *German Politics*, vol. 3 (April), pp. 1–17.

Pulzer, P. (1995a) *German Politics. 1945–1995*, Oxford: Oxford University Press.

Pulzer, P. (1995b) 'Nation State and National Sovereignty', *German Historical Institute London Bulletin*, vol. 17, no. 3, pp. 5–14.

Pulzer, P. (1995c) 'Pointing the Way: the Electoral Transition from the Bonn Republic to the Berlin Republic', *German Politics*, vol. 4, no. 2 (August), pp. 141–51.

Quintessenzen aus der Arbeitsmarkt- und Berufsforschung, 4, 1994.

Raith, W. (1995) *Organisierte Kriminalität*, Hamburg: Rowohlt.

Ress, G. (1994) 'The Constitution and the Maastricht Treaty: Between Cooperation and Conflict', *German Politics*, vol. 3, no. 3, pp. 47–74.

Richardson, J., Gustafsson, G. and Jordan, G. (1982) 'The Concept of Policy Style', in J. Richardson (ed.), *Policy Styles in Western Europe*, London: Allen & Unwin, pp. 1–16.

Roberts, G. (ed.) (1995) '*Superwahljahr*: The German Elections in 1994', *German Politics*, vol. 4 (August), special issue.

Rose, R. and McAllister, I. (1989) *When Voters Begin to Choose*, Beverly Hills: Sage.

Rotfeld, A. and Stützlre, W. (eds) (1991) *Germany and Europe in Transition*, Oxford: Oxford University Press.

Rüdig, W. (1988) 'Outcomes of Nuclear Technology Policy: Do Varying Political Styles Make a Difference?', *Journal of Public Policy*, vol. 7, no. 4, pp. 389–430.

Rühe, V. (1993) 'Shaping Euro-Atlantic Policies: A Grand Strategy for a New Era', *Survival*, vol. 35, no. 2, pp. 129–37.

Rupprecht, R. (1993) 'Innere Sicherheit', in W. Weidenfeld and K.-R. Korte (eds), *Handbuch zur deutschen Einheit*, Frankfurt/New York: Campus.

Søe, C. (1995) 'The Free Democratic Party: A Struggle for Survival and Identity', in D. Conradt *et al.* (eds), *Germany's New Politics: Parties and Issues in the 1990s*, Providence and Oxford: Berghahn.

Sachverständigenrat zur Begutachtung der gesamtwirtschaftlichen Entwicklung (SBGE) (1994) *Jahresgutachten 1994/5: Den Aufschwung sichern-Arbeitsplätze schaffen*, Bonn: Metzler-Poeschel.

Saeter, M. (1980) *The Federal Republic, Europe and the World*, Oslo: Universtetsforlaget.

Schäfer, W. (1993) 'The Unification of Germany, the DM and European Monetary Union', in A. Ghanie Gaussy and W. Schäfer, op cit.

Scharf, T. (1994) *The German Greens: Challenging the Political Consensus*, Oxford: Berg.

Scharpf, F., Reissert, B. and Schnabel, F. (1976) *Politikverflechtung: Theorie und Empirie des kooperativen Föderalismus in der Bundesrepublik*, Kronberg: Scriptor.

Schaüble and Lamers (1994) 'Reflections on European Policy', CDU/CSU Fraktion des Deutschen Bundestages, Bonn.

Scheuch, E. and Scheuch, U. (1992) *Cliquen, Klüngel und Karrieren*, Reinbeck: Rowohlt.

Scheuch, E.K. (1991) *Wie deutsch sind die Deutschen? Eine Nation wandelt ihr Gesicht*, Bergisch Gladbach: Bastei Lübbe.

Schindler, P. (1994) *Datenhandbuch zur Geschichte des Deutschen Bundestages 1993 bis 1991*, Baden-Baden.

Schlaich, K. 1994) *Das Bundesverfassungsgericht – Stellung, Verfahren, Entscheidungen*, Munich: Beck., 3rd rev. edn.

Schlegel, U. (1992) *Frauen in Sachsen. Zwischen Betroffenheit und Hoffnung*, Leipzig: Rosa Luxemburg Verein.

Schlesinger, H. *et al.* (1993) *Staatsverschuldung ohne Ende?*, Darmstadt: Wissenschaftliche Buchgesellschaft.

Schlör, W. (1993) 'German Security Policy', *Adelphi Paper 277*, London: Brassey's for the IISS.

Schmid, J. (1990) *Die CDU: Organisationsstrukturen, Politiken und Funktionswesen einer Partei im Föderalismus*, Opladen: Leske und Budrich.

Schmid, J. and Tiemann, H. (1992) 'Gewerkschaften und Tarifverhandlungen in den fünf neuen Bundesländern; Organisationsentwicklung, politische Strategien und Probleme am Beispiel der IG Metall', in Eichner, Volker *et al.* (eds), *Probleme der Einheit*, 12; Organisierte *Interessen in Ostdeutschland*, vol. 2, Marburg: Metropolis Verlag.

Schmidt, M. (1995) 'The Parties do Matter Hypothesis and the Case of the FRG', *German Politics*, vol. 4, no. 3.

Schmidt, M.G. (1990) 'Die Politik des mittleren Weges. Besonderheiten der Staatstätigkeit in der Bundesrepublik Deutschland', *Aus Politik und Zeitgeschichte*, vols 9–10, pp. 23–31.

Schmitt, K. (1993) 'Politische Landschaften im Umbruch', in O. Gabriel and K. Troitzsch (eds), *Wahlen im Zeiten des Umbruchs*, Frankfurt: Lang.

Schmitt, K. (1994) 'Im Osten nichts Neues?', in W. Bürklin and D. Roth (eds), *Das Superwahljahr*, Köln: Bund Verlag.

Schöllgen, G. (1994) 'National Interest and International Responsibility, Germany's Role in World Affairs', in A. Baring, *Germany's New Position in Europe*, Oxford: Berg.

Schoonmaker, D. (1995) 'Unifying the Greens', in P. Merkl (ed.), *The Federal Republic at 45*, New York: New York University Press.

Schramm, F. (1994) 'Arbeitslosigkeit in Ostdeutschland', in Hildegard Maria Nickel, Jürgen Kühl und Sabine Schenk (eds), *Erwerbsarbeit und Beschäftigung im Umbruch*, Berlin: Akademie Verlag.

Schwarz, H.-P. (1985) *Die gezähmten Deutschen: Von der Machtbesessenheit zur Machtvergessenheit*, Stuttgart: Deutsche Verlags-Anstalt.

Schwarz, H.-P. (1994a) *Die Zentralmacht Europas, Deutschlands Rückkehr auf die Weltbühne*, Berlin: Siedler Verlag.

Schwarz, H.-P. (1994b) 'Germany's National and European Interests', in A. Baring (ed.), *Germany's New Position in Europe: Problems and Perspectives*, Oxford: Berg.

Schweitzer, C.C. and Karsten, R. (1990) *Federal Republic of Germany and EC Membership Evaluated*, London: Pinter.

Seibel, W. (1994) 'Das zentralistische Erbe. Die institutionelle Entwicklung der Treuhandanstalt und die Nachhaltigkeit ihrer Auswirkungen auf die bundesstaatlichen Verfassungsstrukturen', *Aus Politik und Zeitgeschichte*, vols 43–4, pp. 3–13.

Seiters, R. (1995) 'No Magic Formula for Europe', *German Comments*, vol. 40, pp. 6–12.

Sheehan, M. (1996) *The Balance of Power: History and Theory*, London: Routledge.

Simon, H. (1994) 'Verfassungsgerichtsbarkeit', in E. Benda *et al.* (eds), *Handbuch des Verfassungsrechts der Bundesrepublik Deutschland*, 2nd rev. and enlarged edn, Berlin: de Gruyter, pp. 1637–77.

Sinn, G. and Sinn, H.-W. (1992) *Jumpstart: the Economic Unification of Germany*, Boston: MIT.

Smith, E. (1994) *The German Economy*, London: Routledge.

Smith, G. (1992) 'The "New Party System"', in G. Smith, W. Paterson, P. Merkl and S. Padgett (eds), *Developments in German Politics*, Basingstoke: Macmillan.

Smith, G. (1993) 'Dimensions of Change in the German Party System', in S. Padgett (ed.), *Parties and Party Systems in the New Germany*, Aldershot and Brookfield: Dartmouth.

Smith, G. (1995) 'The Moderate Right in the German Party System', in P. Merkl (ed.), *The Federal Republic at 45*, New York: New York University Press.

Smith, G., Paterson, W., Merkl, P. and Padgett, S. (eds) (1992) *Developments in German Politics*, Basingstoke: Macmillan.

Smyser, W. (1992) *The Economy of United Germany: Colossus at the Crossroads*, London: Hurst.

Starck, C. (ed.) (1983) *Main Principles of the German Basic Law*, Baden-Baden: Nomos Verlagsgesellschaft.

Starck, C. (ed.) (1991) *New Challenges to the German Basic Law*, Baden-Baden: Nomos Verlagsgesellschaft.

Stares, P. (ed.) (1992) *The New Germany and the New Europe*, Washington: The Brookings Institution.

Statistisches Bundesamt (1995), Statistisches Jahrbuch 1995, Wiesbaden: Statistisches Bundesamt.

Stern, K. (1993) 'General Assessment of the Basic Law – A German View', in P. Kirchhof and D. P. Kommers (eds), *Germany and its Basic Law*, Baden-Baden: Nomos Verlagsgesellschaft, pp. 17–36.

Sternberger, D. (1990) 'Verfassungspatriotismus', in D. Sternberger, *Schriften*, vol. x, Frankfurt: Insel.

Storbeck, J. (1995) 'Europol: Chance für eine Verbesserung der gemeinsamen Verbrechensbekämpfung in der Europäischen Union', *Aus Politik und Zeitgeschichte*, vol. B23/95, pp. 20–7.

Stratman, P. (1988) 'Arms Control and the Military Balance: the West German Debate', in Karl Kaiser and John Roper (eds), *British–German Defence Co-operation: Partners Within the Alliance*, London: Jane's, pp. 90–112.

Sturm, R. (1985) 'Die Politikstilanalyse. Zur Konkretisierung des Konzeptes der Politischen Kultur in der Policy-Analyse', in H.-H. Hartwich (ed.), *Policy-Forschung in der Bundesrepublik Deutschland*, Opladen: Westdeutscher Verlag, pp. 111–16.

Sturm, R. (1989) *Haushaltspolitik in westlichen Demokratien*, Baden-Baden: Nomos.

Sturm, R. (1991) *Die Industriepolitik der Bundesländer und die europäische Integration*, Baden-Baden: Nomos.

Sturm, R. (1995) 'Nicht in einer Generation zu erreichen – Die Angleichung der Lebensverhältnisse', in Altenhof, R. and Jesse, E. (eds), *Das wiedervereinigte Deutschland*, Düsseldorf: Droste, pp. 191–216.

Sturm, R. (1996) 'Party Competition and the Federal System: The Lehmbruch Hypothesis Revisited', in C. Jeffery (ed.), *The Challenges of Unification. German Federalism in the 1990s*, London: Leicester University Press.

Sturm, R. and Wilks, St. (eds) (1995) *Wettbewerbspolitik und die Ordnung der Elektrizitätswirtschaft in Deutschland und Grossbritannien*, Baden-Baden: Nomos.

Szabo, S. (1990) *The Changing Politics of German Security*, London: Pinter.

Taylor, A. J. P. (1967) *Europe, Grandeur and Decline*, London: Pelican.

Thatcher, M. (1993) *The Downing Street Years*, London: Harper Collins.

Thiemann, Heinrich, Schmid, Josef, and Löber, Frank (1993) 'Gewerkschaften und Sozialdemokratie in den neuen Bundesländern', *Deutschland Archiv*, vol. 26, no. 1.

Thietz, K. (1992) *Ende der Selbstverständlichkeit. Die Abschaffung des 218 in der DDR, Dokumente*, Berlin: Basis Druck.

Tietmeyer, H. (1996) 'European and International Responsibility in Monetary Policy', *German Comments*, January, pp. 39–47.

Toepel, K. (1995) 'Regionale Strukturpolitik in den neuen Bundesländern unter Berücksichtigung des EU-Engagements', *Aus Politik und Zeitgeschichte*, vol. B23/95, pp. 31–7.

Verheyen, D. and Søe, C. (1993) *The Germans and their Neighbours*, Oxford: Westview.

Verträge zur deutschen Einheit, Stand Oktober 1990, Bonn: Bundeszentrale für politische Bildung.

Vesper, D. (1995) 'Milliardengrab Ost?', *Deutschland Archiv*, vol. 6, pp. 572–8.

Voigt, D., Voss, W. and Meck, S. (1987) *Sozialstruktur DDR*, Darmstadt: Wissenschaftliche Buchgesellschaft.

Wallace, W. (1990) *The Transformation of Western Europe*, London: Pinter.

Walter, B. (1994) 'Interpretationen und Tatsachen. Staatsgrenze – Kontur oder Limes?', *Kriminalistik*, vol. 1/94, pp. 47–52.

Walter, N. (1993a) *Der neue Wohlstand der Nation*, Düsseldorf, ECON Verlag.

Walter, N. (1993b) *Weniger Staat, Mehr Markt: Wege aus der Krise*, Bonn: Verlag Bonn Aktuell.

Wassermann, R. (1995) 'Kriminalität und Sicherheitsbedürfnis. Zur Bedrohung durch Gewalt und Kriminalität in Deutschland', *Aus Politik und Zeitgeschichte*, vol. B23/95, pp. 3–10.

Wattenberg, M. (1996) *The Decline of American Political Parties*, 4th edn, Cambridge: Harvard University Press.

Webber, D. (1995) 'The Second Coming of the Bonn Republic', discussion paper, Birmingham, Institute for German Studies.

Webber, D. and Sally, R. (1994) 'The German Solidarity Pact: A Case Study in the Politics of the New Germany', *German Politics*, vol. 3, no. 1, pp. 18–46.

Weidenfeld, W. (ed.) (1990) *Die Deutschen und die Architektur des Europäischen Hauses*, Cologne: Verlag Wissenschaft und Politik.

Weidenfeld, W. and Zimmermann, H. (eds) (1989) *Deutschland Handbuch. Eine doppelte Bilanz*, Munich: Hauser.

Weisser, U. (1992) *NATO Ohne Feindbild: Konturen einer europäischen Sicherheitspolitik*, Bonn: Bouvier.

Weizsäcker, R. von (1992) *Richard von Weizsäcker: Conversation with Gunter Hofman and Werner Perger*.

Wellenreuther, H. (ed.) (1990) *German and American Constitutional Thought*, Oxford: Berg.

Wiesenthal, H. (1993) *Blockaden, Asymmetrien, Perfektionsmangel: ein Vergleich der Reprentationschancen sozialer Interessen im Transformationsprozess*, Arbeitspapiere: Berlin Max-Planck-Gesellschaft.

Wiesenthal,. H. (ed.) (1995) *Einheit als Interessenpolitik: Studien zur sektoralen Transformation Ostdeutschlands*, Frankfurt/Main: Campus.

Willis, F. (1965) *France, Germany and the New Europe 1945–63*, Oxford: Oxford University Press.

Wilson, M. (1993) 'The German Welfare State: A Conservative Regime in Crisis', in A. Cochrane and J. Clarke (eds), *Comparing Welfare States: Britain in International Context*, London: Sage.

Winkler, G. (1994) 'Social Policy at the Crossroads', in M. Hancock and H. Welsh (eds), *German Unification: Process and Outcomes*, Boulder, Col.: Westview Press.

Winkler, G. (ed.) (1992) *Frauenreport '90*, Berlin: Verlag Die Wirtschaft.

Wollmann, H. (1985) 'Housing Policy: Between State Intervention and the Market', in K. von Beyme and M. G. Schmidt (eds), *Policy and Politics in the Federal Republic of Germany*, Aldershot: Gower, pp. 132–55.

Woolcock, S., Hodges, M., and Schreiber, K. (1991) *Britain, Germany and 1992: The Limits of Deregulation*, London: Pinter.

Zachert, H.-L. (1995) 'Die Entwicklung der Organisierten Kriminalität in Deutschland', *Au Politik und Zeitgeschichte*, vol. B23/95, pp. 11–19.

Zahn, I. (1995) *Frauen in Deutschland*, Internationes Basis Info 13.

Zelle, C. (1995) 'Social Dealignment versus Political Frustration', *European Journal for Political Research*, vol. 27, pp. 319–45.

Zimmermann, H.-M. (1992) 'Kriminalprävention – Neue Wege in der Kriminalitätskontrolle', in *Schriftenreihe der Polizei-Führungsakademie*, 2.3/92, Lübeck: Schmidt-Römhild, pp. 5–13.

Zitelmann, R. *et al.* (eds) (1993) *Westbindung: Risiken und Chancen für Deutschland*, Berlin: Propyläen-Verlag.

Index